IN THE CLASSROOM WITH KENNETH BURKE

IN THE CLASSROOM WITH KENNETH BURKE

Edited by
Ann George and M. Elizabeth Weiser

Parlor Press
Anderson, South Carolina
www.parlorpress.com

Parlor Press LLC, Anderson, South Carolina, USA

© 2023 by Parlor Press
All rights reserved.

Printed in the United States of America
S A N: 2 5 4 - 8 8 7 9

Library of Congress Cataloging-in-Publication Data on File

978-1-64317-332-0 (paperback)
978-1-64317-334-7 (pdf)
978-1-64317-333-4 (epub)

1 2 3 4 5

Book design by David Blakesley.
Cover design by Ross Tidwell.

Printed on acid-free paper.

Parlor Press, LLC is an independent publisher of scholarly and trade titles in print and multimedia formats. This book is available in paperback, hardcover, and eBook formats from Parlor Press on the World Wide Web at http://www.parlorpress.com or through online and brick-and-mortar bookstores. For submission information or to find out about Parlor Press publications, write to Parlor Press, 3015 Brackenberry Drive, Anderson, South Carolina, 29621, or email editor@parlorpress.com.

Contents

Abbreviations	*viii*
Acknowledgments	*ix*
Introduction M. Elizabeth Weiser and Ann George	*xiii*

I. Encountering Burke   1

1 Use Everything: Doing Rhetorical Analysis with Kenneth Burke   3
Jack Selzer

    Demonstrating the rhetorical parlor for textual and contextual analysis across course levels.

    Rhetorical Analysis Assignment   16

2 Learning Cluster Analysis with Undergraduates:
Perfected by the Other   19
Annie Laurie Nichols

    Increasingly sophisticated cluster analyses for analysis and invention with a range of undergraduates.

    Perspective by Incongruity and Identification Lessons   39

3 Rhetoric, Identity, and Conflict: Engaging Burke,
Engaging Culture   50
Bryan Crable

    Equipping advanced undergraduates with Burkean perspectives and vocabulary needed to "size up" their own situations and act.

    Rhetoric, Identity, and Conflict—Week by Week   56

4 Illuminating Kenneth Burke, Engaging Publics   73
David Blakesley

    Using multiple media platforms to encourage graduate student engagement with theory.

    Graduate Theory Syllabus   94

II. Specific Applications   105

**5 Identification with the Imagined Community:
The Museum of Us**   107
   M. Elizabeth Weiser

> *Using an assignment of self-made museum exhibits to teach identification and division to undergraduates.*

   Identification Assignment   122

**6 Pathographies as Identification Medicine:
Forming Empathetic Poet-Professionals in the
Health Writing Classroom**   127
   Jarron Slater

> *Teaching identification to future health-care professionals through a series of narrative assignments.*

   Identification Assignment   141

**7 Burke, Feminism, and Community Engagement Projects:
Finding Common Ground**   143
   Rachel Chapman Daugherty

> *Using feminist pedagogy in a community engagement project to teach critical analysis of identity-based appeals.*

   Community Engagement Assignment   156

**8 Dramatism, Archives, and Assembled Trajectories:
"As Rhetoricians, We'll Do Things"**   166
   James Beasley

> *Applying multiple layers of pentadic analysis as undergraduates interrogate and reframe local history archives.*

**9 North with Burke! Symbolic Action and the
Pentad in Political Science**   185
   Jouni Tilli

> *Teaching pentadic analysis to political science students in a graduate seminar.*

   Parsing of the Pentad Handout   200

III. Equipment for Living   *203*

10 Attitudes toward a Historiographic Seminar on Burke   *205*
    Ann George

    Training graduate students to engage with Burke in his rhetorical scene.

    Syllabus for a Graduate Seminar and Topic Handouts   *226*

11 Multiperspectivism: Educating Social Science Students to Become Symbol-Wise Practitioners   *241*
    Laura Van Beveren and Kris Rutten

    Encouraging symbol-wise critical reflection with students of clinical psychology and social work.

    Assignment Prompts   *258*

12 Muscular Drooping and Sentimental Brooding: Kenneth Burke's Crip Time–War Time Disability Pedagogy   *261*
    Shannon Walters

    Combining Burkean pedagogy and disability studies pedagogy to practice symbolic analysis.

13 Burke for Undergraduates: Equipment for Thinking, Working, and Living   *285*
    Elvera Berry

    Demonstrating the lasting power of a general undergraduate seminar on Burke.

    Undergraduate Theory Syllabus   *302*

Appendix A: Further Resources on Burkean Education and Teaching Burkean Concepts   *305*

Works Cited   *311*

Contributors   *327*

Index   *331*

Abbreviations

ATH	*Attitudes Toward History*
CS	*Counter-Statement*
GM	*A Grammar of Motives*
LAPE	"Linguistic Approach to Problems of Education"
LSA	*Language as Symbolic Action*
PC	*Permanence and Change*
PLF	*The Philosophy of Literary Form*
RM	*A Rhetoric of Motives*

Acknowledgments

We thank the authors for their generous contributions toward continuing Burke's legacy in the classroom. We would also like to thank students for their assistance in bringing this book to fruition: David Isaksen for his research pulling together the initial list of Burke pedagogical resources, Ross Tidwell for their cover design, and Jared Jameson for his helpful copyediting. Finally, we acknowledge Texas Christian University and The Ohio State University at Newark for their support toward the production of this text.

*Dedicated to those students of Burke who taught us
and those we have taught in turn.*

Introduction

M. Elizabeth Weiser and Ann George

> "With this to start from, teacher and class are on a voyage of discovery together."
> —Kenneth Burke, "Linguistic Approach to Problems of Education"

Why teach Kenneth Burke? Why teach him today, in the twenty-first century—is he relevant? He's hard enough to read in graduate school, much less teach to anyone, isn't he? Where to begin?

We've all heard this—perhaps we've even said it. What the authors in this book aim to demonstrate is that Burke's ways of studying and teaching about language are accessible to students in everything from a first-year composition course to an advanced graduate program—in rhetoric, in writing and communication, in political science, education, even the health professions. We believe his approach—teaching students to be "symbol-wise" rather than "symbol-foolish" about the world around them—can be flexibly applied to many fields, and further, that its lessons are vital not simply to students in a successful class but to citizens in a functioning nation. As Burke noted in his description of his own popular course "Language as Symbolic Action," the goal of the course was to "sharpen awareness of the ways in which terms are related to one another, and of the momentous role that terminology plays in human thought and conduct" (Letter to Bowman, qtd. in Enoch 275–76). In an era when words and images fill our lives from the moment we wake up and pick up our phones, Burke's focus on symbol-wisdom is a critical corrective.[1]

---

1. We thank Carolyn Skinner, Beverly Moss, and Kelly Whitney for their insightful comments on an earlier draft of this introduction.

Becoming symbol-wise, sharply aware of terminology's role in framing experience, is a skill teachable—and relevant—to all students of our communal life, and people have been doing it successfully, teaching thousands of students, for multiple decades. The chapters in this volume pull together some of the long-standing icons of Burkean pedagogy and some of its newest voices to show how you, too, can teach Burke's concepts of symbolic analysis, incorporating his ideas into full courses, assignment sequences, or single units.

Before we discuss *how*, though, we aim to show *why* studying Burke and his methods is still vital. We argue that Burke is vital because humans make sense of their world through language, and Burke, the "word man," spent a lifetime considering the ways that understanding language—and symbols more broadly—would help us better understand ourselves and our relationships to each other. This understanding, in turn, helps to mitigate our destructive tendencies and better promote our constructive ones. As Jessica Enoch puts it, "For Burke, the overriding purpose of education is for students to reflect on the complicated relationship between language and human relations" in all its ironic complexities (280). In the ironically complex times in which we live, when we are awash in confusingly competing symbols, such a purpose continues to drive rhetorical education and our hopes for deeper insight about our world as we transfer critical reflection to future generations. Robert Asen, Gerard Hauser, Cheryl Geisler, Christian Kook, Lisa Storm Villadsen, and others have long advocated for the importance to democratic societies of education in the discourse practices of responsible citizenry, not only as producers of rhetoric but also as its critically aware consumers. As Kook and Villadsen note, "Rhetorical citizenship is concerned with citizens' output as well as their critical engagement with public deliberation. Careful monitoring of the public deliberation they hear or see is an important part of their deliberative engagement" (5). Burke's pedagogical methods are all focused on this "careful monitoring" and constructive use of the often-contentious, pluralistic public discourse that a diverse modern society needs in order to thrive.

There are four key reasons to incorporate Burke's approaches into your classroom. We'll elaborate on each below:

1. Burke's proposed attitudes promote a citizen engagement model in which people build together a better life for all;

2. Burke's emphasis on dialectical inquiry aims to subvert the competitive instinct engendering the division, scapegoating, and war that threaten our current public life;
3. Burke's symbolic analysis is designed to train students to respond with critical awareness to the flood of information and misinformation swamping us today;
4. Burkean ideas continue to infuse modern rhetorical studies, and his methods for symbolic analysis undergird undergraduate communication and composition texts.

1. Burke's proposed attitudes promote a citizen engagement model in which people together build a better life for all.

Shortly after the November 2020 election, Ibram X. Kendi wrote an article in the *Atlantic* questioning the premise of our current times being a "battle for America's soul." "The battle for the soul of America is actually the battle *between* the *souls* of America," he wrote—the soul of justice and that of injustice. Both souls "have been battling in the same nation." The soul of justice needs to fight off the soul of injustice. The engaged citizen is not one who naively overidentifies with opponents, nor one who demonizes them. Instead, as Burke pointed out in his review "The Rhetoric of Hitler's 'Battle,'" engaged citizens make it their goal to learn from opponents, to see what "medicine" their medicine-men are concocting in order to devise preventatives and antidotes.

This clear-eyed critical awareness is at the heart of the Burkean movement for a rhetorical education based on symbolic analysis. As Jeffrey St. John notes in his review of Ann George and Jack Selzer's *Kenneth Burke in the 1930s,* vibrant citizenship is the result of a dialogue between cultural context and individual drive: "However, [Burke] also intuits that citizens rely on their physical senses for cues about citizenship in much the same way that they rely on those same senses for cues about love, politics, faith, and economics. What we see and hear in our midst is, for Burke, ineluctably constitutive of who we believe we are and what we believe we can do" (416). The shifting patterns of governance in so many nations make clear how very much our scene impacts how we view ourselves and others in our societies, and how necessary it is to be aware of that scenic influence, as our sense of selfhood determines what we think we can and should do together.

What we should do *together* is the key question: since the early 1930s, Burke has defined "the good life" as "a project for 'getting along with people'" (*ATH* 216). Critics rightly point out that "getting along" has historically put more onus on some bodies than on others, as across the world societies are not equally acting together. Asking members of oppressed communities to just "get along" with dominant power structures is not equality, and Burke was adamant that adequate food, shelter, health, and safety should be givens in any society—and to the extent that they are not, we must "commit . . . to open conflict" with those "who would use their power to uphold [unjust] institutions" (*PC* 272). "Getting along" was never Burke's recipe for quiescence. As George notes in her *Critical Companion* to Burke's signature work, *Permanence and Change*, "getting along" is something altogether different from and more complicated than passively "going along" (109). "To get along" in a Burkean sense, as Gregory Clark insists, all "individuals must change in response to each other, must listen as well as speak, and must learn as well as teach. They must revise and adapt" (*Civic Jazz* 3)—and they do so with "shrewdness" about the ways injustice is perpetuated; they do so not with "*passiveness*, but [with] *maximum consciousness*" (*ATH* 166, 171). In other words, at the heart of Burke's pedagogical mission to create a "properly equipped citizenry" lie the eminently teachable rhetorical practices—criticism, composition, communication, revision—needed to collectively build communities dedicated to human welfare and cooperative enterprise (Burke, "New State" 3). In the increasingly interconnected twenty-first century, our very survival depends, in part, on how fully we embrace Burke's mission and how well we teach the crucial rhetorical practices he identified.

2. Burke's emphasis on dialectical inquiry aims to subvert the competitive instinct engendering the division, scapegoating, and war that threaten our current public lives.

Heather McGhee ends her bestselling *The Sum of Us: What Racism Costs Everyone and How We Can Prosper Together* by noting that

> this moment is challenging us finally to settle this question: Who is an American, and what are we to one another? . . . Politics offers two visions of why all the peoples of the world have met here: one in which we are nothing more than competitors and another in which perhaps the proximity of so much dif-

ference forces us to admit our common humanity. The choice between these two visions has never been starker. (288)

Burke saw a similar form of destructive competition playing itself out during the Cold War, and his response was his 1955 article, "Linguistic Approach to the Problems of Education" ("LAPE"). As observed by Jessica Enoch and Scott Wible, in Burke's linguistic education, students are *not* taught how to more aggressively debate or judge. They are instead taught to patiently analyze, to ask questions from multiple perspectives, to be humble about their conclusions, even as they reach a conclusion they think is best in that situation.

Burke in "Linguistic Approach" described this as a practice of thoughtful critical awareness: "A linguistic point of view would be not so much a step 'up' or 'down' as a step to one side. It offers a technique for stopping to analyze an exhortation precisely at the moment when the exhortation would otherwise set us to swinging violently" (284). Students in a Burkean classroom learn to step back from their too-quick first response and "systematically let the text say its full say.... Students with a dramatistic attitude would be patient and tentative; their modus operandi in class would be to 'watch and wait' while they examine language" (270–71). Even as such an attitude of patient engagement remains absent in today's public discourse, that absence is bemoaned by everyone from scholars to politicians to public celebrities. Burke's linguistic education provides both *attitude* and *method* for turning escalating recrimination into engaged dialogue. He named his linguistic approach to productive discourse *ad bellum purificandum*, toward the purification of war, because he saw in his own time, as we see in ours, that heated but appropriately engaged debate ("purifying war") is always preferable to its alternatives: alienation or violence.

In the classroom, the investigation can go even further than in the rest of life, Burke thought, because the classroom is a space for critical contemplation apart from the world at large. "Education must be thought of as a *technique of preparatory withdrawal*, the institutionalizing of an attitude that one should be able to *recover at crucial moments*," he wrote ("LAPE" 273). He envisioned education as a four-runged ladder. Indoctrination (teaching just one "truth") is on the lowest rung, followed by competition (teaching the opponent's truth in order to win against them), knowledge (teaching to appreciate or tolerate others as a kind of benignly interested anthropology), and finally what he termed "dialogue":

One would try to decide how many positions one thinks are important enough to be represented by "voices" and then . . . do all in one's power to let each voice state its position as ably as possible, [not just for fair play but] . . . for ways whereby the various voices, in mutually correcting one another, will lead toward a position better than any one singly. That is, one does not merely want to outwit the opponent, or to study [them], one wants to be affected by [them], in some degree to incorporate [them], to so act that [their] ways can help perfect one's own—in brief, to learn from [them]. ("LAPE" 284)

The idea that we can learn from our opponents—patiently and tentatively parsing the multitude of voices asserting their own realities—is not one in much favor these days. But learning from one's opponent does not mean blithely accepting all their beliefs; it might include incorporating more effective rhetorical strategies or better understandings of human identity formation. And as our authors explore in this volume, it is a helpful attitude for the tentative, multiple perspectives of students growing into their roles in the world.

3. Burke's symbolic analysis is designed to train students to respond with critical awareness to the flood of information and misinformation swamping us today.

"To say that the current state of public discourse is abysmal seems self-evident. Toxic rhetoric has become a fact of everyday life, a form of entertainment, and a corporate product." John Duffy's 2012 assessment is sadly only truer today, and, as Duffy notes, is often overlooked "even in academe"—except in the first-year composition class, which he marks as a place that, in providing a rhetorical education, "engages students, inevitably and inescapably, in questions of ethics, values, and virtues." Marie Secor and Davida Charney, in their preface to *Constructing Rhetorical Education*, in turn extend that vision for rhetorical education beyond first-year writing: "A rhetorical education is not limited to teaching freshman composition (or any specific writing course), and the contexts in which it occurs are not limited to classrooms. An effective rhetorical education certainly results in the growth of writing skills, but its larger goal is to foster a critical habit of mind" (ix). This rhetorical education can also extend well beyond schools: Peter Smudde and Bernard Brock point out in their introduction to *Human-*

istic Critique of Education that education as symbolic analysis envisions learning as a lifelong process (xiv).

As the symbol-using animal, just as we always engage in symbolic action, so must we perpetually be aware of it, ready to step to one side, as Burke put it:

> For [education] develops to perfection one stage in the confronting of a problem, the stage where one steps aside as thoroughly as possible and attempts, in the spirit of absolute linguistic skepticism, to mediate upon the tangle of symbolism in which all [people] are by their very nature caught. ("LAPE" 287–88)

This "linguistic skepticism" is not merely the debunking and fact-checking that pits one side's supposed truths against another's, leaving everyone distrustful of everything. Burke's pedagogical approach is different—it involves stepping outside one's certitude and imagining other possibilities: "You counteract 'slanting' [bias] not by trying to decide [if something is true or fair] but by leaving unquestioned the facts as given and merely trying to imagine different ways of presenting them, or by trying to imagine possible strategic omissions" ("LAPE" 287). Engaging the imagination as well as the intellect involves students in a more liberating, more creative form of linguistic skepticism than simply debunking another's truth, making "a citizenry truly free" from the machinations of powerbrokers seeking to influence their perspectives ("LAPE" 285) while simultaneously helping students understand the power of their own language to shape the world around them.

Burke developed a number of rhetorical tools to assist in the shrewd practical analysis of rhetoric in everyday life. As James Beasley and Jack Selzer note in a recent article, Burke presented his ideas at the very first Conference on College Composition and Communication (CCCC) in March 1950, describing "some of the practical rhetorical moves that he was recommending to composition teachers and that he expected to publish shortly in his 'War of Words' manuscript," including "the 'Bland Strategy,' 'Spiritualization,' and what he called 'Deflection'" (45)—modern rhetorical devices Burke saw operating in the rhetorical misinformation campaigns of his time. Beasley and Selzer note:

> The composition teachers who listened to Burke speak in 1950 before the release of *A Rhetoric of Motives* were exposed to . . . how conventional and uncritical journalistic and bureaucratic

communications were conditioning Americans to accept the stark possibility of an even more catastrophic war[;] Burke was testifying to the importance of their enterprise and to the importance of rhetoric as foundational to the teaching of composition. . . . And given the belligerent elements that pervade our current culture, [these ideas] remain highly instructive about the international, national, and local discursive situations that we find ourselves in today. (46)

Burke's concerns about—and rhetorical response to—misleading media were extensive. For instance, the recently rediscovered "War of Words" manuscript includes a long section documenting "Scientific Rhetoric," which analyzes the ways the media shape national attitudes that lead toward particular actions. Elizabeth Weiser notes in a review of the edited book,

> Beginning with the insight that "we act on the basis of reality as we know it" yet "much of what passes for 'reality' necessarily reaches us solely through the medium of the news" (172), Burke analyzes the linguistic mechanisms by which "just the facts" become rhetorical. Interpretation, selectivity and reduction, . . . "tithing by tonality" (a discerning examination of microaggressions), and the continual competitive need for news as "drama" result in not lies, as he repeatedly emphasizes, but the "tendentious selection of hard facts" (221) that can mislead even more than actual (fictive) dramas. . . . This section alone would make for an excellent addition to today's rhetorical discussions of "fake news." (Rev. of *War of Words* 244)

Burke's concerns with propaganda, bias, and the linguistic tools manipulating society went well beyond the media. Other devices in *War of Words* that Burke thought would help a student of symbolic action analyze the ways in which geopolitical forces worked to convince the public to support their aims include tactics he termed Shrewd Simplicity, Undo by Overdoing, Yielding Aggressively, Spokesman, Reversal, Say the Opposite, Making the Connection. That he included under each of these strategies multiple examples pulled from the public discourse of his day, and that these categories expand on those he was already recommending to composition teachers at CCCC, demonstrate Burke's great interest in helping students read with greater insight the persuasion occurring all around them in their communal life.

Indeed, Burke provides particularly valuable pedagogical tools with which to create symbol-wise students and citizens precisely because for decades he attended to the power of everyday discourse—persuasion that flies under the radar: "We must often think of rhetoric not in terms of some one particular address, but as a general *body of identifications* that owe their convincingness much more to trivial repetition and dull daily reënforcement than to exceptional rhetorical skill" (*RM* 26). A *New Republic* essay from the mid-1930s, "Reading While You Run: An Exercise in Translation from English into English," for instance, instructs readers to note the ideological work accomplished by blurring the distinctions between *industry* and *business* (an insight he got from Thorstein Veblen) or between *manufacturer* and *owner*, "whereby the man who operates a manufacturing machine is *not* a manufacturer" while the man "who does *not* operate a manufacturing machine but juggles dividends for himself" *is* a manufacturer (36). Today, when "alternative facts" are created by persistent retweeting and political discourse is filled with dog whistles, Burke's methods for detecting the "almost imperceptible choice of words . . . that draw lines at the wrong places" are critical for our classrooms (37).

Burke used these practical tactics in his own many teaching engagements at colleges ranging from Bennington, where he taught for two decades, to the University of Chicago, the New School for Social Research, Penn State, Stanford, Princeton, and Harvard (among others). His tools for students included some of the same linguistic techniques he used himself to analyze texts, including his pentad of questions to look at any situation from multiple perspectives and his system of indexing to look for the clusters of key terms in an artifact and use them to consider the author's motivations and those of their society. His books are full of examples of these analyses that one could well imagine him bringing into the classroom. Assignments would then move students to similar types of analyses. For instance, Burke's chapter in the 1954 text *Symbols and Values* focuses on a lengthy analysis of James Joyce's *Portrait of the Artist as a Young Man*, which he introduces by saying that "this essay is part of a project called 'The Theory of the Index' [whose aim] is to make the analysis of literary symbolism as systematic as possible" ("Fact, Inference, and Proof" 283). In it, Burke describes ten "rules of thumb" for students attempting indexing:

1. "Note all striking terms for acts, ideas, attitudes, images, relationships" (296);

2. "Note oppositions," particularly "shifts whereby the oppositions become appositions" (296);
3. "Pay particular attention to beginnings and endings of sections or subsections," and consider the points of transition (296);
4. "Watch names, as indicative of essence" (297);
5. "Watch also for incidental properties of one character that are present in another"—a possible indication that different figures share a common motivation (298);
6. "Note internal forms"; consider their more generalized themes (298);
7. "Watch for a point of *farthest internality*," places where stylistic elements are strongest (298);
8. "Note details of *scene* that may stand 'astrologically' for motivations affecting character, or for some eventual act in which that character will complete himself": these may be restating in scenic terms the action of the piece, thus providing an interpretation of the action (298);
9. "Note expressions marking secrecy, privacy, mystery, marvel, power, silence, guilt," and also terms for the hierarchal order we develop to establish our place (300);
10. "Look for *moments* at which, in your opinion, the work comes to *fruition*." He calls this the "entelechial test"—a kind of short-cut to identifying key terms by starting from those terms present in the stylistic climax of the text (301).

In an interview with Daniel Fogarty from around the same time, Burke describes how he finished his indexing lessons by having students abstract from their particular findings to do what he called *essentializing by entitlement*: "Burke would suggest to students applying his index system that they give titles to the acts of a play, or to the parts of a novel, or to the stanzas of a poem, in order to force themselves to decide what might be the essence of each step of the total development of the play, novel, or poem" (Fogarty 84n109).

In other examples, Enoch (281–86) outlines three classroom techniques Burke used repeatedly to help students understand the role of language, tools she labels *what equals what, revising the news*, and *Burkean debate*. In *what equals what*, or what Burke termed "equations," students look for the author's key terms and determine what they mean in this context. As he wrote in *PLF*, "The work of every writer contains a set of implicit equations. He uses 'association clusters.' And you may, by examining his work, find 'what goes with what' in these clusters—what kinds of acts and images and personalities and situations go with his notions of heroism, villainy, consolation, despair, etc." (20)—in other words, what (largely unconscious, often social) attitudes the writer is bringing to each key term. *Revising the news* is Burke's way of dealing with news bias, or "slanting," as we saw above—an imaginative tool to demonstrate the power of terministic screens that linguistically select and deflect from the reality they purport to be reflecting. Finally, *Burkean debate* reflects Burke's sense that dialogue, not competition, is the highest rung of the educational ladder. "Through this Burkean form of debate, students would compose two opposing positions along with a 'third piece' that would transcend questions of 'for' or 'against' by 'analyzing the sheerly verbal maneuvers involved in the placing and discussing of the issue'" (Enoch 286). Such a focus on the means and motivations by which all arguments are made, Burke hoped, could produce the shrewd humility that allows a symbol-wise person to work effectively in the world. "We would try . . . to perfect techniques for doubting much that is now accepted as lying beyond the shadow of a doubt," he wrote. "A mere inculcating of 'tolerance,' 'good will,' 'respect for the rights of others,' and such, cannot be enough" ("LAPE" 272). Instead, the good life is built by people who are continually aware of the power of language to influence their actions and those of their fellow citizens.

With the rise of domestic terrorism and toxic racialized politics, academicians are taking increasing note of this need to reclaim the role of rhetorical education in fostering a critically aware public engagement. As Cheryl Glenn notes in her introduction to the collection *Rhetorical Education in America*, a critical habit of mind "enables people to engage in and change American society" (viii). Yet engagement among those actors most open to change remains low, while, as public education scholar John Holbein notes, the schools that see increased engagement are those that "get teens and tweens to discuss contemporary political issues [and] encourage students to become involved in civic and political action"—in other words, schools that practice rhetorical education. As we go to press, legislatures in both our states are trying to ban the teaching of "divisive concepts"—part of a nationwide backlash against reckoning with systems of injustice. If they succeed, students will learn a truncated national identity and (as Holbein notes) be less engaged in that learning and therefore in the civic engagement necessary for a functioning democracy. As an antidote to this fearful narrowing of the scope of dialogue, Burke's pedagogies call for maneuvering that space where one puts "identification and division ambiguously together" (*RM* 25) by close reading of both text and context, stepping aside from a debate to analyze the specific forms it takes, determining the motives behind the symbols, and aiming for engagement with others for the good of the community. In some ways, his work has never been more important to the vision of rhetorical education.

4. Burkean ideas continue to infuse modern rhetorical studies and undergraduate education in composition and communication.

As we can see, Burke's methods and multiple theories are embedded into what we today call rhetoric. While rhetorical studies have taken many exciting new paths since the days of the New Rhetoric, Burke's original ideas on such rhetorical commonplaces as terministic screens, identification, and perspective by incongruity remain the substance of rhetorical thought. In the past five years, there have been forty-nine articles in rhetoric journals that specifically include Kenneth Burke as one of their subject terms (Aristotle is a subject of only four articles more). But looking only at pieces that are overtly indebted to Burke obscures the foundational importance of his ideas. Some four hundred other articles reference his work, on themes as varied as "Theorizing Race and Gender in the Anthropocene," "Memory and Lost Communities: Strange Methods for Studying Place," "Bathroom Bills, Memes, and a Biopolitics of Trans Disposability," and "The Work of the Digital Undead: Digital Capitalism and the Suspension of Communicative Death." The field of rhetoric may move into ever new directions, but the foundational influence of Kenneth Burke moves with it.

This influence is also apparent in the textbooks used to introduce new generations to our fields. As a 2011 *Composition Teacher* article notes, "Undergraduate textbooks in rhetorical criticism, rhetorical theory, and communication theory typically include coverage of Burke's theory of dramatism" (Krueger 81)—and these include texts still updated to address today's students, including Foss (2017); Foss, Foss, and Trapp (2014); Goodwin et al. (2020); Griffin, Ledbetter, and Sparks (2018); Hart, Daughton, and Lavally (2017); Herrick (2017); and West and Turner (2020). Composition texts following a process-based pedagogy include similar coverage as they emphasize

Burke's dramatistic approach, including bestsellers such as *Becoming Rhetorical*, *Everything's an Argument*, and *They Say/I Say: The Moves that Matter in Academic Writing*.

Students of Burke have been publishing essays on Burkean pedagogical praxis since the late 1970s (see Appendix A: Further Resources on Burkean Education and Teaching Burkean Concepts), but despite his well-documented influence on and sophisticated resources for rhetorical education, only two book-length studies on the teaching of Burkean concepts exist. The earliest, David Blakesley's *Elements of Dramatism* (2002), offers a clear and in-depth look, particularly for newcomers to Burkean ideas, to such analytical tools as dramatism, form, terministic screens, and cluster criticism. The book is a useful text for the teacher who wishes their class to have a firmer grasp of Burke's theories, and a number of our authors incorporate it into their classrooms, as you will see in the syllabi and exercises provided in this book. The second, Peter M. Smudde's edited collection *Humanistic Critique of Education: Teaching and Learning as Symbolic Action* (2010), is a guide to the ways in which Burke's ideas can improve education in democratic societies. It considers both broad policy and specific pedagogical concerns, and its authors show how symbolic analysis is a humanistic solution to the ongoing crisis of our overly utilitarian, competitive educational system. Our book accepts that argument and provides a range of practical approaches for how to carry it out.

If we should be teaching Burkean methods for symbolic analysis, how do we do it? That is the question this volume explores. Too many teachers fail to recognize just how often we already use Burke's theories and analyses, and how large a role they play in our understanding of rhetorical education as a force that makes for a better society. This book aims to show that you don't need to be a Burke expert to teach students with Burkean pedagogies. It provides you with ideas and lesson plans that you can incorporate into your own classrooms, helping your own students in whatever their circumstances to be more symbol-wise as they face their world.

The exigence for teaching Burkean ideas, therefore, is greater than ever. But delving into Burke with the determination to teach his ideas runs into the familiar concern: He has, as Wayne Booth noted to himself (see Booth's teaching notes in this volume), "a kind of over-denseness" that can be hard to work into the lesson plan for tomorrow's class. He is also expansive—what should one cover among the multiplicity of Burkean thought? Our book, therefore, focuses on practical approaches—lessons and syllabi that have worked for us as we spend time "in the classroom with Kenneth Burke."

The Structure of the Book

We divide our book into three sections. In the first, Encountering Burke, we present four approaches to engaging students new to Burke. Jack Selzer demonstrates how Burke's rhetorical parlor (a model of how discourse circulates in an ongoing cultural conversation) and methodological plea to "use everything" can generate rich, often surprising contextual analyses—in this case of Leslie Marmon Silko's "The Border Patrol State." Selzer's rhetorical analysis assignment engages undergraduates at all levels in substantial primary research; the prompt includes procedural steps, a timeline, and evaluation criteria. Next, Annie Laurie Nichols leads readers through a series of increasingly sophisticated cluster analyses, arguing for their value in helping undergraduates map their worlds and engage empathetically with other voices, particularly those of underrepresented groups. Nichols also provides hands-on, in-class activities with accompanying handouts to teach perspective by incongruity and identification to students in argument or visual rhetoric courses. Then, Bryan Crable details a semester-long undergraduate course on identity and conflict designed to enable students to engage Burke's theories in *Permanence and Change* and *Attitudes Toward History* in order to compose original analyses of cultural conflicts. Crable offers detailed commentary on both texts, explaining central concepts and successfully orchestrating undergraduates' first encounter with Burkean theory and criticism. Finally, David Blakesley explains how his graduate seminar, "Illuminating Burke, Engaging Publics," foregrounds Burke's continued relevance for both rhetorical studies and social justice pedagogy. His syllabus offers multiple rationales and specific methods for studying Burkean concepts, as well as examples of using multiple media platforms to encourage graduate student engagement with theory, with other Burke scholars, and with the larger public.

In the second section, Specific Approaches, we present five lesson plans that promote student understanding of two of Burke's key principles, identification and pentadic analysis. Elizabeth Weiser includes a detailed assignment sequence to help a range of undergraduates experience and, thus, more profoundly understand identity formation and identification by curating and sharing a "display of me" for a hypothetical museum exhibit. Drawing upon new museology and Burkean theory, her project prompt ultimately asks students to analyze how these individual displays become a "museum of us" that reflects (or deflects) twenty-first-century life. Jarron Slater then describes a medical humanities unit designed to teach identification to future health-care professionals through the reading, writing, and sharing of pathographies, or illness narratives. His pathography assignment, which draws upon Burke's understanding of a rhetoricized aesthetic, enables students to experience vulnerability and practice empathy—skills they'll need to see patients as whole human beings. Next, Rachel Chapman Daugherty theorizes a feminist approach to teaching second-year composition students to use and critique identity-based appeals. Her "Community Campaign" assignment sheet outlines a series of scaffolded writing tasks through which students design rhetorical interventions into local controversies involving the common good. James Beasley outlines a unit in a rhetoric and digital humanities course in which advanced undergraduates use pentadic analysis to recursively interpret and "recurate" artifacts and photos in local history archives. This chapter features students' work to foreground St. Augustine's history of segregation and later civil rights activism through student infusions of new metanarratives into the public discourse. Finally, Jouni Tilli models pentadic analysis for graduate political science students by examining discourse surrounding the 2011 far-right terrorist attack in Norway, particularly how politicians framed the attack's causes to suit their political agendas.

In the final section, Equipment for Living, we include four essays that explore how and why to engage students across a semester. Ann George walks readers through her graduate seminar, designed to emphasize Burke's lifelong—and still highly relevant—civic mission: to equip citizens with the rhetorical skills and embodied ethics needed to build a better life. Her syllabus illustrates how to teach Burkean theory as a rhetorical act that deliberately intervenes in specific cultural scenes and teach Burke himself as a committed public intellectual. Laura Van Beveren and Kris Rutten then discuss the multiperspectival pedagogy they developed and implemented to encourage symbol-wise critical reflection about disciplinary language and professional practice with master's students in clinical psychology and social work. Their assignment sheet for critical analyses of verbal and visual representations of poverty demonstrates how instructors might employ the Burkean concepts of terministic screens, multiple ways of seeing, and trained incapacity to help non-rhetoricians discover how disciplinary training hinders our ability to envision and enact more effective praxes. Shannon Walters argues for understanding Burke as a teacher of disability pedagogy—a pedagogy that values nonnormative ways of being and learning and that critiques traditional images of the ideal student as quick and competitive. Students so thoroughly trained for conflict, Burke warned, would only exacerbate Cold War tensions. It is Walters's hope that bringing Burke's teaching strategies into conversation with disability studies in writing classrooms will nurture students' deliberateness and blunt their aggressiveness in our own violent times. The book ends with Elvera Berry's reflection on the lasting power of her general studies' undergraduate seminar on Burke's scholarship. Using students' own reflections, Berry insists that undergraduates not only *can* be but *should* be taught Burkean concepts that offer invaluable methods for gauging how language constructs experience, as well as lessons in appreciating patient discovery, inevitable complications, and multiple perspectives. For Berry's students, Burke has indeed proven to be "equipment for thinking, working, and living."

I. Encountering Burke

Figure 1. Kenneth Burke in a seminar at (then) Central Washington State College, ca. 1967. Photo by John Foster appears courtesy of Dr. James E. Brooks Library, Archives and Special Collections; Central Washington University Faculty Papers, John Foster; Central Washington University.

1 Use Everything: Doing Rhetorical Analysis with Kenneth Burke

Jack Selzer

> *Demonstrating the rhetorical parlor for textual and contextual analysis across course levels.*

It is a truth universally acknowledged that rhetorical analysis is a fundamental, ubiquitous activity in composition courses. (In other words, you really can't teach rhetoric and composition without orchestrating rhetorical analysis as a common assignment or class activity.)

What is not so ubiquitous is any particular, agreed-upon approach to rhetorical analysis. That's because there are so many legitimate approaches to the practice. (There are some not-so-legitimate ones, too.) As I tried to demonstrate not so long ago,[1] the host of options available to analysts can be classified broadly as "textual" or "contextual," depending on their emphasis—but there's also everything in between and plenty of overlap. On the one hand, many approaches to textual analysis attend closely to textual dynamics and "close reading" of the individual item under consideration by itself. These are the approaches summarized in my Bazerman essay and in the notes to Meagan Parker Brooks's recent study of Fannie Lou Hamer's speeches.[2] On the other hand, a host of "contextual" approaches basically attend to recovering and reanimating

---

1. Selzer in Bazerman. See also Chapter Five, "Analyzing Written Arguments" in *Good Reasons with Contemporary Arguments*, fifth edition, a textbook that Lester Faigley and I authored. Portions of this essay derive from that chapter.
2. For a list of works that promote or interrogate textual criticism, see Brooks's *A Voice That Could Stir an Army: Fannie Lou Hamer and the Rhetoric of the Black Freedom Movement*, page 255, note 23.

the rhetorical situation that prevailed when the item under scrutiny was created. Whether these contextual approaches are called "environmental" or "new historical" or whatever, they all basically share a commitment to reading an artifact as part of an interconnected web or network of other artifacts and to uncovering the "fingerprints" of that original rhetorical situation that are visible in the strategies and tactics employed by the rhetor. I'll be discussing here how I teach students to use primary and archival sources to place the text they are analyzing into its particular rhetorical moment.

I do not want to overemphasize the differences between these textual and contextual readings, for they are frequently employed in unison. After all, even in the act of "normal" reading, people usually read critically (to one degree or another) as well as for content, and the two activities of reading and reading critically aren't really separable. But you get the point of my comparison: Rhetorical analysis, however it is done, is an effort to read interpretively, with an eye toward understanding a message fully and according to how that message is crafted to earn a particular response. Together or separately, textual and contextual approaches serve to interpret the purpose(s) behind a given rhetorical artifact—whether that artifact is a text, a speech, a photo, a song, a physical monument or other material artifact—and to turn up the persuasive strategies and tactics employed to carry out those aim(s). Like every other kind of practical criticism, rhetorical criticism strives to teach; rhetorical analysis is meant to demonstrate new information about the item under scrutiny for the benefit of those out to understand it better. The result is a heightened awareness of the message under consideration and how that message is conveyed. It's almost as if rhetorical analysts are eavesdropping on what someone is saying or writing or creating for someone else, with the purpose of understanding better how it is said or written or created. In any event, when people read rhetorically, when they engage in rhetorical analysis, they not only react to the message, but they also appreciate how (and often how well) the producer of that message is conveying the message to a particular audience, whether that intended audience includes the analyst or not. And through that process, rhetorical analysts, especially student analysts, learn to refine their own strategies and tactics in their own persuasive work.

And that brings me to Kenneth Burke. Since I've spent much of my career attempting to decipher Kenneth Burke's endlessly captivating and compelling and (often) intricate works, my thinking about rhetorical analysis has naturally been guided by him. Burke was many things, but he was most fundamentally a rhetorical critic—someone who performed a host of analyses on a staggering variety of what he called "symbolic actions," but who also theorized what he was doing and advised others on how to do it, too. In the title essay of *The Philosophy of Literary Form*, for example, he laid out the principles of textual/contextual/subconscious analysis that were guiding his thinking at that time and then applied those to his commentary on Coleridge's "Rime of the Ancient Mariner." During and after World War II, he published *A Grammar of Motives* and *A Rhetoric of Motives*, which offered theoretical and practical guidance on the conduct of human communication, considering both contextual considerations and textual dynamics. *A Rhetoric of Motives* begins, memorably, with a rhetorical analysis of Milton's *Samson Agonistes*. Burke also worked on the *War of Words*, intended as a part of *A Rhetoric of Motives* and made up substantially of textual analyses of postwar journalism that were guided by both contextual and textual considerations. He later published a multitude of rhetorical analyses of poems, stories, plays, art objects, and essays, collecting many of them in *Language as Symbolic Action*. He conducted those analyses in multiple ways—textual, contextual, and a combination—and even offered a study of his own novel *Towards a Better Life*. Perhaps his best-known stand-alone analysis is the one he performed in "The Rhetoric of Hitler's 'Battle,'" which combines textual and contextual approaches in the service of uncovering once and for all Hitler's nefarious intentions. That essay, reprinted in *The Philosophy of Literary Form*, illustrates especially well the power and utility of his methodological thinking and some of the powerful terminologies or "interpretive schemes" he employed (such as the "scapegoat").

What to do, therefore, in the face of all the dizzying possibilities that Burke laid out? "Use everything!"—Burke's well-known exhortation to critics arguing over the value of textual versus contextual criticism—is great advice, and I encourage everyone to read Burke thoroughly to discover for themselves the merits of his various thoughts.[3] Sometimes Burke modeled traditional close reading techniques to call attention to the particular rhetorical tropes that he had learned from Aristotle and other ancients.[4] In *The War of Words*, he invented a host of other con-

---

3. Burke's exact words in *Philosophy of Literary Form*: "The main ideal of criticism . . . is to use all that is there to use" (23).
4. For example, he detailed "Four Master Tropes" (metaphor, metonymy, synecdoche, and irony) in an essay published in *Kenyon Review* and in an appendix

temporary schemes and tropes as a way of updating and complementing Aristotle's catalogue of tactics. But more often, and against the rising tide of the New Criticism, Burke was a contextualist. He offered all sorts of methods for getting at the contextual matters at play in a given work. Some of them are quite well known, such as his important meditations on *identification* (which is the angle of his discussion of *Samson Agonistes*) or the *scapegoat* mechanism or the famous pentad that Clarke Rountree ("Instantiating 'The Law'") has shown to be so useful. Annie Laurie Nichols illustrates Burkean cluster analysis in this volume, as does Scott Wible in his depiction of Burke's teaching methods ("Professor Burke's Bennington Project"). David Isaksen, meanwhile, has extensively researched indexing, the method Burke most often taught his own students (for instance, "Indexing: Kenneth Burke's Method of Textual Analysis"). Others are very usefully detailed and illustrated in *Landmark Essays on Kenneth Burke* and *Landmark Essays on Rhetorical Criticism*. And David Blakesley's endlessly useful *The Elements of Dramatism* will give readers new to Burke an accessible overview and appreciation of the variety and power of everything that Burke has to offer to analysts.

My own Burkean appropriations, however, derive mostly from the famous parlor metaphor that Burke articulated in *The Philosophy of Literary Form*:

> Imagine that you enter a parlor. You come late. When you arrive, others have long preceded you, and they are engaged in a heated discussion, a discussion too heated for them to pause and tell you exactly what it is about. In fact, the discussion had already begun long before any of them got there so that no one present is qualified to retrace for you all the steps that had gone before. You listen for a while until you decide that you have caught the tenor of the argument; then you put in your oar. Someone answers; you answer him; another comes to your defense; another aligns himself against you, to either the embarrassment or gratification of your opponent, depending upon the quality of your ally's assistance. However, the discussion is interminable. The hour grows late, you must depart. And you do depart, with the discussion still vigorously in progress. (110)

---

to *A Grammar of Motives*. (See Tell.) And he was comfortable with the host of other specialized terms for stylistic maneuvers (e.g., antithesis, hyperbole, antimetabole, etc.) and argumentative strategies (e.g., *ethos, pathos, logos*), terms that are laid out, for example, in Corbett's *Classical Rhetoric*.

To understand any specific contribution within the parlor conversation, this passage makes clear, you have to take others into account. If extreme forms of textual criticism fetishize the bounded text, contextual criticism does the opposite: it demands attention to other items in the conversation (or network or communication chain: call it what you will). Contextual critics create a thick description of the cultural conversation that existed when the rhetorical event took place and then depend on that recreation to produce clues about the persuasive tactics and appeals that are visible in the performance in question. Contextual criticism can be relatively easy to do when the context is obvious (as it can be when classes turn to the analysis of a recently composed contemporary speech or op-ed or film or literary work, published in a familiar venue). But when students are faced with understanding something more remote in time, they have to learn to use primary and archival sources to locate the work under scrutiny in a particular moment. That means doing some research.[5]

Let me explain the benefits and illustrate the methods of textual and contextual analysis by reference to an essay by Leslie Marmon Silko that I have found perpetually teachable. Silko's "The Border Patrol State," published in 1994, "teaches" so well because its subjects—the cultural identity of minority peoples and the conduct of border police—remain very timely; because our quarter-century-now distance from the essay allows current students to experience the text without their being quite so disabled by current attitudes and events and politics; because it's available via the Internet; and because students find it highly readable and artistically accomplished no matter their position on the issues at play in the essay. To put it another way, it is a beautiful and powerful essay with lots to teach about the art of rhetoric and the art of rhetorical analysis.[6]

---

5. Before I turn to how rhetorical analysis works in practice, I'm tempted to call attention to an especially instructive (and favorite) example of the merits and conduct of contextual criticism, the one that Ann George and I once applied (George and Selzer 67–70) in an effort to understand a review of John Dos Passos's novel *1919* that was written by Malcolm Cowley in 1932. Ann and I (especially Ann), with reference to an understanding of its venue (*The New Republic*) and with a consideration of personal letters between Burke and Cowley, demonstrated that Cowley's review of Dos Passos is also a review of Burke's novel *Towards a Better Life*—even though neither Burke nor his novel is ever mentioned in the review!

6. The version that I refer to here is the one published in *The Nation* because most students can access it that way. It was also included in Silko's 1996 collec-

(Here I recommend that you interrupt your reading of this essay so that you can take in Silko's short argument.)

A Textual and Contextual Analysis of Silko's "The Border Patrol State"

How would Kenneth Burke analyze "The Border Patrol State"? Textual analysis would serve him well as a start. Everything in the article itself shows that Silko is taking issue with the practices of the Border Patrol of the Immigration and Naturalization Service (INS), and her explicit aim is equally clear from the text: she is out to disclose how the INS is reenacting the subjugation of Native peoples and to propose a radical reduction in the power of the Border Patrol. She supports this central purpose with two explicitly stated propositions: "the Immigration and Naturalization Service and Border Patrol have implemented policies that interfere with the rights of US citizens to travel freely within our borders" (par. 8); and efforts to restrict immigration are doomed and consequently of "no use; borders haven't worked, and they won't work" (par. 16).

Burke would also easily use textual analysis to turn up the details of Silko's logical, pathetic, and ethical appeals. When she explains the futility of trying to stop immigration, Silko appeals to her readers' reasonableness: constructing walls at the border with Mexico is foolish because "border entrepreneurs have already used blowtorches to cut passageways" through barriers (par. 15), because "a mass migration is under way" (par. 15), and because "the Americas are Indian country, and the 'Indian problem' is not going away" (par. 17). The *pathos* inherent in Silko's argument comes through dramatically in what Burke would call her "representative anecdote" [7]: Silko's single example of a personal experience with the Border Police, sustained throughout, stands in for the treatment of a great many Native Americans. The emotion also is apparent in her use of charged imagery (e.g., the Border Patrol is constructing an "Iron Curtain" that is as destructive to human rights as the one the Soviets erected around Eastern Europe after World War II [par. 15]); stereotypical American values (e.g., "old Bill Pratt used to ride his horse three hundred miles overland . . . every summer to work as a fire

---

tion *Yellow Woman and a Beauty of the Spirit*.

7. The "representative anecdote" (explained fully in *A Grammar of Motives*) is pretty much what the term suggests: a story or incident that persuades through its power and representativeness.

lookout" [par. 1]); and telling comparisons (e.g., Border Police tactics are chillingly reminiscent of the "Argentine police and military officers who became addicted to interrogation, torture, and murder" [par. 3–5]). The most emotional moment in the essay may be when Silko describes how the Border Patrol dog, trained to find illegal drugs and other contraband, including human contraband, seems to sympathize with Silko and those she is championing: "I saw immediately from the expression in her eyes that the dog hated them" (par. 6); "the dog refused to accuse us: she had an innate dignity that did not permit her to serve the murderous impulses of those men" (par. 7).

Burke doesn't often talk about *ethos*, but he would certainly acknowledge how an author's persona assists the art of persuasion. Here Silko, through a variety of textual moves, creates a narrator who appeals to the readers' sense of what is legal, constitutional, fair, and honorable. Early in the essay (par. 3), she establishes her credibility by reminding readers that she is a respected author who is on a book tour to publicize her novel *Almanac of the Dead*. Then she bolsters her credibility throughout by quoting widely from books and reports to demonstrate that she has studied the issues thoroughly. She speaks not only of her own experiences with the police but also of the experiences of others whom she lists, name after careful name. She connects with traditional American values—what Burke would call "god terms"[8]—such as freedom, tolerance, and ethnic pride. Because of its anti-authoritarian theme, the essay certainly articulates politically progressive values, but overall Silko herself comes off as reasonable, hard-working, honest, ethical, educated, even patriotic. All of these are relatively easily identifiable by students after even a basic grounding in rhetorical terms.

Finally, Burke, in the course of textual analysis, would consider matters such as arrangement and style. Silko observes the traditional way of presenting an argument—with a clear beginning, middle, and end. She opens with an introductory anecdote to hook the reader and to prepare for the thesis that is expressed in paragraph 8. After the introduction comes the point-by-point defense of the thesis, that is, an evaluation of the unethical nature of INS policies (par. 11–13), which is followed by the enumeration of practical difficulties of halting immigration (par. 14–15). Then comes Silko's surprising and stirring conclusions (par. 16–17):

---

8. In *A Grammar of Motives*, Burke describes "god terms" as words and concepts that are sanctified by members of a community—terms which thus inspire people to think and act in a certain way.

"The great human migration within the Americas cannot be stopped; human beings are natural forces of the earth, just as rivers and winds are natural forces." The mythic "return of the Aztlan" is on display in the box cars that go by as the essay closes. To support all this, Silko employs the kind of simple, unadorned, reportorial style that you might find in the daily newspaper. There are typically one- or two-clause sentences, frequently brief paragraphs and sentences, infrequent metaphors or other tropes, and simple diction and punctuation.

Notice that all this text-based analysis ignores the fact that Silko's "The Border Patrol State" was originally published in *The Nation* on October 17, 1994. Matters of time and place are extraneous to textual analysis. Nor does it matter to textual criticism which people were reading the essay, what their reaction was, or what other people were saying about immigration (and related topics) at the same time. But all those matters are critical to contextual analysis. If textual criticism can proceed as if the item under consideration "speaks for all time," as if it were a museum piece unaffected by time and space, contextual criticism attends to time-specific cultural meanings and considerations. Contextual analysis requires that texts be considered through the lens of their environments: how do rhetors size up the rhetorical challenges presented by a particular cultural moment and then devise strategies and tactics to answer those challenges?

Burke's commentaries on Hitler's *Mein Kampf* and Milton's *Samson* and Coleridge's "Rime" show how he attended to contextual matters. Since contextual analysis proceeds from an initial description of the rhetorical situation that called it into existence, Burke typically considered the ongoing contemporary conversations that were in play in each case. If each communication is a response to other communications and social practices, if the item under scrutiny is anything but self-contained, then his analyses required him to assess the challenges faced by the author at a particular moment.

And so Burke did his homework on his authors and their circumstances—did some impressive research—to turn up the attitudes and values of the communities that sustained the individual contributions that he was interested in. What challenges did Hitler and Milton and Coleridge face in order to persuade? What strategies and tactics did they employ to achieve their persuasive aims? What does a knowledge of the author's history contribute to an understanding of a given utterance?

If we consider Silko's "Border State" under Burke's tutelage, then, we might first learn all we can about her, especially her life before "Border Patrol" appeared in the mid-1990s. (Well, maybe not "*all* we can": Burke studied Coleridge repeatedly and thoroughly for many years, but such detailed, exhaustive research over a long period is seldom required by rhetorical analysis.) Actually, the essay itself tells readers quite a bit about Silko—most obviously, for example, that she is a Native American writer of note who lived in the Southwest when "Border Patrol State" was written. Some additional poking on the Internet, though, indicates that she is the product of a multicultural upbringing, the offspring of a Laguna Pueblo Indian mother and an Anglo-American father, with Mexican relatives. Born in 1948 and living now in Tucson, she was reared on the outskirts of Laguna Pueblo in New Mexico, was educated there and at the University of New Mexico, and has been producing award-winning poetry, fiction, and essays since publishing her novel *Ceremony* in 1977.

All that is absolutely relevant to an understanding of her essay. Perhaps most relevant to "Border Patrol State" is her 1991 novel *Almanac of the Dead*, the book that Silko refers to in paragraph 3. Set mainly in Tucson, *Almanac of the Dead* centers on a Native American woman psychic who is in the process of transcribing the lost histories of her dead ancestors into "an almanac of the dead"—a history of her people. This history is thus written from the point of view of the conquered, not the conqueror. Thus "The Border Patrol State," it seems, is something of an essay version of *Almanac of the Dead* in that Silko protests what has been lost—and what is still being lost—in the clash between white and Native American cultures that is at the root of her personal upbringing and identity. The essay is a protest against the imperialistic, culture-effacing tactics of the Border Police.

Or is it?

A consideration of the conversations swirling around it (i.e., contextual analysis) reveals that "Border Patrol State" is just as much about immigration policy as about the civil rights of Native Americans. The essay appeared in *The Nation*, a respected, politically progressive magazine that has maintained its political and cultural points of view for many decades. Published in New York City, in 1994 it covered (as it still does) theater, film, music, fiction, and other arts; politics and public affairs; and contemporary culture. If you wanted to know what left-leaning people were thinking about an issue in 1994, *The Nation* would be a good magazine to consult. Silko's essay thus reached an audience of sympathetic readers—people who would be receptive to her message. They would be inclined to take Silko's word for things that she reports and likely to heed her arguments.

What is more interesting is that Silko's essay appeared on October 17, 1994, in a special issue of *The Nation* given over to "The Immigration Wars," a phrase prominent on the magazine's cover on that date. Silko's was one of several articles that appeared under that banner, a further indication that Silko's argument is not just about the violation of the civil rights of Native Americans but also about the related issue of immigration policy. "The Border Patrol State" appeared in *The Nation* after David Cole's "Five Myths about Immigration," Elizabeth Kadetsky's "Bashing Illegals in California," Peter Kwong's "China's Human Traffickers," two editorials about immigration policy during the Clinton administration, and short articles on immigration by *Nation* regulars Katha Pollitt, Aryeh Neier, and Christopher Hitchens. Together the articles mount a sustained argument that Congress and the president should together liberalize immigration policy.

Immigration was not just a topic for *The Nation*, and there was good reason why *The Nation* chose "The Immigration Wars" as a title. October 17, 1994 was just weeks before the 1994 election. When the 1965 Immigration Act was amended in 1990, during the presidency of George H. W. Bush, it was a bipartisan effort (introduced by Democratic senator Ted Kennedy and signed by Republican President Bush) to stem illegal immigration and increase legal entry into the United States. The already strong flow of immigrants to the US was therefore increasing substantially in the first years of the Clinton Administration (i.e., after 1992). While many immigrants before 1965 came to the United States from Europe, through Ellis Island and past the Statue of Liberty, now they were arriving from Asia, Latin America, the Caribbean islands, and Africa and taking up residence in Florida, Texas, Arizona, and California. The arrival of all those immigrants revived old fears—that they take jobs away from native-born citizens, that they undermine national values by resisting assimilation and clinging to their own cultures, that they reduce standards of living by putting stress on education and social-service budgets. Many people were countering those fears by pointing out that actually immigrants create jobs and wealth, that they enhance the vitality of American culture, that they become the proudest of Americans and serve in the armed forces, and that they contribute substantially to the tax base. But those counterarguments were undermined when a tide of illegal immigrants—up to a half-million per year—was arriving as Silko was writing.

The immigration wars were verbal wars. During the 1994 election season, Republicans had united—often uneasily, but they united—under the banner of "A Contract with America." Some three hundred Republican congressional candidates, drawn together by conservative leader and House of Representatives member Newt Gingrich, agreed to run on a common platform in an ultimately successful effort to gain control of the House. Among a number of its initiatives, the Contract with America promised to curtail immigration; to reduce illegal immigration; and to deny health care, social services, and educational access to illegal residents. The Contract with America also offered support for Proposition 187 in California, a so-called "Save Our State" initiative designed to "prevent California's estimated 1.7 million undocumented immigrants from partaking of every form of public welfare," as Kadetsky explained in her contribution to "The Immigration Wars." In short, the Contract with America and Proposition 187 together constituted the nation's leading domestic issue in October 1994. The war of words about the issue was evident in the magazines, books, newspapers, talk shows, barbershops, and hair salons of America—just as it remains today.

In this context, it is easy to see that Silko's essay is about more than the reform of the Border Patrol. It testifies in favor of relatively unrestricted immigration, especially for Mexicans and Native Americans, and it offers a direct refutation of the challenges offered in the language of the Contract with America and Proposition 187. Proposition 187 stated that the people of California "are suffering economic hardship caused by the presence of illegal aliens . . ., that they have suffered and are suffering personal injury and damage caused by the criminal conduct of illegal aliens, [and] that they have a right to the protection of their government from any people or persons entering the country illegally." But Silko answered that challenge by turning the claim around: It is the Border Patrol that is behaving illegally. It is the Border Patrol that is creating economic hardship. It is the Border Patrol that is inflicting injury and damage through criminal conduct. Finally, it is the government that is acting illegally by ignoring the Treaty of Guadalupe Hidalgo, which "recognizes the right of the Tohano O'Odom (Papago) people to move freely across the US-Mexico border without documents," as Silko writes in a footnote. Writing just before the election of 1994, situated firmly in that specific cultural moment, Silko had specific political goals guiding her rhetorical choices. A contextual analysis of "The Border Patrol State" thus reveals that the essay is, among other things, an eloquent refutation of the Contract with America and Proposition 187—even though those items are not even mentioned explicitly in the essay!

Rhetorical Analysis by Students

So that's how Burke might do a rhetorical analysis of an essay like Silko's. But can students do analyses like this? My experience has convinced me that they certainly can. After all, there's nothing especially intricate in the commentary that I've just provided. The textual terminology that I've used to interrogate the essay is very basic; it uses the concepts that are commonly found in introductory composition courses. And, believe me, the research required to contextualize the piece could easily have been done by any conscientious student.

But don't take my word for it. Immediately following this essay, you'll find the assignment sheet I've given over the years to first-year composition students, to students in a sophomore-level elective, and to students in a senior seminar: it describes the rhetorical analyses that I have expected my students to complete, usually as the "big assignment" in the course. And if you'd like to see examples of how students have responded to that assignment, take a look at the "Rhetoric of the Civil Rights Movement" website, which I currently manage: sites.psu.edu/civilrightsrhetoric/. There you'll find a number of sample student rhetorical analysis essays on a variety of artifacts: on speeches (e.g., the address on "Black Power" that Stokely Carmichael presented at Cobo Hall in Detroit on July 30, 1966), on songs (e.g., Bob Dylan's "Only a Pawn in Their Game," which he sang at the March for Jobs and Freedom in Washington on August 28, 1963), on written documents (e.g., the 1964 Supreme Court decision Heart of Atlanta Motel v. United States, which vindicated the Civil Rights Act of that year), or on various other objects of analysis (e.g., Julian Bond's appearance on *Meet the Press*, January 30, 1966). Feel free to have students imitate those examples or take issue with them, as you and they see fit.

Let me conclude on a lofty note, that is, a Burkean note. As Elvera Berry also notes to close out this volume, when you teach the art of rhetorical analysis to students after the example of Kenneth Burke, you will first and foremost be teaching them an art of living. A teacher himself, Burke always fancied himself to be doing important work: preparing students to be more sophisticated (and joyful) consumers and producers of rhetorical artifacts themselves. Anyone who is adept at perceiving the designs that others have on their attitudes, beliefs, and actions, Burke felt, would in turn become more successful at resisting bogus appeals and influencing the attitudes, beliefs, and actions of others. A "War of Words" and symbols rages about us, perpetually, and managing modern life successfully requires survival skills.

But there is even more at stake, Burke felt. It's worth pointing out that Burke did much of his thinking about rhetorical analysis at a time of great crisis himself, namely, during the unfathomable destruction of World War II and under the postwar apocalyptic threat posed by The Bomb (see Weiser, *Burke, War, Words*). Just as Burke gathered his thoughts on rhetorical analysis, ultimately, so that people might find antidotes for disastrous human conflict, so too our pedagogical efforts can contribute to an increase in the sum total of human concord and understanding at a period when we are daily threatened with discord and misunderstanding. I give Burke the last word, therefore, from the conclusion to his chapter entitled "The Devices" in *The War of Words*:

> We take the War of Words to be inevitable. Indeed, a project that looks "towards the purification of war" should hope for not less of such battles, but many more. It is only that grim disease of cooperation, nationalistic "total war," that must be outmoded, unless the human race is to be outmoded. War, in the sense of conflict and competition, is synonymous with vitality. But the more of it there is in civilized forms, the less need of it there may be in those burlesques of primitive substance-thinking we find in modern nationalism. (167)

Rhetorical Analysis Assignment

English 487, Assignment #2: Rhetorical Analysis

The purpose of this assignment is to give you a chance to inform consumers of our course website about the details of a piece of civil rights discourse that is poorly or incompletely understood—and to give you a chance to develop research, analytic, and writing skills that will pay off for you down the line. That is, you have an opportunity to do original scholarship on a rhetorical issue that you care about—and a chance to share your findings with fellow students and other readers (because successful papers will be posted on the class website).

Assignment

Do a scholarly, informed, and informative analysis of a piece of civil rights rhetoric that has not received enough attention or that has been misunderstood. Choose a piece of symbolic action that you are curious about and passionate about so that you are eager to give it your best effort. What you want to do is to produce "the authoritative essay" on your topic: the best scholarly analysis available.

As you consider which object of analysis to pick, think about your interests, explore the course website (particularly the Timelines), overview the suggestions on the course syllabus, and talk with me personally. Usually, the best papers come from your engagement with a speech or document or song (or whatever) that you are especially curious about. If there is a specific person that you are curious about (James Baldwin? Septima Clark? Bayard Rustin? Pauli Murray? Someone more contemporary?), pick something produced by that person—a speech, a document, a song, a film or photo or work of art.

Then become an expert on your topic by studying it thoroughly: to learn about it, use secondary sources and the primary sources that are available via our class "Resources and Analyses" site and make use of suggestions from our librarians (who love to serve as consultants to student researchers). Aim to explain the rhetorical event so well, so completely, and so authoritatively that your essay will stand as the one that others depend on.

Due dates

- You must send me a proposal (attached to an email) asking me to approve your topic, hopefully by _____ and definitely by _____ at the latest. (But why wait until then? Get started early.) The goal of your proposal is to get my approval: I don't want you taking on something too big or too small.
- On _____, be prepared to share informally your list of research sources.
- Your rough draft is due _____. (Note that what I mean by a "rough draft": it's nothing very rough at all, but rather is a fairly finished effort that is ready to be shared with classmates so that you can get suggestions.)
- Final draft is due _____. Or before. After I return your papers, you will have a chance to revise—and qualify to have your essay included on the class website or entered in the Africana Research Exhibition competition and/or submitted for publication in *Young Scholars in Writing*.

Some Suggestions (and Evaluation Criteria)

- Because one purpose of the assignment is to get you into the habit of making detailed research efforts that use both primary and secondary sources, be thorough in your research. Ask me and the library's history experts for assistance as needed. Your finished paper should demonstrate that you know how to investigate thoroughly—learn! learn! learn! —and that you know how to document sources professionally.
- Of course, your essay should display your abilities as a rhetorical analyst as well. Draw from our experiences in class and from your other rhetoric courses as you collect your thoughts on strategies and tactics.
- Be strategic in deciding which features of your topic you want to emphasize and which ones you should deemphasize; focus on the most interesting or problematical features while also being attentive to the whole. Ask me for help in narrowing your topic?

- It is unusual for undergraduate essays to use explanatory notes, but I encourage them as a means of subordinating less important but still relevant information.
- Be sure that your essay develops a clear thesis, that it defends it with a carefully organized and evidence-saturated argument, and that you express yourself clearly and effectively. In short, be a professional in terms of presentation. A common format is to offer an introduction describing the rhetorical challenge faced by the person whose artifact you have chosen, and then to fill the body of your essay with accounts of the strategies and tactics used by the author to meet those challenges. Look at some of the papers on our class website for guidance!
- Length and format: Length is determined by the task—but I'll try to approve only those proposals that I think will generate a paper of 8–12 pages (double-spaced). Format is also a function of task: in this case follow MLA guidelines (i.e., double space with one-inch margins; use paper clips and not staples; and follow MLA advice about type size and style as well as documentation and the correct way to insert photos).

2 LEARNING CLUSTER ANALYSIS WITH UNDERGRADUATES: PERFECTED BY THE OTHER

Annie Laurie Nichols

> *Increasingly sophisticated cluster analyses for analysis and invention with a range of undergraduates.*

In a time when it sometimes feels like everything is fracturing into meaningless lines with no discernable links, students are eager for methods of mapping their worlds and critically grappling with the patterns that run through them.

My students have latched onto cluster analysis as this method. Sure, it lets them untangle ideological assumptions and notice patterns, but it's not any old method: cluster analysis is rooted in rhetorically listening (Ratcliffe) to another in a radically inclusive manner—a skill as desperately needed today as it was in Burke's time (Weiser, *Burke, War, Words*). Its inductive approach asks the critic to engage empathetically with the text—another radical act in our world (Caswell and Cifor). Cluster analysis's form makes it also well-suited to center vernacular and marginalized voices; map visual and multimodal texts; track through multiple fragments; and analyze across layers of close, middling, and distant readings (Nichols).

Cluster analysis also functions as compositional logic: it is both inventional and organizational, and it offers an alternative to linear argumentative moves. Highlighting relationships between concepts and how meanings are being made (Burke, *PC* 14, 35), cluster analysis has proven particularly helpful as an inventional tool when students know what their main points are but not how to clearly explain them. As a means of arrangement, cluster analysis works especially well with nonlinear thinkers and students who come from witty oral cultures—those who are often excluded by more hegemonic forms of composition.

The difficulty of teaching cluster analysis is that, like much Burkean fruit, the concept ripened slowly over many years. Fortunately, Burke uses a well-developed form of cluster analysis in "The Rhetoric of Hitler's 'Battle'" and that, with some explanatory assistance from the four rungs of pedagogy in his essay on education,[1] may be used to great effect to demonstrate the use and power of cluster analysis to undergraduate students.

Unlike Burke's more famous method, the pentad, cluster analysis is not well known or well used, even among Burkeans. So, before I launch into a lengthy account of how I teach it, or even a compelling narrative of why, let me explain just what it is I am talking about.

I teach Burke differently to different classes, of course: to fit the amount of time we have to spend on learning the method, to fit the course level and focus, and to fit the level of sophistication of the students. I also progress students through cluster analysis as Burke himself progressed through it (Nichols).

I always start out with a more equational form, like the cluster analysis Burke sketched in the "Dictionary of Pivotal Terms": "Clusters: Significance gained by noting what subjects cluster about other subjects (what images b, c, d the poet introduces whenever he talks with engrossment of subject a)" (*ATH* 232).

Simply looking at what terms have been grouped in a text facilitates great insight and allows student-critics to attend to the patterns and pieties of others before being asked to contribute their own interpretations or analyses. Foregrounding the meanings of the text on its own terms allows students to exercise the perspective-taking so essential to understanding another's point of view.

You may have caught that "equation" is not a super-Burkey word—and indeed, it smacks of the sort of scientistic thinking that Burke resisted in much of his work. Although he seemed to be using "equation" in a more relational than mathematical sense—he even uses equation and

---

1. Rung 1: taking a stance; "a mode of indoctrination"; Rung 2: listing importance; knowing the enemy so as to be better equipped to combat them; Rung 3: objective appropriation; "describe and 'appropriate' other groups"—basically collecting and describing in a cataloging sense—one might say "for truth and science!"; Rung 4: learning from the other; "to so act that [their] ways can help perfect one's own" ("LAPE" 283).

relationship in clusters together (*PC* 280; *Dramatism and Development* 20)—he eventually shifted away from the term altogether, using "relationship" instead.[2]

Concomitant with this shift from equational to relational cluster analysis is a shift in Burke's focus from using the method to dive ever deeper into a single text to, instead, build meanings outward from a text. For example, in "The Rhetoric of Hitler's 'Battle,'" he analyzes a specific text, then its relationships to its cultural context, then its implications for Burke's cultural context, building a 3D chess-style multidimensional reading of Hitler's autobiography using cluster analysis.

Such an analysis is sophisticated, involved, and complex, and I have not yet attempted to teach it outside a 400-level rhetorical criticism course. I always teach such students the equational form first, just as one teaches 2D chess first, and then we add on.

Besides equational and relational cluster analysis, the third form is compositional logic: using cluster analysis as a form of invention and organization—doing cluster analysis on one's own notes, thoughts, and other prewriting material as a means of thinking. This form is, admittedly, neo-Burkean. I have no evidence that Burke used his method this way; I have just found it a useful practice in my own writing and have therefore folded it into my lessons with students. However, I only teach this method to students who have already learned the first two—I don't want to lead anyone astray!

The remainder of this chapter follows this same arc: first, I detail how I teach the equational form of cluster analysis in both beginning and upper-level undergraduate courses. Second, I explain how I build on that foundation to teach upper-level students a more sophisticated, multilayered, relational version. Third, I elaborate how I use cluster analysis for invention and organization, and I outline how I teach its compositional logic to students. I conclude with a reflection on cluster analysis and rhetorical listening.

Equational Cluster Analysis: Cluster-Link-Analyze (Detailed 2-D Mapping)

Criticism of Media and Society is a 400-level course that serves two primary functions in the communication curriculum. First, it brings students to mastery of core elements of the program, such as "perform

---

2. For an extensive treatment of this transformation, see Nichols, pp. 14–46.

theoretically grounded critiques of mass media artifacts that address diversity and incorporate global perspectives." Second, it teaches analytical methods of research, providing an overview of a variety of methods that are immediately applied in critical analyses of media texts. The course covers formal, ideological, and feminist approaches, among others, and cluster analysis. Not the pentad. Cluster analysis.

I know that, to some, those are fighting words. In defense, let me offer this: Burke taught his own students cluster analysis at Bennington College (Wible). That's not why I do it, though. We all know that poor pentadic analysis tends to be little more than a list of who/what/when/where/how/why—a list from which it is difficult to generate insight (for ways to teach this better, see Tilli's and Beasley's chapters in this volume). In contrast, even basic-level cluster analysis—looking only at the adjectives and phrases immediately surrounding a particular word in a text—may yield great insight. Thus, cluster analysis serves as a better gateway to Burkean method, one which scaffolds more smoothly, yields across a wider range of levels, and which can serve as a foundation to other canonical concepts, such as terministic screens, piety, identification and division, substance, terms of order, the scapegoating and redemption cycle, symbols of authority, motive, and so on. Cluster analysis also lays the groundwork for pentadic analysis by attuning students to the relationships between words.

The form of cluster analysis that I teach, quilted from Burke's explanations and examples, consists of three iterative steps: cluster, link, and analyze. In other places I have referred to this as relational cluster analysis ("No Tangle So Hopeless"), as the "link" step highlights the relationship between the terms. I present these steps as a series of substeps:

I. CLUSTER

- Determine your key terms, those crucial to your text (or your research questions).
- Begin with one term.
- Find every instance of that term in your text, and every reference to it, however oblique.
- Note the concepts (synonyms, adjectives, adverbs, opposites, insults, metaphors, etc.) that appear with your key term, especially those which appear *frequently* (in tone or number).
- Draw a circle and write your key term inside it. Write the concepts around it.

- Group concepts by *where they appear in the text*. Not by their meaning. Words that appear together in the text should be closer to each other—clustered together.
- Make more frequent concepts larger or a brighter color or some such to distinguish the *degrees of relationship*.

II. Link

- Consider HOW each concept is related to your key term:[3]
    - Of the same kind =
    - Transforming from one thing to another -->
    - Linked by being dissimilar to =/=
    - In opposition to |

III. Analyze

- Consider the implications of these linkages. Are any of them unexpected?[4]
- Is there anything here that is contradictory? If so, which side seems to be winning out?[5]
- If we remember that every word choice is a selection, a deflection, and a reflection, what are some things that have NOT been chosen that one might reasonably expect to find?[6] What are some things that have been chosen NOT to say? That is—what may have been overlooked? What was purposely left out?

---

3. With the exception of the fourth ("in opposition to"), which is my own addition, these symbols and their use are detailed in *PLF*, 74–75, 77.

4. Burke explains that one way to do cluster analysis is to note "discontinuities in procedure," e.g., where opposites are linked or where terms frequently show up together and are made to stand in for each other. These discontinuities "are particularly valuable as 'leads' for the critic who would track down the meaning of symbols," Burke writes, adding, "we consider this method essential to analytic exegesis" (*ATH*, 194).

5. This step is drawn from Burke's claim that "by charting clusters, we get our cues as to the important ingredients subsumed in 'symbolic mergers.' We reveal, beneath an author's 'official front,' the level at which a lie is impossible. If a man's virtuous characters are dull, and his wicked characters are done vigorously, his art has voted for the wicked ones, regardless of his 'official front'" (*ATH*, 233). See also Burke, *GM*, 108, 114; Burke, *RM*, 89; Burke, *LSA*, 19.

6. We cover this Burkean concept earlier in the semester: "Even if any given terminology is a reflection of reality, by its very nature as a terminology it must be a selection of reality; and to this extent it must also function as a deflection of reality. . . any nomenclature necessarily directs the attention into some channels rather than others" (*LASA*, 45).

- What is reflected here that you have seen elsewhere? Are you reminded of anything? Is this imagery typical elsewhere? Where do these adjectives tend to be used? What are their associations? What is the cultural history of these concepts?[7]
- What identifications are being made here? What divisions?[8] What lines of piety are drawn?

These three steps can be done at each of the four stages outlined above: relationships between term and attitudes, relationships between clusters of terms, relationships between cultural contexts and clusters of terms, relationships between the contextual cultures and our own (or other) cultures.

When I first introduce cluster analysis to my students, I explain it by means of an example. Here is a passage from Douglas Adams's *The Hitchhiker's Guide to the Galaxy* (35) that I use in my 100-level Intro to Communication Theory course (Figure 1). I highlight references to humans and all the adjectives and phrases associated with them. Those are isolated into a cluster, with "human being" at the center (Figure 2). This immediately makes clear Ford Prefect's views toward humans, as well as illuminating the basics of the method.

---

7. Burke explained to Cowley in a 1950 letter that cluster analysis was meant "to find out *what goes with what* in a book, so that one's analysis is internal; yet to note the social relevance of such 'equations'" (Jay, 291–92); note that this terminology is parallel to his description of style and piety: "Style is a constant meeting of obligations, a state-of-being-without-offense, a repeated doing of the 'right' thing. It molds our actions by contingencies, but these contingencies go to the farthest reaches of the communicative. For style (custom) is a complex schema of *what-goes-with-what*, carried through all the subtleties of manner and attitudes. . . . The normal tendency to refrain from the murder of one's allies is 'rational' only because it reflects an unquestioned taboo, an undeviating sense of what goes with what. And an obedience to such customary values is not cowardice, but piety" (Burke, *Permanence and Change*, 269–70; emphasis added).

8. Again, we cover identification and division earlier in the course. This dialectic is a central pairing in Burke's work. See, for example, Burke, *RM*, 16–58; Burke, *PLF*, 227–29, 306–11; Burke, *ATH*, 263-73.

Learning Cluster Analysis with Undergraduates 25

> One of the things Ford Prefect had always found hardest to understand about human beings was their habit of continually stating and repeating the obvious, as in It's a nice day, or You're very tall, or Oh dear you seem to have fallen down a thirty-foot well, are you alright? At first Ford had formed a theory to account for this strange behavior. If human beings don't keep exercising their lips, he thought, their mouths probably seize up. After a few months consideration and observation he abandoned this theory in favour of a new one. If they don't keep on exercising their lips, he thought, their brains start working. After a while he abandoned this one as well as being obstructively cynical and decided he quite liked human beings after all, but he always remained desperately worried about the terrible number of things they didn't know about.

Figure 1. In-class cluster exercise from Douglas Adams's *The Hitchhiker's Guide to the Galaxy* (35).

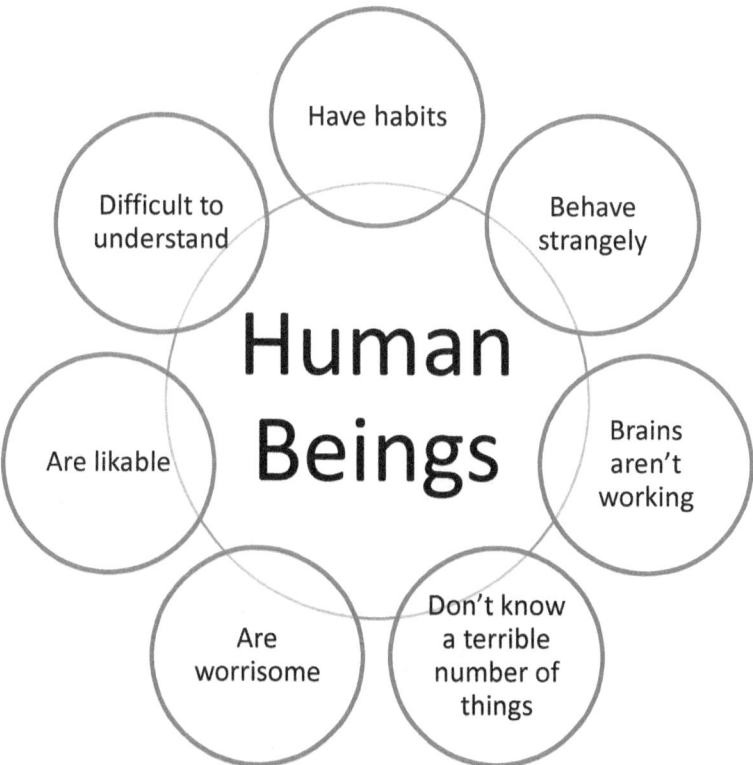

Figure 2. In-class cluster exercise designed by the author.

Once students understand how the concept works, I give them a text to work with, say, a newspaper article about basketball superstar Zion Williamson (e.g., Ellentuck; I choose something current that folk are passionate about) and have them repeat the exercise themselves: Find all the references to Zion. Find all the synonyms, adjectives, and phrases that surround those references. Pull them out and write them down. Looking at that group, draw some conclusions about overall attitudes.

For even better effect, I sometimes give two or three different articles from different points of view on the same topic to different groups of students and then compare the attitudes in the large group discussion. Students are surprised to note that Williamson is described as bestial (beast, monster), elemental (hurricane, whirlwind), and even architectural (pillars, skyscraper, tower), but never as a human. These observations lead to discussions of US cultural narratives of the Black body (nonhuman, dangerous) and some of the implications of those narratives (police officers defending themselves, necessary use of excessive force, nonhuman bodies of Black men).

This is as far as I go in 100- or 200-level courses, but it allows us to cover quite a lot of ground in a single class period: we establish that terms have attitudes, that those attitudes are expressed in clusters, that we can critically analyze those attitudes by mapping those clusters, and that this is a form of close textual analysis that yields insight, helps make more sense of motive and action, and gets students excited about doing criticism (when was the last time you went from zero to insight in seventy-five minutes? It's a great feeling!).

For the 400-level course, we keep on. Having encircled our key figure in a cluster, we pause to discuss the types of relationships between terms:

- Of the same kind =
- Transforming from one thing to another -->
- Linked by being dissimilar to =/=
- In opposition to |

And we look at another example. Students connect each term in their cluster to the key term in the center using the appropriate symbol and note any relevant connections between terms, as well. We pause to discuss any new insights.

At this point we have gotten to the second stage of cluster analysis—looking at the relationships between terms in a cluster. This is generally plenty of new content for one class meeting, so we use the remainder of our time to map other key terms in the article and mark the relationships between them—opponents, coaches, teammates, gravity, normal humans—splitting the students into groups to do so. When they've finished, we transfer their work to the board, and they explain it to the class.

As homework, each student maps the concepts that recur around key terms they've previously identified in the media artifacts (a film, music album, speech, advertising campaign, Instagram account, sculpture, cartoon, etc.) that they've been working with all semester. They are instructed to bring these maps—complete with relational markers—to class next meeting.

At the beginning of the next class meeting, I copy the example cluster analysis map back onto the board, with the additional key word clusters ringing it. We pull out the example text again and look for relationships between the key terms themselves: are they equal, transitioning, linked by their dissimilarity, in opposition to? What are the implications of each? Are any culturally unusual?

After working through the example on the board, I give students some time to work with the cluster maps they brought in. By this point in the semester, they are well acquainted with their media artifacts, so I walk around the room and troubleshoot, but students are generally able to pull up their piece of media and work with it readily.

When everyone has a solid grasp of this step, I offer a further example. We discuss how we might take this cluster analysis of a single article about a single basketball player and situate it as one part of a larger cluster of texts—are male athletes covered differently than female? Does race matter? Sport type? How are young Black men described in other contexts? How is Zion Williamson described by reporters in other countries? Looking at these clusters of texts would answer different questions—but we would still need to follow the same process: Cluster, link, analyze!

This brings us to the third stage—comparing clusters to their cultural contexts. What are the implications of describing Zion Williamson as a "beast," "superhuman," with "pillars of stone" for legs? What are some of the things article authors are NOT choosing to say—or choosing NOT to say? What cultural connections can we make here? Why might it be a problem to only talk about a young Black man's body or to dehumanize it? Are there any unusual choices here? We continue to work together on the example text for two-thirds of the class time, before students switch to adding to the cluster maps for their own media artifacts.

The difficulty of using cluster analysis for a third of my course is that—as with many Burkean concepts—KB developed it slowly, with many meanderings, over a long period of time (Nichols). The entry in his "Dictionary of Pivotal Terms" (*ATH*, 232–34) for cluster analysis is quite green when compared to the cluster analysis in *Rhetoric of Religion*. Consequently, there is no single passage one can assign to students to let them learn cluster analysis from Burke, in Burke's voice. In the end, I see this as an opportunity. Burke is at his best when he is explaining the "so what?"—and one of his most brilliant, most captivating, most bold and brassy so what's is his rationale for "The Rhetoric of Hitler's 'Battle.'" Rather than asking students to meander through Burke's multidecade maturation of cluster analysis (much though I wish I had the time), I teach them how to use it, giving them an overview in class myself. When we are ready for stage four, the stage that corresponds with the fourth rung of Burke's pedagogical ladder—"one does not merely want to outwit the opponent, or to study [them], one wants to be affected by [them], in some degree to incorporate [them], to so act that [their] ways can help perfect one's own—in brief, to learn from [them]" ("LAPE" 284)—then I assign Burke. We read "The Rhetoric of Hitler's 'Battle.'"

So far, this has always been a hard class. We don't like to think that, were we in Nuremberg in 1934, we probably would have cheered. It is so much more comfortable to condemn others than to change ourselves. So, I bring cupcakes. We sit in a circle. And we digest. I teach them about KB's four rungs, and we look at their cluster analyses again. "Which rung are you on right now?" I ask. "Are you indoctrinating? Combatting? Appropriating? Learning? What do you need to do to climb up?" I don't know if it's the Burke or the sugar that kicks in at this point (probably the sugar), but it's here that the students get really excited. I usually have to remind them to pack up when the class period ends.

For homework, each student must turn in their complete, detailed cluster map of their media artifact. Next class period we start on the multilayered cluster analysis modeled in "The Rhetoric of Hitler's 'Battle'" as students begin to connect their analyses and insights with larger cultural norms, implications, and takeaways.

Relational Cluster Analysis: 3D Chess

In teaching students to turn their detailed 2D cluster maps into rich 3D topographies, I find it useful to introduce them to a simple form of pieties (which I refer to as norms or "normals"). To do so, I make use of some examples of my own cross-cultural work in Russia and Azerbaijan. I find it helpful to start with cross-cultural examples because, as Gerry Philipsen put it, paying attention to another culture's linkages can help us note our own, usually taken for granted, associations. However, it can be equally effective to use a cultural group with which students are intimately familiar–the culture of one's particular educational institution, for instance. Here I give an example of how I introduce the concept of cultural norms as linked to cluster analysis to students, using cross-cultural experience as a starting point:

> It was my friend's birthday today, so I stopped by the store to buy her some flowers. I already had been warned that flowers in even numbers symbolize death, so I carefully chose three roses. I decided on yellow, as yellow roses symbolize friendship where I come from.
>
> But not in Russia. There they mean, "I'm breaking up with you. Goodbye." Why someone would buy roses to do that, I really don't know. Thankfully, my friend was gracious and accepted the flowers along with their American meaning.
>
> I wonder what the people working in the flower store thought.

Each of us makes assumptions every day about what's correct, what's good, and what's normal, I tell my students. These assumptions seem like common sense to us, perfectly normal: how could anyone think otherwise? But we learn them, typically through interactions with other people. And these shared assumptions about what is normal, correct, and good comprise culture. They connect us to each other, allow us to understand each other, and hold us together as communities. Our sense of what is normal allows us to connect but also separates us from those who have other normals. Community is constructed through terms that unite and divide us, making connection messy and difficult.

When I lived in Russia from 2007 to 2011, I found out that most of the things I thought were normal were, in fact, American. Living in another culture for four years does rub off on you, though; when I came back, all my American friends thought I was weird—I had the wrong set of normals. But you don't have to go to another country to do the wrong thing or misunderstand others; right now, Americans are having a hard time understanding each other's normals. My social media feeds are filled with people shouting at each other, or, worse, everyone saying what I already agree with. What I don't see a lot of is trying to connect to others and understand their normal. Some may argue that we shouldn't try to understand others, that some beliefs are so vile that we should stamp them out as much as possible. These folks are much more in favor of punching Nazis than listening to them. But punching doesn't heal community, or help us understand each other, or make it possible to live together.

When Adolf Hitler wrote a memoir, most Americans dismissed it as evil and condemned the German people for going along with it. But there was one social critic who was humble enough and wise enough to take Hitler's writing seriously. Kenneth Burke wrote in 1939:

> Here is the testament of a man who swung a great people into his wake. Let us watch it carefully; and let us watch it, not merely to discover some grounds for prophesying what political move is to follow Munich, and what move to follow that move, etc.; let us try also to discover what kind of "medicine" this medicine man has concocted, that we may know, with greater accuracy, exactly what to guard against, if we are to forestall the concocting of similar medicine in America. (*PLF* 191)

Burke's solution was not to dismiss Nazis, but to pay attention to how they created the connections that held them together—and which might, conceivably, hold others together as well. The solution? Understand so that one will not get the same illness. That is, Burke treated understanding the connections between Nazis as a kind of inoculation against hate speech.

Burke gives us a way of talking about community, identity, belonging that focuses on their communicative root. In his cluster analysis of Hitler's "Battle," he also gives us a way through the problem. When we map people's connections, we are able to understand them. But we are also able to transcend them, generate new connections, and replace connections that destroy with connections that facilitate stronger community. We often do not notice what we take for granted as normal until it is challenged. So how do we figure out what is normal for someone else? For this, Burke developed cluster analysis: a method of mapping the connections that constitute identities, communities, and cultures by linking together objects, experiences, and interactions. Adults know that one thing can belong to many categories (my niece's *daddy* can also be my *brother*), but we still tend to choose things out of particular categories over and over, and these repeated choices constitute our habits, character, selves, communities, culture. These are our "normals."

So, to understand what is normal to people, we need to map their links. What do they group together? What do they think "properly goes with what," as Burke puts it (*PC* 269–70)?

When my students and I have worked through the concept of cultural norms and linked them to cluster analysis, I introduce the concept of layers or stages of analysis. Each stage is linked to an increasingly abstract level of culture, from very specific subgroups to the imagined communities of nations. Not all projects require analysis at all stages, but it is useful to be versed in all of them.

1. In the first stage of cluster analysis, we map the relationships between terms and the attitudes formed by their associations and transformations.
2. In the second stage, we consider the relationships between the clusters themselves—clusters of clusters, as it were.
3. In the third stage, we elucidate the relationships between these associations and society, critically examining the implications of the sense of normality these links create. This provides a robust analysis that focuses on the rhetorical moves and relationships in the text and how they work together to create a particular view of the world.
4. In the final stage of cluster analysis, we explain what one can learn from that point of view and how one can incorporate insights from it into one's own orientation.

To make the layers clear I use some of my own work on nationalism in Azerbaijan to explain these stages to students. I focus on how different ethnographic groups define their place in the new nation and how the government is working to draw the many disparate groups together to create a sense of being Azerbaijani. If time allows, we also work through data on #BlackLivesMatter protests in Baltimore, Maryland in 2014 surrounding the death of Freddie Gray as an example of a non-nationalist application of the stages.

It is not necessary to do this work with a culture as geographically removed as the people groups of Azerbaijan are from rural Pennsylvania, but I have found it helpful to choose a topic with which students are unfamiliar to highlight the power this method may have in fostering understanding of both familiar (famous basketball stars and US race relations) and unfamiliar (the fractured nationalism of far-off lands) subjects. I have also found that students want to jump to the "drawing conclusions" step rather than attending to what the text actually says; using texts from contexts they are unfamiliar with forces them to focus on the text and work through the process of analysis from a listening rather than an analytical stance before applying judgment. I take this to an extreme by using ethnographic texts from rural Azerbaijan, but it can be done with archival documents, historical speeches, MySpace profiles, or Supreme Court proceedings—any texts that students lack great context for should suffice.

Using some of my ethnographic fieldnotes to work through how the isolated Xinaliq people understand self and place (Figure 3), we discuss how texts can be constituted in conversation as much as by publishing them or producing them by more formal means. We connect Xinaliqi experiences to the students' everyday lived experiences, their own vernacular voices, and what they've learned in prior courses about narrative, identity formation, and social cohesion. We also discuss how important it is to listen to how people define themselves, in their own words, and the terms and relationships they use to do so, and we note how cluster analysis allows us to focus on words and clusters before we apply any lenses.

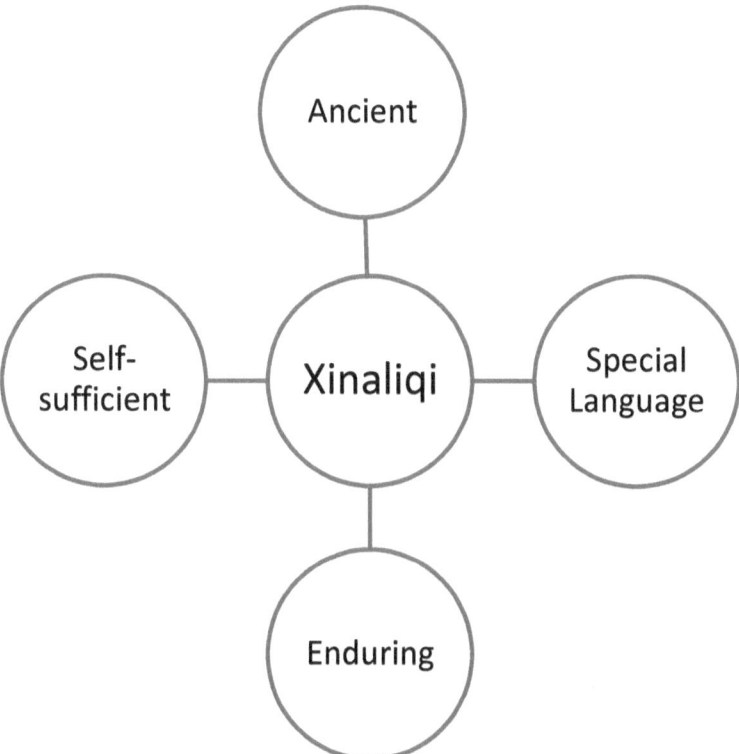

Figure 3. Demonstration of first level of relationship clusters; slide by the author.

Moving up one level of relational abstraction from the relationships between terms and attitudes in a text or community to the relationships between groups of communities, we discuss how the majority ethnic group of Azerbaijani people, the Azeri, living in the largely modernized capital city of Baku, talk about themselves and their place in the world.[9] We also discuss the relationships between the Xinaliqi and the Azerbaijani viewpoints, as well as how rural and city folk talk about each other (Figure 4), reinforcing how to use our symbol system of relationships between terms and clusters.

---

9. I emphasize that the people I spoke with in Baku, like the people in Xinaliq, were choosing how to portray themselves to a random American lady who showed up and talked to them for a long time in the middle of the winter one month, and that we needed to understand their stories in that context—how important it always is to discuss stories in their context, especially when comparing them to each other.

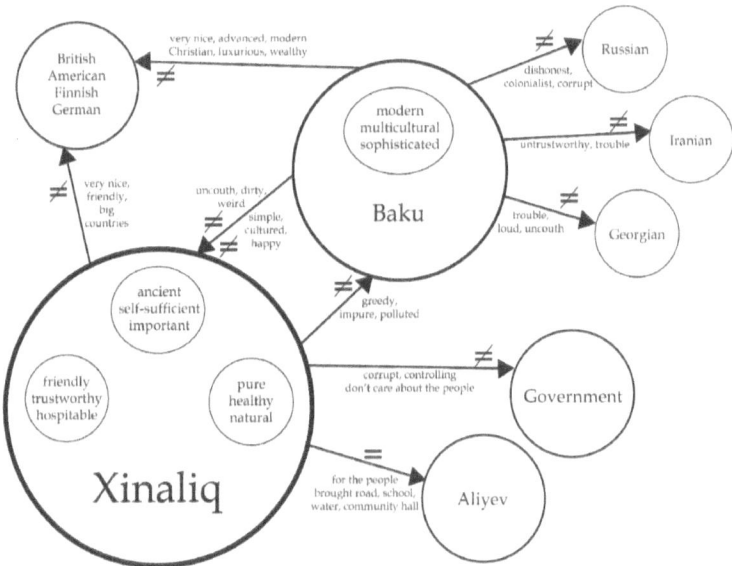

Figure 4. Demonstration of second level of relationship clusters; chart by author.

I introduce the next relational level, relationships between community associations and society, as a challenge that the government is presently trying to address: What is Azerbaijan? We discuss the differences between the viewpoints of the Xinaliqi in Xinaliq and the Azerbaijani in Baku. Then we look at a national symbol that has done some work to draw the groups together: the buta (Figure 5), a paisley-type shape common in the region that holds a variety of meanings for the people of Azerbaijan.

In the final level, we ask the question that I learned from Elvera Berry (see her chapter in this volume) when I was an undergraduate student: "so what?" What can we learn from these groups of people, far away in a country most of us can't spell and many of us can't locate on a map? We discuss this for a while. Eventually we come to something like this: Creating a transcendent national identity that connects very different communities requires balance, a framing of one value in terms of another. In America, there has been a breakdown of these sorts of transcendent values, and to make America a community, "American values" must be explained in terms that bridge groups. If there's time, we take a look at some campaign speeches or ads to see whether they do this effectively.

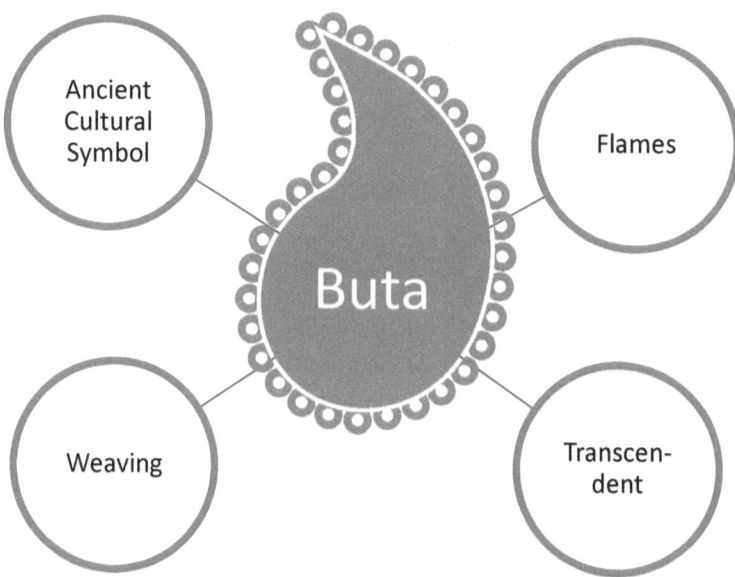

Figure 5. Cluster relationship of a unifying national symbol; slide by author.

I take the time to teach this multilayered version of cluster analysis because it provides a method that is inductive, rooted in the meanings, connections, and assumptions of the community, rather than the researcher. Most methods can show me—and my students—whether people are doing things that *I* consider normal, but they are not as good at mapping out what others consider normal. In this multilevel variant, my own culture is inserted only at the very last. This means that I am listening to the community and its connections for the majority of my critical endeavor—even when conducting ethnographic research, where I am the instrument of data collection—rather than centering my own expertise and experience.

Teaching students a method of analysis that automatically centers the voice of the text, that focuses on listening to the community by design, is invaluable. One of the most difficult skills to master as a critic is how to balance insightful analysis and critical distance. Cluster analysis has that balance baked in, so budding critics can focus on the work and developing their insight, rather than juggling. Working inductively also grounds their analysis in the text, forcing students to work from *what is there* to their claims, rather than the other way around, an all-too-common challenge for beginners. At the same time, mapping key meanings and their relationships, considering them in their contexts, and learning from them gives students an opportunity to take on the orientation of the text in a nuanced and empathetic manner—the principle of education that Burke described as "the most mature of the lot, and the one that would surely be aimed at, in an ideal world of civilized and sophisticated people" ("LAPE" 284).

Cluster Analysis as Compositional Logic

Cluster analysis's grounding in the text also works well for grounding a writer's thoughts. The method can serve as a powerful part of the writing process because it highlights the relationships between terms, amplifies the connections between concepts, and raises up the transformations occurring. It's also a great way to suss out one's own pieties and to find where one's thinking on a piece is still murky.

When I teach this method to students, they already have created detailed cluster analyses of their media texts. But the insights generated by doing those analyses must be combined with previous work on the forms and ideologies of the text. They need to think about how to integrate their insights to create a cohesive final paper.

We start much like any outlining: What's unusual, different, important about this text? Put those ideas in big circles. Do any of those ideas have ideas that go with them? For example, in my project—I always have an ongoing research project to use as an example—one of the main ideas is that a lot of people troll because they are lonely, and the subideas are that trolling demonstrates their in-group status, separates the sheep from the trolls, and allows them to perform their commitment to the group. Those ideas can be added as smaller circles around the large one, with the appropriate relationship marked.

Now, are there other concepts or information that are important to your paper? Are they connected to any of your circles? If not, add them around the edge or write them on another piece of paper, and we'll add them as we figure out where they go. Sometimes you just need a "background" or "context" section where a bunch of that stuff goes together. Sometimes you don't. But we'll see.

Now, are any of these new terms/concepts or circles connected to each other? How? Add the appropriate relational marks. Remember that things can be connected in more than one way! Finally, looking at this, are there any places where things are unclear or missing?

Working through this process helps those thinkers who, like me, do better with visual information. But it goes beyond that—it's not just a weird version of a mind map. It's a visual format that emphasizes the *relationships* between the components, not just that organizes the components themselves. That's a step that both mindmapping and traditional linear outlining don't get to. So, yes, the visual aspect of organizing a paper with clusters is useful to my visual learners and nonlinear thinkers—but it does more than that. It is also inventional.

Using cluster analysis to organize their thoughts doesn't just get students to the cluster—it also gets them to the analysis. The method forces them to lay out their pieties and examine the relationships their thought has formed—that is, to lay bare their insights. And, like tilling a garden to lay bare the earth, this occupation can be quite generative, helping them to create new meanings, insights, and relationships. For example, preparing to write about the *SpongeBob SquarePants Movie*, one student mapped the values of the title character for a major section of their paper. In noting what SpongeBob cared about, the student realized that the character underwent a significant maturation process from childhood to adolescence while maintaining the same primary motivation of achieving personal goals and maintaining positive self-worth. This realization ended up forming the crux of their paper, as they contrasted the hero's journey of SpongeBob to the selfish route taken to the same goals by the villain (this parallel was also discovered during cluster outlining).

Conclusion: Clustering as Rhetorical Listening

Even though Burke developed cluster analysis over decades, it may be effectively taught to undergraduate students at a variety of levels, from an intro course to a senior seminar. Moreover, the method may be taught as focusing on a single text in detail (2D chess), as a text in relation to other texts (3D chess), or as compositional logic. All three forms are best taught by use of examples, but the second benefits from working through Burke's "The Rhetoric of Hitler's 'Battle'" and excerpts from "Linguistic Approach," giving students a framework for increasing the complexity of their analysis with the assistance of a pithier Burkean source.

When it comes down to it, I teach cluster analysis not because it's easy for students to grasp, because it yields immediate insight, or because it's elegantly and powerfully scalable. I teach cluster analysis because it engages students' critical imaginations. Beginning with the key terms in the text and then tracking the concepts and relational links that surround them causes the critic to engage the text on its own terms first, long before bringing their own critical insights to bear. This inductive structure yields two jewels: first, students do good criticism that is grounded in the text—not a small thing; second, they practice rhetorical listening, or as Burke might say, a willingness "to be affected by" the text ("LAPE" 284). This sort of perspective-taking is a crucial skill of close textual analysis as well as a vital part of a functioning society. Formal analysis is great and all, but it does not make categorically better people.

Perspective by Incongruity and Identification Lessons

1. Perspective by Incongruity: *Florilegia*

I introduce the concept of perspective by incongruity in this lesson. I begin by giving students the "Florilegium" handout (Handout 1), explaining the concept and history of gathering a bouquet of quotes, either topically or haphazardly. We then explore topical florilegia with the "Perspective by Incongruity" handout (Handout 2).

I break students into groups of 3–4, and each group must write a single-sentence definition of perspective by incongruity, which they then share with the class. I compile these on the board to create a multi-version, and we discuss the similarities and differences between groups' definitions. Typically, we spend most of our time on the incongruity half; I find that students have a strong understanding that things ought to be approached from multiple perspectives (even if they do not always know how to execute that imperative).

We then practice perspective by incongruity while exploring the haphazard sort of florilegia through an in-class activity.

2. Perspective by Incongruity: Find a Connection

Close your eyes and take two magazine cut-outs from the box [I bought one copy each of *Time, Ebony, Airbnb Magazine, Fermentation, Backcountry, Southern Living,* and *Yoga Journal* and cut out all the images. Any assortment of magazines with a wide range of pictures will do.] Choose another from the dictionary box [I bought a dictionary for $3, cut out miscellaneous columns, and put them in a box; see Handout 4 "Argument Words" in the next lesson for examples].

Using at least one of the words from the dictionary clipping, create a composition on a piece of cardstock using the cut-outs that highlight one or more relationships between the two images. You may add other words, drawings, symbols, designs, etc. as necessary to illustrate this relationship.

Homework

Read Anne Demo's article "The Guerrilla Girls' Comic Politics of Subversion" for class on Tuesday. You don't have to understand everything but try to figure out what she means by perspective by incongruity and strategic juxtaposition and pay attention to how the Guerrilla Girls use remix to deliberate. These questions might help:
- What do the Guerrilla Girls remix (ideas? images? words? values?)? Why?
- What is their main message?
- Are they successful in shifting the conversation or bringing attention to their cause or issue? How?
- Are there any downsides to their approach? What?

Learning Cluster Analysis with Undergraduates 41

https://en.wikipedia.org/wiki/Florilegium

Florilegium

In medieval Latin a *florilegium* (plural *florilegia*) was a compilation of excerpts from other writings. The word is from the Latin *flos* (flower) and *legere* (to gather): literally a gathering of flowers, or collection of fine extracts from the body of a larger work. It was adapted from the Greek *anthologia* (ἀνθολογία) "anthology", with the same etymological meaning.

Meanings

1. a collection of botanically accurate paintings of plants, done by botanical illustrators from life

2. a patristic anthology in Christian literature

3. the title of a scholarly journal published annually by the Canadian Society of Medievalists / Société canadienne des médiévistes

4. the title of various literary anthologies, e.g., by Johannes Stobaeus

5. the title of certain collections of musical compositions, e.g., by Georg Muffat

2. Medieval Usage

Medieval florilegia were systematic collections of extracts taken mainly from the writings of the Church Fathers from early Christian authors, also pagan philosophers such as Aristotle, and sometimes classical writings. A prime example is the *Manipulus florum* of Thomas of Ireland, which was completed at the beginning of the fourteenth century. The purpose was to take passages that illustrated certain topics, doctrines or themes. After the medieval period, the term was extended to apply to any miscellany or compilation of literary or scientific character.

1. Flowers

The term *florilegia* also applied literally to a treatise on flowers or medieval books that are dedicated to ornamental rather than the medicinal or utilitarian plants covered by herbals. The emergence of botanical illustration as a genre of art dates back to the 15th century, when herbals (books describing the culinary and medicinal uses of plants) were printed containing illustrations of flowers. As printing techniques advanced, and new plants came to Europe from Ottoman Turkey in the 16th century, wealthy individuals and botanic gardens commissioned artists to record the beauty of these exotics in Florilegia. Florilegia flourished in the 17th century when they were created to portray rare and exotic plants from far afield. Modern florilegia seek to record collections of plants, often now endangered, from within a particular garden or place. Florilegia are among the most lavish and expensive books to produce because of all the work required to produce them.

Handout 1. *Florilegium*, by the author.

"'perspective by incongruity,' a kind of vision got by seeing one order in terms of another." ●

"Midway between an old weighting and a new weighting, is the realm we have called 'perspective by incongruity' (a term that designates one way of transcending a given order of weightedness.) The concept, as we see it now, was the other side of Remy de Gourmont's formula for the 'dissociation of ideas.' De Gourmont was concerned with the methodic blasting apart of verbal particles that had been considered insepa|rable; 'perspective by incongruity' refers to the methodic merger of particles that had been considered mutually exclusive." ■

"It appeals by exemplifying relationships between objects which our customary rational vocabulary has ignored." ■

perspective by incongruity brings "together terms which we had unconsciously classed as mutually exclusive." —

"The universe would appear to be something like a cheese; it can be sliced in an infinite number of ways--and when one has chosen his own pattern of slicing, he finds that other men's cuts fall at the wrong places." ■

"As soon as one tries to carry his pattern of cuts beyond the classifications recognized in common speech, one strains at the limits of 'good taste,' since good taste is manifested through our adherence to the kinds of relationship already indicated by the terminology of common sense." ■

Kenneth Burke
perspective
by Incongruity

"analytic processes whereby a non-A or counter-A is explicitly shown (by 'organized bad taste') to have been implicit in the term A." ■

"we contend that 'perspective by incongruity' makes for a dramatic vocabulary, with weighting and counter-weighting, in contrast with the liberal ideal of neutral naming in the characterization of processes." △

"Perspective by incongruity is a way of seeing two ways at once." ⬟

The stage between piety and impiety "involves a shattering or fragmentation" -- aka a ■ perspective by incongruity

● Counter-Statement ●
■ Permanence and Change ■
△ Attitudes toward History △
Language as Symbolic Action
⬟ On Human Nature ⬟

1931 1935 1937 1966 2003

"One sees perspectives beyond the structure of a given vocabulary when that structure is ■ no longer firm."

"a word belongs by custom to a certain category--and by rational planning you wrench it loose and metaphorically apply it to a △ different category."

perspective by incongruity is "when a term that has come to seem natural in one context is suddenly jammed into a different ⬟ and hitherto alien context."

Handout 2. Perspective by Incongruity, from Kenneth Burke, constructed by the author.

3. Perspective by Incongruity: Verbal and Visual Arguments

Note: This lesson immediately follows the lesson on Florilegia in my course.

Perspective by incongruity is a key concept in my visual argument course, so I introduce it early. We begin by reading and discussing Anne Demo's article "The Guerrilla Girls' Comic Politics of Subversion," looking at examples of strategic juxtaposition and perspective by incongruity and teasing out what makes them so strategic.

We then practice by creating conflicting, multifaceted definitions of argument in an in-class activity (Juxtapositions of Argument; see below). I distribute four different definitions of "argument" or "rhetoric" to students (Handout 3 "Argument Definition"), with each student getting just one definition. Each student is tasked with rewriting the definition into plain language, then using adjectives from random dictionary pages (Handout 4 "Argument Words" handout) to create other meanings of argument. Finally, they add their own words and images to round out the composition.

Next, we refresh our memories on perspective by incongruity and discuss how we might use it visually. I present perspective by incongruity in visual argument as having two main goals: to put things together that haven't been together before, or to take things apart that have habitually been grouped together. After giving several examples, I give the students a pair of visual collage tasks that allow them to practice visual perspective by incongruity (Strategic Juxtapositions 1 and 2). I purposely chose a challenging topic for this assignment because I have found that an issue with clear stakes is more straightforward for them to grasp quickly. We do half of the assignment as an in-class activity, and students complete the second part as a homework assignment.

Juxtapositions of Argument

You will receive a definition of argument (Handout 3 "Argument Definitions"). Your task is to:

1. Remix the definition into the vernacular (rewrite it into everyday language that normal people can understand).
2. Choose some of the "Alliterative Argument" words to collage in (Handout 4 "Argument Words").
3. Find or create images to collage in that illustrate existing or add additional points.

Your goal should be to create 2–3 different perspectives on what argument is.

Activity 2: Strategic Juxtaposition 1

Go to www.humansofnewyork.com/tagged/refugee-stories and choose one story.

Juxtapose some of the images and words from that story with images and words of "terrorists" to create a visual argument about whether or not refugees belong in that group.

Homework: Strategic Juxtaposition 2

Use the same story you chose for Strategic Juxtaposition 1. Juxtapose some of the images and words from that story with images and words of "The American Dream" to create a visual argument about whether or not refugees belong in the same cluster or group of concepts.

> "the art of discovering in any given case the available means of persuasion"
> Aristotle

> "the art of enchanting the soul"
> Plato

> "a claim supported by reasons"
> Dale Hample

> "a symbolic means of inducing cooperation in beings that by nature respond to symbols"
> Kenneth Burke

Handout 3. Argument Definitions, constructed by author.

Learning Cluster Analysis with Undergraduates

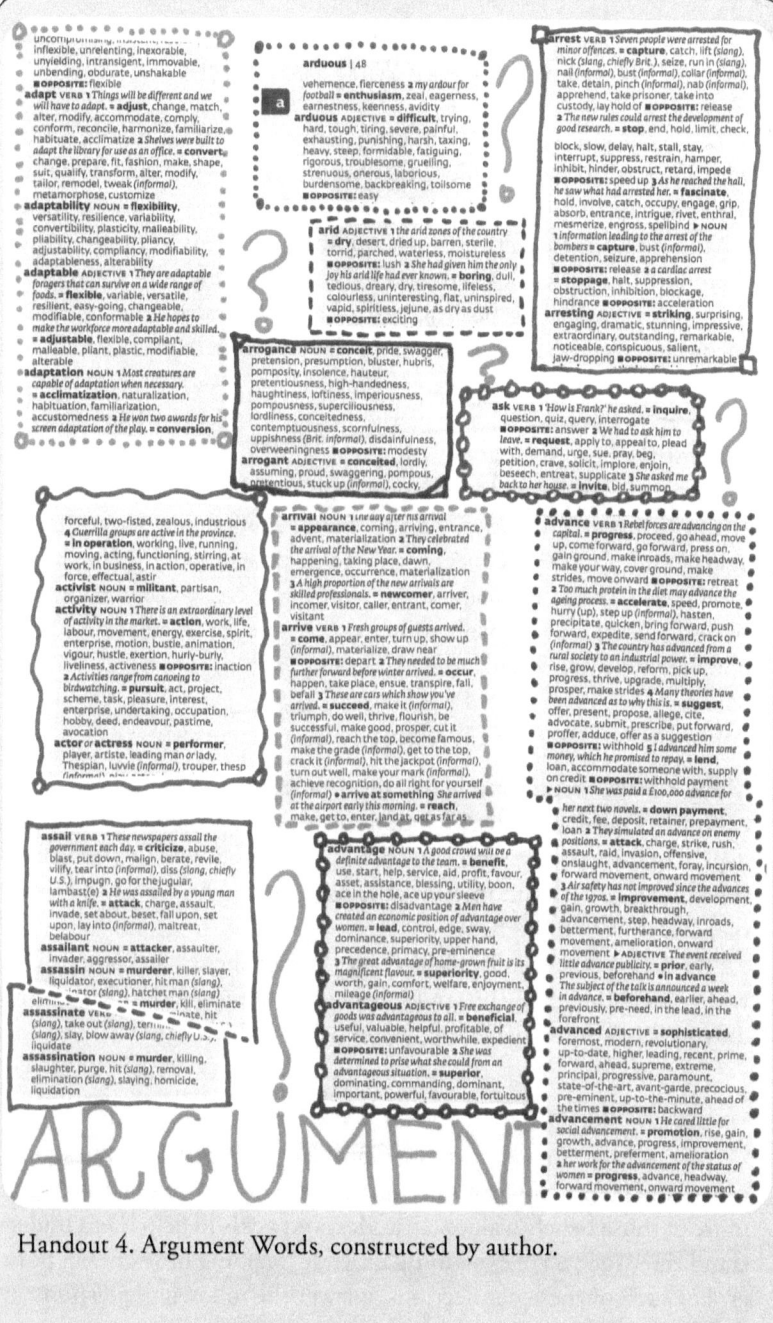

Handout 4. Argument Words, constructed by author.

4. Identification/Division: How Closely Are You Connected?

When we begin to discuss building connections with others, I start with Burke's dialectic of identification/division. As I explain that we use language in an attempt to bridge our differences, I give students a handout of some pithy Burke quotes housed in a jigsaw puzzle (Handout 5 "Identification & Division Definitions"), illustrating the concepts of being both joined to and separated from others. I encourage them to add illustrations, their own definitions, and notes to this page as we discuss the concepts.

Next, we consider some of the factors that can affect strength of identification, such as how important an issue is and how much overlap one has with the other person on that issue (Handout 6 "Identification & Division Range" handout). I then give students a chance to try out this concept with an in-class activity (below).

Finally, we discuss using identification to create connections between people, and identification as the basis for persuasion. Their homework builds on this understanding.

Identification and Division of Relationships

Make a large graph on a blank sheet of paper. Using the "Identification & Division Range" handout of issues, label one axis with the degree of importance each issue has for you, from low to high. Label the other axis with the amount of agreement you have with the statement, from low to high.

Based on this exercise, which speakers of these statements could you be friends with? Who could you not be friends with? How strong do you think your friendship would be? Why?

Homework

Choose one person you know. Consider their beliefs, values, attitudes, and goals. Now consider three ways you can connect to one or more of those beliefs, values, attitudes, and goals to help them understand the issue you're explaining on your [ongoing project of a] poster. For each of these connections, answer the following questions:

1. How strong is this identification going to be for them? Why?
2. How positive is this identification going to be for them? How do you know?
3. How can you create this identification using only a few words?
4. How can you create this identification using a visual image?
5. Is this person in a group who you would normally expect to be supportive/understanding/knowledgeable of this issue? Why/why not?

Chart each statement from the "Identification & Division Statements" handout on the graph. You may create a shorthand or symbol system instead of writing the statements but be sure to include a key so we can read it.

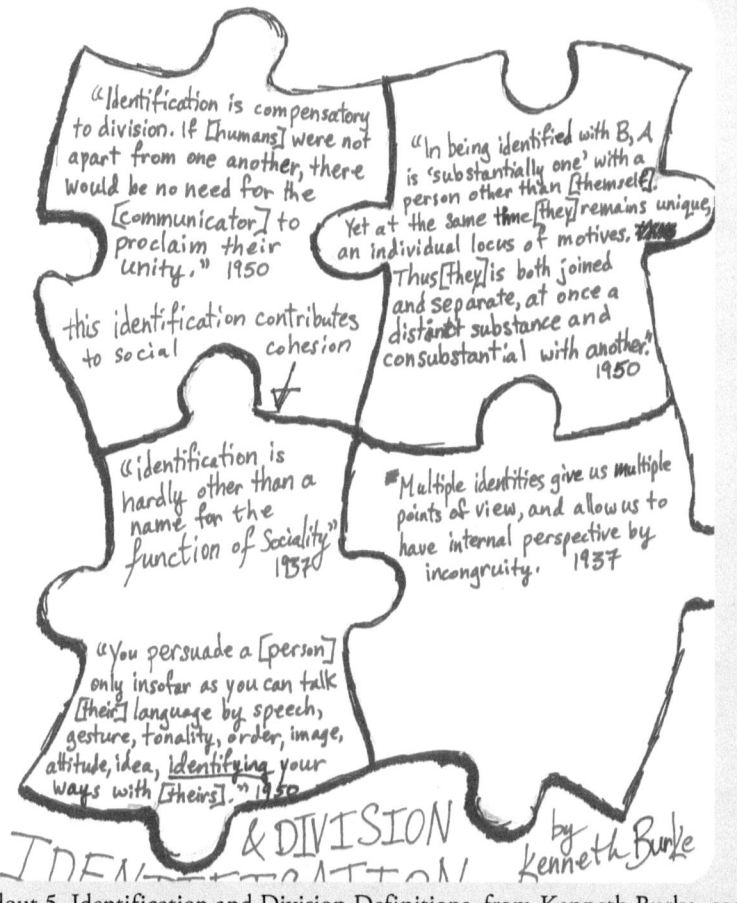

Handout 5. Identification and Division Definitions, from Kenneth Burke, constructed by author.

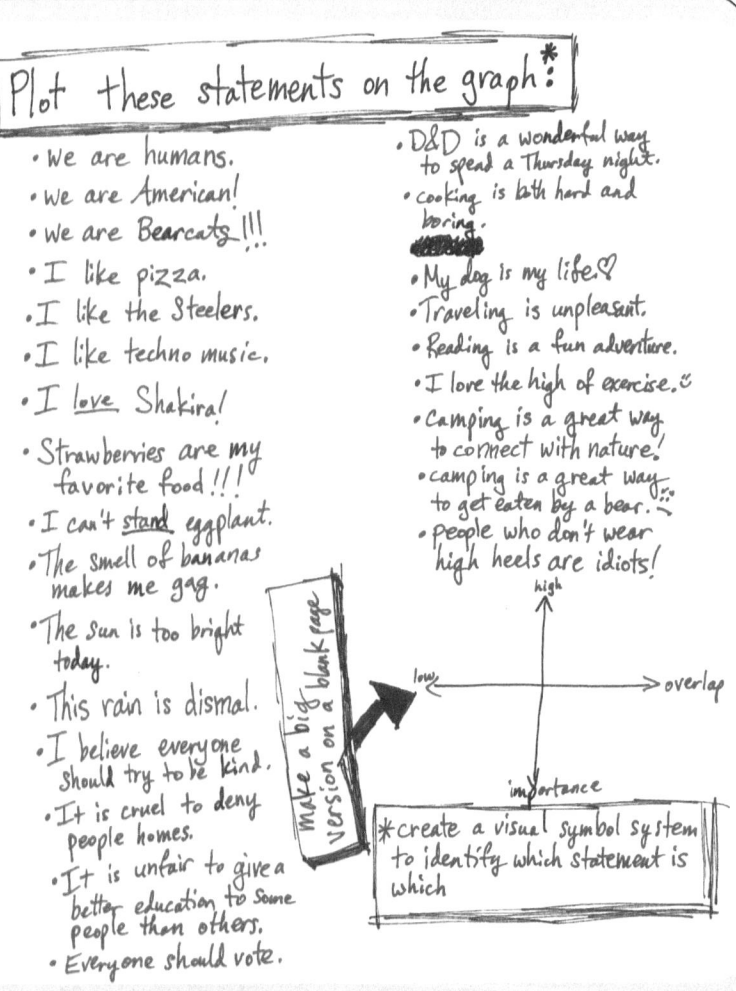

Handout 6. Identification and Division Range, constructed by the author.

Handout 7. Identification and Division Graph, constructed by the author.

3 Rhetoric, Identity, and Conflict: Engaging Burke, Engaging Culture

Bryan Crable

> *Equipping advanced undergraduates with Burkean perspectives and vocabulary needed to "size up" their own situations and act.*

Despite the lasting influence Burke has had upon my scholarly development, I can honestly confess I never wanted to teach a course centered upon him and especially not one geared to undergraduates. My students, though, changed my mind. Let me explain.

When I embarked upon my career, I felt an obligation to make sure that I was covering the entirety of rhetorical theory. Thus, for the first decade or so, I occasionally taught Burke's writings but avoided the kind of sustained (let alone hagiographic) presentation of them that I had witnessed in my graduate education. When our undergraduate curriculum was revised about fifteen years ago, though, my students convinced me that I had, perhaps, overcorrected. During this revision, I added a new course to our rhetoric curriculum: Rhetoric, Identity, and Conflict. My intention was for students to spend the semester analyzing and critically engaging sites of social conflict and the kinds of identity issues that reflect or challenge dominant public meanings. Although I designed the syllabus to end with Burke's *Attitudes Toward History*, I felt that I had to supplement too much of the book to make it comprehensible to an undergraduate audience. At the same time, it was nonetheless clear that my class responded quite positively to Burke's text: students almost unanimously chose Burke to drive the arguments in their term papers, and several of them took to carrying their drafts around at all times, proudly referring to them as their "babies." Even more striking, a few months after the semester ended, one of my students sent a lengthy email detailing her experiences in Teach for America. Her posting was in the South, in an impoverished school district, and she wrote that she and her fellow volunteers were having regular conversations about the school and its students—and that during those sessions she invariably took *Attitudes Toward History* off the shelf to cite as a reference, as it helped her make sense of what she was seeing.

That comment really resonated with me, and so when the course rotated back around in the departmental offerings, I decided to substantially revise the syllabus. In a decision whose perversity I feel that Burke himself would have applauded, I determined the only way to make *Attitudes Toward History* even more legible to (and useful for) my students was to *add more Burke to the syllabus*. I resolved that my students were going to read *Permanence and Change* at the beginning of the semester, which would provide the preparation they needed to grasp and make better use of *Attitudes*. Further, I decided to bookend these two volumes with essays that specifically applied Burke's work to the analysis and interpretation of human social life; through such examples, I felt, students would feel further challenged (and inspired) to produce their own Burkean readings of significant rhetorical topics. These readings would not necessarily be anything Burke himself would have written, though his ideas would be what made them possible. That is, a Burkean conceptual framework would allow students, as it allows scholars, to go beyond Burke to engage the topics and texts that matter to us today.

I had a small (and outstanding) group of students sign up for this new version of the course, and together we spent the semester reading these works by and about Burke. They subsequently converted his insights into term papers exploring a broad range of topics, all of which showed me the value of a class oriented around Burke's thought. One student, who found herself at odds with family members in law enforcement, turned this experience into a paper on Black Lives Matter versus Blue Lives Matter, drawing heavily on the "Dictionary of Pivotal Terms" from *Attitudes Toward History*. Another, fresh from a summer abroad, used the "Poetic Categories" to analyze the strengths and shortcomings of a girls' empowerment program in Zanzibar. Other papers used Burkean insights to engage such topics as the Wikileaks controversy, rhetorical framings of mass shooters (as "insane" or "psychotic loners"), Caitlyn Jenner's transition, and the cult comedy movie *We're the Millers* and its rhetorical work surrounding race. As a group, these papers were truly exceptional, and I was incredibly pleased with the quality of these students' engagement with Burke's work. As far as I was concerned, this new design was a roaring success.

I have taught the course three times since then and have found that this "pilot" experience was no anomaly; my undergraduate students are, as a rule, capable of outstanding and innovative Burkean analyses if they are given the space to engage his ideas clearly and systematically. In fact, one of my students in spring 2019 was inspired to apply Burkean concepts in an eerily prescient way, since her term paper focused on piety, orientation, and the rhetorical insularity of anti-vax discourse! I have since experimented with a version of the course for graduate students, yielding similarly outstanding final papers (such as one on action and motion in Jordan Peele's *Us,* which forever changed the way I read that movie, and an essay on Burke and queer theory that was brilliantly heuristic). However, for the duration of this chapter, I want to focus on the class as I designed it for undergraduates, as I have found it to be a consistently engaging and transformative experience for them (see Ann George and David Blakesley in this volume for examples of graduate syllabi). I can honestly say that I have witnessed undergraduate students suddenly "seeing around the corner" of their accustomed perspectives. I have actually *seen* a decisive, world-changing intellectual shift register on their faces as they read and talk through Burke's writings (e.g., *ATH* 269). So, for those interested in using Burke to help inspire the same kinds of transformative experience in their students, I offer a brief treatment of the course objectives and assignments, the course schedule, and the approach I take to these readings—in order to help flesh out how I teach this, my too-long-deferred "Burke course."

Overview of the Course and Assignments

Since Rhetoric, Identity, and Conflict is not a required class and often attracts students who have not previously had me as a professor, I operate under the assumption that few know much about rhetoric, let alone about Burke himself. I therefore start the first day of class very basically, with the quote that opens my syllabus: "Meanwhile I ponder the morality and immorality of rhetoric, asking: How can a world with rhetoric stay decent, how can a world without it exist at all?" (Letter from Kenneth Burke to Malcolm Cowley, 22 October 1946). I tell my students this brief quotation captures the foundational premise of the course: human beings are necessarily *rhetorical* beings, which is both something to celebrate *and* something to fear. I identify the course as an examination of the role played by rhetorical discourse in the struggles over identity—both individual and community—and in the creation and alleviation of conflict of all kinds. Since this topic touches equally upon the personal and the political charges of our symbol use, I emphasize that it will allow us to discuss both the rhetorical obstacles to and the means toward social change.

To make sure we are all on the same page, I also give them a foundation for our communal studies of the rhetorical. I start by highlighting two senses of "rhetoric" they might be familiar with. The first is what I call "rhetoric as shameful," the kind of practice that, as I tell them, would make your family ashamed—style over substance, lies rather than truth. This, I repeatedly stress, is *not* how they should understand the term "rhetoric." Second, they may equate rhetoric with persuasion, as in the traditional definitions that tie it to the study of politics, law, and ceremonial speaking (h/t Aristotle). However, I emphasize, Burke calls on us to expand the scope of rhetoric, to see it as much more complex, spontaneous, and communal than "persuasion" allows—that rhetoric more broadly entails the production of identities and communal realities through the strategic (though not necessarily deliberate) employment and redeployment of symbols, bodies, and material objects. Yet, even here, I note, we are only beginning to touch on the complexities of the rhetorical. After all, to speak of an individual's identity is already to point toward a rhetorical encounter: the process by which a human being is brought into sociality and into a meaningful (symbolically charged) world. In other words, as Burke tells us, there are no individuals existing outside of the rhetorical. Second, to speak of rhetoric as uniting communities is to also imply the opposite: that rhetoric can (and often does) produce division even as it produces unity. In short, as Burke's pithy comment to Cowley suggests, rhetoric may not simply be a way to smooth over conflicts—it may instead represent the driving force behind the conflict.

With this foundation, I end the first day of class with a discussion of the class assignments, beginning with their final term paper. I frame the project as their intellectual contribution to the class as a whole, their synthesis of our semester together, applied to a topic that matters—in some way—to them. By the end of the semester, they will generate a fifteen-page paper that analyzes some specific and relevant topic by drawing upon a theoretical framework arising from our course readings. This paper's focus is entirely up to them; it should entirely reflect *their* (and not *my*) personal, professional, academic, or civic interests and drives. Here I cite some of the topics explored in past semesters: the 9/11 Memorial, "dog whistle" politics, ways of seeing and not seeing in *Bird Box*, the naming controversy over the nation of "Macedonia," reactions to interracial romantic relationships, war rape in Bosnia, race and Milo Yiannopoulos, the transformative nature of studying abroad, Rachel Dolezal and "transracial identity," and toxic masculinity and the Gillette "Best a Man Can Be" campaign.

When I transition to the remaining assignments in the course, I frame them as the necessary preparation for the students' final project—in other words, reassuring the class that the other assignments they complete will help carry them, step by step, to the term paper. The first of these is what I call Daily Questions (DQ), an assignment that carries out several key functions: it takes the place of exams, it guides students' reading of Burkean texts, it helps me gauge their degree of comprehension of the course material, and it directs each day's lecture and discussion. Generally speaking, at the end of each class I provide a question or two related to the content of the next assigned reading. DQ answers are not supposed to be lengthy (no more than two typed, double-spaced pages), but they must fully answer the question and demonstrate understanding of the relevant pages of text. These answers, like their corresponding readings, are due at the beginning of the next class period; since we talk about their answers in class, this means that I do not accept late DQs. I require students to answer at least ten of these questions but allow them to answer as many as fourteen (and I "count" only their ten highest scores), giving them a chance to "get the hang of" reading and writing about Burke without suffering too much of a grade penalty. I also require them to complete at least five DQs by the midpoint of the semester. I emphasize that this assignment will assist them greatly in developing a facility with Burke's ideas.

I have two other built-in assignment "checkpoints" along the way, both of which are designed to assist in the completion of their term papers. The first is the Final Paper Proposal, due at midterm, which requires students to outline a project and Burkean approach for their term paper, the specific topic that they want to examine through a Burkean lens, its significance, and some specific arguments or concepts from our course readings that might be their focus. This paper is to be accompanied by an annotated bibliography of at least four good sources on the proposed topic—and I emphasize that these are typically going to be nonscholarly sources, such as blog posts, magazine features, or substantial newspaper articles.

This paper proposal is also designed to give the class ample time to prepare for the next central assignment, the Topic Briefing. As with the proposal, the Topic Briefing is intended to help students refine their ideas before handing in the final paper, since it requires them to design and carry out a class presentation on their final project about *one to two weeks before* they hand in the paper. Since it is a "briefing," I tell the students that the presentation should introduce the class to the topic at the heart of their paper and outline the direction of their final argument, including discussion of the specific concepts and passages from Burke they are drawing upon in their analysis. I encourage them to bring in multimedia or other creative elements to help capture their topic and their ultimate Burkean argument.

I also require students to run a Q & A session at the end of their briefing. I typically say nothing at all to allow the rest of the class to offer their reactions, comments, and suggestions. This includes not simply aspects of context or topical details that need to be clarified but Burkean concepts the presenter might not have considered or alterations in the paper's thesis the presenter might pursue. I repeatedly frame this not as adversarial but as a collaborative effort to help one another make their papers stronger. I encourage students to listen closely to their peers (I take notes so they don't have to), and I also provide my own written feedback afterwards—typically noting which pieces of advice they might especially consider following and which might simply lead to a different or muddled analysis. I devote the last two(ish) weeks of the semester to these Topic Briefings, scheduling two students per day. This not only alleviates the burden of reading new material as they work on their papers but also allows each student to get detailed feedback from me and from their peers prior to handing in the final draft.

Every semester I look around during the Q & A to see students furiously flipping through their Burke books, looking for a reference, concept, or passage to assist a classmate. It reminds me of nothing more than the spirited sessions I have witnessed (and participated in) at Kenneth Burke Society Triennials over the years—and I take the quality of these sessions to be an early bellwether of how the final papers will look. Students regularly reflect on this presentation as one of the most challenging, yet most helpful, exercises that they have ever had in an undergraduate class.

Having outlined all of these assignments, I typically end the first class session by encouraging the students to see this course as one where they will be challenged to gain a new perspective on their social world. Before they walk out the door, I provide them the first DQ of the semester, fitted to their first reading: "The Rhetoric of Hitler's 'Battle.'" Let me now shift to a consideration of each week of the course, focusing on the reading assignments, concepts covered, and the DQs that ask my students to gain and develop their Burkean chops.

Rhetoric, Identity, and Conflict—Week by Week

My course is typically two class sessions per week, each of which spans an hour and fifteen minutes. However, in what follows I organize the course schedule by week for simplicity's sake. Each week is broken down into readings, corresponding DQs, and the key topics of the class session.

Week One: Introduction to Burke and the Course

Reading 1: "The Rhetoric of Hitler's 'Battle.'" DQ: Explain why the Jewish scapegoat represented such an effective *"noneconomic explanation for economic ills"* (p. 204).

Since I devote an entire class period to orienting students to the course, I have only one reading the first week. I spend the first day (as detailed above) explaining the course and preparing the students to think about what rhetoric is—and, just as important, what it is *not*. However, I do not spend much time introducing them to Burke himself; I leave this for the second day of class. Instead of focusing too much attention on the "man behind the book," I give them a brief oral description of Burke's life and early years. Given Villanova's geographical location, I make sure to mention Pittsburgh as his birthplace, Greenwich Village as his formative intellectual years (quoting his "I want to be a genius" comment to Cowley), and Andover as his rural haven from the crowds of New York City. I also help set the stage for the course readings by delineating some of the key features of life in the 1930s—and pointing to the commonalities between that era and our own. Here I am typically guided by the introduction to Ann George's excellent *Kenneth Burke's* Permanence and Change*: A Critical Companion* and the first chapter of my first book, *Ralph Ellison and Kenneth Burke*, the latter of which sketches out the social and personal contexts shaping both men prior to their introduction. (For graduate students, I have them read both of these texts, but for the undergraduate classroom I summarize the relevant points myself). I also use the example of Ellison to again emphasize the overall goal of the course: for each of them to draw from Burke the concepts needed to engage a topic they find compelling. Just as Ellison was motivated to use Burke's writings to engage matters of race (even though, as I contend, that interest was not wholly reciprocated by Burke), I ask them to find in Burke the tools needed to carry out *their* own project, regardless of whether it matches Burke's.

But what was Burke's project? With this background in hand, I answer this question by pivoting to his essay on *Mein Kampf*. Instead of framing the discussion for the students, I begin with their voices. As with each day of the semester, I open by asking the students for what I call "responses/reactions/questions," the points that they want to make sure we talk about, the passages that they had special difficulty with, and the aspects of the text that they really responded to in a negative or positive way. In this particular case, students are typically most interested in engaging Burke's critique of Hitler's perversion of religion and Burke's identification of the possibility of an American version of Hitler—an issue that especially resonated with the students I taught in the fall of 2016, as they grappled with the (ultimately successful) Trump candidacy for the presidency. I am careful to emphasize the aspects of the argument that connect to the DQ, as this also allows me to engage the merger of Marx and Freud Burke creates in the essay—something that, I tell the class, will be a hallmark of both required books for the course.

I conclude, though, by emphasizing the date of Burke's original presentation of the lecture: June 1939. I do this to highlight the prescient nature of Burke's analysis of Hitler's virulent rhetoric. My message to students is that Burke arrived at his analysis of *Mein Kampf* by applying the concepts and terminology he had developed in our required course texts. Their challenge, I tell them, is to do the same; in other words, their task is to develop a facility with Burke's concepts of the 1930s and use them to produce their own brilliant, creative, theoretically rich analysis of an important rhetorical text or topic. And with that challenge, I send them off to begin the second week of the course and their systematic engagement with Burke's ideas.

Week Two: Introduction to Permanence and Change: Orienting ourselves

Reading 1: *PC*, prologue, 3–18. DQ: Burke says, "Orientation can go wrong" (p. 6). Explain this point, drawing on the terms "trained incapacity" and "means-selection."

Reading 2: *PC*, 19–21, 29–49. DQ: Explain the relationship between motives, situations, and orientations.

In week 2, I focus primary attention upon addressing the assumptions about language, thought, and reality that they likely hold entering the class. I specifically focus upon the necessity of interpretation (Burke's trout example on page 5) and upon the systemic nature of such interpretive moves—extending the point about the trout's reading of the signs of "bait" to the more complex situation faced by human interpreters. Here I try to shift them away from the pressures of individual experience—which tend to overly individualize human beings and downplay the communal nature of symbolicity—to the human reliance upon the interconnected network of linkages that, for Burke, is named "orientation." An orientation, as he makes clear, is a system of meanings that indicates how we should identify and relate ourselves to significant elements in the environment. I also point to Burke's passages about the connection between our orientation and our "empirical" observations of the world; to adopt an orientation, as Burke makes clear, is to prepare ourselves to see some things and not to see others—or solely to see them through the lens of our orientation. This, I suggest, is why the problem of social change is not a "facts" or "information" problem—why you cannot simply show someone evidence of why their orientation is problematic. Further, I emphasize Burke's quotations about the "fitness" (or lack thereof) of our orientations, the notion that "orientation can go wrong" (6), that our successful internalization of a particular orientation may eventually prove to be our undoing, should conditions change.

The second part of this week involves detailed attention to Burke's arguments about the term *motive*. Again, I focus upon trying to combat the assumptions that follow the students into the classroom—and especially the assumption that motives are internal, psychological, and the cause of our actions. Instead, following Burke, I emphasize the relationship between language, communal orientation, and motives. In other words, we focus on motives as words, as summarizing titles for situations that are sufficiently regularized as to require a name; as I tell them, you cannot have a motive that others do not recognize, that is purely unique to you (and if you have such a motive, or claim to, that will most likely end in your involuntary institutionalization). To internalize an orientation, then, is to internalize a set of terms to use in defining situations and adopting the appropriate conduct; we talk about these as individual psychic entities, but really they are internalized meanings, drawn from our linguistic community, that prepare us for action. Further, I use this point to highlight the cultural critique that runs parallel to Burke's conceptual argument throughout the book; in the 1930s, though contemporary culture is little different, Burke is identifying a fundamental instability in the dominant cultural orientation, which betrays itself in a lack of agreement over our own and others' motives. I end by pointing to his discussion of "occupational psychosis" and its associated critique of the technological or scientific—the critique that, for Burke, will point to the need for a new orientation and associated set of motives.

WEEK THREE: PIETY AND THE SEARCH FOR MEANINGS

Reading 1: *PC*, 69–79, 80–87. DQ: Why, according to Burke, is a "drug fiend" pious, but an evangelist impious?

Reading 2: Edward Schiappa and Mary F. Keehner, "The 'Lost' Passages of *Permanence and Change*," *Communication Studies* 42 (1991): 191–98. DQ: Compare and contrast the arguments Schiappa and Keehner make about the "lost" passages of *PC* to the explanation that Burke makes in the prologue to the 2nd edition.

At the third week of the course, I begin by stepping back to again remind the students of the dual nature of Burke's argument; he is offering us both a theoretical account of orientation and a cultural critique based upon this theoretical account. I remind them to keep track of both of these layers while they read and to note where he is placing his emphasis in particular sections of the text. Similarly, I remind them of the overall structure of the text: the emphasis upon orientation for part one, the movement from one orientation to another in part two, and the new orientation that, for Burke, should replace the old.

With this in mind, then, I turn to the discussion of these pages by emphasizing what is at issue within them: the inseparability of intellect and emotion in discussions of orientation. Through his discussions of "piety," Burke is challenging us to remove—at one level—the morality from the term. If we expand it beyond the confines of the religious, in other words, we are able to grasp something important: within the context of orientation, "is" equals "ought." In other words, an orientation *drives* our actions, as we seek to embody it in all aspects of our lives. However, this also means that any attempt to challenge our orientation is met with fierce, even violent, resistance—since such challenges are felt to be impious, to be violations of the moral (and not simply intellectual) order. I end this section by emphasizing that this is not Burke's argument against changing another's orientation, but instead a warning that we must go about such matters delicately and with the understanding of why we are met with resistance. I frame this as Burke's attempt to theorize the complexity of producing social change—the diagnosis of the problem we face if we try to shift another's orientation.

In the second half of this week, we look more closely at the cultural critique that follows from this argument and, specifically, engage Burke's advocacy for communism as the needed complement to the poetic orientation in the first edition of the text. I use Schiappa and Keehner's article to address this, since they indicate just how to reconstitute the first edition from the second/third edition—and include the passages that were cut in the 1954 revision. I ask the students to reflect upon their argument regarding the situated nature of rhetorical theory and the need to recontextualize our writings within the political and social issues of our day. I use this opportunity to both situate Burke in time and space, and to ask students to reflect on the way in which their own academic work contributes to (or erases) the pressing matters of our contemporary moment. I end this week by asking them to keep the Schiappa and Keehner article close at hand when they read, so that they are prepared to insert the "lost" passages as needed into their text. I even encourage them to put in asterisks at the relevant places, so that they can be reminded each time they return to the text to consider the importance of what was removed in the 1950s.

Week Four: Perspective by Incongruity, Cultural Instability, and the "Rock of Certainty"

Reading 1: *PC*, 97–124. DQ: Burke advocates "perspective by incongruity" as the best way to address the contemporary social situation, with its lack of stable orientation. Why would that be a better approach than a scientistic one?

Reading 2: *PC*, 125–34, 142–47, 155–63, 167–78. DQ: Burke says, "Speech in its essence is not neutral" (p. 176). Explain what this means and why this demonstrates the value of the poetic over the scientistic orientation.

In beginning this week, I connect the previous week's discussion of pieties and orientation to Burke's concern with science and scientism more specifically, since this is also part of his move toward cultural critique. Because those within an orientation are committed to it, other orientations may be "unthinkable"—or, at best, viewed as impious challenges. In this section of the text, Burke addresses the question this raises: how do we judge the adequacy of an orientation? Through its successes? Through scientific tests? Here we spend time on Burke's critique of "tests of success" (100), where he asks us to consider what constitutes "success" in the sphere of human social life. Is the application of a chemical weapon to human beings "successful" if it deploys as intended—injuring, killing, and disabling thousands? Is the use of growth hormones in cattle "successful" if they produce more milk—though the hormones subsequently appear throughout the human population? Here we see Burke's emphasis upon the inherent link between orientation and "reality," which throws the "tests" of science into question. I emphasize that the engagement with another's orientation is not a matter of "proving" them wrong, but of attempting to *convert* them—the key point that Burke wants to make in these sections. After discussing psychoanalysis as an example, we end on his discussion of "perspective by incongruity," and I ask them to note the several different means of achieving this that are highlighted in George's *Critical Companion*.

This discussion sets the stage for our more extended discussion of Burke's critique of scientism and advocacy of the poetic. These passages include a series of arguments related to the poetic, which prepare us to accept his overall argument for its superiority to the scientific. There is much going on in these pages, of course, but I particularly emphasize his argument about being versus becoming as central to his critique of the scientistic or technological orientation; we are accustomed, as Burke writes, to accepting science as having replaced magic and religion due to its superior rationality and intellectual clarity, but he attempts to change our view of this shift. In this discussion, I highlight Burke's arguments for the emphasis upon the poetic orientation's "being" versus the scientistic emphasis upon "becoming" or "progress." We spend the majority of our time, however, upon his arguments about language—and specifically his contention that the scientific orientation is built upon a faulty theory of language. I conclude this session by looking closely at his discussion of thinkers who "went 'nudist'" (172), as it tends to give students trouble. I emphasize the key point: when a dominant orientation is in tatters, when confusion, complexity, and a welter of perspectives abound, we also see a tendency to try and cut through the clutter and *simplify* the entirety of social life. Although, as Burke says, nudism (literally) expresses this point, I instead point to fundamentalist movements (like the Taliban or MAGA) and to cultural products they are familiar with that do the same work, such as *The Walking Dead* (and its spin-offs) or *The Purge* films. These texts similarly depict a situation where our technologies, laws, and social customs are stripped away, leaving us with the utter simplicity of kill-or-be-killed. I use this as a way to again set up Burke's project—since he, too, wants to envision an underlying foundation that we can build upon but one rooted in communication rather than conflict, connection rather than limitless violence. I end the week on this point, as a way for them to consider the arguments that conclude *Permanence and Change*.

Week Five: Concluding PC: Transitioning to ATH

Reading 1: *PC*, 179–87, 218–24, 232–36. DQ: Explain what Burke means by "metabiology" (sometimes also called "dialectical biologism").

Reading 2: *PC*, 250–72. DQ: What does Burke mean by "recalcitrance," and why is it an important addition to the "poetic metaphor" or "poetic orientation"?

We pick up the discussion of the text where we left off—Burke's own "rock of certainty." The text spends a good bit of time developing the emphasis upon human permanence that Burke identifies lying beneath our confusion of contingencies. Though Burke is never, to the students' satisfaction, clear about what exactly he means by "metabiology" (and he seems to indicate this dissatisfaction in the preface to the 2nd edition), we spend most of the session unpacking the relationship between materialism, idealism, and Burke's proposed alternative, "dialectical biologism." Though I generally loathe to be anachronistic in teaching Burke, I tend to use his later formulation of "bodies that learn language" as a way to unpack the dialectical relationship between the biological and the linguistic that is captured by "metabiology." In this, I specifically emphasize the passages discussing our engrained tendency to draw the lines between "inside" and "outside" the human body—and Burke's critique of this division as arbitrary (e.g., 232–34). I also use this as a way to engage the *rhetorical* realism at the heart of the poetic orientation; a point of view, as he tells us, is definitively real and a very consequential part of the universe. This, Burke argues, helps indicate the insufficiency of the scientistic orientation and the need for the poetic as a corrective.

We build upon this point in our discussion of *Permanence and Change*'s ending. Specifically, I focus on the link between pseudo-statements, statements, and recalcitrance; the linkages that he traces among these help explain why he is willing to defend (to a point) D. H. Lawrence and his statements about the sun, crops, and the moon. Since Burke's discussion tends to be more abstract (and centered on authors they likely have little familiarity with), I tend to focus on environmental examples that reflect the same point. For example, Americans long engaged in a collective pseudo-statement: we treated the earth *as if* there were a limitless supply of petroleum to fuel our industry. As recalcitrance rose to meet our pseudo-statement, we revised it: we treated the earth *as if* it were a steady supply of petroleum to fuel our industry, but *only if* we expand our efforts and develop new techniques of extraction (like fracking or drilling in Indigenous Nations' territories). However, to the extent that recalcitrance continues to build in response to even this revised pseudo-statement, we are not only prevented from arriving at the accuracy of a full "statement"—in Burke's sense—but we are faced with mounting evidence that our guiding orientation itself needs to change if we are to better meet the disruptions and crises produced by industry-fueled climate change. We conclude this part of the text by reflecting upon the book's ending, both in the original 1935 version, and in the revised 1954 and 1984 versions. I ask the students to consider Burke's call to action and evaluate its adequacy for meeting our current moment—

asking, in essence, to what extent it remains adequate "equipment for living" in the twenty-first century.

Week Six: Attitudes Toward History: Frames of Acceptance and Rejection

Reading 1: *ATH*, Introduction, 3–5, 19–33. DQ: Burke argues that frames of acceptance are not passive (p. 20). Why is this the case?

Reading 2: *ATH*, 34–56. DQ: Explain the distinctions that Burke makes between comedy, tragedy, humor, and the epic.

Having spent the first five weeks working through *Permanence and Change*, I open our discussion of *Attitudes Toward History* by pointing to the many terms that drop away—including, but not limited to, the poetic orientation. However, I also point to the many commonalities between the projects represented by these books and especially the focus on how we should best understand the need for, and difficulties surrounding, social change. With *Attitudes Toward History*, I emphasize, Burke is even more focused on the difficulties that arise when an insight, a concept, or an instrument is embodied in a social texture; the result is an emphasis upon the need for continual reflexivity, at the level of both the individual and collective. I encourage them to begin by equating "frame" with "orientation" but then develop the distinction that Burke draws between individual frames—the frames of "acceptance" or "rejection" covered at the beginning of the text—and dominant historical frames, the meaning systems that function as an *orthodoxy*, an accepted vocabulary for distinguishing the "friendly" forces from the "unfriendly," a vocabulary that is embodied in institutions, technologies, rules, norms, and laws, and that prepares us collectively for action. I conclude by emphasizing Burke's tracing of the relationship between collective and individual frames: to the extent that a dominant historical frame outlives its accurate fit with prevailing conditions (an inevitability, due to the by-products that its bureaucratization generates), then the resulting conflict requires those within the culture to decide between accepting or rejecting that frame. I emphasize that this is the foundation for Burke's engagement with social change in the remainder of the book.

We build upon this foundation in the discussion of Burke's "Poetic Categories," examining works of art as individual symbolic products that serve as early warnings of significant shifts in relation to a dominant historical frame (as in the example of Shakespeare Burke cites). It is in this context that we approach his categories, since he divides them into forms of art that enact and encourage an attitude of acceptance and those that enact and encourage rejection. We spend the most time on the four categories listed in the DQ, since those are among the most dominant that they encounter. I emphasize Burke's point about the inaccuracy of the epic's form of acceptance under non-"primitive" conditions, and I cite examples of cultural texts that are built around a heroism that is too easily adopted for oneself. For example, tying this point to the concerns of our current moment, I cite films like Bob Odenkirk's *Nobody*, which celebrates the heroism of an "ordinary" white man. However, I spend more time distinguishing humor from comedy, a point that I find severely understressed in the rhetorical literature; the comic, as I repeatedly emphasize, is often not funny. Examples of gender "comedies" typically provide helpful examples of humor, of works that reduce the complexity and seriousness of the patriarchy enshrined in our dominant historical frame to the minute nature of its characters. I typically point to works like *Hannah Gadsby: Nanette*, a stand-up comedy special that functions far more like Burke's comic frame than like humor; the special's focus on anti-LGBTQ+ actions and misogyny are wrenching, perspective shifting, and often quite grim. Yet, to the extent that Gadsby encourages recognition of our necessarily limited perspectives and engages in some systematic "perspective by incongruity," she begins to arrive at the kind of comic insight Burke advocates in *Attitudes Toward History*.

Week Seven: Frames, Poetic Categories, and the Comic Corrective

Reading 1: *ATH*, 57–69, 92, 99–107. DQ: Explain the case that Burke makes for the widespread adoption of the comic frame as the "most serviceable for the handling of human relationships" (p. 106).

Reading 2: *ATH*, 111–13, 124–26, 139–41, 150 (footnote only), 166–75. DQ: Explain the differences and the connections Burke draws between material and spiritual alienation.

I approach this section of text as Burke's more extended meditation upon the pressures resulting in the need for an individual to adopt a frame of acceptance or rejection in relation to a dominant historical frame. We look closely at his discussion of the ideal scenario (68), whereby a dominant historical frame encompasses all the significant features of the social situation and where those within it feel themselves to be at home—allowing them to adopt a frame of acceptance without discomfort. However, as Burke points out, such a situation, if it ever exists, cannot be permanent, insofar as the dominant frame begins to generate by-products that cannot be accepted by all those within it. Here, though, we see Burke trace the difficulties with adopting an attitude of rejection, since such a posture (and corresponding line of action) typically results in excommunication from the orthodoxy in all respects, which is often combated by the generation of a heretical countermovement—though this itself is prone to further splintering, until there is little in the way of a "united front" in the struggle for social change. Alternately, we can find individuals attempting to "accept" these by-products, to create some form of symbolic transcendence that eliminates the discomfort between dominant and individual frame. As we conclude this discussion, here we see Burke's emphasis upon the value of the comic frame: it allows for a broader frame of acceptance than one tied to a particular dominant historical frame, and its form of acceptance enables one to grapple with the pressures of rejection without the demoralization of splintering and the associated "war of words" that follows.

This discussion builds into the next series of pages, which allow us to engage Burke's use of these ideas for cultural critique—and his advocacy of the comic frame. I focus a great deal of our discussion on alienation, as I find it to be both incisive and crucial to the comic frame. We discuss the ways in which an individual can be alienated from a dominant historical frame—either materially, through deprivation of some material necessity of life, or spiritually, through deprivation of meaning or significance—the loss of a sense of "at-home-ness" within a dominant frame. We discuss the permutations that follow from this scheme; one might be materially alienated but not spiritually alienated (and thus content with the orthodoxy), spiritually alienated but not materially alienated (as Marx was), or *both* spiritually and materially alienated (as with those who galvanized the #BlackLivesMatter movement). I draw on this discussion to engage the case Burke makes for the comic frame as the most well rounded, since it is designed, as Burke says, to combat the forms of alienation that result from the need for rejection—and to enroll us in a program of action that might more accurately diagnose and remedy the problems with a dominant historical frame. However, as I end this discussion, they should note the kind of acceptance that characterizes the comic; it is not a pure acceptance of "what is," since, as Burke contends, it cannot simply "transcend" the forms of alienation that accompany (for example) capitalism or leave us content with an unfit and unjust orthodoxy (174–75). The comic, in short, is neither a simple refusal nor a meek acquiescence; it is instead a *revolutionary* frame of acceptance.

Week Eight: Ritual and Symbolism

Reading 1: *ATH*, 179–215; Dictionary of Pivotal Terms (DPT): *identity, identification; alienation; "earning" one's world; repossess the world; being driven into a corner; opportunism; casuistic stretching; perspective by incongruity (308–309 only)*. DQ: Explain the connection between symbolic transcendence (of the self), acceptance/rejection, and rituals of rebirth. [Option 2 DQ: Explain the connections between the DPT terms for the day.]

Reading 2: *ATH*, DPT: *problem of evil; sect; stealing back and forth of symbols; bridging device; salvation device; secular prayer; transcendence*. DQ: Explain the connections between the DPT terms for the day.

Drawing upon the discussions leading up to this point—most of which have focused upon the nature of dominant historical frames and the kinds of organized struggles that emerge in relation to them (both on their behalf and against them)—I note that, in the last chapter of the book, Burke more specifically attends to the question of identity and to the individual's use of symbols in response to a dominant historical frame. Here we see his attempt to craft an approach to identity that not only refuses the isolated, pure subject of liberal humanism but also points to the value of engaging individual symbolic works in order to more robustly analyze and understand the pressures of acceptance and rejection characteristic of a particular historical moment. Burke also draws upon this portrait of individual identity to add to his advocacy of the comic frame; to the extent that we are to realize the full potential of human life, he contends our crafting of individual identity should incorporate the materials of the comic frame—so that we transform ourselves into a "poet-plus-critic," the Burkean ideal (213). This, again, is Burke's call to action, his entreaty to internalize and apply this conceptual system to our own lives.

As we move beyond this third chapter to the last part of the book, I describe the "Dictionary of Pivotal Terms" (my favorite part of *Attitudes*

Toward History) as a recapitulation-plus, a section of the book that repeats previous passages and concepts but from a different angle—and, often, in ways that shed new light on the arguments appearing in earlier pages. As such, I divide the DPT into clusters of terms, all of which I see to be meditating upon a related set of issues or questions; instead of going back through these terms one by one, I spend these portions of the class asking for students to try out their DQs on the rest of the class—to begin with one of the day's assigned terms and then logically move, one by one, through the rest of them, showing how they interconnect. Since, as Burke tells us, these terms are so mutually dependent that one can begin with any and arrive at the rest, I typically ask the students to drive these class sessions—I have volunteers demonstrate the specific connections they have identified and the sequence of terms that made the most sense to them. Not only does this allow us to cover these terms in depth, reinforcing the ideas from our earlier class periods on *Attitudes Toward History*, but it also illustrates Burke's argument about the systemic nature of his vocabulary.

Week Nine: Concluding ATH and Burkean applications

Reading 1: *ATH*, DPT: *rituals of rebirth; cluster; cues (236–41 only); imagery; symbolic mergers*; Conclusion. DQ: Explain the connections between the DPT terms for the day.

Reading 2: Ralph Ellison, *Invisible Man* (New York: Vintage International, 1980), 3–14, 572–81; A. Cheree Carlson, "'You Know It When You See It': The Rhetorical Hierarchy of Race and Gender in *Rhinelander vs. Rhinelander*," *Quarterly Journal of Speech* 85 (1999): 111–28. DQ: Drawing upon Ellison, Carlson, and Burke, explain the relationship between race and visibility.

After spending another day with the students' tracing their paths through the DPT, I conclude their discussion of *Attitudes Toward History* by having them evaluate the "equipment for living" it provides and have them compare and contrast the persuasiveness and utility of both of the semester's key works. I also frame this as the foundation for their own critical analyses and introduce the remaining days of the course as examples of the kind of analyses Burke's ideas can inspire—and, therefore, as exemplars they can use to refine their own projects and prepare for their topic briefings. I also encourage them to draw from these works if they find aspects of the theoretical framework useful as supplements for *Permanence and Change* and *Attitudes Toward History*.

The first day of Burkean applications returns to the beginning of the semester and the work of Ralph Ellison. I have the students read the "Prologue" and "Epilogue" from Ellison's famous novel, *Invisible Man*, both of which clearly demonstrate the Burkean framework at the heart of Ellison's project—the ways in which Ellison harnessed Burke's insight that "ways of seeing" function simultaneously as "ways of not seeing" and applied it to matters of race in the United States. Similarly, I have them engage Cheree Carlson's brilliant analysis of an infamous legal case centered on the intersection of race and gender—whose arguments similarly reflected the sedimented American "ways of seeing" race and their rhetorical (and malleable) nature, especially when connected to the corresponding ways of seeing gender. I describe these articles as exemplifying a Burkean perspective applied to whiteness as a dominant cultural frame and challenge the students to identify (especially in Ellison's novel) the many Burkean turns of phrase, concepts, and arguments that he marshals in an antiracist project. I close by reminding the students that Burke would not have written either of these works, though his ideas were what made them possible; I again challenge them to do the same, to develop a Burkean conceptual framework that allows them to engage the questions, topics, or rhetorical texts that matter to them, regardless of whether Burke specifically talks about them in his writings.

Week Ten: Burkean applications (con't.)

Reading 1: Abhik Roy, "The Construction and Scapegoating of Muslims as the 'Other' in Hindu Nationalist Rhetoric," *Southern Communication Journal* 69 (2004): 320–32; A. Cheree Carlson, "Gandhi and the Comic Frame: 'Ad Bellum Purificandum,'" *Quarterly Journal of Speech* 72 (1986): 446–55. DQ: Using Burke's tragic and comic frames, compare and contrast Gandhi's and Shiv Sena's approaches to the "enemy."

Reading 2: Robert Wade Kenny, "The Rhetoric of Kevorkian's Battle," *Quarterly Journal of Speech* 86 (2000): 386–401; Robert Wade Kenny, "A Cycle of Terms Implicit in the Idea of Medicine: Karen Ann Quinlan as a Rhetorical Icon and the Transvaluation of the Ethics of Euthanasia," *Health Communication* 17 (2005): 17–39. DQ: Drawing upon Kenny's discussion of both Jack Kevorkian and Karen Ann Quinlan, explain the difference between a *discursive (or rhetorical) agent* and a *rhetorical icon*.

The final week of assigned course content continues in a similar vein, presenting students with examples of published research applying Burke's concepts in ways that release new insight into the struggles of social life. The first pair of readings are designed to help the students grasp more fully what it means to engage the "Poetic Categories" from *Attitudes Toward History* and apply them outside the bounds of literature. I use these two works together since they sharply contrast in emphasis, though both draw on *Attitudes Toward History* and both focus on a global (rather than US-centric) context. Though not recent, Roy's article engages an urgent current problem (Hindu nationalism and the violence directed against India's Muslim community) and approaches it from the standpoint of the scapegoat, the focus of Burke's tragic frame; his analysis is a clear explication of the characteristic features and grave consequences of such a frame, when used by a group such as Shiv Sena. By contrast, Carlson's pioneering work applies the comic frame to the understanding of a social movement: Mohandas Gandhi's strategic, collective struggle to radically change the nature of Indian society and its relationship to Great Britain. Placing these two analyses side by side gives the class a strong sense of what it might look like to similarly engage this dimension of Burke's *Attitudes Toward History*.

The final day of assigned readings is devoted to two works by Kenny that develop Burkean thought in complex and nuanced ways. The essay on Kevorkian begins to use Burke to theorize the importance of the "rhetorical icon" in critical moments of social disruption—a figure that Kenny identifies not as the author or *subject* of rhetorical discourse but its *object*. Using the example of the infamous Dr. Jack Kevorkian, Kenny points to the disruptions surrounding end-of-life experience wrought by contemporary technology; using Burke as a guide, he develops the clear contrast between Kevorkian as a rhetorical agent and a rhetorical icon. As Kenny demonstrates, Kevorkian's own discourse positions him as *anything but* an advocate of those seeking a humane death—it instead positions him as something far more brutal, as drawing quite near the doctors of Nazi Germany. However, as Kenny indicates, given the instability of the dominant cultural frame surrounding the end of life, Kevorkian *became a figure for others to argue about*—an object of rhetorical discourse, one whose own words contributed little, if anything, to the public depictions of who he was or what motivated him. Kenny builds upon this in his essay on Karen Ann Quinlan, who was literally unable to speak for herself—but who served as a site for others' rhetorical discourse about euthanasia. In this sense, she was a perfect rhetorical icon, purely the object of discourse, not its subject; Kenny draws this concept together with the "Poetic Categories" from *Attitudes Toward History* to offer a complex account of how rhetorical icons can contribute to either the protection of a dominant frame under attack or to the revolutionary attempts to replace it with an alternative. Though Kenny's arguments are complex, I have had students draw upon them to great effect; most notably, the papers that students wrote on Caitlyn Jenner and Rachel Dolezal demonstrated the potential of the "rhetorical icon," connected to Burke's work of the 1930s, to shed powerful light on contemporary social struggles.

By Way of Conclusion . . .

Following these last two classes, the assigned readings stop, and students spend the remainder of the semester working on their final papers. Subsequent days of the course are filled, first, with the Topic Briefings assignment, and, subsequently, with paper workshop class periods, in which students work with me individually on the final details of their arguments and on any remaining conceptual questions they might have.

Although at this point the semester itself is at an end, I require students to meet during our final exam period, where I ask them to share a brief (about five-minute) synopsis of their final argument with the class and emphasize what they gained from the comments on their Topic Briefings. I tell them to make their informal presentations as engaging as possible, since there will be a vote afterwards for the *Kenneth*—an award for the coolest-sounding paper in Rhetoric, Identity, and Conflict. (I emphasize "coolest-sounding" and indicate that the award is no guarantee of a grade, simply a measure of their peers' admiration.) The *Kenneth* comes with a framed plaque and a gift of my choice—and the presentations and vote invariably yield great conversation, laughter, and cheers for the eventual winner of this hotly contested award.

For me, the degree of excitement surrounding the *Kenneth* is one measure of how successful the class has been. Another is how much clear packing tape I have to use to patch the new cracks in the bindings of my books; if we really studied the books carefully together and had strong discussions, then I know that new splits, perhaps many of them, will have emerged during the semester. More seriously, though, the proof of a successful engagement with Burke is always in their papers. When I read these at the end of the semester, I can honestly say that I am invariably convinced all over again by my students: they *need* a course like this, one that asks them to think in Burkean fashion about their social world, and I was remiss in avoiding it for so long. If a world without rhetoric is unthinkable—yet one with it threatens disaster—then this course equips students with Burke's quintessential, thoroughly *reflexive* symbolic hypochondriasis . . . something that, in our current moment, represents a truly vital, even irreplaceable, form of rhetorical education.

4 Illuminating Kenneth Burke, Engaging Publics

David Blakesley

Using multiple media platforms to encourage graduate student engagement with theory.

I have been fortunate to have the opportunity to teach numerous graduate seminars on Kenneth Burke and rhetorical theory over the years. Student interest in such a course has remained steady, one sign that Burke's work continues to be relevant for students in rhetoric and composition, communication, and related areas.

The Students and the Classroom

The course I describe in this chapter included twenty-one students: thirteen first-semester MA students and eight PhD students. The MA students specialized in either English (literature) or Writing, Rhetoric, and Media. The PhD students in the rhetorics, communication, and information design program included a cohort of on-site students and another that only attended courses from a distance. The on-site students, sixteen total, met in a technology-rich classroom in Clemson's Watt Family Innovation Center. Online students attended synchronously via Zoom with the help of a Meeting OWL, which facilitates group video conferencing across physical spaces. The room itself had three large displays, high quality video and audio support, and mobile furniture. The classroom has been well designed to take advantage of a variety of new technologies that support interaction, collaboration, and engagement.

Figure 1. Room 218 in the Watt Family Innovation Center, site of the seminar. Photograph by Tullen Burns. Used by permission.

Overview of the Approach

Naturally, a graduate seminar like this one has multiple objectives. Most traditionally, I want students to learn about rhetorical theory through their engagement with Burke's texts and others that illuminate them or present contrasting, alternative, or derivative conceptions of rhetoric. I envision this course, like most of my courses, as the parlor that stages the unending conversation of history (*PLF* 110–11). We listen for a while to get our bearings, then we put in our oar. That, of course, stands as the ideal. To achieve it, I provide students with multiple ways of voicing their assertions, one of which includes synchronous discussion of course content, in plenary or smaller group formats. Students can join the unending conversation asynchronously and in numerous other ways that I describe later in the chapter.

Illuminating Burke

With the term *illuminate*, I allude to the illuminated manuscripts of the late Middle Ages through the Renaissance, when illuminating texts became a high art. Early in its development, illumination involved adorning or embellishing texts, often with gold or silver paint, to give the impression of a luminous text. During the medieval period, illumination evolved to include illustrations representing key principles or incidents in the text and fostering spiritual or intellectual enlightenment. Elaborate borders (called *marginalia*) established visual motifs or themes. These marginalia evolved into what we know today as annotations or glosses. *Illuminate* has its origins in the Latin *illuminatus*, sharing roots with *luminary* and *elucidate*: To illuminate means to enlighten, to alight, or to make clear. To elucidate means to explain and clarify through analysis. Illuminating Burke, then, involves both enlightenment and elucidation, which I hope to accomplish through a wide variety of supplements from audiovisual assets that reveal concepts more clearly or shine new light on Burke or rhetoric. We also illuminate a subject with other texts that throw it into relief by shifting the angle of approach or changing the situation or scene in which particular ideas act. An interanimating power of the verbal, visual, and textual generates and elaborates perspectives. Burke's own work comprises most of the course readings, but contemporary work in rhetorical theory, including feminist, antiracist, and activist approaches, broadened the focus. The full list of readings appears in the course description that follows this chapter.

Practically speaking, I want students to see, hear, and read how others have attempted to illuminate Burke and rhetoric. I provide already published or work-in-progress student examples, as students typically respond most enthusiastically to what previous students have created, making them critical to illuminating Burke. I include several examples to end this chapter.

Engaging Burke

A popular ideal in pedagogical circles, engagement refers to the student's degree of connection, interaction, or assimilation of course content. In this sense, engagement measures attention and focus. Engaging with course content precedes change and growth. Similarly, instructors want to make the content of a course engaging, capable of effectively appealing to students' interests and desires. Course content should spark curiosity and create exigency, thus raising the stakes of learning by virtue of the quality and value of knowledge about and around, in this case, Burke and rhetoric. Engaging Burke means learning why his work matters now, what it helps us understand, what difference it makes, and what we gain though that engagement. For these reasons, I think of engaging Burke as a kind of praxis—the actualization of theoretical principles in contexts that matter.

I also have in mind another scene of engagement involving people working (or playing) in professional communities, the sort of activity that characterizes the intellectual life of an active scholar. In the parlor, identities form and reform through interaction, connection, contribution, and even selflessness. In classical terms, Burke's *polis* embodies the Wrangle of the Market Place or the Human Barnyard (*RM* 23). Engagement with local and global publics promotes learning and acting in the world.

When I ask students to engage and create opportunities that I hope motivate their engagement, I have both kinds of engagement in mind: engagement with the content and with the community of knowledge that make that engagement meaningful. These underlying principles ground students with a (Burkean) sense of being in the world and becoming part of it.

Social Change / Social Justice

As Ann George so effectively demonstrates in her critical companion to *Permanence and Change*, Burke's more theoretical pronouncements form the basis of a new rhetoric for "civic pedagogy to save the world" (*passim*). In our age, rhetoric applies to everything because so much needs to be understood, particularly in our political lives. Applied rhetoric enacts civic engagement when the exigencies of the moment draw the attention constantly. Our social-political problems have been perpetuated for too long by those with the power to sustain the status quo. We need rhetoric more than ever to help us expose and challenge what has been repressed in the interest of nationalism and its offshoots or cousins, such as fascism. We must recover what has been lost in our detachment from humanity.

More than ever, students have social justice and civic engagement on their minds and in their futures. The publication of *The War of Words* and George's call for a civic pedagogy inspire new ways to bring Burke's ideas to bear on social issues and, importantly, to suggest ways that social movement rhetoric can lead to significant change. As I will discuss in the sections on the Podcast and Multimedia projects, I hoped for and witnessed most students accepting this invitation to express their desire by gauging the situation and formulating a response to it, to loosely paraphrase Burke. They acted, in other words, on their world as they've come to experience it and remade it, even if only in some small way (see James Beasley's chapter in this volume for another example of remaking the world via digital technologies and Rachel Chapman Daugherty's for engaging students with their community). Students want to change the world, yet so much competes for their attention that they may set that motive aside in the exigency of the moment. I therefore invited Ann George, Anthony Burke, Jack Selzer, and Kyle Jensen to join the class during a Zoom session, in the hope that they might show students the stakes and the ways Burke might help them develop a strategy for their own engagement.

The Range of Rhetorics

Theory should not be a luxury to postpone for later, Burke argued in "War and Cultural Life." We must understand how we got here, what we should have seen coming but didn't. Rhetorical theory, which theorizes generative principles and elaborates ambiguity, can help us unravel these mysteries. To start, we need more than ever the widest ranging elaboration of rhetoric as applied, its praxis, so that we see its machinations and magic. To understand how rhetoric applies to present contexts, to see the theoretical foundations these applications or performances stand on, we can work backward to generative principles. The method of glossing the present exemplifies rhetorical invention in reverse, one of Plato's principal methods. We see the conclusions everywhere, so theoretical inquiry means unraveling the threads that led to them: How did we get here?

A generative principle of the course therefore involved tracking down the implications of our terminologies, which in this case began with *rhetoric*. At the very start of this or any course on rhetoric, I try to illuminate the ways that preconceptions can (and should) be challenged. As TL (The Lord) says repeatedly in Burke's "Dialogue: Prologue in Heaven," "it's more complicated than that." In some respects, I walk Burke's path in *A Rhetoric of Motives* when he inveighs that rhetoric "must lead us through the Scramble, the Wrangle of the Market Place, the flurries and flare-ups of the Human Barnyard, the Give and Take" (*RM* 23). Can we track the implications of rhetoric? How far do they range?

Enhancing Student Engagement with the Course Content

In this particular instance of the course, I introduced several specific communication technologies that I believed could support the goal of energizing class dialogue across multiple channels—from our live Zoom sessions to synchronous social media posts on Twitter and asynchronous threaded discussion on Yellowdig.

Yellowdig as the Burkean Parlor

Yellowdig (yellowdig.com/) touts itself as a community-building, asynchronous discussion board designed to improve student engagement with course content. In some respects, it functions like many other threaded discussion boards, but Yellowdig stands apart from them in a number of key ways. Yellowdig "gamefully" fosters dialectical inquiry. Students automatically earn points for a variety of actions in addition to posting and responding to each other. If their posts reach a certain number of words, they earn points. Their comments earn points after forty words. Authors who receive comments also earn points. Students can upvote each other's pins ("love" or "like," for example) with a wide variety of emojis. Instructors can give out "accolades" (like badges), which likewise earn points and serve as both incentives and models with course content. Yellowdig makes it easy to add links, embed video, and attach files to posts. Instructors set a point goal per week, and grades for this aspect of the coursework tally automatically (see figure 2 for the configuration of the points system). Yellowdig's founders used to refer to all this play-for-point *gamification*. In Burkean parlance, we might call it *competitive cooperation*.

At first use, the gamification seems a little too behavioristic, especially for a Burke seminar where we began by discussing trained incapacity and well-educated chickens. But the gamification magically works. Students wrote extensively, responding to prompts I supplied each week, starting new topics of their own, and commenting enthusiastically and frequently on each other's writing. All twenty-one of the students earned the maximum number of points for the semester. Because Yellowdig tallies the points automatically and feeds them back to the Canvas grade book, I spent my time reading and responding right along with them, as I should be, not grading, counting words, or simply recording posts.

(It's hard to put in your oar in the parlor if you spend all of your time keeping score.)

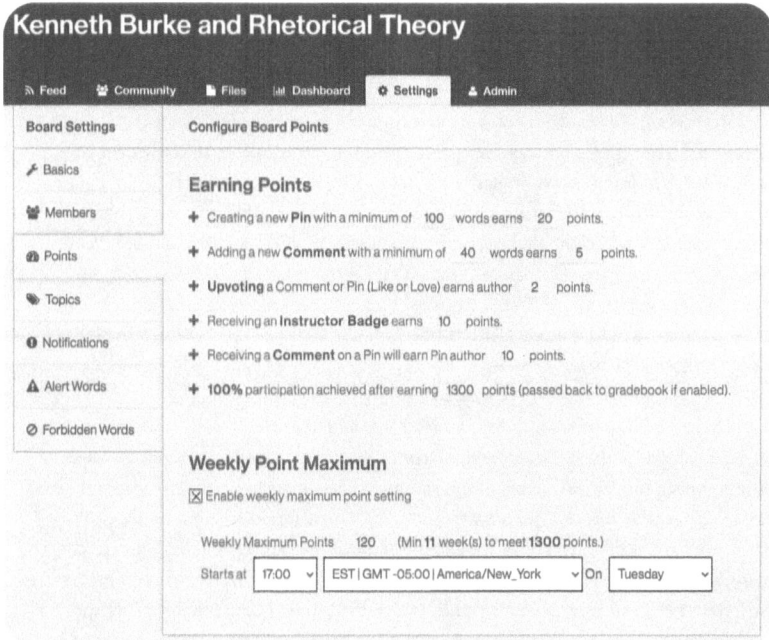

Figure 2. The Yellowdig point configuration screen.

While most discussions supported, elaborated, or extended Burke's ideas, quite a few threads took issue with problematic (or largely absent) statements about racial ethics, the patriarchal, white privilege of his public role as a critic, and other controversial positions that warranted more attention than he gave them. We should take seriously Burke's admonition to seek transcendence through competitive cooperation. Yellowdig became the students' parlor where they felt free to engage with Burke and rhetoric without the formal and social constraints of synchronous, oral discussion. See figure 3 for a typical post.

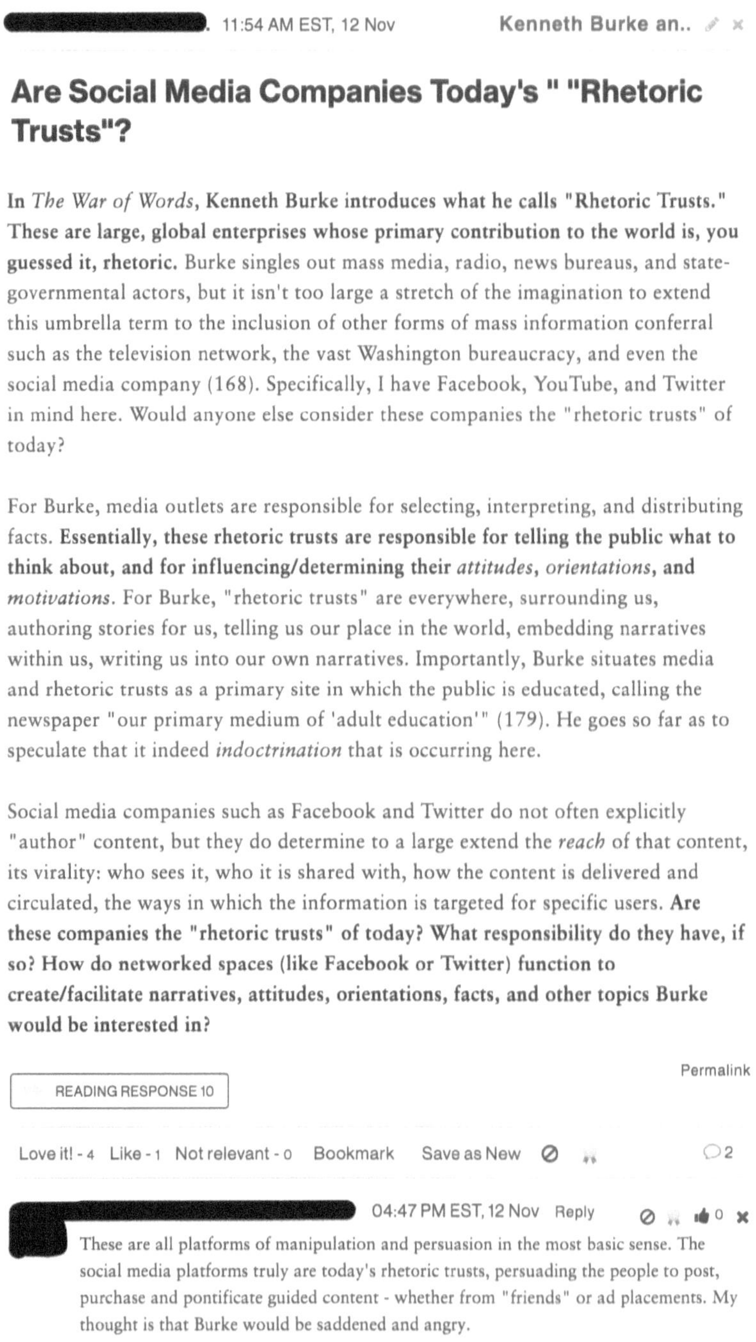

80   David Blakesley

■■■■■■■■■■■■■. 11:54 AM EST, 12 Nov   Kenneth Burke an.. ✏ ✕

Are Social Media Companies Today's " "Rhetoric Trusts"?

In *The War of Words*, Kenneth Burke introduces what he calls "Rhetoric Trusts." These are large, global enterprises whose primary contribution to the world is, you guessed it, rhetoric. Burke singles out mass media, radio, news bureaus, and state-governmental actors, but it isn't too large a stretch of the imagination to extend this umbrella term to the inclusion of other forms of mass information conferral such as the television network, the vast Washington bureaucracy, and even the social media company (168). Specifically, I have Facebook, YouTube, and Twitter in mind here. Would anyone else consider these companies the "rhetoric trusts" of today?

For Burke, media outlets are responsible for selecting, interpreting, and distributing facts. Essentially, these rhetoric trusts are responsible for telling the public what to think about, and for influencing/determining their *attitudes, orientations,* and *motivations*. For Burke, "rhetoric trusts" are everywhere, surrounding us, authoring stories for us, telling us our place in the world, embedding narratives within us, writing us into our own narratives. Importantly, Burke situates media and rhetoric trusts as a primary site in which the public is educated, calling the newspaper "our primary medium of 'adult education'" (179). He goes so far as to speculate that it indeed *indoctrination* that is occurring here.

Social media companies such as Facebook and Twitter do not often explicitly "author" content, but they do determine to a large extend the *reach* of that content, its virality: who sees it, who it is shared with, how the content is delivered and circulated, the ways in which the information is targeted for specific users. Are these companies the "rhetoric trusts" of today? What responsibility do they have, if so? How do networked spaces (like Facebook or Twitter) function to create/facilitate narratives, attitudes, orientations, facts, and other topics Burke would be interested in?

Permalink

| READING RESPONSE 10 |

Love it! - 4   Like - 1   Not relevant - 0   Bookmark   Save as New ⊘ 👍   💬 2

■■■■■■■■■■■■■■■■■■■■■■■■ 04:47 PM EST, 12 Nov   Reply   ⊘ 👍 👍 0 ✕
These are all platforms of manipulation and persuasion in the most basic sense. The social media platforms truly are today's rhetoric trusts, persuading the people to post, purchase and pontificate guided content - whether from "friends" or ad placements. My thought is that Burke would be saddened and angry.

Figure 3. A Yellowdig post showing the tagging and gamification interface, with a sample comment.

In future incarnations of this course, I plan to be less directive with my suggestions for weekly topics. I want students to forge their own paths, but when I provide (or even just "suggest") topics, they focus attention on what I have in mind, which may not be where they need or want it to be. With asynchronous discussion, the richest communities with the highest degree of student engagement evolve organically and dialectically. When I steer the conversations, students respond at the last minute and usually only to what I post.

TWEETDECK

Tweetdeck, a Twitter application, allows anyone to aggregate tweets from a variety of sources or hashtags. Tweetdeck often appears in public spaces on large video displays to show current conversations about topics of current or local interest. You'll sometimes see Tweetdeck displays at conferences or even in panel sessions to highlight relevant ongoing discussions. I introduced Tweetdeck into the Burke seminar to give students another way to share their thoughts in real time. In a large seminar with talkative graduate students, it can sometimes be difficult to get a word in edgewise, so I wanted another stream of conversation. I displayed Tweetdeck (see figure 4) on a large video display and could glance at it during the session to see questions and comments. I wanted the opportunity to tweet during class to engage students in new ways or let them focus their attention productively. Students could use a pseudonym to keep identities private.

Tweetdeck proved to be an interesting experiment and prompted occasional chuckles during class when someone tweeted something witty, but in the end Tweetdeck proved to be more distracting than engaging. As the instructor trying to manage a course session with fifteen students face to face and another six on Zoom while leading class discussion, I barely had a moment to see what transpired on Tweetdeck, even though it displayed on a large screen in the fairly small room. Some students forgot about it. A handful of experienced tweeters kept the feeds moving along, but those people told me later that they felt like they spoke to an empty room. Tweetdeck disappeared like white noise after a while, but that didn't ruin the engagement. We had other ways to engage, including in the synchronous chat room in Zoom. If anything, I learned that engagement could become a distraction when it demands too much of our attention.

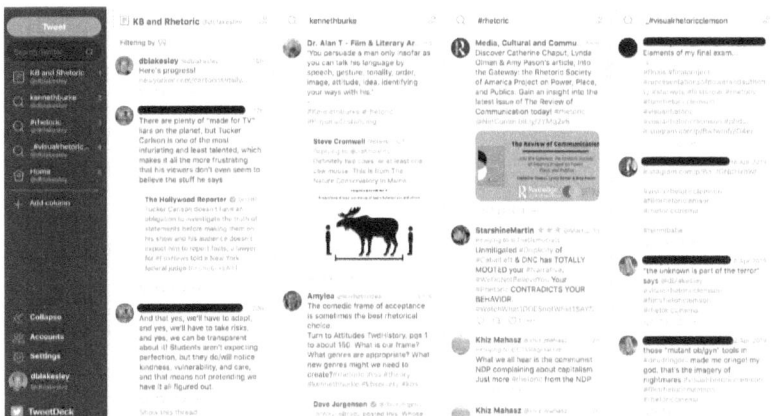

Figure 4. The Tweetdeck display shows four columns of content, each one collecting tweets from a different hashtag or source. Column 1 shows tweets by students in the KB and Rhetoric class only. Column 2 shows tweets using the hashtag #kennethburke. Column 3 shows collects #rhetoric tweets. Column 4 shows tweets with the hashtag #visualrhetoricclemson, a session-specific hashtag used just on a particular day.

Fostering Engagement with Wider Publics

I also wanted students to engage with the broader community of scholars in rhetoric, to learn what others in the parlor have been saying but also to put in their oars. In addition to meeting by Zoom with Burke scholars, students chose a new form (for them) to engage wider publics.

Podcast Project

In the podcast project, students created an episode of "The Parlor," a podcast series planned for launch in 2024 and focused on rhetoric, Burke, and "American Words." Students chose a particular key term; one they had been researching throughout the semester and writing about in Yellowdig. They sought scholars in the field with expertise on the subject, then recorded interviews produced and packaged as future segments for the series. The key terms and concepts included *casuistry, disability rhetorics, myth, attitude, piety, purposive forgetting, dialectic, logomachy,* and *orientation*. Podcasts potentially appeal to wider publics, and most of my students listen to them regularly. Most have never produced a podcast, however. An ideal way to engage with the broader scholarly community, podcasts invite students to put in their oar while also inviting the public to join the fray. Students retained author/producer rights for the work they completed, so all of them have podcast production credits on their CVs and podcast episodes in their professional portfolios.

Engagement Project

This project gave students opportunities to contribute in practical ways to the field of Burke or rhetorical studies, to do the heavy lifting that sustains a field and a discipline. Students were given a wide variety of options and then chose their path. Those options included reviewing manuscript submissions, writing reviews of recently published journal articles about Burke, responding to new work published in *KB Journal*, tracking down assets for a multimedia Kenneth Burke timeline, writing book reviews, conducting an accessibility study of *KB Journal*'s website, and updating the Burke bibliographies. Students shaped their contributions into manageable units, then I helped them develop and refine their work. Everyone can now list new editorial work, reviews, or publications on their CVs. More importantly, students come to appreciate the crowdsourced development of resources for scholarly research.

Print or Multimedia Project

The major project in all of my Burke seminars encourages students to produce publishable work, either a traditional article/conference paper or a multimedia project that might be published by an online journal or website. I want them to publish ("make public") content that elaborates or exploits ideas, terms, readings, and concepts discussed or read in class and that radiate from or focus on Burke's work and, more generally, rhetorical theory. Here's the longer explanation:

> If you choose to develop an article, you could focus specifically on issues in Burke, drawing on secondary sources as needed to support your discussion. Or you could draw on Burkean concepts to illuminate some other topic in your area(s) of interest. If you apply Burke, the application should be richly textured so that the concepts you apply represent Burke's own work complexly but clearly. If you choose another form for your project, such as a conference presentation, you could do much the same, but your presentation should be supported by content that will keep

your audience attentive. Visual or other content should support your paper/presentation. If you decide to develop a multimedia or other project, it should be one that fills a need in Burkean or rhetorical scholarship and that could be presented online or at a conference as an installation (for example). You can imagine that whichever option you choose, your final project will be suitable for publication or presentation in a venue where Burke and rhetorical scholars will find it a genuine contribution to "Burkology."

Students write a contract proposal, conduct their research, draft and review prototypes, then submit projects at the end of the semester. Along the way, some learn to play roles relatively new to them, such as those of scholar/writer or public intellectual. They learn the process of tracking down copyrights and how to request permissions from rights holders, which challenges all archival researchers, creative artists, and mash-up remixers. Many follow through by publishing their project online, sometimes in journals but also on YouTube, Vimeo, Spark, or at conferences.

Student Examples

I want to conclude this chapter with a gallery of student projects that you can find online now or in the very near future, all from iterations of this particular course. Their work speaks for itself impressively. Some of the projects stun for their creativity and imagination in both content and presentation. All have made and continue to make important statements in the unending conversation of history. Each screenshot includes a caption that provides some context. Their projects have been of all sorts over the years, and I only have space to mention a handful of them here. You'll run into the others somewhere down the road.

Hypertext Essay

"Kenneth Burke's Definition of Human" (1998) by Jerry Ross

After watching "Kenneth Burke: A Conversation," the Harry Chapin video interview with KB, Jerry Ross seized on the illustration of the "Definition of Man" that Burke explicates while Harry asks him questions. The illustration appears on the wall in the kitchen at Burke's home in Andover. Jerry captured the image from the video, cleaned it up, added a few of his own illustrations (such as the "Wo" before "Man") and then created a hypertext essay that elaborated each frame. The hypertext essay appeared at the Virtual Burkeian Parlor in a section called "Taking Burke On(line): The Kenneth Burke Bibliography and Archival Project," a curated archive of projects on Burke that I created in 1997. The essay received many thousands of hits and stood as one of the first, if not *the* first, hypertext essay on Burke ever published.

Years later in a discussion with Phillip K. Thompkins, I discovered that the illustration had been produced by an artist's group associated with his Burke seminar taught at SUNY Albany in 1974. The students presented Burke with the artwork, and it still hangs on the wall in the kitchen in Andover. Figure 5 shows an enhanced screen grab of the illustration from the video and a photograph of the source illustration.

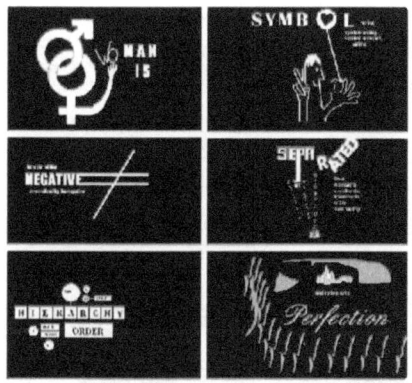 

Figure 5. The illustration of Burke's definition of human that anchors Jerry Ross's hypertext essay (left) and a photograph of the source illustration in Burke's home (right). Photograph by the author.

Archival Projects

"Road to Victory" by Elaine Burklow (1998)

Elaine Burklow read this passage in *A Grammar of Motives* and felt compelled to track down any information she could about the photograph:

> In an exhibit of photographic murals at the Museum of Modern Art, there was an aerial photograph of two launches, proceeding side by side on a tranquil sea. Their wakes crossed and recrossed each other in an almost infinite variety of lines. Yet despite the intricateness of the tracery, the picture gave an impression of great simplicity, because one could quickly perceive the generating principle of its design. Such, ideally, is the case

with our pentad of terms, used as generating principle. It should provide us with a kind of simplicity that can be developed into considerable complexity, and yet can be discovered beneath its elaborations. (xvi)

Elaine first found a guide to MoMA's past exhibits, which gave her enough information to write for more information and a copy of the actual photograph. Like many archival projects, this one led to further discoveries, such as the broader context in which the photograph appears (an exhibition meant to stoke patriotism at the start of World War II). "The Road to Victory," including many of its images and the supporting text written by Carl Sandburg, can now be viewed online: www.moma.org/calendar/exhibitions/3038.[1] The image in the online exhibition appears on the twenty-ninth slide in the lower left corner. To our surprise, the photograph of the two launches appears in a larger exhibition context that Burke ignores in *A Grammar of Motives*. Other photographs show images of war, including the bombing of Pearl Harbor, battleships (the "two launches"). We see the imagery and instruments of killing. Burke implicitly suggests that the pentad can reveal the motives we attribute to war, patriotism, and violence.

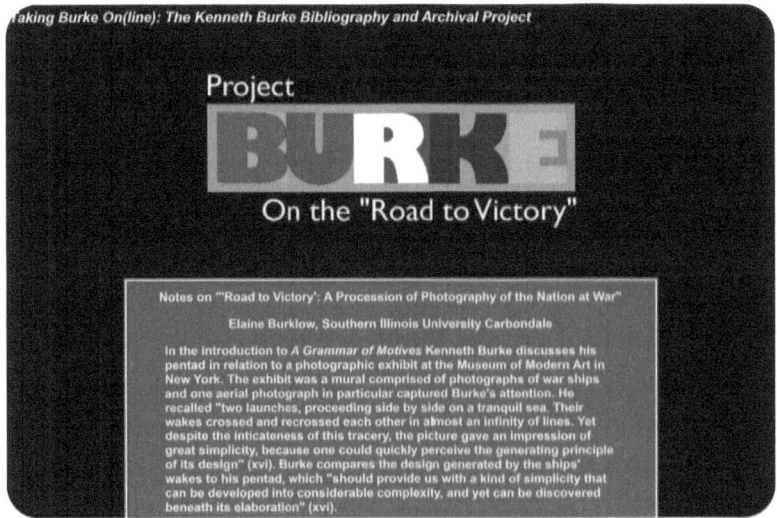

Figure 6. Elaine Burklow's project at the Virtual Burkeian Parlor in 1998. It included an image of the photograph Burke mentions in *A Grammar of Motives* to explain the nature of the pentad as an analytical method.

---

1. See also Debra Hawhee and Megan Poole, "Kenneth Burk at the MoMA: A Viewer's Theory." *Quarterly Journal of Speech*, vol. 105, no. 4, 2019, pp. 418–40.

Kenneth Burke's FBI Files by Todd Deam (1999)

Todd Deam correctly surmised that there would be an FBI file on Burke, so he wrote a Freedom of Information Act (FOIA) Request to the FBI and received a redacted copy of the complete file a couple of months later. After scanning and transcribing the documents, they appeared at the Virtual Burkeian Parlor in 1999. The files focus primarily on activity around the 1935 American Writers' Congress sponsored by the League of American Writers in New York City and where Burke delivered his well-known speech "Revolutionary Symbolism in America."

Home » Issues of KB Journal » Volume 13, Issue 1 Fall 2017

Kenneth Burke's FBI Files

David Blakesley and Todd Deam

Todd Deam requested Burke's FBI Files in February, 1999. The Justice Department responded within several weeks to say that the files would be made available in "due time." Due time turned out to be only 45 days, in part because the files had been requested previously and thus didn't need to be censored again.

The packet contains twenty pages in all, some of which are inserts of an FBI form indicating that one or more pages is not being released because of exemptions specified in the Freedom of Information Privacy Act. Because of their location in the entire file, the missing pages appear to be from the mid-1950s, but that conclusion is only speculation. You can download the entire FBI file without annotations here. Otherwise, you can review each page and a transcription below.—*DB*

FEDERAL BUREAU OF INVESTIGATION

FREEDOM OF INFORMATION/PRIVACY ACTS SECTION

COVER SHEET

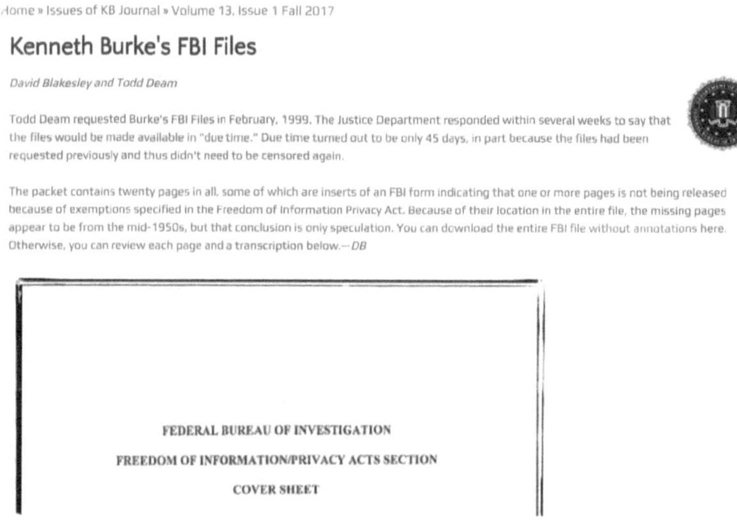

Figure 7. In 2017, Burke's FBI files were published at *KB Journal* and now include an accompanying essay by this author. See kbjournal.org/fbifiles.

Application of Burke's Ideas in a New Field (2019)

"Burkeian Applications in Enhancing Interface Design" by Kylie Carlson

Kylie Carlson's course project applies Burke's theories of metaphor, form, individuation, and symbol to the challenges of interface design and user experience design in an Adobe Express Page (a scrolling, multimedia presentation format made by Adobe). After the course, Kylie successfully reworked the project and presented it at the University of Alabama Digitorium Conference in October 2020.

Figure 8. Screenshot of Kylie Carlson's multimedia project on interface design (2020). express.adobe.com/page/5nGXvLcMceLMc/

Video Projects

"KB: A Conversation with Kenneth Burke" by Ethan Sproat (2014)

With the permission of the Kenneth Burke Literary Trust and Sandy Chapin, Ethan Sproat digitized the fifteen-minute video featuring Harry Chapin interviewing Burke at the Andover farm in the late 1970s. The KB video sold on the *KB Journal* website soon after. This project also led to Ethan's creation of the Kenneth Burke Digital Archive (kbjournal.org/kenneth-burke-digital-archive), which expanded to include collections of audio and video recordings of KB, one of which became central to Victoria Carrico's film adaptation "Eye-Crossing: From Brooklyn to Manhattan" (figures 12–15).

"2Minute Thinker: Burke" by Stephen Lind (2011)

Stephen Lind accepted the challenge of trying to summarize Burke's contributions to the study of rhetoric and created a video and YouTube channel that launched the "2Minute Thinker" project. His own video appeared first in the series and captures KB in two minutes, or at least as much of him as anyone could reasonably expect. Stephen also premiered the short film at the 2011 Triennial Conference of the Kenneth Burke Society at Clemson.

Figures 9 and 10. 2MinuteThinker Project by Stephen Lind (2011). youtu.be/iYjpjVDG6zs. The project now includes videos about Aristotle, Cicero, Erasmus, Richard Weaver, and others, with new submissions encouraged: www.youtube.com/user/2MinuteThinker.

Three Short Film Adaptations by Jimmy Butts (2011)

Jimmy Butts focused on Burke's fiction, but rather than write a traditional academic paper, he chose the much more difficult task of trying to adapt the fiction to film. To make the process manageable, he chose three of Burke's (very) short stories: "Parabolic Tale, with Invocation," "The Excursion," and "Scherzando." These three stories challenge readers in part because they repurpose a familiar form, such as the parable or quest narrative. That quality granted Jimmy considerable license. He had to formally request permission to adapt the work from the Kenneth Burke Literary Trust. Jimmy premiered the short films at the 2011 Triennial Conference of the Kenneth Burke Society at Clemson, and they appeared in *KB Journal* in 2013.

Figure 11. Screenshot from Jimmy Butts's film adaptation of "Parabolic Tale" (2013). kbjournal.org/three-short-film-adaptations-jimmy-butts.

"Eye-Crossing from Brooklyn to Manhattan" by Kenneth Burke. Video, Captioning, and Artist Statement by Victoria Carrico (2019)

Victoria Carrico's thirty-minute film interprets and represents Burke's long poem, "Eye-Crossing from Brooklyn to Manhattan." When Victoria first proposed this project, I cautioned her that this long and complex poem would take a substantial amount of work to interpret and adapt well. We both watched Alejandro Mos Riera's interpretation of T. S. Eliot's "The Waste Land" (2017), which includes audio of Sir Alec Guinness reading the poem (vimeo.com/213670858). We worried about the challenge of finding a suitable narrator, but I remembered that Burke recites the poem in an interview with Howard Nemerov in 1968 that had been collected in Ethan Sproat's digital archive and published at *KB Journal* (kbjournal.org/kenneth_burke_wustl_reading1). Maybe it would be possible to use that audio. Victoria went to work. She told me afterward that she spent three and a half hours of work for every one minute of film, which didn't surprise me. (When you watch the film, you won't be surprised either.)

Despite its length and circuitous path, Burke called the poem a lyric, and in the words of Gregory Clark, it thus "invites readers to identify themselves with the poet by adopting as their own the attitude the poem expresses toward circumstances that they share" ("Sinkership"). In this respect, Burke's poem motivated Victoria's own lyrical adaptation of this poem's themes, which move from the inscrutability of change to the alienating character of rapid urbanization and dehumanizing technologies. The poet sees America in decline as he struggles himself with anxiety about his own aging. Burke followed the path that Walt Whitman mapped in "Crossing Brooklyn Ferry" poem in *Leaves of Grass*. Victoria describes her path in a reflection on the film,

> I decided to bring "Eye-Crossing from Brooklyn to Manhattan" to life by creating a visual accompaniment to the poem in order to increase the "consubstantiality" between readers and Burke. By adding a visual element to the poem, viewers will be able to experience Burke's apprehensions, fears, and thoughts expressed in this poem in a new medium, deepening their understanding of his ideas.

Because she also managed to collect and edit Burke's reading of the poem, as the film unfolds the poet speaks directly to us. A beautiful and moving lyrical performance in its own right, Victoria's film debuted at *KB Journal* in 2021: kbjournal.org/carrico.

Illuminating Burke, Engaging Publics 93

Figures 12–15. Screenshots from Victoria Carrico's adaptation of "Eye-Crossing: From Brooklyn to Manhattan (2020).

Graduate Theory Syllabus

Kenneth Burke and Rhetorical Theory

Reading List

These are the primary course readings. The books are available at the Clemson University Bookstore. The course calendar (syllabus) specifies what should be read and when.

Blakesley, David. *The Elements of Dramatism*. Longman, 2002. Free digital copy provided.
Burke, Kenneth. *Counter-Statement*. 1931. U of California P, 1968.
—. *Permanence and Change: An Anatomy of Purpose*. 1935. 3rd edition. U of California P, 1984.
—. *Attitudes Toward History*. 3rd ed. U of California P, 1984.
—. *A Grammar of Motives*. 1945. U of California P, 1969.
—. *A Rhetoric of Motives*. 1950. U of California P, 1969.
—. *Language as Symbolic Action: Essays on Life, Literature, and Method*. U of California P, 1966.
—. *Here and Elsewhere: The Collected Fiction of Kenneth Burke*. Godine, 2005. Free printed copy provided.
—. *Essays Toward a Symbolic of Motives, 1950–1955*. Ed. William H. Rueckert. Parlor Press, 2007. Free digital copy provided.
—. *The War of Words*. Edited by Anthony Burke, Kyle Jensen, and Jack Selzer. U of California P, 2018.
George, Ann. *Kenneth Burke's* Permanence and Change: *A Critical Companion* (Studies in Rhetoric/Communication). U of South Carolina P, 2018.
Glenn, Cheryl. *Rhetorical Feminism and This Thing Called Hope*. Southern Illinois UP, 2018.
Thompson, Clive. *Smarter Than You Think: How Technology Is Changing Our Minds for the Better*. Penguin, 2013.
—. *Coders: The Making of a New Tribe and the Remaking of the World*. Penguin, 2019.

Digital Coursepack: These readings will be listed on the calendar and appear in the Files section of Canvas. The collection includes primary and secondary readings on rhetorical theory and Burke. This collection of files will grow as the semester develops.

For Further Reading: Burke

Here are some more books by and about Burke. For primary and secondary bibliographies, check out Works by KB and Works about KB at *KB Journal*.

Burke, Kenneth. *Equipment for Living: The Literary Reviews of Kenneth Burke.* Ed. Nathaniel Rivers and Ryan Weber (Parlor Press, 2010)

—. *Kenneth Burke on Shakespeare.* Ed. Scott L. Newstok (Parlor Press 2007)

—. *Late Poems, 1968–1993 Attitudinizings Verse-wise, While Fending for One's Selph, and in a Style Somewhat Artificially Colloquial.* Ed. by Julie Whitaker and David Blakesley. University of South Carolina Press, 2005.

—. *The Rhetoric of Religion: Studies in Logology.* 1961 (University of California Press, 1970)

—. *On Human Nature: A Gathering While Everything Flows.* Ed. William H. Rueckert and Angelo Bonadonna (University of California Press, 2003)

Coupe, Laurence. *Kenneth Burke: From Myth to Ecology.* (Parlor Press, 2013)

Crable, Bryan. *Ralph Ellison and Kenneth Burke: At the Roots of the Racial Divide.* (University of Virginia Press, 2012)

—, editor. *Transcendence By Perspective: Meditations on and with Kenneth Burke.* (Parlor Press, 2014)

Crusius, Timothy. *Kenneth Burke and the Conversation after Philosophy.* (Southern Illinois University Press, 1999)

George, Ann, and Jack Selzer. *Kenneth Burke in the 1930s.* (University of South Carolina Press, 2007)

Henderson, Greig. *Literature and Language as Symbolic Action* (Parlor Press, 2023)

Rickert, Thomas. *Ambient Rhetoric: The Attunements of Rhetorical Being.* (University of Pittsburgh Press, 2013)

Selzer, Jack. *Kenneth Burke in Greenwich Village.* (University of Wisconsin Press, 1996)

Selzer, Jack, and Robert Wess, *Kenneth Burke and His Circles*. (Parlor Press, 2008)

Weiser, Elizabeth. *Burke, War, Words: Rhetoricizing Dramatism*. U of South Carolina P, 2008.

Description

This course will consider Kenneth Burke as an exemplary figure in the genesis of rhetoric, composition, communication, cultural studies, and literary theory in the twentieth century. The focus will be on his continuing relevance for our understanding of key rhetorical principles (identification, division, context, terministic screens, dramatism, symbolic action, and more), of emergent topics and trends in rhetoric as a field of study and application, and the relationships among rhetoric and other areas of the inquiry. Course readings will include primary Burkean texts and secondary work by other rhetoricians, theorists, and critics. Coursework will include weekly written responses to the readings in Yellowdig, an engagement project, a major print or multimedia project, and contributions to a podcast or documentary film related to Burke and rhetoric. Some student projects may be developed for submission to *KB Journal*, which is hosted and edited here at Clemson.

Coursework

Further details about each of these projects are available in Appendices below and will be discussed in class:

Asynchronous Online Discussion: Yellowdig

Access the Yellowdig assignment the first time through its associated assignment page. At least one pin each week should add to our running discussions of Burke and rhetorical theory (choose one of these as the Topic of your pin). Other pins, replies, and comments can be about what we read, view, or discuss throughout the class. You will be given some time during class to post and respond on Yellowdig, but most of your responses will need to be written outside of class. Some of this writing will be prompted, but you may also post on any topic relevant to the course at any time. The goal is to accumulate 100 points per week. Points are earned by creating a new pin (20), adding a new comment (5), upvoting a comment or pin (1), receiving an instructor badge (10), and receiving a comment on a pin (5). (30% of course grade, or 300 points)

Tweetdeck

Although this aspect of the course won't be graded, we're going to use Tweetdeck as a «Tweet Board» during and sometimes between class sessions to enrich class discussion and involve everyone in sharing ideas, thoughts, resources, and more while a class session unfolds. To use Tweetdeck, you'll just need a Twitter account from which you can tweet, reply, like, retweet, and more. Your account can be anonymous if you choose. You'll be able to watch and post to Tweetdeck during class, either remotely in a separate browser window or in class projected on a large display screen or on your computer. You can post questions about class content/discussion, start subthreads, reply to others, share/link to resources, and more. When your post directly relates to Kenneth Burke, you should use the hashtag #kennethburke so that it also gets picked up by the KB Journal Twitter feed. In terms of good practice, "be genuine and non-deceptive and provide value." You can tag others in the class, use hashtags (other than those for the class session, and send direct messages to others in the class, whom you should also follow.

Podcast Project

Develop the topic and content for a podcast episode of The Parlor (a new podcast on Burke, rhetoric, and American Words). You'll work in teams of two or three (if needed) to plan, research, script, produce, and publish an episode of The Parlor. (15% of course grade, or 150 points)

Curating Content for *The Wordman*

The aim of this project is to curate or create some content for a documentary film on Kenneth Burke, The Wordman. See spark.adobe.com/page/9FOCxFUzTe96H/ for some back-ground. (5% of course grade, or 50 points)

Engagement Project

The engagement project will be tailored to individual student interest but will focus on some aspect of the production and distribution of a professional, open-access resource about Burke and/or rhetorical theory. (10% of course grade, or 100 points)

Major Print or Multimedia Project

At the end of the semester, submit a research essay or multimedia project that draws on course readings and any other work relevant to your subject matter and that advances a position on a topic of potential interest to others in your field of study. You'll be provided with detailed guidelines for this project in Week 6 and be required to submit work-in-progress reports in class. Length: 4,000 – 8,000 words or the equivalent. You may think of this project as a conference proposal and presentation or the draft of a project to submit for publication to a journal. (40% of course grade, or 400 points)

RESOURCES

KB Discussion List. In existence now for 20 years, this list includes approximately 240 members from many different fields of study. I would like each of you to join the list and "lurk" or participate (as you choose). List traffic is usually light but will pick up now and then as people ask questions or introduce topics. To learn about how to join the list, visit kbjournal.org/mailing. I am the list moderator. Please email me by the start of Week 2 to let me know that you have successfully joined the list.

KB Journal: www.kbjournal.org. In addition to newly published articles on Burke, the journal features discussion forums, bibliographies, information about the Kenneth Burke Society, announcements, and more. *KB Journal* is hosted at Clemson. The bibliographies will be especially useful for your research.

GRADING

Yellowdig Discussion	30%
Podcast Project	15%

Curating Content for The Wordman	5%
Engagement Project	10%
Print or Multimedia Project	40%
Total	100%

The criteria for evaluation of assignments will be spelled out on the assignment. You'll receive feedback along the way throughout your inquiry project from your peers and me, as well as a grade on each completed step.

Podcast Project

Prompt

In teams of two or three, plan, script, and produce a 20-to-25-minute podcast in Adobe Audition that includes an interview with at least one outside "expert" that focuses on one key term or concept in rhetoric as discussed/elaborated in Kenneth Burke's work.

Discussion of the Prompt

Once your teams have formed, you'll need to select the key term or concept that you want to elaborate in your podcast. You can review the glossary in *The Elements of Dramatism* for some ideas or simply select one from any of the course readings. You'll want to choose a term/concept whose meaning is not unambiguous, one that can be elaborated, extended, defined in a variety of ways depending on contexts, and that is also one that others will be interested in learning more about, that helps them understand an interesting or important aspect of rhetoric.

Good podcasts tell stories with sound effects, music, narration, and interview(s). In the resources section, you'll find some links to videos and information about podcasting generally, as well as tools and content that will help you collect assets for the project. There are also examples of some podcasts that you can use for inspiration. You probably also like some podcasts of your own, so draw on them for inspiration and technique.

Identify one or more experts on your term/concept and ask them if they'd be willing to meet via Zoom for a short interview/discussion about the term/concept. Explain the context of the project and how the interview may be used/published.

Steps in the Process

- Identify your term/concept and say a few words in class about your choice. (In-class, October 1.)
- Identify possible interview subject(s). (In-class, October 1). Email the interview subject(s) to invite them to participate. (Complete by October 8.)
- Scripting/Interview Questions: Develop and share your interview questions with the subject in advance, then conduct and record the interview in Zoom. (October 22).
- Write and record your opening and closing narration. (October 29)
- Add sound effects, music, and other elements to your podcast. Be prepared for peer review in class. (November 5)
- Submit your podcast file in Canvas as an MP3 file. (November 12)

Review of Your Work

Along the way, you'll receive feedback from your peers as we try to help you develop a first-rate podcast. You should also feel free to email me or stop by my office with questions at any time.

Resources

- Making the Burkean Parlor Podcast: https://express.adobe.com/page/7pGxJ2Aeekljx/
- Intro to Podcasting (from Adobe Course): edex.adobe.com/pd/course/podcasting/e/workshop/podcasting191/step/3
- Tutorial 1— Creating a Podcast from Edge Gain on Vimeo.
- Producing Audio in the Classroom: edex.adobe.com/pd/course/podcasting/e/workshop/podcasting192/step/8
- Creating Audio Recordings and Podcasts with Audition: edex.adobe.com/en/resource/36ac6–49#

- Adobe Audition Downloads (Sound Effects, Music Loops and Beds, Soundbooth Scores): offers.adobe.com/en/na/audition/offers/audition_dlc.htm

Some Fun Podcasts
- This American Life: www.thisamericanlife.org/
- The Allusionist: www.theallusionist.org/
- Lore: www.lorepodcast.com/
- Pedagogue: www.pedagoguepodcast.com/

Engagement Projects

The engagement project will be tailored to individual student interest but will focus on some aspect of the production and distribution of a professional, open-access resource about Burke.

Here are some possible projects (for one person, unless otherwise noted)

1. Edit *KB Journal* articles. Using guidelines provided, copy-edit 2–3 journal articles and then prepare them as simple HTML files for uploading to the *KB Journal* Drupal site.
2. Update the "Works about KB" bibliography. Involves adding sources published in the last two years. See the current site here: kbjournal.org/worksaboutkb.
3. Update the "Dissertations about KB" bibliography. Content up to 2016 has already been collected.
4. Launch an online photo sharing site. For collecting images from KB conferences, including the most recent. Then help people contribute as needed during its launch.
5. Assist with KB Timeline development. Help Dr. B. wrap up a Kenneth Burke timeline.
6. Review a new book about Kenneth Burke for possible publication.
7. Propose and develop a new feature for the *KB Journal* website. You could also revive the conference paper repository. See kbjournal.org/content/conference-paper-repository.
8. Create your own contribution. Come up with an idea for enhancing or improving *KB Journal* with new content; cre-

ate a new crowd-sourced Burke/rhetoric project that is both engaging and can evolve over time.
9. Digitize archival video. Dr. B. has video content from past KB conferences that needs to be digitized.
10. Complete a usability study of current *KB Journal* website (in a team of 2–3), with specific recommendations for updating the Drupal site.
11. Fix the Twitter feed functionality at the *KB Journal* website. See the front page and kbjournal.org/twittersphere.

Major Print or Multimedia Project

At the end of the semester, submit a research essay or multimedia project that draws on course readings and any other work relevant to your subject matter and advances a position on a topic of potential interest to others in your field of study.

Discussion

You have a number of format options for your project, but what should be common across all is content that elaborates or exploits ideas, terms, readings, concepts and the like discussed or read in class and that radiate from or focus on Burke's work and, more generally, rhetorical theory. If you choose to develop an article, you could focus specifically on issues in Burke, drawing on secondary sources as needed to support your discussion. Or you could draw on Burkean concepts to illuminate some other topic in your area(s) of interest. If you apply Burke, the application should be richly textured so that the concepts you apply are represented as complexly as they are in Burke's own work (as much as possible). If you choose another form for your project, such as a conference presentation, you could do much the same, but your presentation should be supported by content that will keep your audience with you. So visual or other content should support your paper/presentation. If you decide to develop a multimedia or other project, it should be one that will fill a need in Burkean or rhetorical scholarship and that could be presented online or at a conference as an installation (for example). You can imagine that whichever course you choose that your final project would be suitable for publication or presentation in a venue where Burke and rhetorical scholars will find it a genuine contribution to "Burkology" (written with tongue-in-cheek, as Burke would have it).

Steps in the Process

- Contract Proposal, posted as a Pin in Yellowdig in which you explain your subject, suggest some parameters for your research, and indicate why the subject interests you and how studying it will be beneficial. You should also mention how or where your work might be published. You'll be asked to summarize your proposal in class. (Suggested length: 250 words)
- Draft or Prototype in which you present key elements of the final project for peer review. The draft need not be complete, but it should be a component that is polished and ready for feedback.
- Polished Final Project should be submitted on the Canvas site.

Review of Your Work

Along the way, you'll receive feedback from your peers as we try to help you develop a first-rate project. You should also feel free to email me or stop by my office with questions at any time.

Possible Approaches and Topics

In addition to the article or conference presentations options, you may also choose to create a multimedia project of some type. Here are some possible technologies/interfaces that may give you some ideas:

- An augmented reality display or print project using Artivive or other AR software.
- Conference proposal and paper/presentation. Prepare a proposal for the next conference of the Kenneth Burke Society.
- A complex Express or Prezi presentation that introduces some key concept in Burke.
- A video that adapts or explains a Burke concept, work of fiction, or poetry.

II. Specific Applications

Photo 2. Kenneth Burke teaching a class. Photo courtesy of Pennsylvania State University archives.

5 Identification with the Imagined Community: The Museum of Us

M. Elizabeth Weiser

Using an assignment of self-made museum exhibits to teach identification and division to undergraduates.

It is a truism in Burke studies that identification is a key component of the Burkean theoretical framework. Humans form their sense of self as "beings who by nature respond to symbols" by identifying themselves with the symbols of shared beliefs, occupations, attitudes, and objects, and identifying with the others who share these allegiances. Thus, the persuasive force of rhetoric is found not in rational argument but in human interactions: "You persuade a man only insofar as you can talk his language . . . *identifying* your ways with his," as Burke put it in arguably his most famous sentence (*RM* 55).

We know this is profound. But when I present it to students they tend to say, "okay." I give them examples from conversations we've had in class, where someone mentions that they're from, say, Cleveland, and immediately anyone else from a surrounding suburb will pipe up. Or they're studying psychology—"I am too!" "I thought about psych before switching to social work." "My brother's girlfriend majored in psych." See? I say. "Oh. Okay," they respond. It is such a truism that it seems self-evident—why would someone have to *theorize* this?

Of course, we can explore the theory more deeply. But my undergraduates, most taking anything I teach as their one and only rhetoric or writing class, don't want to read theory. So, instead, I came up with a way for them to experience firsthand some of the implications of identification by calling on my work in museology, and that is through the assignment sequence I call the Museum of Us. The objective of the Museum of Us is to get students to explore *identity* as a rhetorical action, *identification* as a means of persuasion, and the *personalizing of essence* as a force in public identity-building. (Jarron Slater's pathologies work in this volume demonstrates another way to help students understand many of these concepts.)

I have used the Museum of Us in both an introduction to rhetoric survey for (mostly) non-majors and a more advanced course on rhetorical theory and criticism that I call Spaces and Place for (mostly) majors. I have taught the assignment sequence both in person and online. The assignment sheet following this essay will present a hybrid model that can be adapted to either format.

The assignment is simple: Somewhere just after the first month of class, and after an introductory lecture on identification and basic museum components, students are asked to choose five objects that symbolize their life for a museum exhibit called "Life in the Twenty-first Century." They create a display of these objects (the Display of Me) with an interpretive panel describing each object and placing it within the context of their life story, and everyone then shares these "displays" across the entire class. Each student's display becomes one (virtual) vitrine in the exhibit describing life in this era. I then ask students to analyze how these disparate displays become The Museum of Us as they reflect (select, deflect) life in the twenty-first century—including their own life.

In the rest of this chapter, I delve into the theoretical underpinnings of this assignment in both Burke studies and new museology, show a few examples, and end with the full assignment.

Preparing for the Museum of Us

We start with the notion of *identity formation*. William Penuel and James Wertsch describe how identity is not an essence-in-itself but the end result of an ongoing process of identity formation: "a form of action that is first and foremost rhetorical, concerned with persuading others (and oneself) about who one is and what one values to meet different purposes" (91). Students can easily identify both times and places where they have recently worked to persuade others—and themselves—of some new aspect of their identity. I point out to them that both of the fields I work in—rhetoric and museum studies—historically aim to have the rhetor/curator identify (or call into being) their audience/visitors, while at the same time recognizing that audiences are made up of individuals who come to the discourse not as blank slates but as participants in the dialogue. We discuss the notion that identity—both individual and communal—is a reciprocal action between audience/visitor and rhetor/curator, with both actively engaged in building a narrated identity that does not exist outside the interplay of actor and scene. *Was our country different when your grandparents were your age? Would you be different if you came from different families/had different friends/went to a different college?* Just as the individual's identity is situated, audiences make sense of that identity-in-context in their own situation because, as Penuel and Wertsch note, identity "is always addressed to someone, who is situated culturally and historically" (91).

To whom is this identity addressed? We next consider James Porter's understanding of *audience* not as the end recipient of the information-dissemination process but as a "discourse community" actively engaged with the rhetor, working with them to build not only a common story but also a common identity (see *Audience and Rhetoric*). In this way, rhetor and audience are engaged in a Burkean dialectic, the unending conversation of the rhetorical parlor or the conversation as it "may be thought of as voices in dialogue or roles in a play, with each voice or role in its partiality contributing to the development of the whole" (Burke, *GM* 403). As a conversation, I stress, Burke's dialectic was not the point/counterpoint of courtroom dramas—or war—but a plurality of partial voices that together would determine a new perspective by falling on the bias between various positions.

We then bring these somewhat abstract ideas into materialized practice in the museum. We may compare Lisa Roberts's work in *From Knowledge to Narrative* with John Falk's *Identity and the Museum Visitor Experience*. Roberts emphasizes the differences in visitor *experiences*, noting:

> in any given museum, visitors will probably encounter the same raw material: an entryway, exhibits, and perhaps a restaurant or gift shop. However, each will come away with an individually unique experience and interpretation because every visitor is engaged in constructing a narrative about what he or she sees. (137)

Falk emphasizes the similarities in visitor *roles* as he describes the way visitors are encouraged to perform one of five identity-roles in a museum (Explorer, Facilitator, Experience seeker, Professional/Hobbyist, Recharger) (64). Individuals may be choosing the role they wish to play, but the rhetorical scene of the museum persuades toward particular roles, I note. We can look at the website of the British Museum (britishmuseum.org), with its strong emphasis on "exploring" its multiple pathways, as an example.

I use the analogy I used in my book *Museum Rhetoric* to describe the way individual and communal identity are intertwined in a museum:

> It is as if the visitor were handed a sheet of paper with the vague outline of the nation on it and a box of crayons and were encouraged to draw a picture. The crayons are not limitless; they are constrained—there are ten of them, say, or twenty. The colors selected are multiple but compatible. Thus, each picture drawn is unique to the visitor, fitting more or less into the given outline, but each will be in some kind of harmony with the drawing of every other visitor, and different from the drawings done in museums of other nations, with their own outlines and color schemes.
>
> Kenneth Burke said this more theoretically in *A Grammar of Motives*, writing that the paradox of individual and collective motivations, "such as a concept of class, nation, the 'general will,'" seems to subsume individuals into a collective not of their making (37). It may appear, then, that collective motivation negates individual will, but to Burke this is a paradox precisely because individual identity itself is already derived from the collective in which one lives: "Yet despite this position as dialectical antithesis of the individual motive, the collective motive may be treated as the source or principle from which the individual motive is familially or 'substantially' derived in a 'like begets like' manner" (37). To return to the outlined page at the museum, individual visitors who add to the drawing of any collective identity depicted in a national museum "choose" their scene, but they do so with its general boundaries already in view and its limited palette of colors already seeming largely (if not wholly) appropriate. (Weiser, *Museum Rhetoric* 20)

Developing the Display of Me

I then introduce the assignment. While there are practical reasons (the syllabus sequence) for placing the assignment about one-third of the way into the semester, I also aim at this point to turn students' attention away from a focus on me and my "facts" toward a fuller sense of the persuasive impact of their own and each other's stories on the perspectives that shape their positions. It is helpful to let students express in the exhibit where they've come from and what is important to them as we move increasingly from teacher lecture to class discussion. One of the major issues that comes up when teaching rhetoric to this purple-state mix of students from a diversity of backgrounds is how we can look at the same evidence and come to such different conclusions. *How can that or he possibly persuade you? Why don't they persuade you?* As Burke would say, "The universe would appear to be something like a cheese; it can be sliced in an infinite number of ways—and when one has chosen his own pattern of slicing, he finds that other men's cuts fall at the wrong places" (*PC* 103). The jangling incongruities of the cuts made explicit by the differing exhibits help students recognize that those other cuts are possible—and also that surface similarities and differences do not necessarily correspond to differences in values. As an example, in the first class I did this assignment in, the evangelical Christian farm girl and the Muslim immigrant boy realized that they were the only two students who had placed faith at the center of their exhibits, and they bonded over their obvious shared joy in discussing their faith lives with others.

We begin to construct the exhibit by first looking closely at any good online exhibit (this could be done as a field trip to a museum, as well, if one were nearby). I like the ongoing major exhibit *Many Voices, One Nation* at the National Museum of American History (NMAH) (americanhistory.si.edu) for this phase, as it foregrounds polyphony and the dialectic of unity and diversity. This close examination of a professional exhibit helps those students who have limited experience with museums to consider how to materialize abstract ideas and provide concise interpretations that both describe the artifact in itself and integrate its meaning into the larger exhibition theme—in this case the idea that many voices make a nation. Because the exhibit promises to explore the question "How did we become US?" it also allows a class to discuss the significance of Burke's dictum that "vocabularies that will be faithful *reflections* of reality" will necessarily develop "vocabularies that are *selections* of reality" that sometimes "function as a *deflection* of reality" ("Tactics" I.27). Who is *selected* in this view of US? Of whom are they *reflections*? Who is *deflected from* the American identity? The musealized depiction in the NMAH exhibit of the full swath of American history makes this concept easy to discuss.

Students are now ready to choose their own five artifacts, and I remind them that the overall theme of our exhibit is "Life in the Twenty-First Century." I make a point of noting that they can interpret "Life in the Twenty-First Century" either diachronically or synchronically—as a chronology of their years or as a slice of their life right now—but either way they will end up with a unity that joins their diverse roles and pathways into a "me." We discuss narrative psychologist Dan McAdams's "lifestory theory of identity" (187), in which, he says, we develop an adult identity by integrating the various roles and pathways of our lives into our unified story of self—much as the US is narrated from "many voices" into "one nation" in the NMAH exhibit. The unity needed for an identity, a sense of "me," says McAdams, is achieved through interpreting our lives in a manner that unites the different synchronic roles we play (rhetorician, spouse, parent, garage-band member) and the different possible diachronic pathways for our lives (a first marriage, a year in Argentina, a PhD) into one coherent timeline (188–89). The question the exhibit attempts to answer, then, is not only "who am I?" but "how did I become ME?"

Armed with this background, students construct their exhibits. Students first choose five artifacts that represent their own "life in the twenty-first century." They post these as a "draft" to a class folder (or discussion board) first, with a simple short narrative explaining what they are, so that they can see each other's initial choices. This serves both to help students who might have a hard time imagining their life via material objects and also as an analytical tool in the later part of the assignment, as we shall see. I tell them that they can change out any objects from the draft in their final version of their display.

The actual display format they produce can be varied by course, depending on class size, format, design skills, and space considerations. At the most material end, each student can place five physical objects on a table. They may combine this with the more common display of five objects/photos of objects on a large poster board, decorated as they wish to represent "them." In the online version of the class, students produce five slides of their objects. Depending on the class, it is certainly possible to have them contribute to a class website or upload a video walk-through. Whatever their format, I have them title their exhibit with something more than their name, to include a summarizing title that defines/unifies their exhibit. (See figure 1 for an example.) In this way they can experience the power of Burke's "ultimate terms," words and phrases that have sufficient scope to sum up all aspects of an ongoing discussion (*RM* 186). As the students quickly discover, ultimate terms—the display titles they've chosen—also have the power to influence the *selection* of the reality they are narrating.

Whatever the format chosen, I ask students to produce an accompanying short narrative that includes a phrase describing the artifact and its provenance, a brief summary of approximately two sentences of why this artifact was selected (what aspect of the personal identity represented by the ultimate term does it represent), and a final sentence that relates the artifact back to the exhibit theme of "Life in the Twenty-First Century" (see figure 2 for an example).

ELIZABETH WEISER
At Home in My Worlds

Figure 1. Title slide example with "ultimate term" title, constructed by the author.

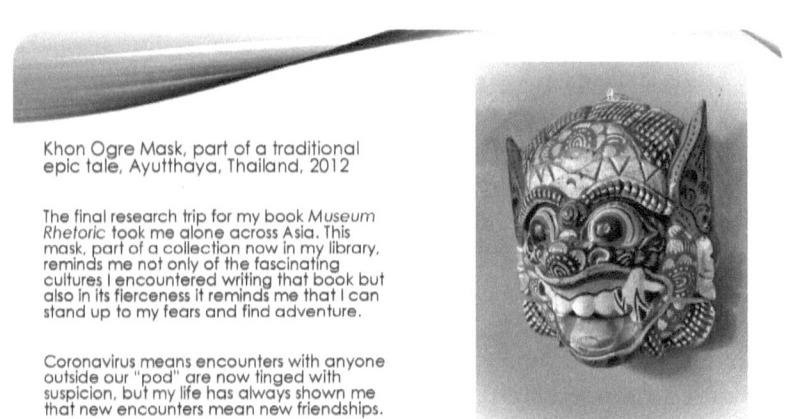

Figure 2. Example slide of one object and narrative, constructed by the author.

Students also arrange a recommended pathway through their exhibit, indicated by numbers on a table, lines on a poster, order of slides, perhaps links in a webpage. Some students choose to narrate a chronological life story with a definite starting point and clear trajectory for the audience, some give greater emphasis to the ultimate term and cluster their various artifacts around it, others follow a more synchronic narrative where visitors can explore artifacts in any order. They choose their arrangement, and we can then discuss together the effects of that choice on the narrative.

What we end up with is a musealization of what John Falk describes as the "malleable, emergent rather than permanent" process of identity formation:

> Our identity is a reflection [of] and a reaction to both the social and physical world we consciously perceive in the moment, but identity is also influenced by the vast unconscious set of family, cultural, and personal history influences each of us carries within us. Each is continuously constructing and maintaining, not one, but numerous identities which are expressed collectively or individually at different times, depending upon need and circumstance. (72–73)

Presenting the Exhibit

In face-to-face classes, students divide into "curators" and "visitors" on different days, with some percentage of each class serving as interpreters-for-a-day to clusters of the rest of the class, which wanders from display to display, as in a poster presentation. Curators explain the selections and arrangement of their displays, and visitors ask questions. I take photos of each display to post online for future analysis or, in an online class, simply upload all student slideshows into one document available to all, like an anthology. In a discussion post for each student-curator, student visitors respond to all exhibits (or, in a large class, a portion of them) and can reply to questions about their own. (Discussions also take place synchronously over Zoom.) While this is the part of the assignment that students find most interesting as they get to know each other, the important part of this aspect of the assignment is that students will naturally fall into discussions over commonalities, identifying their "speech, gesture, tonality, order, image, attitude, idea" (*RM* 55) with those of the various curators.

This, then, leads students naturally to the concept of *identification*, "any of the wide variety of means by which [a rhetor] may establish a shared sense of values, attitudes, and interests with [an audience]" (*RM* 243). Identification, we discuss, is the necessary companion to effective persuasion because persuasion is not purely rational. This is easily demonstrated after the student exhibits because there is always someone who, by this point in class, has shared an opinion that some other student disagrees with. "How can they be persuaded by *that*?" Oftentimes, the student's exhibit makes their position more understandable and therefore more persuadable. For example, one student's uncompromising devotion to absolute gun rights—a position not shared by many students in the aftermath of the Parkland shooting—became clearer to all as his exhibit showed his weapons alongside the recently deceased grandfather who used to take him hunting and whose example (and military career) this student was determined to emulate. Did he persuade his classmates? His editorial later in the semester received the highest number of peer votes for rhetorical argument—many with the caveat, "I don't agree with his position, but I can see why he would argue this way." Another student used her poster to describe her recent move from a strict religious upbringing to embracing feminism and atheism, and while her positions were equally foreign to a number of these sophomores, her dedication to discovering for herself what she really believed, like the other student's devotion to a beloved relative, struck a chord with many of them and engendered supportive discussions where she had been afraid of ostracism. As students stroll around the room or scroll through the webpages, I ask them to identify which materialized attitudes/values/interests they find themselves identifying with, how, and why. I also ask them to consider the selection *patterns* they see across exhibits—what recurs across exhibits, what is anomalous—to consider the collective identity the exhibits have engendered, what is more universally selected for and deflected from by the class. Students during the lockdown semester of fall 2020, for instance, commented on how a majority of this online class included in their exhibits something related to their increased video gaming and music making as pandemic coping mechanisms.

The experience of focusing on these musealized life stories not only makes clear the persuasive power of identification. It also points out what I think is an important nuance of identification, well known to creative writers: We do not need to identify with others' *experiences* in order to identify with their *attitudes* and *values*. When a well-written character loses a beloved child to cholera or aliens, we don't (thank goodness) have to have experienced the same event to identify with either their heartbreak or their decision to relentlessly seek a cure or join the resistance. We call on similar feelings invoked from our own distinct experiences. Similarly, presented with simple, material evidence of the touchstones of another life, students spontaneously identify with others' underlying values, attitudes, even interests. Have you spent years perfecting your hesitation dribble? I work daily on a Liszt piano concerto—we share values of perseverance (or obsession). Or equally, we may share similar *experiences* (as the two students with strict faith backgrounds) while having grown to have different *attitudes* and *values* (evangelism/atheism)—but still we can share our origins as a starting stance for dialogue even as our differences allow us to clarify our own values. Just as in a novel, the secret to empathy with the abstractly universal Other is its materialization in the concretely specific, the locus of identification.

Moving from the Exhibit of Me to the Museum of Us

When we move to looking at how the individual exhibits contribute to a museal whole that transcends yet encompasses students' individual lives, I point out something like the description of the ongoing (2004–2021) exhibit *Our Universes* at the National Museum of the American Indian (americanindian.si.edu), which states in part:

> *Our Universes* focuses on Indigenous cosmologies. . . . [T]he exhibition introduces visitors to indigenous peoples from across the Western Hemisphere who continue to express the wisdom of their ancestors in celebration, language, art, spirituality, and daily life. The community galleries feature eight cultural philosophies—those of the Pueblo of Santa Clara (Espanola, New Mexico, USA), Anishinaabe (Hollow Water and Sagkeeng Bands, Manitoba, Canada), Lakota (Pine Ridge Reservation, South Dakota, USA), Quechua (Communidad de Phaqchanta, Cusco, Peru), Hupa (Hoopa Valley, California, USA), Q'eq'chi' Maya (Cobán, Guatemala), Mapuche (Temuco, Chile), and Yup'ik (Yukon-Kuskokwim Delta, Alaska, USA). The design of these galleries reflects each community's interpretation of the order of the world.

The museum, that is, gave each group of community curators an overarching theme and asked them to design an exhibit that described their belief systems using visual as well as textual symbols. In similar fashion, each student was given an overarching theme—"Life in the Twenty-First Century"—and found the visual and textual means to personalize that theme. The resulting "museum" demonstrates that any version of "us"—even an us as constrained as one classroom of central Ohio Buckeyes—is a polyphonous entity. Its various manifestations are not only variations on a theme; they are completely different, competing pieces of music playing seemingly discordant notes. "Life in the Twenty-First Century"—just like "America" or "Generation Z" or any other supposed audience group—is an ambiguous entity. As Burke realized as early as *Permanence and Change*, if we do not recognize this mutual ambiguity, these polyphonous experiences, as equal parts of our collective identity, then we cannot be persuaded to dialogue, we cannot allow rhetoric to happen.

It is here that I discuss sociologist Benedict Anderson's assertion that national identity is a story we tell ourselves to define who we are beyond family groups. Our concept of nationhood, Anderson wrote, relies on a sense of shared activities in geographic space: "An American will never meet, or even know the names of more than a handful of his 240,000-odd fellow Americans. He has no idea of what they are up to at any one time. But he has complete confidence in their steady, anonymous, simultaneous activity" (26). In Anderson's titular phrase, a nation "is an imagined political community" (6). If we accept only one version of that "steady, anonymous, simultaneous activity"—and here I play the Fourth of July song "It's America"—if our national identity is only "kids selling lemonade" in a front yard while listening to Springsteen (Atkins), then we are self-evidently deflecting from the reality of the lives depicted by some of our classmates right in the room with us.

With that we can turn to the notion of the action that results from an ambiguous sense of *collective identity*, a condition rife for rhetoric. As Gregory Clark describes, rhetoric for Burke becomes "the process of negotiating with others our notions of individual and collective identity" (*Rhetorical Landscapes* 3). One simple way to demonstrate the issues involved in negotiating a collective identity is to have the class, in groups of about five, write the opening signage for the whole "museum." "The Museum of Us is . . ." what? What is included/excluded or foregrounded/ backgrounded? Whose voice gets the most play? What artifact(s) would be featured on a web homepage or guide cover? Why? (The example of the NMAH exhibit helps them identify how this works.) With several groups' attempted statements, we can look as a class at these multiple constituted identities and consider again how the way reality is narrated shapes our view of that reality.

By naming our space The Museum of Us and giving our exhibit the ultimate theme of "Life in the Twenty-First Century," and then by actively participating in its constitution, we establish a space/time for a necessarily selected collective identity and identify our own story as a part of it. On a larger scale, the ability to imagine that our national community—a purely verbal reality—is real, and to incorporate that reality into our sense of self, demonstrates the unconscious power of Burkean identification. As we discuss, such an identity may not be consistent with each individual's personal life story, or even with their understanding of the life story of "Us," but the external constraints imposed by our structure serve to encourage individual identification along certain lines more than others and thus to incline the collectivity toward a narrowed range of narratives—which range, in turn, influences the choice of artifacts deemed relevant to display in "our" museum, whether that museum is a class, a community, or a nation. For instance, during fall 2020 student exhibits focused very much on individual activities (cooking, gaming, playing guitar)—and we discussed how that *reflected* what was then eight months of the pandemic, while also *deflecting* from the pandemic itself, as no one displayed any COVID-related artifacts (masks, sanitizer). I pointed out how frequently they defined "life in the twenty-first century" as "life in 2020," noting that this was both a producer choice and also an audience-awareness decision for people who spent most of the twenty-first century as children: the Now is what is important. As Clark notes, individuals are prompted by the material provided to endow what they are looking at with collective meaning and then to determine their stance on that meaning: they are "prompted to recreate themselves in the image of a collective identity" (4).

Analyzing the Museum of Us

I introduce a final Burkean concept as we consider that one way to look at the identification process is through the lens of what Burke called in *A Rhetoric of Motives* a *personalizing of essence* (15) in which the individual characteristics that make up one's personal identity narrative (here, the Exhibit of Me) are translated into an abstract reflection (the Museum of Us), then retranslated back into a narrative now larger than oneself—in other words, into a persuasive narrative of self-in-society. This personalizing of essence is *how*, rhetorically, individuals grow to identify with Anderson's imagined community. Their individual identity (here a hybrid of visitor and museum creation of people living in the twenty-first century), is presented back to them as a piece of the collective identity of all the other individuals similarly engaged in translating upwards from the disconnected personal to the collective abstract, then downwards back into the personal—a personal now infused with a collective narrative with which one is invited to identify. I point out to them that some of them chose to change some of the objects they included in their exhibit after seeing what everyone else had included in the first discussion-board "draft," while others chose to keep theirs, and we talk about how in both cases the collective narrative was influencing their choices of self-representation as an individual in the collective.

As Burke wrote, an essence (timeless presence) is translated into a narrative (temporal framework) "by conceiving of its kind according to the perfection . . . of which that kind is capable" (*RM* 13–14)—either through its origin story or its ultimate goal. Burke notes that narrative must by its nature historicize occurrences that do not actually happen sequentially, because narrative requires linearity—one thing must follow another. Placing essence into time means translating personal (time-bound) narrative into abstract (timeless) philosophy, then retranslating that philosophy back into narrative—a narrative now larger than oneself, situating oneself within the space/time of others. For example, I don't just *choose to wear a face mask*, I *participate in the communal evidence-based response to a global pandemic.* I identify with the kind of person who has always "trusted science" and "cared about others." So, my personal choice to wear a mask in the grocery store becomes infused with a moral identification with all the others living in "my America." The fact that "my America" is perhaps half of the people I actually see in my specific grocery store does not weaken my identification with the imagined community I trust is out there because I see it, as Anderson pointed out, in the media (here a larger discussion for a different day!). Participating in that particular imagined community furthers my personal identification with that collective sense of self.

By the mere fact of one's participation, whether the imagined community is the masked community or the classroom Museum of Us, one absorbs a part of the collective identity as a *personalized* version of the larger story. This personalization of the essence of the collective identity, I tell them, may well feel like "What I learned about myself" in this museum, this community event, or simply this individual event that I can now imagine is being carried out by other individuals across a nation I will never meet. As we had earlier discussed, "It may appear . . . that collective motivation negates individual will, but to Burke this is a paradox precisely because individual identity itself is already derived from the collective in which one lives" (Weiser, *Museum Rhetoric* 20).

The course sequence ends, then, with a reflective essay asking students to consider what they learned about their individual identity from curating their display, what impact the collective identity had on their individual understanding, and perhaps how their individual display influenced the collective. The assignment asks students whether they would change anything now that they've seen the exhibit as a whole, and what that decision says about identity formation. And finally, the assignment asks them to reflect on which aspects of American life in the twenty-first century were reflected by the class exhibit and which were deflected from: who was not included in this representation of communal identity?

Thus, we can end with dramatism and the understanding that language does not simply convey meaning in the world; it makes meaning—and meaning makes action. Dramatism assumes that words and other symbol systems generate attitudes (as we saw in the Museum of Us experience), that attitudes shape our perception of reality (what is life in the twenty-first century?), and that differing perceptions cause us to experience differing motivations for the courses of action we choose to follow. Because words affect our actions, Burke insisted, these imaginary perspectives created by words are in fact quite real, made of "real words, involving real tactics, having real demonstrable relationships, and demonstrably affecting relationships" (*GM* 57–58). In dramatistic terms, then, a class, like a nation, talks (and writes and displays) itself into being because of the ways in which its individuals name their communion with the "speech, gesture, tonality, order, image, attitude, idea" of some classes of strangers (*RM* 55) and not others. The Museum of Us makes this ongoing identification process, this always occurring interplay between self and society, more explicit, while allowing students to experience the Burkean concepts involved.

IDENTIFICATION ASSIGNMENT

THE MUSEUM OF US

Overview

Identity—both individual and collective—is something we construct, a reciprocal action between an actor and their scene, a rhetor and their audience, a curator and their visitors. As both curators of our own life story and engaged audience for others', our individual narratives interact to form collective identity narratives, like those of a class or a nation, with which we are invited to identify—and these collective identities turn back again to continue shaping our individual narratives.

This two-week assignment sequence will help you understand the concepts of identity, identification, and the interplay between individual and collective identity, the personalizing of essence, as you "musealize" your own life story into a class exhibit in the Museum of Us.

Objectives

- To gain an understanding of the rhetorical concepts of identity, identification, and personalizing an essence.
- To practice the Burkean dictum that any attempt to reflect reality in symbols must necessarily select certain aspects and deflect from other aspects in the narrated reality.
- To consider the interplay between individual and collective identities and our role in constructing both.
- To identify with classmates as we continue to debate throughout the semester.

Directions

Before Class 1

1. We've looked at the National Museum of the American Indian exhibit Our Universes and the way they incorporated the displays of community curators. Now you'll do the same.

2. We're going to be building and analyzing our own museum exhibit over the next two weeks. You have been given the task of being a community curator, contributing one exhibit to a larger museum exhibit. The museum is the Museum of Us, and the overall exhibit is Life in the 21st Century. Your contribution to that exhibit is your personalized display case of five objects that depict your life in this century—the Display of Me.
3. In a Discussion post, upload photos of five objects—material objects, things—that you could point to make sense of your lifestory. You can tell as much or as little of your life as seems significant to you (twenty years? five?) but you only have five objects.
4. Don't work too hard getting the photos perfectly organized in the post—this is just your initial notes toward what comes next. Just find your objects and then throw the photos up here, with a brief explanation of what they are.

During Class 1

1. We'll discuss the two ways we form a unified identity—synchronically and diachronically—and you'll add two sentences to your photos post unifying your story each way.
2. We'll go over the practicalities of the exhibit you will develop.
3. We'll look together at the National Museum of American History exhibit One Nation, Many Voices to discuss the exhibit's polyphony and rhetorical ultimate terms.

After Class 1: The Display of Me

1. Select your five material objects to represent your display of your life in the twenty-first century. You can choose to depict "your life" any way you want, but you must have five objects that you can photograph. If you want to modify your objects after scrolling through the Discussion posts—if somebody else's gave you a new idea—you can of course do that.
2. Take the best photo you can of each.
3. Open PowerPoint, choose New. Theme templates appear; you can use the search bar to find more or click "Presenta-

tions" under the search bar. Follow its directions to modify your chosen template to fit "you."
4. Use the title slide to give your exhibit a name—include your own name and an ultimate term that encompasses/defines/makes an argument for the global unity of your exhibit. (see my first example slide above)
5. Click for a New Slide. Under Layout choose a Two Content option and place your first photo and text onto a slide (see my second slide above)
6. Write an interpretive text for each object:
    - In one sentence or phrase, describe WHAT the object is
    - In at most two sentences, describe WHY it is a symbolic representation of an aspect of your life
    - In about one sentence, describe HOW it is indicative of twenty-first century life
    - Repeat four more times.
7. Save your completed slideshow (as a pptx, of course, by default). You'll use this slideshow to present your display to us.
8. Save your slides a second time: This time click "Save As an Adobe PDF."
9. Upload the PDF to the assignment dropbox here. NOT the PowerPoint, the PDF (this way your formatting will be saved when they're all combined). I will combine your PDFs into one big "Museum of Us" file and share it back to you for next week's analysis.

Online Class 2: The Museum of Us
1. You'll present your display to the class in a presentation of no more than thirty seconds per slide.
2. Make notes as you listen, and then again as you scroll back through each of the exhibits in the Museum of Us. Like the two Smithsonian exhibits, we have a polyphonous exhibit of identity depictions. Make notes to yourself on two things:
    - What five artifacts or experiences from others' exhibits do you most identify with? These might be material ("same poster!") or experiential ("I was also in band!") or attitudinal ("I felt like that, too!")

- What specific patterns do you see across the exhibits—which symbols or experiences come up more than once, which come up in similar (but not the same) ways, and which are anomalous, unique to one person?
3. Comment on the displays. You can make one unified post, just make it clear who the comment is for—and obviously, if everyone is commenting on "Sarah's" exhibit, try commenting on John's or Jane's—we all want to be recognized. Feel free to reply to a thread that contains your name over the next week.

During Class 3 (and possibly for homework together)

There's a blank document set up for each group of four. You'll use it to write together an introduction to the exhibit, no more than one hundred words, and also choose the five photos from the exhibit that you decide together best represent the scope and reduction of the exhibit (that is, broad enough to encompass the exhibit, focused enough to be specific to THIS exhibit). You will also, if you wish, tweak the title of the exhibit, now that the displays are in: Is "Life in the Twenty-First Century" the appropriate ultimate term for this exhibit?

1. Scroll together through the Exhibit.
2. Connect with your small group and negotiate with them, using the Many Voices, One Nation exhibit intro as an example. Think about:
   - What is the exigence of your visitors? (Let us pretend, in fact, that this would be a real exhibit in the Wexner Center on the Columbus campus next spring.) How will you encourage the larger audience to identify with this exhibit?
   - Consider any patterns you see—what's exactly repeated across exhibits? What general categories are repeated (this is often the most interesting)? What is anomalous but you want to make sure you include?
   - Which five of all the photos in our exhibit will your group choose to illustrate the cover slide?

- How will you work together to select pieces that reflect the reality of our exhibit while *also* negotiating what you deflect from in your introduction?
3. Upload your group's statement and photo choices to the group assignment folder. Looking at each group's intro statement, we'll discuss the narrated nature of the imagined community and collective identity. We'll then explore how that imagined collective identity comes back around to influence us through the personalizing of essence.

After Class 3: Reflection Paper
1. What did you learn about your individual identity from your participation/exploration of the Museum of Us? What aspects of the collective identity do you most identify with, and which do you find most unexpected/alien?
2. What did you learn about the collective identity of "life in the twenty-first century"? Do the attitudes/experiences of the collective impact your personal identity—and how do you impact the collective?
3. Having done this once and seen the final "exhibit," would you change anything about your own display of individual identity? (or maybe you did after seeing the initial discussion?) Why or why not, do you think? Consider the intersecting roles of collective and individual identity.
4. If we were to expand this outward to the larger community, how would the exhibit change? In other words, by defining the twenty-first century with these particular displays, what (and whose) reality are we selecting, and what (who) are we deflecting from?

6 Pathographies as Identification Medicine: Forming Empathetic Poet-Professionals in the Health Writing Classroom

Jarron Slater

> *Teaching identification to future health-care professionals through a series of narrative assignments.*

Allow me to begin with a brief pathography, or illness narrative: Once upon a time, there lived a sixty-eight-year-old man named Kenneth Burke, who was diagnosed with a bilateral inguinal hernia and needed an operation. His friend, the poet-doctor William Carlos Williams, advised him to go to one doctor, but Burke stumbled upon another who would do the operation immediately and locally for only two hundred dollars plus hospital expenses. Burke accepted the proposition. But on the morning of the surgery, and after Burke was lying on the operating table almost entirely anesthetized, suddenly everyone realized that the surgeon was forty-five minutes away eating breakfast. When the surgeon finally did arrive, the operation, which should have taken less than an hour, ended up lasting two hours, and when the procedure was over, Burke felt confused that any mention of this frustrating experience to the health professionals whom he was paying to take care of him seemed to be the equivalent of saying "an unforgivably dirty word." While Burke's hypochondria probably made him a difficult patient, these workers became annoyed and frustrated with Burke's real concerns about his health. One intern, fed up with Burke, claimed that "writers talk too much" and denied Burke adequate sedation so that he lay awake at night, feeling more like a prisoner than a patient (East 199–200).

The doctor saw Burke once the next day, but that was before the swelling began. As Burke's swelling increased, so did his pain and the fear both he and his wife Libbie felt. When Burke and Libbie tried to call for help, they were told "we can't do anything for him until the doctor sees him," but the doctor had also cut off Burke's hospital phone line so that Burke could not "bother him" (East 197). The fear, pain, and frustration increased until the third day, when the doctor finally provided relief. Yet, even after Burke had been released from the hospital, he did not get enough sedation until a week after he was home because the doctor (whom Burke calls "my clown") was hunting in Maine. Even then, the amount of medicine prescribed was insufficient, so Burke doubled the dosage on his own. Libbie felt angry that this doctor lacked any compassion for his patients (East 198), while Burke, who wrote to Williams about this difficult experience, profoundly wished that he "could . . . have had a humane guy like you to attend me" (East 200).

All of that happened in 1965. One hopes that this lack of compassion and empathy among health professionals is a thing of the past, that doctors and health professionals are educated today to be both medically knowledgeable and humane. While in many ways things are far better now, sadly, and too often, stories like Burke's can and do still happen. Scholars have discussed how medical education often tends to dehumanize students, whose capacity to empathize decreases as they attend medical school (see Kleinman, *The Soul of Care*; *The Illness Narratives*). Hence, the suggestion that one critical factor in humanizing patient care is humanizing the education of health professionals (see Cole et al., *Medical Humanities*).

This chapter describes how Burke helps me to humanize the education of health professionals in a medical humanities unit in a course on writing in the health professions. Van Beveren and Rutten in this volume discuss using Burke to help health-professions students gain critical reflection skills; my goal is to help them develop their affective side as well. I aim to form health professionals who can heal and not just diagnose, who empathize and not just treat, and who listen and not just hear. To teach students empathy, which is closely related to identification, I invite students to anticipate, read, write, and share a pathography, or illness narrative. With Burke's notion that "everything is 'medicine'" (*PLF* 293) in mind, students and I discuss and discover how pathographies are medicine for those who are transformed by writing, reading, and sharing them. The sharing of a story of suffering increases understanding between class members, thereby creating identification and transforming identity. Pathographies, like other works of art, mold the desires of those who experience them, enable readers to vicariously experience some of what another person has experienced, and thereby facilitate identification among students of the health professions through knowledge of their mutual vulnerability. In short, genuine listening to narratives of suffering can bring people together.

Being in the health professions writing classroom with Burke can be a transformative experience for both instructors and their students. After all, Burke recognizes not just a connection between doctor-poet Williams's capacity for humane care (*LSA* 282–91) or his desire to have "a humane guy like [Williams] to attend [him]" (East 200), but also that "we are all poets" (*PC* 76). Thus, I argue that teachers who bring out health professional students' innate capacity for creating and participating in aesthetic culture also invite those same students to an increased capacity for humane care and empathy.

Given that the anticipation, reading, writing, and sharing of a pathography are all held together by Burke's notion of form, I begin there. Since the sharing of pathographies requires a high level of trust among class members, I also describe in-class activities that prepare class members for the writing and sharing of their pathographies. The activities help students "anticipate another part" of the course and then be "gratified by the sequence" (*CS* 124) when they finally do share their illness narratives. In that way, preparing for the pathography assignment is a necessary and inseparable part of the pathography itself. And, even though that assignment does not come immediately, the eventual fulfillment can be more satisfying when it is delayed (*CS* 31).

Formal Course Design: Creating Expectations for Empathy, Equality, and Pathography

An understanding and application of Burke's notion of form as "the psychology of the *audience*" (*CS* 31), the "arousing and fulfilling of desires" (124), "a way of experiencing" (143), and "the creation and gratification of needs" (138) lie at the core of my pedagogical technique. Just as highly formal works withstand repetition, and just as we find not less but more delight quoting an especially eloquent passage of poetry or listening to a sublime musical work, so courses based on the psychology of form rather than the psychology of information withstand repetition. Richard Thames argues that both students who take a course only once and teachers who teach the same course many times should not merely consider course material as one piece of information after another solely for rote memorization, but "as moments to be experienced and contemplated in the context of a larger story" (138).

Burke's notion of conventional form, the fulfilling of expectations held by or invoked in the audience (*CS* 126–27), helps me teach students empathy through reading, writing, and sharing a pathography. Most of my students are studying nursing, but some are studying premedicine, health sciences, or health-care leadership. To understand—and thereby to begin to work to fulfill—the desires that students bring with them to the course itself and to each individual class period, I simply ask students what kinds of desires they have upon enrolling in the class. What do they *want?* Students describe their desires to care for, to heal, or to improve the lives of others. Students long for engagement with patients; they want a more humane health system. Some even tell stories about a physician or nurse who cared about them deeply and who influenced them to want to do the same for others. Once students voice these desires, I can show them how the course is more than just a program requirement, how it will help them to fulfill their desires. Or, as Burke put it, "If people believe something, the poet [or here the instructor] can use that belief to get an effect" (*CS* 161).

Understood in this way, Burke's conception of form also explains how a class community might be created. The health-professions students I teach begin to identify with one another when they notice their common desires, hopes, and expectations for humane care, empathy, and equality. While not every class can be taught in a seminar room with windows and a large conference table around which all class members sit on adjustable swivel chairs, class members at my institution can sit in a circle, and I can sit in a different place each day so that no expectation is created that there is a "front" of the classroom. In addition, students can teach one another by giving presentations and leading class discussions.

Anticipating the Pathography: Discovering a Relationship between Health, Humanities, and Communication

Although the pathography comes at the end of the medical humanities unit, everything class members do anticipates it. During the first week of class, students receive two assignments that create expectations for the pathography, as well as for equitable treatment, empathy, and humane care. First, students sign up to give brief presentations on a topic relating to medical humanities that anticipate the pathography because they provide students with opportunities to share and read stories of suffering. Topics include the construction of disease, health and medical education, medicine and technologies, the health of populations, death and dying, aging, poetry and moral imagination, goals of medicine, health and disease, medicine and power, justice and healthcare, religion and spirituality in health care, bioethics, and other issues addressed in Thomas Cole, Nathan Carlin, and Ronald Carson's *Medical Humanities*. One or two students present each day, providing the springboard for that day's class discussions and writing exercises. During their presentation, students ask at least two discussion questions to the audience to invite class members to interact with one another. Students already have a lot to say about these subjects. Although such issues are brought up in their other classes, students want more opportunities to talk about them and to say what they think, rather than just hearing someone else tell them about them. This presentation assignment creates the expectation that all class members, instructor included, perform some of the same work. These presentations can be successful ways to introduce subjects because students who speak to other students more often speak "the language of a voice within" (*RM* 39). They are also successful because students learn best when they have to teach someone else what they are learning (see McGuire).

A second assignment, which asks students to clearly articulate in writing their understanding of the relationship between humanities, health, and communication, provides additional anticipation of the pathography. Students prepare a three- or four-page discovery paper in which they consider how art—including the texts, stories, poetry, and plays like those we read in class—changes, adds to, or enriches their understanding of the relationship between humanities, health, and communication. One part of this assignment invites students to reference the presentations (discussed above) of three other students, an invitation that further reinforces the idea that each student has something important to say.

These two assignments, the presentations and the discovery paper, are designed to help fulfill students' pre-existing desires to prepare to help those who are sick, infirm, disabled, or unwell. To that extent, these assignments prepare students of the health professions to listen to, empathize with, be moved by, and humanely help others through their own stories of illness—their pathographies.

Reading Pathographies: Narrative, Medicine, and Narrative Medicine

Through the initial readings and assignments, students learn about the prominence of narrative in health and medicine. Together, class members and I study how many of the most important stories in medicine include patients' autobiographical stories and suffering narratives that enable a diagnosis and how "much of the central business of caring for patients is transacted by means of narrative" (Hunter 5). We discuss examples of how "medicine is fundamentally narrative" and why "its daily practice is filled with stories" and organized by storytelling (Hunter 5–6). We also study Rita Charon's assertion that physicians need both scientific ability and narrative competence, or "the ability to acknowledge, absorb, interpret, and act on the stories and plights of others" ("A Model for Empathy" 189). We consider how narrative medicine can be understood as a counterpart (an *antistrophos*) to medical and health humanities, and we weigh arguments that the study and teaching of narrative and the humanities to health professionals and physicians can help to guard against dehumanizing tendencies of science and medicine, can teach empathy and genuine listening, and can help health professionals to treat people like people and put patients over profits. The time spent gaining narrative competence is not wasted but invaluable. Poetry, drama, stories, the arts, and the humanities are not time-wasting, fact-neglecting, practicality-lacking subjects but are paramount to helping health professionals—and anyone, for that matter—empathize and practice humane care for others.

To introduce students to the concept of narrative medicine, I teach Burke's profound insight, made during an examination of proverbs, that "everything is 'medicine'" (*PLF* 293). Burke quickly generalizes his conclusion about proverbs to literature, or "proverbs writ large," and from there to art, aesthetics, and even to "life in general." Burke's examination suggests that, as medicines, literature, the arts, and the aesthetic supply *"strategies* for dealing with *situations"* (296). As strategies, or attitudes, the aesthetic does more than fix problems; it also facilitates healing (297). Thus, the aesthetic is medicine, or equipment for living, because it can provide people with healing attitudes or strategies, and even metastrategies (304), for dealing with the infirmities, disorders, and complexities of life.

With this in mind, I ask students, "When has a work of art, a story, or a poem acted as medicine for you?" I also ask, "What was that story and why was it medicine?" Students write about these and other questions in a journal they use most days in class. Sometimes I stress that, contrary to what some students believe, these low stakes writing exercises are not busywork; they help us to learn and discover ourselves through writing (see Anderson and MacCurdy). Students study Heather Mangino's statements about how, as she began to write and reflect on her interactions with patients in a personal journal, she discovered that she was understanding herself better both as a professional and as a person—and that these actions contributed to her emotional growth (192). So, class members complete many of these smaller, writing-to-learn exercises to help them discover who they are and what they are beginning to say, even as they also provide a springboard for in-class discussion.

Students share their experiences and thoughts about when a work of art has been "medicine" for them, and I have found it useful to simply let students talk while the rest of us quietly listen. I do not want to cut these discussions off too soon because, in order to develop trust and empathy, students need time to talk with one another deeply about profound questions. Too much concern for being "on task" can rob class members of the opportunity to listen and identify. Nothing that another person says can be tangential. Students will learn in other classes how to keep the person they are questioning "on task." But in a class that emphasizes trying to humanely see the whole person, students can talk and listen with the intent to get a feeling for the other person without worrying so much about whether or not that person is giving them "information." The emphasis is on the psychology of form rather than on the psychology of information.

As students discuss when a work of art, a story, or a poem has acted as medicine for them, some weigh the term *medicine* with the term *therapy* because it can seem more common to talk about stories and art as *thera-*

py. Students then scrutinize the two terms and speculate why writers like Burke and Charon both deliberately use the word *medicine*. After all, "a focus on object *A* involves a neglect of object *B*" (Burke, *PC* 49). We speculate that *medicine* may be a stronger term, perhaps even approaching ultimate-term status when it becomes a metaphor or myth that orients attitudes and values (see Ann Hawkins). When we further consider how forms manifest themselves as rhythms on a page that also set up corresponding rhythms in the body (*CS* 140), we understand form's close relationship with desire and the physical body (see Hawhee's *Moving Bodies*), and we conclude that stories, art, music, and the aesthetic are medicines insofar as they are bodily.

Students then discuss how narrative and story provide ways of knowing that, while different from scientific ways of knowing, are complementary to them. Thus, we consider how questions of art, narrative, and story begin, not from questions of truth/falsity or even epistemology but from drama and action (Burke, "Counter-Gridlock" 374). To do so, students and I read about gastroenterologist Richard Weinberg's patient whose severe abdominal pain could not be discovered or attended to by objective means but only by genuine listening to the story, even the drama, of the patient herself ("Communion"). Students write in their journals about how Weinberg's genuine listening enabled the patient to begin to heal. They also write and explore, using Shields's words, why narrative knowing "strikes at the heart of the quest for patient-centered approaches to care and collaborative decision making" (Sheilds 713). Such questions and discussions further reinforce the prominence of story and drama in medicine—and prepare students to write, read, and share their own stories of illness.

The "signature method" of narrative medicine, close reading, can help health professionals to improve care in a variety of ways, including deepening empathy (see Charon et al. 157–79; Charon, *Narrative Medicine*). Burke, as we know, was an expert in close reading and provides a variety of methods for doing so. One helpful question that Burke asks students of literature is this: since "all works are 'medicine,'" "what is the work a cure for?" (East 172). To practice asking what a given work is a cure for, we read Margaret Edson's Pulitzer Prize-winning drama *Wit* (supplemented by a few of John Donne's *Holy Sonnets*). Interestingly, when the play opened at the Union Square Theatre in New York City, audience members had such a strong emotional reaction to it that they just sat in their seats, weeping, long after the play had ended. In response, the producers hired psychologists to hold therapy groups and postshow discussions to help audience members better understand the intense feelings the drama produced (Charon, *Narrative Medicine* 18). In addition to *Wit*, we also study Theresa Brown's memoir *The Shift* and summaries of longer pathographies. According to Arthur Frank, the dramas of illness "are the dramas of all of our lives," and "they bring everyone to life, by allowing us to see ourselves in the lives of others" (394). Since narrative medicine is "medicine practiced with the narrative competence to recognize, absorb, interpret, and be moved by the stories of illness" (Charon, *Narrative Medicine* vii), activities that provide students with opportunities to listen to, ponder, and closely read texts anticipate the writing and sharing of a pathography.

Empathy as Emotional Identification Among Health Professionals-Rhetoricians

When class members present, write, discuss, and then when they anticipate, write, and share one another's pathographies, they discover that their "interests are joined" (*RM* 20). So, while students and I do not study much rhetorical theory in my health professions writing class, we do read some crucial snippets about identification from *A Rhetoric of Motives*. As we do so, I invite students to substitute "health professionals" for words like "rhetorician" or "orator." After all, whether or not Plato's Gorgias correctly stated that rhetoricians can persuade patients better than doctors (*Gorgias* 456b), it is true that doctors, nurses, and other health-care professionals constantly use rhetoric as they teach, care for, invite, and persuade others. Through substitutions like these, we read about how health professionals, as rhetoricians, "seek to display the appropriate 'signs' of character needed to earn the audience's good will," and how, while the health care professional as rhetorician may have to persuade the patient to change something, the professional can only do so insofar as the professional "yields" to the patient "in other respects" (*RM* 55–56). Thus, the health professional's identification with the patient—and therefore the professional's persuasion of the patient—will be "more effective" when it is "genuine" (56). People—and here we also read patients—are persuaded, Burke reminds us, when others "talk [their] language" and thereby identify with them (55). In sum, Burke's theory of identification can help students of the health professions to learn to care for and empathize with others, including their patients.

Closely related to identification, I tell students, is empathy. As Gregory Clark observes, empathy might be a "a good analogue" for identification, and an experience of empathy can be understood in terms of a shared identity (*Civic Jazz* 131–32). Insightfully, Burke writes about how works of art, such as stories, music, and paintings, only "come to life" for people when those people empathize with them ("A Theory of Terminology" 242). Students and I discuss how the empathy that we employ when we read texts can be transferred to people and how understanding the relationship between empathy and identification can help students of the health professions to increase their capacities for them through practice.

To practice empathy, students read and discuss a chapter from Theresa Brown's *Critical Care* in which Brown, a registered nurse, describes what it was like for her to take a painful fall and end up as a patient at the same hospital where she worked. While some of the other workers teased her for what seemed to them like no big deal, Brown felt frustrated until she went to a specialist who finally understood both her problem and how much pain she was actually feeling. From this experience, Brown understood better how patients feel when they lose privacy, self-reliance, and even a portion of their own dignity because she, too, was for a time unable to dress herself, use the bathroom, or get herself food or drink. Students also read brief summaries of longer pathographies. These summaries, conveniently found in *Medical Humanities*, tell of Oliver Sacks's leg becoming lifeless and unknowable (*A Leg to Stand On*), William Styron's descent into the depths of depression and despair (*Darkness Visible*), Lucy Grealy's rare survival of Ewing's sarcoma and the jaw cancer that resulted in the removal of part of her face (*Autobiography of a Face*), and Aaron Alterra's story of caring for his wife as she suffered from Alzheimer's (*The Caregiver*). Students read the summaries to one another and consider why illness might prompt writing and reflection, what some potential benefits and drawbacks might be of writing about illness, and how pathographies might influence readers.

A Transformative Rhetorical Aesthetic in Writing and Sharing Pathographies

When students prepare to write their own pathography, I invite them to consider Susan Sontag's famous statement:

> Illness is the night-side of life, a more onerous citizenship. Everyone who is born holds dual citizenship, in the kingdom of the

well and in the kingdom of the sick. Although we all prefer to use only the good passport, sooner or later each of us is obliged, at least for a spell, to identify ourselves as citizens of that other place. (3)

I then ask students to write for ten minutes about these questions: "What does it mean, and what does it feel like, to be a citizen of 'that other place'? When have you been a citizen of 'that other place'?" When they finish, they talk about what they have written in small groups, and they listen. As they consider these questions, some students draw on the reasons they decided to study the health professions in the first place, reasons that we discussed together as a class at the beginning of the semester. Others recount things that have happened or are currently happening to them. As each student considers what it feels like for them and for others to be citizens of Sontag's "other place," they begin to see how challenges and difficulties give people a story to tell, and they begin drafting their own illness narrative.

Then we discuss together how each person is a storyteller, even an artist—a poet-professional. Each of us creates worlds in which our readers dwell, given the etymology of "poet" as a maker or even creator. Students consider Burke's observation that "we are all poets" (*PC* 76), and we talk about how the poet-audience relationship can be mapped onto the doctor-patient relationship (see Woods). In this way, class members and I hearken back to our earlier discussion of Burke's statement that "everything is 'medicine'" as we discuss the *homo poeta* as a *homo medicus* (see *PLF* 64), a poet-professional who works through the principles of form and identification: speaking of the poet as a "medicine man," Burke writes that "it is only in so far as his situation overlaps upon our situation, that his strategy of encompassment is felt by us to be relevant" (64).

As class members then write a pathography, they reflect on how the experience with suffering changed them. To do so, we read short excerpts from Dr. Steven Hsi's pathography, *Closing the Chart*. Hsi's perspective on medicine as a family physician changed when he underwent heart surgery. As he reflects on his experience, he laments that his doctors were silent on what he felt were the most important questions; he longed to be asked: "What has this . . . done to your life? What has it done to your family? What has it done to your work? What has it done to your spirit?" (6–7). Students ponder these questions, write about them in their journals, and incorporate their findings in their own pathography.

Then, after students have developed trust and respect for one another over a number of weeks, have identified with each other, have studied narrative medicine, read several pathographies, and written a pathography of their own, they are ready to share their pathographies. To provide students with a model and to show them that I am not exempt from the vulnerability that this activity invites, I also read a pathography of my own that talks about growing up with tinnitus and what it was like to get my first pair of hearing aids at age nineteen.

The listening skills that we have practiced on other texts we now practice on one another. Students distribute their pathographies electronically, and when the author reads the pathography aloud, class members follow along. In this way, everyone in the room has a shared experience as we hear the single voice penetrate the silence and captivate those who listen. Listeners then type a comment to the reader. Some students tell painful vignettes about the things that close family members or friends have suffered. Others describe an eating disorder, debilitating depression and anxiety, or quest to find healing from a toxic relationship. Still others describe a treasured relationship with a family member or beloved friend who has since passed on. It takes about a week and a half for every student to read their pathography to the class, but it teaches us timeless lessons about our shared identity as members of a community that includes future health professionals who empathize with and humanely care for others.

After we experience one another's pathographies, as the instructor I want to know how this experience has impacted and even changed students—specifically how their capacity for empathy and humane care has been influenced over the course of the unit. We talk about how the acts of writing, sharing, and listening to others' pathographies does something to us and about how the form of a pathography works to invite identification with others and provides them with opportunities to practice empathy. Students and I remind ourselves of the universal appeal of form in *A Rhetoric of Motives*: "You are drawn to the form, not in your capacity as a partisan, but because of some 'universal' appeal in it" (58). Although people experience different kinds of suffering, the universality of suffering enables comprehension of specific instances of suffering by other symbol-using creatures. No two class members have had the same experience, but by listening to one another's uses of symbols that enable them to share their experiences, listeners nevertheless feel in their own body the formal patterns that the poet-professional induces in them, and when that happens, they begin to hold an "attitude of assent" towards the writer (*RM* 58; Slater). Suffering might well be one of the unnamed "innate forms of the mind" that enables people to feel some part of what others have felt (*CS* 46). As class members listen to and identify with one another, they start to see a bit of their own story in the pathography writer's story. They imagine what it would have been like to experience what the writer experienced, and they grow and are transformed as a result.

At this point, class members and I have a shared understanding that the rhetorical aesthetic of writing, reading, and sharing pathographies can provide students, teachers, and others with a transformative experience. As Gregory Clark explains, there is much more inherent in the aesthetic than merely making or producing: it also functions rhetorically to form, shape, change, and transform the identities of those who experience it (*Rhetorical Landscapes* 52). Part of that transformation involves the identification and even vicarious experience of another person's story. Insofar as the aesthetic is "medicine" that provides people with "*strategies* for dealing with *situations*" (*PLF* 296), a rhetorical aesthetic of pathographies builds a community as it fosters capacities to understand, empathize, and be more humane health professionals.

Pathographies, like other works of art, mold the desires of those who experience them, inviting participants to hold what Burke calls "attitude[s] of collaborative expectancy" (*RM* 58). Pathographies also can be understood as case studies of the rhetorical aesthetic of the creative act. Since sharing stories of suffering also enables the sharing of the burdens caused by suffering, pathographies can facilitate identification because they teach people, such as students of the health professions, about their mutual vulnerability by way of vicarious experience.

Conclusion: Attending to the Aesthetic Culture of Medical Humanities

Burke believed and taught that "literature was still of central importance and that the critic had a crucial role to play in making the deep and complex insights of art available to the rising generation" (King, "Kenneth Burke" 44). This statement is true not just for "the critic" and "the rising generation" but also for teachers of rhetoric and writing and students. Studying, creating, and experiencing narratives, drama, poetry—the art—of suffering alongside Burke, narrative medicine, and medical humanities, can help health professionals to see beyond a narrow diagnosis to the whole person, a symbol-using creature with attitudes and values and a life far beyond that person's current journey to the kingdom of the sick. Ethics easily slips into aesthetics (see Burke, *PC* 266).

Burke's description of the good life, "getting along with people" (*ATH* 256), looks toward a poetic orientation that fosters democratic participation, a culture that values most of all "people, and particularly their social relationships" (George, *Kenneth Burke's* 96). As such, living the good life also includes empathizing with one another and giving and receiving the humane care that Burke wished he had had when he experienced his painful and difficult operation. Living the good life in this way—and helping others to do the same—can be facilitated by reading, writing, and sharing pathographies, acts that invite us to hold expectations of mutuality, empathy, and vulnerability as we vicariously experience some part of what another person has suffered and collectively transform our identities. The attributes of trust, empathy, and an understanding of what vulnerability feels like are among the most crucial attributes for health professionals—and even citizens in general—to acquire.

IDENTIFICATION ASSIGNMENT

ENGLISH 205 WRITING IN THE HEALTH SCIENCES—PATHOGRAPHY ASSIGNMENT

BACKGROUND

Susan Sontag writes, "Illness is the night-side of life, a more onerous citizenship. Everyone who is born holds dual citizenship, in the kingdom of the well and in the kingdom of the sick. Although we all prefer to use only the good passport, sooner or later each of us is obliged, at least for a spell, to identify ourselves as citizens of that other place" (*Illness as Metaphor* 3; Farrar, Straus and Giroux, New York, 1978).

What does it mean—and what does it feel like—to be a citizen of "that other place"? This next assignment asks you to tell your own illness narrative, or that of someone close to you. This personal illness narrative is actually a subgenre of autobiography and biography. Since it combines elements of both biography and the things that people experience and suffer (pathē), it is called pathography.

PURPOSE

Considering the above quotation, write a first-person account of your own experience with (an) illness or that of someone close to you. Whatever your approach, be specific about your thoughts, emotions, and responses to the illness. Writing a pathography and listening to the pathographies of other class members will help us learn to empathize with, trust, and learn from those who make themselves vulnerable to us.

GUIDELINES

One model for this may be Chapter 4 of Theresa Brown's *Critical Care*, in which Brown describes what it was like to go to the emergency department at the same hospital at which she was a nurse. We have heard similar narratives from Jason, the young doctor in *Wit*, and from his patient, Vivian Bearing, his former teacher dying of ovarian cancer. Your job is to tell your story of an illness, or the story of an illness of a friend or loved one.

The narrative may focus on one incident, or a set of incidents. We want you to use your best skills as a storyteller to help us understand and feel what your experiences have taught you. If you desire, you may also tell why this experience has helped you decide what you want to do and be. In other words, you might also consider telling your history with health care, and how it informs your life and goals. You could tell us how you got from there to here, as a nursing major, or exercise science major, or pre-med student, or prospective physician assistant, or whoever you now are.

Write this in APA format. Shoot for 4–5 pages, excluding the title page. Though references are not required, if you reference any books or articles, please cite them according to APA guidelines.

In-Class Reading

Please prepare to read your paper out loud to the rest of the class. These read-aloud exercises will provide you with the opportunity to focus on saying exactly what you want to say exactly how you want to say it. They will also help you to think of your audience as you write because you will read word-for-word what you wrote to the rest of the class.

7 Burke, Feminism, and Community Engagement Projects: Finding Common Ground

Rachel Chapman Daugherty

Using feminist pedagogy in a community engagement project to teach critical analysis of identity-based appeals.

In my experience teaching Burke's theories, I have found students respond positively to identification because it gives name to phenomena they experience at school, in their work, and most of all, in their social media circles—active appeals for personal connection. Identification is, as Burke tells us in *A Rhetoric of Motives*, the "simplest case of persuasion" because it allows us to see the everyday arguments in identity-based appeals, like those on social media or in cultivated news feeds. Students also recognize that "identification is compensatory to division" through their online experiences because they see connecting to some people means disconnecting with others (*RM* 22). Digital algorithms have cultivated a growing awareness of the ways that identity markers like race, gender, class, sexuality, nationality, ability, and ethnicity can be used to encourage *and* discourage group affiliations. However, this cultivated awareness does not prepare or encourage students to analyze identity-based arguments. Thus, students can recognize identification but struggle to *critique* identity-based appeals in news reporting, social media settings, or their local communities.

A feminist pedagogical approach to Burke's identification theory can address this gap between recognition and critique. Feminist pedagogical strategies like collaboration, reflection, intersectional analysis, and community engagement can encourage students to apply Burke's identification as a rhetorical tool for analyzing how identities can shape perspectives, influence research, and provide opportunities for persuasion (see Elizabeth Weiser in this volume for another example of identity-formation work). As Laura Micciche notes, feminist pedagogy is a "flexible basis from which to launch intersectional pedagogical projects—projects focused on a dialectic of multiple identity categories rather than, for instance, on gender or sex alone" (129). A feminist pedagogical approach to identification would analyze the intersectional appeals between the topic and the audience to understand how race, gender, class, sexuality, nationality, and ethnicity are factors in these identifications. As a collaborative and reflective tool for analysis, Burke's theory of identification provides students with rhetorical tools to critique intersectional appeals for identification and gain agency in these connections. When we apply Burkean identification to feminist goals for community engagement, these rhetorical tools enable students to compose meaningful interventions for the common good.

And yet, some feminists might be surprised at such a Burkean pedagogical pairing: could the marriage finally be saved, as Phyllis Japp once asked? Feminists in rhetoric and composition have long critiqued Burke as part of a patriarchal tradition within rhetorical theory that excludes non-male and non-white experiences. Japp argues that Burke's tradition should not be thrown out, but "for feminist critics, as well as for others who refuse to disengage their intellectual lives from their social responsibilities, reclamation of Burke must not only provide strategies for personal survival; it must emphasize the power of Burke's system in the struggles for social change" (129). Similarly, Celeste Condit has argued that rhetorical scholars must maintain Burke's concept of "sub-stance" in order to understand the basis from which Burke determines how and which "bodies . . . learn language." Condit encourages feminist scholars to recontextualize Burke's theories of bodily experience using feminist epistemologies. Krista Ratcliffe's *Rhetorical Listening* exemplifies this feminist re-visioning by considering the limitations of Burke's notion of identification, which Ratcliffe argues "makes space for personal agency and commonalities but not for differences" (58). In my feminist pedagogical context, I argue that common ground does not depend on eliminating differences; instead, it can be a place where commonalities, either in identification or in shared goals, can be highlighted as the foundations for rhetorical action. My feminist approach to teaching Burke's theories retains Burke's concept of *sub-stance* by (as Condit suggests) recontextualizing Burke's theories of bodily experience in an intersectional framework. Doing so recognizes the power of Burke's system for social change but sharpens these rhetorical tools with the feminist theory of positionality, offering students powerful persuasive resources for rhetorical intervention.

In this chapter, I illustrate how a feminist pedagogical approach to teaching identification can be applied to research-based writing assignments and community engagement projects, encouraging students to create rhetorical interventions in their local communities and gain personal ownership over Burke's rhetorical identification as a tool they can apply in their everyday lives. I will demonstrate how Burkean rhetorical concepts are relevant for twenty-first-century feminist pedagogies by sharing my "Community Campaign" assignments, which connect divisive national political arguments to local examples by focusing on common ground between community stakeholders.

The Community Campaign is a feminist pedagogical approach to analyzing and composing intersectional appeals to identification in local contexts. I will show how the collaborative approach of my classroom and assignments allows students to rhetorically engage public arguments by identifying with their local communities, finding common ground between consubstantial audiences interested in the common good. Finally, I will show how one student team designed rhetorical interventions in local problems of the common good, demonstrating direct applications of Burkean concepts in twenty-first-century pedagogy. Ultimately, I will show how Burke's concepts "properly equip" students to understand arguments for connection and to engage in intersectional feminist inquiry.

Teaching Burke's Theories in Feminist Classrooms: The Community Campaign Project

After encountering a range of new perspectives in college, students often welcome the concept that "a way of seeing is a way of not seeing" (*PC* 49) but (like many others) take for granted appeals to their identity and viewpoint, or as feminists describe it, their *positionality*. Positionality is the feminist concept that social and political context influences a person's viewpoint and vice versa, described by Myfanwy Franks as "the way in which individual identity is positioned by *others*" (42). Students can recognize that identity-based appeals are successful strategies for connecting to new communities because they have been encouraged by campus groups to become members based on shared interests, beliefs, and experiences (e.g., gender, race, career goals, political interests, etc.). Through the feminist concept of positionality, students can view these appeals for membership as *rhetorical* acts that use identification to connect or divide individuals into identity-based groups. Positionality provides contemporary feminist context to the substance of identification by identifying how race, class, gender, sexuality, ethnicity, ability, nationality, and so on make audiences consubstantial in rhetorical contexts. As Burke argues, "To identify A with B is to make A 'consubstantial' with B" (*RM* 21). For Burke, to make someone consubstantial in argument is to facilitate identification between the speaker and audience, creating a point of common ground on which an argument can be built. In a feminist classroom, identification and consubstantiality allow students to question *why* they are persuaded to identify with others and *how* these arguments depend on identity-based connections to make them consubstantial.

My feminist pedagogical approach to identification encourages students to analyze identification using reflection, collaboration, and community connection. One goal of the Community Campaign is to humanize hotly debated national topics in which common ground seems impossible (see Jouni Tilli in this volume for another example of approaching contentious national topics through a Burkean lens). I ask students to resist "for" and "against" argumentative frames by using identification to patiently analyze the scope of perspectives on a topic. This ideological shift asks students to consider more than two stances on a topic, working toward the feminist goal of resisting binary ideas and envisioning the multiplicity of ideologies available to audiences. Students have, for example, pursued projects investigating campus carry laws, in which the "for" and "against" stances were challenged by investigating the scope of perspectives and stakeholders. With this topic, students found the range of stances varied among stakeholders like students, teachers, campus staff, administration, alumni, and visitors. Rather than thinking all students were "for" arming teachers in their defense, students found that where they were brought up (which could lead them to have differing experiences with guns) influenced their stance on the topic. In this case, some students who associated guns with self-defense, hunting, and ROTC were "for" carry laws only if teachers had adequate training. Some students from states with more restrictive gun laws were "against" campus carry because they felt guns had no place in educational settings. Yet, some students from these same states argued in favor of campus carry because they had personally experienced or knew someone involved in a school shooting. These factors enabled students to articulate the range of stances on campus carry that challenged binary perspectives. Identification allows students to see how people are connected to topics through their identity and experiences, but with positionality, students can see alternative positions to "for" and "against" national issues by characterizing the intersectional appeals to identification for these issues. Together, identification and positionality provide students rhetorical tools to analyze contextual influences on standpoint and intersectional appeals for consubstantiality.

Students and I share Burke's concerns that competitive, everyday discussions can escalate into situations where "national 'differences' may become national 'conflicts'" ("LAPE" 272). Recent students shared that family members have clashed over nationally debated topics like the results of the 2016 US presidential election, immigration, abortion access, and gun violence—everyday conversations that can turn into discursive boxing matches. I encourage students to examine the ways nationally debated topics affect local communities in a multi-unit Community Campaign project. In their Community Campaign, students use identification and consubstantiality to analyze how language shapes human connection, especially investment in a topic, argument, or community. For instance, students easily identify with arguments against school shootings, which helps them recognize how they are consubstantial audiences in arguments about arming schoolteachers. Students already recognize overarching connections between divisive national political arguments and local examples in their own lives, but the Community Campaign equips students to analyze and intervene in these topics using identification. In the following sections, I will demonstrate how the reflective, process-based approach of the Community Campaign productively interweaves feminist positionality with Burkean identification and consubstantiality to aid student engagement with identity-based arguments.

Step 1: The Argument Analysis and Positionality

Before students work in their Community Campaign teams, they first complete an Argument Analysis in which they individually investigate a national topic about the common good with local connections. The Argument Analysis assignment continues Burke's pedagogical strategy to invite students to grapple with national debates like the threat of nuclear war. Burke used a pedagogy of critical reflection to offer students rhetorical exercises to help them analyze high-stakes arguments without falling into the competitive tendencies of contemporary discourse that cause division (and, in Burke's mind, led to war). While our twenty-first-century teaching situation is certainly different from Burke's in 1955, these pedagogical concerns have endured and have led me to wonder, as Burke did, how students can use education to "meditate upon the tangle of symbolism in which all [people] are by their nature caught" ("LAPE" 288). Jessica Enoch argues that composition classrooms using Burke's pedagogy of critical reflection could offer students alternative paths to conflict and encourage reflection as the first stage of critical investigation:

> Before students even begin to formulate thesis statements and argumentative tactics, they would learn to inspect carefully and precisely those texts that linguistically create certain positions and arguments. Thus, a Burkean pedagogy of critical reflection would teach students to become "symbol-wise" by encouraging them to adopt an attitude of patience and withdrawal—an attitude that necessitates waiting, listening, reflecting, and analyzing before any arguments are made or action is taken. (292)

To become symbol-wise, students need the tools to analyze their own experience and perspective before they can analyze the perspectives of others. In doing so, students patiently engage arguments with a spirit of reflective inquiry into their own positionality. Positionality is individually determined first to gain (1) individual recognition and practice, and (2) self-reflection on their perceptions of sub-stance related to the topic.

Investigating positionality using Burke's pedagogy of critical reflection means that students must situate their own topical perspectives within their experience, thereby recognizing the limitations of their experiential perspectives and the value of multiple perspectives for understanding topics. For example, one student wanted to research a controversy that had reached national prominence in the spring of 2017—athletes kneeling during the national anthem to protest police brutality against Black Americans. The student did not support these athletes and recognized that his perspective assumed that such protests disrespected veterans, the American flag, and patriotic values. In his individual Argument Analysis, this student analyzed news articles that included interviews with veterans and active service members to test his own assumptions. His analysis revealed that many veterans supported the athletes' right to protest, challenging media binaries that put athletes and veterans in opposition. By analyzing veterans' identification with the protesters, this student expanded his preconceived notions of stakeholders in this issue and found common ground. In his reflection, he recognized that his positionality as a white man limited his anticipated scope of identifications with this protest method and that analyzing other stances complicated his notions of "right" and "wrong" for this topic. Enoch argues that using critical reflection can encourage students to delay judgments about an issue to analyze their own positionality and question which people, groups, organizations, and communities identify with particular stances and why (292). Thus, the combined analytical tools of critical reflection and positionality equip students to analyze multiple identifications in arguments by finding connections between language choice, stakeholders, and persuasive goals.

Step 2: The Collaborative Argument Brainstorm and Consubstantiality

In the second phase of the Community Campaign, students collaboratively investigate a local topic about the common good. For the purposes of teaching identification, local connections help students better analyze nationally divisive arguments by investing time in learning about their community. My feminist pedagogical approach to identification follows a long-standing feminist dedication to, as Micciche explains, "connect local, personal experiences to larger contexts of world-making, harkening back to the familiar second-wave feminist maxim, 'The personal is political'" (129). What is important here is that students recognize that identification occurs through the shared experiences of identity *and* place. Feminist theorist Judith Butler argues that identification always invokes "an assumption of place" (99), which, as Krista Ratcliffe asserts, signifies "both bodily and historical/cultural locations" (49). By first identifying their own positionality on this national debate, students practice analyzing why they identify with this topic and how the topic is locally connected. In doing so, students are better prepared to engage— rather than avoid—ongoing political, social, and cultural debates.

Because students have already explored their individual positionality in the Argument Analysis, the collaborative phases of the Community Campaign expand students' understanding of the ways identity is positioned in relation to others as they compare group members' positionalities and intersecting identifications. Students then define how this national topic about the common good has connections to individuals, groups, organizations, and/or communities connected to our shared campus, town, county, metropolitan area, or state. While local connections can help students better grapple with national debates, collaboration distributes agency among students and fosters a decentered investigation of divisive topics. Students in past years have explored such issues as the removal of confederate monuments, DACA, state legalization of marijuana, and access to reproductive services, including abortion. In my classes, students collaborate during active learning in-class activities and in research teams to expand their individual knowledge of positionality into a range of represented positionalities identified with research topics. Collaboration encourages students to seek out multiple consubstantial audiences for their research topics and analyze the intersectional features of these audiences through positionality.

More and more teachers are turning to collaborative student research teams as a feature of their pedagogy, especially for multistage projects. Gail Stygall has argued that "[t]echnologies of talk—such as collaboration—are part of discursive relations in educational institutions. In the writing classroom . . . collaboration acts to displace teacher authority" (254). Feminists find such decentering of teacher authority incredibly productive for student learning because, as Stygall's research reveals, "women fare better in collaborative talk when the feminist teacher explicitly teaches and models new forms of talk" (254). Thus, I model new forms of talk about divisive national issues using feminist collaborative inquiry to question the intersectional identifications with these issues. I thereby turn attention away from defending political parties and toward local audiences affected by these issues. I ask students to share what they learned from their Argument Analysis with their team in a collaborative Argument Brainstorm to determine the stakeholders of their local topic. I introduce this collaborative activity after teams have formed and reviewed each member's research from the Argument Analysis assignment. Identification and critical reflection aid this process because they encourage students to focus on a successful project outcome supported by team collaboration.

Once students have recognized the various identifications they may have witnessed or experienced they are more convinced of their ability to interrogate nuanced differences in beliefs. Students use rhetorical analysis to actively question the intersectional identifications of a controversy's stakeholders to determine which stakeholders are consubstantial in these arguments. To accomplish this task, students use the collaborative platform Google Docs to rhetorically analyze the appeals to intersectional audiences and identify language that makes specific local audiences consubstantial. In this analysis, students need to consider the many identities represented in local audiences for their topic to (1) affirm the local connections to this argument for the common good, and (2) characterize the potential identifications with those audiences. As a result, students analyze their own positionalities to their research topics as part of their collaborative brainstorming process. Using their knowledge of positionality, identification, and consubstantiality, students are better equipped to discover intersecting and overlapping characteristics of their research, including local organizations, school district policies, laws, institutional policies, represented communities, and other shared connections.

For example, students who analyzed gun control debates found that local laws like the Texas School Marshal Program, which trains selected employees to be armed marshals in K–12 schools, were favored in discussions about protecting children but criticized in discussions about students of color feeling unsafe. Local examples like the School Marshal Program challenge students to analyze assumed "universal" concepts like safety in the context of intersectional experiences to define the local range of identifications with this issue. In this instance, the student team recognized how their combined positionalities as white students attending suburban schools did not allow them to envision an armed marshal as a potential threat to their personal safety. Even more, this analysis allowed students to recognize that they needed to seek out alternative positionalities to their own to discover the differences between consubstantial audiences for their topics. These reflective approaches mirror Burke's pedagogical efforts to examine the linguistic identifications and divisions in arguments so students (and citizens) can become "symbol-wise" about arguments for the common good. Thus, a collaborative and intersectional feminist approach to teaching identification expands student understanding of consubstantiality by turning attention to specific, local audiences affected by topics about the common good.

Feminist teachers can interweave intersectional analysis with Burkean identification and consubstantiality as pedagogical strategies to deepen student analysis of national debates about the common good. By collaboratively investigating how audiences identify differently with national topics, students can break the "for" and "against" binaries of national debate and employ fresh approaches that reveal the spectrum of intersecting identifications in their local community. When students investigate the intersecting factors of race, class, gender, ethnicity, ability, nationality, sexuality, and other features of identity, they become symbol-wise to the intersectionality of identifications with debated topics. But during this investigation of identification and consubstantiality, students are simultaneously practicing Burke's theories through course activities and applying these theories to create rhetorical interventions in their local communities. From their analysis of identifications among local communities to their collaborative brainstorm of rhetorical interventions, students learn to investigate different stances in national debates with the goal of finding common ground. Differences then become a source of collaborative insight for discovering the range of consubstantial audiences, available identifications, and paths to rhetorical intervention.

Step 3: The Campaign Texts as Rhetorical Interventions

The Community Campaign concludes with the Campaign Texts, three rhetorical interventions composed in the team's chosen media. In this assignment, students collaboratively create appeals to identification with local audiences, considering the form of each appeal as part of the identification process. Student choice of media is key to this assignment's success—by choosing the form of arguments they will create, students assert agency over the composing process while also negotiating the appeals to identification with their audiences. The Campaign Texts encourage student accountability for *successful* identification, meaning they need to justify how their chosen appeals will reach—or create—consubstantial audiences. In doing so, students illustrate the scope of local stakeholders through rhetorical identification.

The Community Campaign Texts assignment asks students to be accountable to their individual positionalities, their team's collaborative capabilities, and identification with local audiences by creating targeted rhetorical interventions. For example, one team that analyzed the debates about the death penalty developed rhetorical interventions to increase audience identifications with this topic and direct audiences to attend a forum about the intersectional factors of death penalty laws in Texas. After reviewing their Argument Analysis research, the team concluded that many Texans recognized racial injustice in the criminal justice system but did not view those injustices as an exigence for action. In their collaborative Argument Brainstorm, this team found that awareness of injustice does not compel audiences to action *unless* they feel directly impacted by those injustices. As the student team explained,

> [W]e found that many people were aware of these injustices; however, they did nothing to spark change in the situation. After much discussion and consideration amongst our group, we decided to switch our goal from helping our community become aware of injustices to offering potential answers to the question, "What can I do about it?" We hope to evoke change in our community, one person at a time.

The team, made up of white students and students of color, had analyzed their own positionalities relating to this topic and found that direct experiences with the criminal justice system most often led to individual involvement in community action groups. As a result, the team aimed "to facilitate others in taking the next step in this process and acting on this feeling" by encouraging local audiences to connect with community organizations.

To find common ground on this issue and effect change in the local community, this team designed rhetorical intervention strategies to direct citizens in the Dallas–Fort Worth area to act on their knowledge by getting involved in local justice programs and events. These students intended to illustrate to white audiences that racial injustices are a shared concern for all Texas citizens. The team reached out to local police officers and community leaders to show how shared investment in this issue could facilitate mutual understanding and open discussion among differing racial stakeholders. Two of the team's Campaign Texts, an Instagram page and website, shared their Argument Analysis research to increase audience awareness about racial injustices in the criminal justice system and direct audiences to apply that knowledge by getting involved in local organizations like the Innocence Project of Texas. These two Campaign Texts also directed audiences to participate in a student-created and facilitated forum on intersectional factors in Texas death penalty cases on Wrongful Conviction Day.

The team invited guest speakers from their campus police department and the local organization Tarrant County Coalition for Peace and Justice to bridge divides between law enforcement and marginalized communities. The goal of this planned event was to connect consubstantial audiences with community stakeholders currently working together on the criminal justice system and invite audience members to get involved by participating in future events. Ultimately, the student team found an intersectional framework for identification could help shift citizen interest into action by encouraging consubstantial audiences to collaborate and find common ground.

Feminist pedagogy can encourage students to mobilize Burke's theories for community engagement by identifying with local audiences, community groups, and organizations to rhetorically intervene in issues of the common good. As a class, we discuss how feminist theories of epistemology, positionality, and intersectionality can support such investigations by identifying how identity influences perspective and experience. By asking students to focus on the form of appeals to identification with their audiences, students again must consider the local, intersecting connections of this topic: where do these audiences live, work, and gather? What kinds of communication do they encounter daily? What organizations, groups, or communities connect to or represent these audiences? As a result of this critical feminist approach, students often report personal and professional investment in their Community Campaigns because their work contributes to the collective knowledge of our class and directly engages with local community issues. Teachers can use Burke's theories to support student projects committed to cultural and intellectual diversity by using intersectional analysis to characterize the spectrum of perspectives on community issues.

Conclusion

Like Burke's pedagogy of critical reflection, feminist pedagogy encourages a shared vulnerability and exploration of ideas in the classroom, using, as Shari Stenberg describes, "reflexivity and humility, so that the teacher's agenda does not overwrite that of the students" (63). Such feminist goals productively align with Burke's pedagogical goals by providing students with rhetorical tools for engaging with everyday arguments through critical reflection. Burke's rhetorical theories of identification and consubstantiality "properly equip" students to understand arguments for connection as they analyze arguments for the common good in their local community. Because divisive political debates are so often associated with the political parties that represent them and not the evidence that forms these argumentative positions, students must question appeals to identification to collaboratively break "for" and "against" argumentative frameworks and invite intersectional identifications with these topics. While national political debates continually perpetuate binary oppositions and divisions, a feminist pedagogy incorporating Burkean theory can recognize the multiplicity of intersectional identifications in these debates.

Feminist pedagogical approaches like collaboration and community engagement encourage students to use critical reflection to analyze the intersectional factors in appeals to identification. In these collaborative investigations, students use their own reflective experiences to challenge binary arguments and expand the range of stakeholders and positions in arguments about the common good. For students, Burke's theories provide rhetorical frameworks to analyze and compose arguments for local audiences, using identity-based appeals to identification. For teachers, the productive pairing of Burke's theories with feminist pedagogical approaches adds intersectional context to Burke's concept of *sub-stance* and shows the power of Burke's methods to facilitate social change through a pursuit of common ground. Thus, this pedagogical pairing of Burke's identification and feminist positionality offers students transferable tools to pursue common ground in community engagement projects, defy binary stances, and facilitate rhetorical interventions for social change.

Community Engagement Assignment

Community Campaign Activity and Assignments

Collaborative Argument Brainstorm Activity

To define the rhetorical situation around your topic, write with your team on the Campaign Argument Brainstorming document in your Google Drive folder. This initial brainstorming process should be additive—build off your team's comments by adding more ideas, or refining the ideas offered by team members. The goal of this brainstorming process is to create a wealth of content to work from to draft your Campaign Argument Plan.

1. Identify two distinct audiences to appeal to with your campaign, noting how the rhetorical process of identification makes certain people consubstantial in this problem. What are the stakeholders within these audiences? What rhetorical appeals are used to persuade these audiences and why?
2. Brainstorm two distinct forms of rhetorical intervention. Keep in mind: the effectiveness of your intervention will be determined by your awareness of the rhetorical situation. Each form of intervention should demonstrate rhetorical awareness of the audience's identification with the topic, exigence for the topic, and the local connections to the topic.
3. Determine which rhetorical strategies would be best suited to your audiences, topic, and intervention goals. Your team must justify what kinds of arguments are needed to effect a change for the common good. Do you need to increase awareness of the problem? Do you need to draw attention to a specific aspect of the problem? What specific kinds of change are you arguing for? Considering the discourse of the community, your team should use your combined knowledge of identification to demonstrate what rhetorical features make your campaign a meaningful intervention to this problem.

Community Campaign Assignments

> *[S]ocial change can take place in daily interactions when the regular flow of events is objectified, reflected upon, and altered.*
>
> Ellen Cushman, "The Rhetorician as Agent of Social Change"

In this project, you will work in small teams to research a local community's problem. This project spans the entire course, so we will work on this project in small stages throughout the term. This assignment is divided into three major check-in points, but you and your team will self-direct your project progress and account for that progress at the end of the course. While you will work with your team members on these major parts of the assignment, you will also reflect individually in your Research Journal and as a team in Discussions. Your team will use primary research (surveys, interviews, observation) to study problems that affect real people, design effective arguments for specific audiences, and produce arguments in multiple forms (posters, videos, webpages, editorials, social media pages, etc.)

This project contains multiple assignments as part of the larger Community Campaign.

Community Campaign Part 1: Argument Analysis

For this assignment, each team member will write a three-page, double-spaced critical analysis of three texts relating to your team's issue. These texts could be any variety of publications, but must be published through an organization, not independently published (like a blog or personal YouTube video). The main criteria for selecting these three texts are that they directly relate to your issue and the local community, and that they are reputable sources for this topic. A reputable source is a text that the local community would find relevant to the issue under discussion. The benefit of this kind of analysis means that each team will have a wide range of texts from which to draw perspectives and evidence for their Community Campaign.

Your analysis of each text should address the following questions:

- **Authorial perspective:** To what field of study does the author belong? What is the author's perspective, and what is their stake in this argument?
- **Topic/issue addressed:** What is the focus of this argument? What is the author's goal in addressing this topic? Who is the audience? How does the author address the intersectional perspectives of their audience or audience(s)?
- **Rhetorical appeals:** How does the author appeal to the audience using identification? What persuasive strategies does he/she use to convey the exigence and focus to the reader? What evidence from the argument demonstrates these appeals?
- **Mode and delivery:** How do the modes of the argument (blog, news article, scholarly journal article, video, etc.) influence the delivery of the argument?
- **Critical reflection:** What potential flaws exist in this argument, and what do they tell us? What perspectives does the author praise, and what perspectives do they miss or gloss over? What questions or suggestions would you offer this author, considering their goals?

Objective: You will analyze perspectives on an issue, strategies for speaking across difference to identify what about the community's ideology and members make this problem an exigence; as Bitzer calls it, "a thing which is other than it *should* be" (emphasis added). Your team will work together to identify an exigence for change in that community. You will clearly define that exigence within the community's ideology and the rhetorical situation of the common good as defined through this topic.

This assignment has three specific checkpoints:

- **Source Selection and Sharing:** After researching a variety of texts on your team's topic, select the two most relevant sources. Create PDFs of these sources and post them to your team's Google Drive folder.
- **Source Feedback to Team:** After your team members have posted their sources to your team's Google Drive folder, review the articles for relevance to your team's topic. Go to the Source Review document in your Google Drive folder and

provide feedback to each team member about their source selection. The point here is not to critique the source selection of your team, but instead to consider how each source could provide different perspectives and evidence for your team's topic.
- **Submission of Argument Analysis to Dropbox:** Submit this assignment in .docx format to the assignment dropbox by the due date.
- **Sharing Your Argument Analysis with Campaign Team:** After submitting your Argument Analysis to the assignment dropbox, upload your Argument Analysis to your team's Google Drive folder. You need to share these assignments with your team to move on to the next part of your Community Campaign.

Community Campaign Part 2: Research Proposal

For this assignment, you and your team members will create a detailed plan for your Community Campaign research in a 1000–1500-word report written in MLA format. This is the preliminary phase of your research process where you develop a strategic plan for studying your topic based off your collaborative knowledge of rhetorical situations. Your research proposal should outline each step of your research process, including the logistical planning for data collection (focus groups, interviews, observations, artifact collection, field notes), and data analysis. Consider what resources you might need to complete your research, including technology, software, travel arrangements, and most importantly, time!

- **Describe your team's research topic.** After reviewing each team member's Argument analysis assignment, your team should know a lot more about your research topic. This knowledge could shift and/or focus your research topic, like focusing a camera lens. Use each team member's identification of exigence for this community problem to describe your research topic.
- **Summarize the relevant research from each member's Argument Analysis.** After your team researches debates on this topic, work together to conduct an analysis of the stasis

in the topic's rhetorical situation. Who are the audiences for this topic? What are the intersectional features of these audiences? How are these audiences connected through this topic? What potential points of common ground did your team discover in the research? What is still unclear? What is the most likely path for common ground in this rhetorical situation? Write a summary of the relevant research for this topic that provides the grounding for your campaign research.

- **Describe your project's research question.** A research question helps you to you situate your campaign within the ongoing research and debates on this topic. Think of it like a promise you're making to your reader—the scope and detail of your research question determines the possible research you find, and what kinds of arguments you can make. Use your team's knowledge of the rhetorical situation to find the scope, exigence, and audiences for this problem. Your team should use each member's knowledge, experience, and resources in local communities to aid in your research. Then, write a concise and specific research question that captures your team's approach to this research within the ongoing research on this topic.
- **Describe your plan for gathering research data about your community problem.** Your team could design a survey, write questions for interviews or focus groups, conduct observations, or complete a textual analysis to gather data about the community and their experiences with the problem. Describe what kind of research your team will conduct and why this research is the best choice of data for your research question. Your research data should be designed to help you answer this question, and the data should help provide evidence for the exigence of this community problem.
- **Write a timeline for researching your community's problem.** Review the Stages of the Research Process graphic again with your team. Your team should discuss how the data collection process could encounter problems (no or low survey responses, problems scheduling interviews, etc.) and what your contingencies plans your team could put into place. For each research stage, a team member should be designated as

the "Check-In" member who will serve as the point person to keep track of progress in that research stage. Each team member should be assigned as "Check-In" member for at least one stage of the research process.

Community Campaign Part 3: Argument Plan

For this assignment, your team will use the knowledge and evidence gained through your research process to outline the rhetorical situation in which your campaign will intervene. Your team's Campaign Research Plan will be a 1000–1500-word report written in MLA format. Your team will identify the scope of stakeholders in the community issue—that is, the people and groups invested in and affected by the issue—by describing their intersecting identifications with this issue. You and your team will then identify the targeted influencers (at least three) in the community issue—that is, the people and/or groups with the power, access, or ability to effect change on the issue. You will use this information to write a Campaign Argument Plan that outlines how you will address these features of your campaign: objective, exigence, stakeholders, targeted influencers, and rhetorical strategies.

Your team will be responsible for creating three texts to convey the messages of your campaign. Those messages can showcase three approaches to your rhetorical strategy, target separate influencers, appeal to three different stakeholders, or any combination of these. The important thing to remember is that your two campaign texts must be created for two specific writing genres—that it, the channel or system of communication through which the message appears. So, your team could create a poster, video, blog, Twitter account, TED Talk, letter-writing campaign, website, meme, map of survey responses, PSA, video game, billboard . . . the options all depend on the ideal genre for your message.

Your team's Campaign Argument Plan should include detailed responses to the following questions using the provided format:

Objective and Exigence
- What is the goal of the campaign? How does this campaign intervene in a local community problem? How does this campaign make an argument for the common good?

Stakeholders, Influencers, and Audiences
- Who are the stakeholders in this argument? What evidence do you have of these stakeholders from your research?
- What influencers are you hoping to reach with your campaign? What makes these influencers ideal for your topic and research question? Use evidence to support your response.
- What audiences are you trying to reach with your campaign? How will your campaign appeal to these audiences? Be specific about the demographic information for each audience. How will your team account for and/or appeal to the intersecting identifications of your audiences for this campaign?

Rhetorical Strategies and Genres
- What rhetorical strategies will your team use in the campaign? What are your campaign messages?
- What mediums will your campaign use to share these messages with your audiences? Be specific about how these genres are ideal for your topic and how they relate to your campaign's objective.
- What visual choices will you make in this campaign? Consider the placement of visual elements, color schemes, choices of visual and textual elements, cultural references, and your team's approach to this topic.

Team Process
- What specific rhetorical, material, methodological, and technological choices will your team need to make to accomplish your campaign goals?
- Why did you end up pursuing this plan as opposed to others you came up with?

- Who will be responsible for accomplishing these goals? Consider your team's resources, skills, abilities, and time available for this campaign.

Community Campaign Part 4: Community Campaign

For this assignment, your team will design a campaign—multiple arguments intended to persuade a specific sector of the public to intervene in the issue. Your team will identify and analyze audiences to assess the capabilities of your team and the communities through which you could stage your intervention. To accomplish this goal, you will identify distinct audiences that identify with this problem, finding their points of connection to the issue and community involved. You will specifically identify relationships to power for the people involved—that is, which people are affected by this problem, and which people have the power to change it? Why? Consider the institutional resources of the people involved, as well as their community ethos on this topic.

This assignment has two parts that encompass the entire team's Community Campaign, your three Campaign Texts and your Statement of Goals and Choices:

Part 1: Campaign Texts

- **Create three texts** to persuade your campaign audiences, making sure that each text is distinct in its message and medium and message, and has a specific space and time in which the text will appear. Your awareness of the rhetorical situation and exigence of this problem will allow you to describe how make appeals to identification with local audiences.

- **Design each campaign text to publicly intervene in the community's problem.** One of these texts should have significant visual components, whether it is an infographic, billboard, poster, flyer, video, social media posts, or another mode of visual argument.

- **Demonstrate rhetorical awareness** of your topic's problem through the rhetorical features of each campaign text:

- **Distinct Purpose and Message:** The campaign text represents a distinct part of the community campaign with a message that aligns with the goals and style of the campaign argument. Exigence and stasis are reflected through the rhetorical features of the campaign text purpose and message.
- **Research Support and Audience Awareness**: The campaign texts demonstrate rhetorical awareness of the situation through your team's textual and primary research. The campaign text uses persuasive language and rhetorical appeals aimed at distinct audiences and selects the ideal evidence for the situation and topic.
- **Genre, Style, and Conventions**: The campaign texts achieve success in their distinctive genres by capitalizing on the chosen genre's conventions to address the exigence of the problem through stasis. The style and conventions of the campaign text align with the expectations of the genre.

Part 2: Statement of Goals and Choices

In this collaborative reflective essay, you and your team will describe the challenges and successes of your Community Campaign and teamwork process. Your team's Statement of Goals and Choices will be an 800–1400-word reflective essay written in MLA format. Using Jody Shipka's example "Statement of Goals and Choices" from our course reading, you and your team will write a collaborative Statement of Goals and Choices that explains in detail how well your team put your Campaign Argument Plan into action. Because the process of composing and writing means making changes to your original plans, your team will also describe how and why your Community Campaign changed between writing your Research Proposal, your Argument Plan, and completing the Campaign Texts.

Your collaborative SOGC should:

- Describe how all three campaign texts work together to intervene in the community's problem.

- Describe the decision-making process of determining the campaign's focus, goal, and methods of intervention through your choice of text genres.
- Address the following features of your campaign as examples and evidence for your reflection:
    - **Objective**: Communicate the overall goal of the Community Campaign.
    - **Intervention**: Describe the problem that the campaign is addressing, and how your team believes your Campaign is designed to successfully intervene in the problem.
    - **Audience**: Describe the two distinct audiences appealed to in this campaign, and how they are consubstantial in this community problem.
    - **Design**: Describe how the campaign goals are achieved through the rhetorical features of your campaign texts.

8 Dramatism, Archives, and Assembled Trajectories: "As Rhetoricians, We'll Do Things"

James Beasley

> *Applying multiple layers of pentadic analysis as undergraduates interrogate and reframe local history archives.*

As we think about the pedagogy of Kenneth Burke and how to utilize Burke in our pedagogy, I often think of a line that he wrote to Malcolm Cowley when he was teaching at the University of Chicago in 1938, "Am learning a hell of a lot—and have been gratified by the friendliness of the kids, who don't seem to mind that I am better at flushing game than at bagging it" (qtd. in Jay 221). What is almost humorous in this line is to think about what it must have been like for these students to have had Burke in the classroom. "The kids are all right," Burke seems to suggest. I wonder, however, how "all right" they really were. I suspect that it must have been challenging to have been in his classroom. The challenges were even acknowledged by Wayne Booth in his own classes at Chicago. Before Booth taught *A Grammar of Motives* to his students, he engaged in a series of prep sessions: "Reasons for Liking Burke" and "Reasons for Not Liking Burke" (see figure 1). According to Booth's teaching notes, among the reasons for "Not Liking Burke" were an "ignorance of rhetoric," the "superficiality of the modern mind," and "over-denseness in Burke himself."

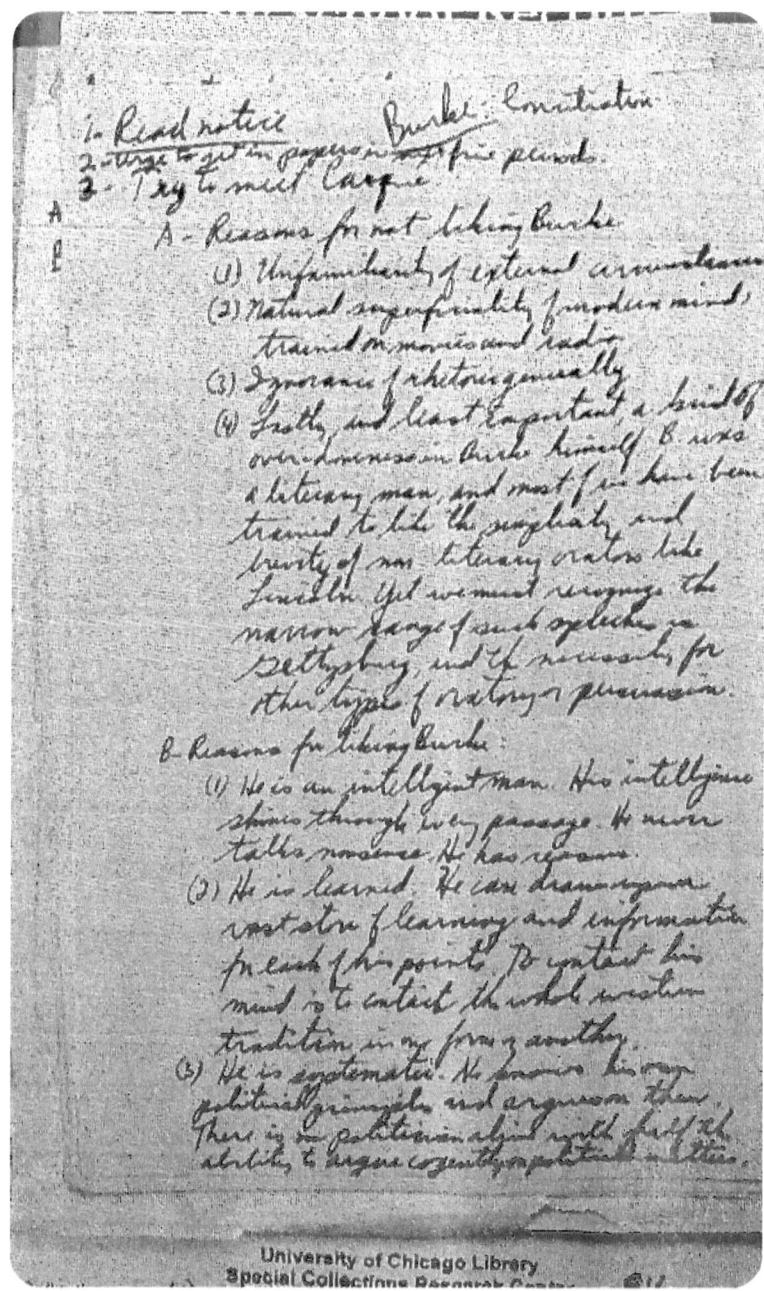

Figure 1. Wayne Booth's teaching notes, courtesy of the University of Chicago Special Collections Research Center.

While Burke's over-denseness has been much discussed, it still confuses and bewilders even some of the most persistent readers. Students encountering Burke for the first time need time to read, time to discuss, time to be confused and to allow that confusion to simmer, and time to reread and rediscuss. Booth also kept a list of the "Reasons for Liking Burke," including "4. He is delightfully allusive, frequently humorous, frequently ironic. There is a constant extra, additional pleasure from observing the play of a superior mind over his arguments" (Booth). Booth knew the satisfaction that comes from prior pieties upended by new knowledge. In teaching Burke's ideas, we can see students' knowledge change in a matter of minutes. It is with both these apprehensions and aspirations that I underscore the use of Burke's dramatism in a digital archives course I regularly teach. In this chapter, I will detail how teaching Burke's pentad not only reveals the "drama in the archives" but also helps students understand archival documents as circulating objects. Teaching students to use the pentad also means that they are able to manipulate the velocity of that circulation for other audiences and purposes outside of the classroom.

Introducing the Archives

One of the first obstacles in teaching archival methods in an English class is student difficulty in understanding why archival study is rhetorical in the first place. As Cara Finnegan's "What is This a Picture Of?" notes, "The suggestion that the archive is a rhetorical construction is hardly new, of course. But I worry that in our desire to trumpet the general uses and benefits of archives, we too quickly gloss over the specific, complex rhetorical negotiations such research often requires" (117). This tendency to "too quickly gloss over" the complexity in archival research is one of the reasons why Burke's dramatism is useful in the archival methods classroom. For students, the pentad is the means by which they are able to slow down their thinking, making these complexities visible. Finnegan writes, "We need to recognize that archives—even seemingly transparent image archives—function as terministic screens, simultaneously revealing and concealing 'facts' at once enabling and constraining interpretation" (117). Because archives, and specifically archival photographs, function as terministic screens, I find it helpful to utilize Burke's dramatistic pentad to make these screens visible to students and other researchers alike.

The use of Burke's pentad in the archives is not new. In Jessica Enoch and Cheryl Glenn's account, they write that Burke's

> dramatistic pentad provides familiar guides for us as we explore the "drama in the archives." Within the archive (the scene), the researcher (agent) engages (agency) in a variety of recovery and recuperative practices (acts) directed toward a specific end (purpose). And the familiar ratio between those key pentadic terms (scene: act, scene: agent, agent: agency, and so on) provides purchase. (322)

The purchase that Enoch and Glenn describe is that students are able to earn their increment; there is a "goes before" initial approach to the material and a "comes after" reflection on new interpretations that using the pentad with archival material can provide. My students, too, have appreciated learning about archival research, learning new information strategies, seeing the disciplinary benefits, and imagining how they might incorporate primary methods in their own teaching. By using the pentad, moreover, these students came to these conclusions through the dramatistic review of their own interpretations about their archival interpretations. This is the "purchase" that using the pentads allows for. After I introduce students to the pentad from *A Grammar of Motives*, then, they create pentads based on the photographs and objects from the St. Augustine Historical Society and Lincolnville Museum and Cultural Center. We then read these pentads alongside Enoch and Glenn's account. I have included sections of the students' pentads and how Enoch and Glenn's descriptions of the "purchase" that they speak of appears in their work.

Using the Archives

While St. Augustine, Florida is one of the most popular tourist destinations in the United States, much of that history is hidden, specifically the history of the historic Lincolnville neighborhood. Lincolnville, a segregated community after the Civil War, was the center of both African American business in North Florida in the 1920s and civil rights marches in the 1960s. The St. Augustine Historical Society and the Lincolnville Museum and Cultural Center are the portals into this history. In an effort to enhance their efforts, I have collaborated with both sites on several projects over the last several years in the undergraduate/

graduate cross-listed course, ENC 4415/5935 Rhetoric and the Digital Humanities.

Rhetoric and the Digital Humanities begins with an introduction to archival methods and some brief research in our university's own special collections research area. The Carpenter Library Special Collections houses the Eartha White Collection, the papers of one of North Florida's most celebrated citizens: an educator, philanthropist, and civil rights activist. Students spend the first few weeks applying readings on archival methods and theory to their own research in this collection. They then read specific narratives of St. Augustine as a tourist space, narratives that completely ignore St. Augustine's history as a center of the civil rights movement in the summer of 1964. We contrast those narratives with resources from the St. Augustine Historical Society and the Lincolnville Museum and Cultural Center. One of the central collections of both institutions is the Richard Twine collection. Twine was an African American photographer who memorialized life in Lincolnville. Students choose photos that are of interest to them, begin collecting groups of similar photographs, and then use the St. Augustine City Directories to enter street, address, occupation, and business information on the subjects of Twine's photos into the curation software program Omeka.

In the next iteration of this course, we utilize the contents of the Lincolnville Museum and Cultural Center's "Lifeways" exhibit, using Omeka to record the metadata available from the city directories but also creating a Neatline map of St. Augustine as a way to replace the durable narrative of traditional city maps, which highlight the Spanish history of St. Augustine, with more ephemeral ones which highlight the civil rights-era history of St. Augustine. Durable narratives are those that, according to Jason Farman, "demonstrate the power dynamics and hierarchies involved in who gets to tell the story of a space" (6). Ephemeral narratives, in contrast, "tend to be done by those without the power and political clout to create durable inscriptions. These inscriptions often serve to stand in opposition to the legal and 'authorized' ways of storytelling about a place" (6–7). The Neatline map in Omeka that is housed online is created by students who do not have access to power and political clout, in order to memorialize very different people than those celebrated through St. Augustine's durable inscriptions, the statues and homes marked on official tourist maps of the nation's oldest city. (See David Blakesley in this volume for further examples of the use of technology in digital humanities classes.)

I want students in this class to take entire collections of photographs and artifacts and organize them into smaller subgroups, to understand the possibilities that are available to them to narrate and renarrate what appears at first to be historical reality. These students were taking the apparently stable archive of the Richard Twine photographs and the contents of the Lincolnville Museum and Cultural Center and then reorganizing them according to the idiosyncratic "what influences the what" of their own descriptions of the pentadic act, Finnegan's "what is this a picture of." Jeremy Tirrell writes in "Latourian Memoria": "The notion of an archive is predicated on a form of stability, wherein stored things remain static. Latour's kairotic temporality denies all of this. Memory cannot be a process of fixed storage and retrieval; it is always a new assemblage in the present moment" (174). Students in this class not only reorganize the archives, but they also reassemble them into a new archive, one that is in flux and in motion. Their pentadic analyses help them to break apart the unconsidered status quo to allow for new considerations as they apply perspective by incongruity to the archives.

Step 1: Initial Analysis Using the Pentad

I use Burke's pentad to help students focus on the archival material as having an effect on the act, using Finnegan's question, "What is this a picture of?" We begin with a focus on one photo, "After the Parade," taken by Richard Twine after the Emancipation Day Parade, January 1, 1921. Students create pentads with "What is this a picture of?" as the act and proceed through Burke's pentad from there. Here is an example of one of the students' log entries for this photo:

ACT: This photograph is a testament to the documentary-like quality of photographs because of how much it can tell us about the time period—for example, the outfits of the two people or their expressions.

SCENE: The where of this photograph is a field probably sometime near the Emancipation Day parade in the 1920s Lincolnville. Since the parade celebrates veterans, I am curious as to whether or not the field behind the young man and woman is actually a cemetery based on our conversation in class about the memorial plaque.

AGENT: The agent of this photograph was Richard Twine because he took the pictures; historians can use these pictures to get an accurate sense of what was important to Twine and/or Twine's community.

AGENCY: Twine likely asked to take a picture of these two young people because he wanted to take some pictures of World War I (WWI) veterans (or representatives, say, wearing a uniform symbolically in honor of those who did serve).

PURPOSE: The why behind this picture is because he wanted to honor those who had served in WWI, especially since he had not gone to war himself. He probably admired this young man in particular.

Biggest Influence: The biggest influence in my interpretation is probably AGENCY because I wrote a lot about the circumstances behind the two people and therefore why they would be okay standing for a picture for Twine.

After completing this first dramatistic pentad, students are able to examine the Twine photographic archives themselves and consider which aspect of the pentad is being highlighted by the photograph's title. By identifying the Burkean agency of glass plate photography as having the greatest effect on the act, this student is able to see around the denotative meaning of the photograph's title ("After the Parade") into the connotative meanings of why these subjects were photographed in the first place, to memorialize Black bodies in a white space. As Finnegan notes, "Before we critically engage the artifacts we discover in the archive, we need critically to engage the archive itself" (118). For this student, the scene "After the Parade" did not have as great an effect as the agency of photography on the act, and so she retitled this photograph "For Richard Twine," as if the subjects of the photo are dedicating the photo of themselves together to the photographer, the one who memorialized their presence in white St. Augustine.

Using the Archive to Extend the Pentad

Asking students not only to reflect on the pentadic elements of "what is this a picture of" but also to indicate which element influenced them the most (via the question "How does the what influence the what?") serves to have them think about the specific kind of data source their interpretation will encourage them to further pursue. For instance, if students said that the scene had the most important effect on the act, they then began researching the street address from the city directories and began compiling that information as further data about that person (what is commonly called metadata, pictured in figure 2) into the Omeka website. However, if they said that agent had the greatest effect on the act, they began researching the occupation of the figures pictured, again from the city directories, and began compiling that information as further data about that person in the Omeka website (see figure 3).

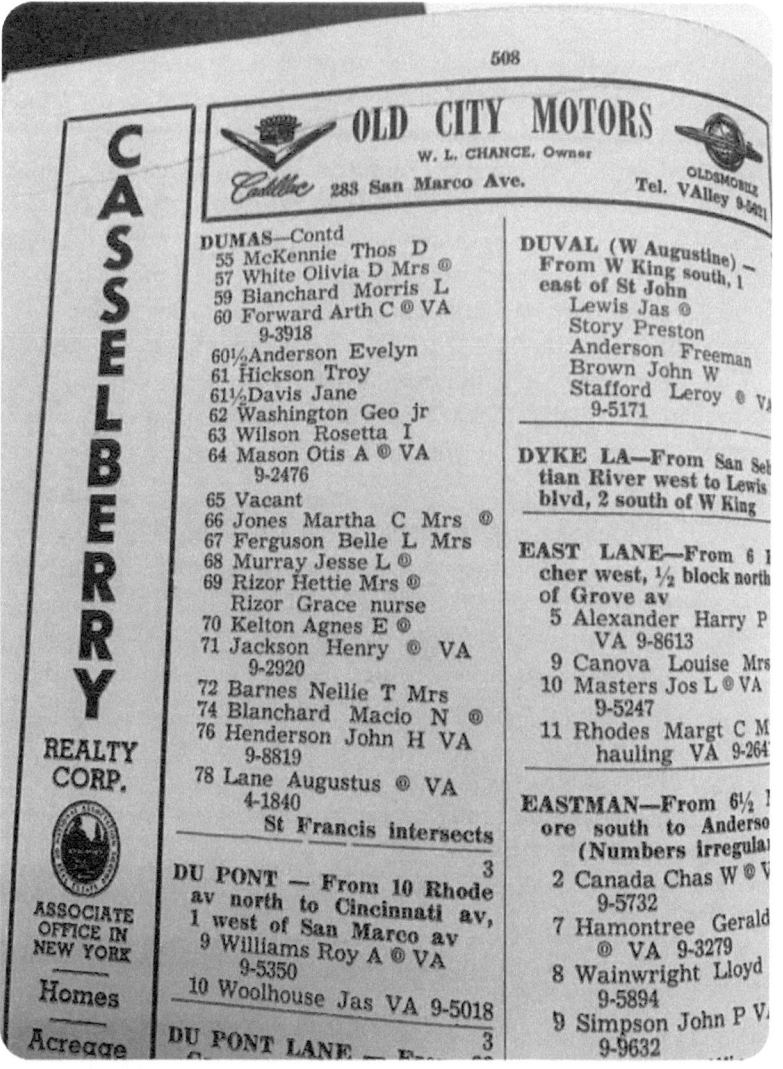

Figure 2. Historic city directory, photo by the author.

City Directory	Mapped to Dublin Core	Example (formatted)	Obligation	Notes
Name	Title		Required	
Address	Description		Required	
Book title	Source	St. Augustine City Directory	Required	
Occupation	Subject		Required if present	
Business	Subject (added input)		Required if present	
Date of publication	Date		Required	

Figure 3. Omeka website database example.

Furthermore, if students said that agency had the greatest effect, they researched the means by which the photographs were taken, the process known as glass plate photography. These plates of Richard J. Twine's were found and given to the St. Augustine Historical Society for preservation. Students who said that the agency had the greatest effect on the act researched characteristics of glass plate photography and entered the citations from that research in the "Source" field of metadata in the Omeka website. An emphasis on "agency," then, changed the source from the St. Augustine City Directories to the specific book or resource on glass plate photography that they had researched.

To demonstrate how this worked with the student pentads, here is an example showing how a student decided that the scene had the greatest effect on the act:

> ACT: This photograph is a pictorial representation of history, especially a family's history. It is a portrait of sorts, depicting a close-knit group who likely kept this photograph as a keepsake.
> SCENE: The where of this photograph is someone's (probably someone in the photo or a relative of someone in the photo) house (i.e., House "127"), or the front porch of that house. (intimate)
> AGENT: The agent of this photograph is a person who is family-oriented, caring, and sentimental, or business-oriented and (possibly) cold or greedy.
> AGENCY: This picture was able to be taken because the photographer was either close with the family (or a member of the family like the bride or groom), he was hired to take the pictures, or a mix between the two (i.e., he was hired to take the pictures because he was a friend with professional camera capabilities).

PURPOSE: A reason behind keeping this photograph at the Historical Society was to provide an example of a wedding in that time period, or to show diversity in the photographer's work in relation to the majority of studio portraits (i.e., this is a more formal picture with the subjects lined up intentionally, but the atmosphere is more natural and relaxed than that of an artificial environment like a studio).

Biggest Influence: The biggest influence in my interpretation is currently the SCENE because of the intimacy of the group of whom the photographer is taking a picture.

Because this student identified the scene as having the greatest effect on the act, she could turn her attention to the city directories, locating the subjects of Twine's photos by their street address. Before getting too comfortable with this "goes after," however, this student admits her own uncertainty when it comes to her newfound pentadic knowledge: "They all sound too similar; that is why I am concerned." Her frustration is not unfounded: the diffusion of the ratios is the subject of much Burkean study. According to Enoch and Glenn, "Our framework, however, entails certain limitations. First is the limitation of this linear format, which demands that we explain consecutively a process that is overlapping, interactional, and (to use Burke's term) 'compellingly corresponding'—even when illuminated by the dramatistic 'ratios'" (118). Enoch and Glenn's recursive use of the pentad in their own archival research illuminates the good company with which our students find themselves and their archival interpretations. Part of teaching Burke's ideas is assuring students that recursively reexamining their interpretations is a part of the investigative process.

Just as Enoch and Glenn revisit each other's archival interpretations, the groups that the students formed around their pentads began to help them understand the "goes before" quality of their pentads and their "comes after" understandings from talking with one another. This student wrote that "we also worked with primary sources again and based on groups, I went to work with other people who said SCENE was their most important factor."

After identifying scene as having the greatest effect on the act (what is this a picture of?), these students, working together, were able to combine the several images they had collected from the overall collection. In this way, we ended up with a collection of photographs organized by scene, agent, agency, and purpose. In other words, students started grouping, or "dividing," photographs from the whole collection into smaller units, based on their descriptions of how a specific ratio affected their description of the "act."

Step 2: Reinterpretation Using the Pentad

In "Drama in the Archives," Enoch and Glenn describe how their own process of using the dramatistic ratios informs their archival work:

> A concerted attention to the "act" of choosing archival documents and locations ("scenes") can enrich our sense of the kind of texts that can contribute to our historical understandings as well as the places where these texts might be found. A greater consciousness of the "agents" in the archive can prompt us to initiate better networks among scholars and to collaborate with archivists as a means to broaden our historiographic vision and deepen our knowledge of what an archive is and can be. And, finally, a consistent reflection on who we are as researchers can call us to think more critically about our "purpose" as we work to interrogate our "agency"—our interestedness in our research agendas, our choice of theoretical frames, and our attention to and regard for the other agents in the archive. (336)

After visiting the Lincolnville Museum and seeing Martin Luther King Jr.'s fingerprint card when he was arrested in St. Augustine in 1964, one student used Burke's pentad to describe this act in the following way:

> ACT: Martin Luther King Jr. is forced to roll his inked stained fingers on a police fingerprint card.
> SCENE: St. Augustine jail, thriving on injustice and racism in an equally constraining society.
> AGENT: Peaceful activist fighting for freedom, change and equality for all.
> AGENCY: Attempting to eat in the Monson restaurant. A simple but forbidden act.
> PURPOSE: The act happens to display the message of peacefully cooperating despite injustice. MLK Jr. imprints his fingerprints on the police's card knowing he has imprinted his beliefs and made a mark on St. Augustine at the same time.
> Purpose = greatest effect on act.

The purpose can become the new act: Displaying the message of peacefully cooperating despite injustice.

Taking what was the "greatest effect on the act" and creating a new pentad based on that interpretation, students create a "goes before" pentad to be followed by a "comes after" pentad. This student took the purpose ratio of the previous pentad to create a new act for a new pentad:

ACT: Florida student realizes they have not been taught the whole truth of the history of where they live.

SCENE: A museum in a town created for freedom, happiness and in celebration of cultural differences but was robbed of this due to racist, evil times.

AGENT: Student desperate to learn about Lincolnville's significant civil rights movement.

AGENCY: Witnessing in person the artifacts of MLK Jr. directly related to St. Augustine and jars of soil from the ground beneath where people were lynched.

PURPOSE: The act happens to make the student angry and therefore become informative to others and raise awareness.

Agency =greatest effect on act.

For this student, the act was no longer just her archival reading but the effect of that reading on the agent herself. By describing the act as "Florida student realizes they have not been taught the history of where they live," she is already opening herself to a perspective by incongruity that will help her understand her trained incapacity as a student of Florida's incomplete history lessons. As Enoch and Glenn write, "We are limited by what Burke refers to as our 'trained incapacities' . . . [but] we think the pentad with its inherent ratios is a useful way to explore the drama in the archives" (322).

For this student, the next steps of her pentad highlight the where and the when of that perspective by incongruity. How she describes the agency of the perspective by incongruity, "witnessing in person the artifacts of Martin Luther King Jr. and jars of soil from the ground beneath where people were lynched," has the greatest effect on the act and helps her then describe the purpose: to make the student angry enough to be a source of information and awareness for others. Actually, this process for this student worked similarly to the way Enoch and Glenn described that it worked for them. They write that "a consistent reflection on who we are as researchers can call us to think more critically about our 'purpose' as we work to interrogate our 'agency'— our interestedness in our research agendas, our choice of theoretical frames, and our attention to and regard for the other agents in the archive" (336). In interrogating her own agency, this student was able to create a purpose for this encounter that would not have occurred without it. For her, there was a very specific "goes before" and very emotional "comes after" that created the impetus for discussing her "earned increment"—the new knowledge she had discovered—with others:

> We went over our informal writings and a great question was brought up about whether digitizing parts of the Lincolnville museum would increase or decrease visitors and/or funders. Additionally, the discussion of funding was a big part of [the] conversation and I liked the connection that was made in class that the amount of funding you give is your amount of commitment to the cause, in this case the civil rights movement. Therefore, St. Augustine could be purposefully not funding or advertising about the museum in order to keep that "ugly" history hidden still.

For Enoch and Glenn, "A greater consciousness of the 'agents' in the archive can prompt us to initiate better networks among scholars and to collaborate with archivists as a means to broaden our historiographic vision and deepen our knowledge of what an archive is and can be" (322). For this student, the Lincolnville Museum and Cultural Center was not just a repository of civil rights memorabilia; its underfunded presence was transformed into a symbolic act of institutionalized racism. Since she identified purpose as having the greatest effect on the act in her pentad, she researched the racism inherent in the ignorance of these museum objects, focusing on Florida history, which ignored their presence. She then tied these objects to these stories of deflected history. After she charted these objects and their presence in civil rights histories, they also became metadata for our class Omeka-curated database.

While in many research courses students are often confused as to where to conduct research or why, we can see in this student's expanding work the passion that she brings to this research. She is looking for evidence of the use of specific artifacts in civil rights narratives in St. Augustine. She began her pentadic analysis describing the act of a student whose history had been hidden from her. She acknowledges that trained incapacity, and it motivates her research work. What is inventive about utilizing the pentads in this part of the research process is that once the gap in their knowledge becomes visible to them, students extend their research past any requirement of mine. They begin to look into court records, genealogy databases, and newspaper files from other libraries beyond St. Augustine. In this particular case, this student was looking for that hidden history in the research as evidence of where the pieties of St. Augustine's narrative need to be broken apart and retold. Further, through her discussions of her own "goes before" with other students, multiple students not only arrived at some startling "goes afters," such as the underfunding of museums dedicated to social justice, but they were able to identify specific sources for further research. The motivation for that research became much clearer. "After all, it is through a perspective by incongruity that researchers make some of their most important discoveries" (Enoch and Glenn 323). This student was then able to curate a collection of other "goes afters" into an Omeka civil rights metadata file.

Step 3: Scope and Reduction

Using Burke's pentad allowed the students to see how far they could take their interpretations, how far they could widen their scope in the kind of stretching that the ratios allow for. This was especially generative for the following student, who wrote:

> Enoch and Glenn write, "Widening the scene of our research creates new opportunities" . . . This quote hit home for me within my paper not only as [I] wrote a pentad from the perspective of having a co-agent. I wrote from a place where I uncovered new artifacts and information since I was having to read the information aloud, for [my daughter] Lucy. As we were in the cultural center, she would ask, "What does that say?" Which I wrote about. This allowed her to take in information as well. "In other words, historiographers, like ethnographers, concentrate on connecting the experiences of someone to the representation of those experiences by someone else" ([Enoch and Glenn] 335). Although Lucy and I are neither historiographers nor ethnographers, there were moments during our exploration of Lincolnville where we shared the feeling and the information within the archive. We also took the time to feel the brick of the AME church.

This student realized that her interpretations were also those of her daughter through her. Her pentads focused on how the (co) agent had the greatest effect on the act (what is this a picture of?) and led her to develop a research grid that emphasized the interaction of text and audience. The question, "What does that say?" may seem to be the starting place for any investigation, but for this student, she had to answer her daughter by describing an act, and as she read the words that were written on the signage, this student went through everything that she had come to realize about the civil rights movement being expressed in the denotative description. This difference between the denotative description that she read to her daughter and the connotative descriptions she was forced to think through during her seemingly short answer, considerably widened the scope of her research. As Enoch and Glenn conclude:

> Archival acts of reading, then, are tethered to the researcher's perceptions and prejudices as well as the theoretical frame used to approach his or her work. As we make these considerations about our own interestedness and theoretical grounding, though, we also consider how these two ideas prompt scholars to acknowledge other important agents in the archival scene besides the researcher and the archivist. (331)

The effect of using dramatistic pentads with an archival object as seemingly innocuous as the canteen this student eventually focused on created the space for the student to think about the rhetorical process of archival description, as "what something says" on the surface is a limited reflection of "what it says" to its audience, as an act in the scene of a museum.

Step 4: Assembled Trajectories

So far, students have created pentads from the objects in the museum, expanded on those pentads to identify how their interpretation led them to specific research sources, and begun entering metadata based on those sources. At this point, they are able to curate a collection based on their findings. Jason Waitman's canteen in the Lincolnville Museum and Cultural Center demonstrates this final step, as it became the centerpiece of this student's collection, exerting an agency on her and how she began curating the metadata of other objects in the Lincolnville Museum. As her collection began coalescing around these objects, she was doing something similar to Jeremy Tirrell's description of "Latourian memoria": "A Latourian memoria denies human's special privilege and embraces a momentary kairotic assembly rather than a chronos-driven durable archive. Within this framework, actors' (human and nonhuman) agential role is to form strong alliances through productive but necessarily contingent and perishable associations" (176). Jason Waitman's canteen tells us in a connotative way about his patriotism towards a country that would not allow him to participate in the rights of being a member of that country because of the color of his skin. In this way, the assembly of this collection is kairotic, being initiated from the specific moment her daughter asked her, "What does this say?"

The curatorial movement among these particular students and their data sources was not just a simple application of theory to practice. The dramatistic pentad was the means by which these "new assemblages in the present moment" could occur, and the new assemblages become the "goes after" of the "comes before." We see another student's pentad become a "goes before," which he then reassembled into a new "goes after":

> I wrote about the jar of dirt that contained ground from Isaac Barrett's lynching and the photograph of Leroy Pappy. For the first object, I described most of the pentad with an invective voice, angry at the memory of a lynching that happened so close and not so long ago. Concerning the picture of Leroy Pappy, I focused on the mystery that Richard Twine created by enveloping half of Pappy's face in light, while the other half was hidden from the camera by darkness.

For this student, it was the agency of the glass plate photography that had the greatest effect on the act. By creating a new pentad changing the agency into a new act, this student was able to see how agency can make us see archival objects from the perspective of different agents, to reassemble an archive based on the needs of varying agents. With some guidance, the student wrote:

> I understood that the Agents (the volunteers at the museum) were also the "covered" [the members of the Lincolnville community], those benefiting the most from museums like the Lincolnville museum. This encouraged me to see that the discriminated were still fighting to this day without any loss of resolve.

As he then created a new pentad based on making this agency the act, he began to see how he could interpret the objects from the museum, not from his perspective, but from the perspective of the Lincolnville Museum curators themselves. He began to develop his research materials not on the materials he thought he should utilize, but on the materials that he guessed the "covered" would want him to emphasize.

Based on the metadata that this student collected, he was able to create an Omeka entry on the site of the Lincolnville Museum and Cultural Center itself, the Excelsior High School. In this way, we were able to utilize the description of the agents of the museum, whom the students described as "the covered," and through the Omeka metadata site, they were able to uncover their lives to make them visible. By understanding that the Lincolnville Museum archivists (who had curated these objects for those whose histories were "covered" by the majority narrative) were themselves a part of uncovering that "covered" history, this student was able to create co-agents out of the archivists themselves. For this student, it was his work with Burke's pentad that became the means by which this knowledge of what an archive can be was accomplished.

Setting It Out to Do Things

Burke's pentad is also the means to understand what an archive cannot be, or in other words, how an archive can disappear in one place and reappear in another. I will conclude this chapter with an example of how one student used his work with Burke's pentad to replace part of a durable inscription with an effective, ephemeral one. His outline of his work plan noted:

> Using the LMCC catalog and link on the course home page, we will identify the photo and object from our Lincolnville visit, as well as the items around and similar to them to identify for our collection. Next, we'll make use of Burke's Pentads to think about where we need to look, so that by the end of class Thursday, we'll be able to curate our items, and the ones around them. By doing so, we'll be able to identify which sources will be most useful to us moving into cataloging for the museum. As rhetoricians, we won't just uncover what happened, we'll set it out to do things.

This student's description here reminds me of Burke's letter to Malcom Cowley, "I'm better at rustling game than bagging it." Burke rustled it, set it out, to "do things," and in this student's log for his photograph of James Washington and the Woolworth's counter where Washington was arrested for ordering a Coke, it is clear just how important this "setting it out to do things" can be:

> While I was able to track down James Washington, my hunt also revealed unexpected insight into St. Augustine's racial underworkings, when I realized that although the Washingtons' name and address were listed in the city directory by name, their residence was skipped in the section of the directory that lists occupants in the street listing. This practice was likely employed by St. Augustine in an attempt to conceal the black population of its streets from people looking to move there.

For this student, the scene of the Woolworth's counter where James Washington was arrested had the greatest effect on the act. If his house was not listed in the St. Augustine City Directory, then this student would give him a new residence, this time using a mapping feature of Omeka, Neatline Editor. By placing a map of St. Augustine in the Neatline editor function, students could superimpose images from the Lincolnville Museum and Cultural Center onto where they happened (see figure 4). Tirrell writes, "Memory is the always new interpretation of the present moment through an assembled trajectory, which invokes a contingent alliance among actors understood as bundles of relations without need of a transcendent metasubstance" (174).

Figure 4. Neatline maps of James Washington's associations, screenshots by the author.

The current location of the Woolworth's counter is a Wells Fargo Bank, with the old Woolworth's store handle preserved at the entrance. This student's use of the pentad enabled him to multiply the associations among James Washington's photo, the lack of information on his home in the 1965 St. Augustine City Directory, the Woolworth's lunch counter, and the Wells Fargo Bank located on its site. Tirrell writes that "memory is not being colonized but multiplied through association with more and better partners. All actors are gaining increased possibilities for association" (175). This student was able to do this "as a rhetorician," and the means by which this rhetorician was able to "not just uncover, we'll set it out to do things," was through the use of Burke's dramatistic pentads.

9 North with Burke! Symbolic Action and the Pentad in Political Science

Jouni Tilli

> *Teaching pentadic analysis to political science students in a graduate seminar.*

A Finnish professor of political science pointed out that before he went to conduct research in Japan in 1986, "no one talked about rhetoric but when I came back in 1988 everyone did" (qtd. in Palonen 2). Despite the rhetorical exaggeration, he correctly dates the change that had begun to take place at the time: Kenneth Burke, Stephen Toulmin, and Chaïm Perelman had entered the Finnish academic scene. From the 1990s onwards, rhetorical analysis has become a legitimate way to interpret social, political, and literary texts.

Rhetoric as such was not a novelty in Finland before the 1980s. Quite a number of books on oratory had been published already in the late nineteenth century and early decades of the twentieth century. The emphasis was on practical advice in giving a speech and eloquent reading of classical prose and poetry. At the same time, however, the importance of rhetoric in the Finnish academy was waning. At the beginning of the early twentieth century, rhetoric existed only as a historical remnant and a marginal part of classical studies; philology or linguistics had replaced it. The fact is surprising. When the first university of Finland (then a part of the Swedish empire) was established in 1640, it had ten professorships, *professor eloquentiae* among them (Keskinen 28–29, 53–54.)

It was the "new rhetoricians" who reintroduced Aristotle, Cicero, and Quintilian to Finnish researchers outside classical studies. Slowly but steadily, Burke and Perelman in particular have become almost household names in Finnish academic circles, particularly in humanities and social sciences. However, as of 2020, there still is no professorship of rhetoric (or argumentation). Research and teaching of rhetorical criticism and history of rhetoric is dispersed among various disciplines at Finnish universities, mainly political science, communication studies, literature and cultural studies, theater studies, even general history and theology.

The purpose of this chapter is twofold. First, I will look at the origins of new rhetoric and Kenneth Burke's ideas in Finland. Second, I will explain how I have taught Burkean rhetorical criticism—with a focus on the dramatistic pentad—to graduate students of political science at the University of Jyväskylä. I argue that Kenneth Burke provides indispensable tools for political scientists. The pentad in particular offers a method that helps to understand persuasion at work: for example, how seemingly simple or "innocent" characterizations of situations point toward acts that seem reasonable, implicit, or even unavoidable in that situation.

On the Origins of "New Rhetoric" and Kenneth Burke in Finland

Hilkka Summa's doctoral thesis from 1989 is the first academic work that went beyond the confines of a traditional understanding of rhetoric. Summa analyzed administrative texts pertaining to housing policy planning and budgetary practices from 1975 to 1987 and understood planning practices as a rhetorical struggle in which the different agencies present their cases for their budgetary share (*Hyvinvointipolitiikka* 224–25). Although Burke is not mentioned in this pioneering text, Summa's work is nevertheless inspired by similar phenomena as Burke's pertaining to symbolic action, named by him as trained incapacity and occupational psychosis.

The first Burkean analysis in Finnish was published in 1991. Its author, Matti Hyvärinen, discusses new rhetoric and analyzes political symbolism in the 1970s Finnish student movement. According to him, the newness of new rhetoric is that rhetoric is expanded from techniques aimed at speaking to masses to those for persuading different types of audiences. He notes that whereas Perelman and his followers are rooted in legal theory, the American rhetorical tradition, represented by Burke and Wayne Booth, was inspired by literary criticism. Expressions of hate, love, or solidarity are not always restricted to argumentation or convincing the audience, but they are all rhetorical, Hyvärinen stressed. Accordingly, he notes that Kenneth Burke's solution is to "ontologize" rhetoric: Rhetoric is reality, not only argumentation about the nature of reality (84–85).

It was not until five years later that the wave of new rhetoric gained momentum. A 1996 collection of articles edited by Hilkka Summa and political scientist Kari Palonen about rhetorical theory and criticism introduced Burke and other new rhetoricians to a wider academic readership. The collection includes a comprehensive discussion of "old" and "new" rhetoric. The editors also present a history of "the rhetorical turn," drawing, for example, on Richard Rorty and Herbert W. Simons. Burke is discussed with Perelman and Toulmin in a chapter written by Summa. For the first time in Finnish, she offers an overview of Burke's major works. Summa also examines in more detail the four master tropes and the idea of humans as symbol-using animals. Identification is used to explain Burke's general approach to symbolic action as well as the principle that powers particular tropes and techniques of persuasion ("Kolme näkökulmaa" 51–60). According to Summa's assessment, Burke is more fruitful for scholars of conceptual history or history of rhetoric than Perelman or Toulmin because their works focus on building systems of their own (61–62). Additionally, Matti Hyvärinen contributed a chapter that explicitly used Burke's concepts. The collection soon became *the* source for new rhetoric in Finland. For more than a decade it was virtually the only textbook in Finnish that included a discussion of new rhetoric and in which ideas of new rhetoricians were applied. The anthology is still widely used as course material.

From the late 1990s onwards, the number of Burkean graduate theses has been increasing. In 2005, Ilkka Mikkola from the Department of Information Science, University of Tampere, examined discourses that resisted the closing down of local public libraries in 1990s Finland using Burke's thoughts on symbolic action. In 2006, James O'Connor from the Department of Political Science, University of Helsinki, analyzed US neoconservatism, applying Burke and Jacques Derrida, arguing that an important trait of US national identity is its formation in opposition to the identities of enemies, allies, and "forces of evil" against which its purity is emphasized. Yannick Lahti from the University of Jyväskylä Department of Language and Communication Studies used Burke's guilt-redemption cycle to conduct a rhetorical analysis of campaign and presidential speeches by Donald Trump in 2016–2017.

Burke was introduced to me by a supervisor of my dissertation, Tuija Parvikko. I tackled the rhetorical problem of how Finnish Lutheran priests supported the war effort against the Soviet Union in 1941–1944. I combined Burke's dramatistic pentad and the notion of dialectical substance to examine how the clerical rhetoric transformed when the military-political situation changed. I used Burkean notions of entelechy, mortification, and the temporizing of essence to tease out the nuances of wartime spiritual rhetoric (Tilli, "The Continuation War").

Going to a Classroom with KB

"How am I ever going to be able to teach this?!" was my first thought after I agreed to give a methodological course based on my dissertation. I have always been interested in methods of rhetorical criticism, but teaching Burkean concepts seemed a formidable challenge. I defended my dissertation in October 2012, and in the same fall I embarked on pedagogical studies to obtain an adult educator's diploma. Thus, the KB course functioned as a "laboratory" for developing my academic teaching skills.

The course I taught in fall 2012 and spring 2013 was titled Kenneth Burke and Rhetoric as Symbolic Action. According to my knowledge, it was the first course in Finland dedicated solely to Burkean rhetoric. In fall 2012, eight graduate students attended the course, while twelve participated the next year. Since then, I have utilized portions of the Burke course several times in teaching introductory courses in rhetoric.

At the time I was getting familiar with Burke's writings pertaining to pedagogy, and I took some of the points discussed in "Linguistic Approach to Problems of Education" ("LAPE") as guidelines for my course development. First, language use is a mode of action, not merely semantic description. For students of political science this means a recognition of the fact that language use and power are inseparable. Words and other symbols induce attitudes, define, express, and exhort. They establish various kinds of orders with different hierarchies. Physical reality, in turn, is always endowed with various kinds of symbolic meanings. For instance, before an army advances or police use force, symbols have been used and misused, and even the setting of a table can be interpreted in many ways. In a word, language as such has a political dimension.

Second, the primary interest does not lie in detecting whether a statement or claim is true or false. Rather, we analyze the relationships prevailing among the key terms of a given text. Thus, the focus is on Burke's seemingly simple question: what is involved when we *say* what people are doing and why they are doing it? (*GM* xv). Consequently, "linguistic skepticism," a wariness toward the symbolicity inherent in language, should not only sharpen kinds of perception that are valuable to the manipulating of symbols; it should also contribute to the study of linguistic tactics in a realm where purely rhetorical devices overlap upon a realm of nonverbal materiality, as with the pronouncements by politicians, diplomats, and editors, whose use of purely symbolic resources is backed by organizational or bureaucratic forces ("LAPE" 294).

The five-credit course I developed had sessions for identification, dramatism, god-terms, the guilt-redemption cycle, and cluster analysis. The first part included five lectures accompanied by exercises on the given topic. Each lecture's theme included a text by Burke and a commentary or an application. For example, for the pentad, we studied excerpts from *A Grammar of Motives*, David Blakesley's *The Elements of Dramatism*, and an article by Michael Overington. After these lectures, students worked alone or with a colleague for four weeks on the topic of their choosing. The assignment included two parts. First, the students were required to write a ten-page analysis using a Burkean method discussed in class. The topic was to be chosen freely. This period included at least one meeting with me, although more guidance was available if needed. Second, I applied a form of the "pedagogic practice of debating" ("LAPE" 287): The students had to present their paper to the group in a seminar session and respond to critical comments by a designated "opponent," a devil's advocate so to speak, in order to help bring the coursework to fruition (see Burke, *PLF* 181). Consequently, each student had the role of a presenter and an opponent. After seminar sessions, students then had a week to finalize their papers before turning them in for evaluation. Assessment of students was based on classroom activity and their course assignment.

Teaching the Pentad in Finnish

The theme of my lecture on the dramatistic pentad was the famous quotation from William Shakespeare's play *As You Like It*: "All the world's a stage, / And all the men and women merely players: / They have their exits and their entrances; / And one man in his time plays many parts" (2.7.145–49). Accordingly, I pointed out that Burke claimed that symbolic action resembles a drama on stage, and it can be understood in terms of roles, acts, scenes, scripts, stages, conflicts, and resolutions.

Because the students were in political science, I introduced them to a way of perceiving politics as drama. Politics takes place in front of people, on the public stage; therefore, it is vital to understand the power of perception and the way people, things, and actions *seem to be*. Drawing on Hannah Arendt, I stressed the importance of common experience. Appearance, that is, something that is seen and heard by others as well as by us, constitutes human reality. This "in-between" is where politics takes place, Arendt argued. Consequently, symbolic action is more than the words and acts of public figures: in the drama of politics, watching or following "the play" of these figures is also symbolic action because watching inevitably leads the political audience to an assessment of its meaning and importance, which in turn promotes the next level of action. Because language is *action*, not representation of action, we need a proper way to approach the human drama of the political scene, and that is "dramatism" (Burke, "LAPE" 271; see Rountree, "Revisiting").

I then started teaching the dramatistic pentad with a discussion of the concept of *motive* in Burke's thought. In general, a situation derives its character from the entire framework of interpretation by which we assess it. Differences in our ways of comprehending a situation are expressed subjectively as differences in our assignment of motive. I particularly stressed that motives are linguistic constructs used to make actions understandable: they tell how a person conceives his or her situation and acts according to it (Burke, *PC* 10–16, 18, 25, 31–36, 150). For instance, here in Finland, Minister of Finance Jyrki Katainen stated in 2008 that the financial crisis was "the winter war of economy," thus comparing the situation to the famous Winter War of 1939–1940, which Finland fought against the Soviet Union. The assessment motivated Katainen's rhetoric further: he even compared critique from the opposition to the infamous "Terijoki government," a short-lived puppet government established and recognized only by the Soviet Union during the war. After facing fierce criticism, the minister apologized that he had likened legitimate parliamentary opposition to treason (Yleisradio). The example showed the students how the Minister of Finance had conceived the situation and constructed the motives of his political opponents accordingly—and how he had to reassess his rhetorical interpretation.

In a word, motive is a configuration of the elements of dramatic action in a given case (Rountree, "Instantiating the Law" 4). I used Burke's famous passage that a rounded statement about motives "must have some word that names the act (names what took place, in thought or deed), and another that names the scene (the background of the act, the situation in which it occurred); also, you must indicate what person or kind of person (agent) performed the act, what means or instruments he used (agency), and the purpose" (*GM* xv). As Burke points out, although there may be strong disagreement about, for example, the purposes behind a given act or about the character of the person who did it, any complete statement about motives will offer *some* kind of answers to these five questions: what was done, when/where it was done, who did it, how they did it, and why (xv.) Attitude was also included as the "how" or manner of symbolic action (443). We discussed the terms at a general level because we would later examine them in more detail in classroom exercises. A formulation by Clarke Rountree summarized the issue nicely for pedagogical purposes: the grammar of motives is universal in describing those general, formal relationships but not the particular content they will carry ("Revisiting").

At this point I encountered the first challenge. It was, ironically, language: how to translate Burkean concepts into Finnish without losing their original intent and flexibility? For example, the word *agency* in English has an organic connection with the *agent*. In Finnish, however, the most common translation of the term, *väline*, refers exclusively to an inanimate tool or instrument. Moreover, the etymology of the Finnish term emphasizes the difference between the instrument and the person using it: the root "väli-" denotes a gap or a distance. In this way, the connection between agent and agency present in the Burkean conceptual apparatus is diminished in the Finnish language.

My solution was to use the original English terms with explanations in Finnish. Although it required more work than using only Finnish, it helped the students get used to searching for points of uncertainty and transformation right from the start. We had a discussion in which I explained my choice to the students, and none of them objected to the bilingual policy.

I also believe that the selection of texts examined in class is crucial when one is teaching a thinker whose work has not been translated. The case studies introduced function as a barker, drawing in students in a way that even a good translation cannot. In addition to their topicality, I chose my text samples because they showed clearly how different root terms function differently in rhetorical motivation. In general, and in retrospect based on my experiences of teaching Burke's ideas in a language other than English, my estimation is that a course including several Burkean concepts and their application is not suitable for undergraduate students whose native language is not English. If an undergraduate course were to be held, it would be best, I would suggest, to organize it around one theme or concept.

After introducing the pentad as a whole and examining the individual terms, I moved on to ratios between them. We spent a considerable amount of time on Burke's insight that there is implied a coherent "dramatistic ratio" between any two given terms. According to the logic of dramatic coherence, for example, certain kinds of acts and agents imply corresponding means and ends just as certain kinds of scenes call forth certain actions. Although every selection of terms amounts to an attempt to locate an act's motivational substance, we must at the same time rely on the other terms of the pentad, since one cannot produce a development that uses all the terms at once, yet each term provides a part of the context by which the other is defined (Burke, *GM* 403, 503–17; Crusius 27–30). At the time when the course was held, there was an ongoing public discussion of measures carried out by different states while waging a "war against terrorism." I used the discussion to illustrate the terministic relationship among the pentadic terms. For example, expectation or even acceptance of exceptional measures is inherent in a declaration of a state of exception. By the same token, it is implied that such a scene needs authorized agents. I was referring to the United States and the Patriot Act of 2001, but a student was quick to point out that in the 1930s in Finland the so-called anticommunist laws gave the president and the police exceptional powers in order to curtail communist influence. A lively discussion ensued, and after it we were able to formulate in pentadic terms the motivational constellation present in the examples: drawing on the scene–act or scene–agent ratio, there is implicit in the quality of a scene the quality of the action that is to take place within it and the character or status of the agents carrying out the action.

After ratios, we moved on to root terms. The pentad can be applied when examining dominant terms that arise in different sections or phases of a text or discourse. In such a situation the focus is on which of the competing pentadic terms is primary (Wess 174). By isolating one term at a time, one is able to use it as a synecdochic key to the whole item under study and to reveal the main rhetorical source of motivation. Such root terms reveal the element by which the substance of any given discourse is generated, with the other terms having a role in relation to this term (149).

During the student discussion, one group made an astute observation in relation to Finnish politics. It seemed to them that in Finnish political rhetoric it is economic necessities that are often used to construct the proposed course of action as the only one possible. In such rhetoric, scene (for example the economic situation or EU demands) is the element that forcefully structures the given discourse by shaping our understanding of the other terms. In contemporary economic rhetoric, the economy functions as a scene that demands certain kinds of acts, which usually consist of cuts to social security benefits as the only viable policy and endow legitimacy to political actors whose platform is in line with the situation. Based on our discussion, I emphasized that for political scientists it is important to recognize that scenic rhetoric is useful because it creates a perspective from which the audience will view the situation as coercive and act accordingly (King 169). Here it is easily forgotten that the initial definition drawing on scenic rhetoric is itself *an act*.

Burke's likening of the pentadic terms to the fingers, which in their extremities are distinct from one another but merge in the palm of the hand, turned out to be helpful in explaining the flexibility and the interconnectedness of the terms. By moving from one finger to another without a leap via the palm, one can detect a new course while respecting the common "ancestry" of the terms (*GM* xxii). I brought a golf ball to class to demonstrate the hand metaphor. The ball represented the phenomenon that was being examined. Picking it up with two fingers at a time illustrated the functioning of pentadic ratios: holding the ball in the middle of the palm offered an overall view but using two fingers it could be scrutinized more closely. In a similar way, using one finger to point at the ball resembled the functioning of a root term.

Finally, I showed the students how scope and circumference could be used in relation to the pentad. For example, scene can be defined as local, historical, or even eschatological, and the choice of "circumference" for a scene, its seriousness or scope, affects the interpretation of the act and the agents. Here I used a dramatic piece of clerical war rhetoric from my dissertation, in which I analyzed how Lutheran priests contributed rhetorically to the war effort of the Finnish state against the Soviet Union in World War II. The war was framed by a Finnish Lutheran chaplain in scenic terms as an event of apocalyptic scope that would, after the inevitable divine judgment, transform the remaining world into something drastically better. By the same token, the animosity and Satanic qualities of the enemy-counteragent were stressed. My example text seemed to work well, possibly because World War II is an important part of Finnish national identity. It is also often used for assessing contemporary politics, for example, in terms of a "debt of honor," whereby a policy or a decision is justified based on a claim that in this way the present generation pays its respect to war veterans. Thus the debt of honor emerges as the foundation of an authoritative symbolic order whose logic is that the course of action suggested by the speaker functions as payment for the "service" of the fallen ones. I also pointed out that the agent is not necessarily an individual human being; it can be "the nation," "the party," or even God, as is characteristic of religious discourse. I emphasized that Burkean scope and circumference are important tools for political scientists because they can be used to analyze how the limits of political action are drawn in a given text. For instance, "economy" is often constructed as an all-encompassing scene outside the reach of democratic decision-making acts.

Before the students conducted their own pentadic analyses, we had a summarizing discussion of the pentad I had presented. Critical dialogue is an essential element of my pedagogical philosophy, and thus I asked each student to describe their impressions about the pentad in their own words as honestly as possible. To my relief no one confessed to being completely at a loss! Instead, most of them admitted that Burke's ideas were interesting and refreshing, if also frustrating, because knowing how and where to start seemed difficult. So, we ventured further with that thought guiding us.

Pentadic Exercises

Classroom exercises were based on texts pertaining to current cultural, social, or political phenomena. The part of the course that dealt with the pentad included two examples of political reactions—two acts of description—to the July 2011 massacre in Norway perpetrated by far-right terrorist Anders Breivik. In the attack, seventy-seven people were killed and over three hundred injured, most of them participants of a social-democratic summer camp on a small island called Utøya. The second text in particular illustrates how the pentad can be used to detect points of ambiguity. As Burke (*GM* xviii–xix) stresses, the purpose of the pentad (with the hexadic addendum) is not to dispose of uncertainties but to identify "the strategic spots" at which ambiguities among competing motives necessarily arise. This is a point that needed to be emphasized regularly. The first example was from a statement by a Finnish historian and a peace activist:

> The massacre conducted by the Norwegian Anders Breivik in July 2011 brought right-wing populism and explosively grown hate speech to wider attention. Breivik is not a mentally deranged individual with his bombs and automatic weapons. He is a product of contemporary society. The present poll ratings of right-wing populist parties reveal a lot of the current political development. . . . Finland's political field was "normalized" in spring 2011 when the [populist] True Finns got the largest victory in the history of Finnish parliamentary elections. The party increased their support [from 4.05 percent in 2007] to 19 percent. (Jokisalo, trans. by author)

First, we assigned initial meaning to each of the pentadic terms: the scene is society ridden with right-wing populism, the act is the mass murder, the agent is Anders Breivik, the agency is bombs and weapons, and the purpose is to get rid of ideological opponents. The last one required some "collective thinking" before we could arrive at this conclusion, based on the writer's use of the word "massacre."

Next, we detected the dominant term of the text. In this case the root term was scene. The second step was to examine carefully how the root term functions. Importantly for political scientists, the example above illustrates how scenic rhetoric can be used to shift the focus from an individual person to the whole society, ideology, or the political situation. Based on the scenic emphasis, the writer claims that the real problem is right-wing populism, not the lone gunman. As a student observed in class, in such rhetoric, the responsibility of the perpetrator is significantly diminished, although this most likely was not the aim of the writer. I pointed out that scene is often so powerful a root term that the situation dominates over the people encompassed within it (Birdsell 268, 270–71)—in this case, Finnish right-wing politics over the Norwegian Breivik himself.

Detecting pentadic ratios and their possible transformations was the third step. Based on the scene-agent ratio, we examined the perpetrator through the pentadic scene as an extension of its qualities. We also noted that, by the logic of the scene-agency ratio, Breivik is in fact relegated into a mere "product" of populism. At this point I generalized our observations: scenic emphasis is common to ideological rhetoric in which human beings are treated as mere cogs in a machine. I also underlined that our initial difficulty with assigning meaning to purpose was connected to scene overshadowing all other terms.

The text we analyzed also includes a critique and a warning pertaining to (at that time) recent election results and the spread of right-wing populism in Finland. As a matter of fact, students were shocked to realize that by the logic of act-scene ratio, the speaker was holding each voter responsible for expanding the potentially dangerous scene by implying that tragedies resembling the one in Norway are probable also in Finland because of "the normalization" of right-wing parties in the political scene—and in any society in which such an ideology has gained a foothold. In this way voters are in fact scapegoated. I also pointed out that the text is a good example of how the pentad can be used to tease out rhetorical ambiguities and transformations: via dialectical transformation, an extremely tragic event, its victims, and even the perpetrator turn easily into an agency in a political struggle.

While teaching the pentadic ratios for the first time, I noticed that the students were indeed able to make astute observations, but "translating" them into dramatism presented a challenge. Students could often detect act, scene, and agent as distinct elements, but developing the observations towards expressing how they function as ratios was difficult at first. For example, "the populist scene" in the text was easy to name, but terministic relationships and the fact that they flow both ways was harder. That a scene may contain acts, but an act may create a scene for further acts (such as voting creating a political scene) needed my assistance. Thus, I gave extra attention to helping them word pentadic ratios in my pedagogical talk.

The second example was from a right-wing Finnish political activist who was also a member of the parliament at the time, representing a populist party:

> The act is heinous, and I fully condemn it. But I am not surprised that it took place in Oslo. You see, ALL (100%) perpetrators guilty of [dozens] of rape attacks are immigrants/foreigners outside the Western world. It is thus justified to think that the whole event is a result of side effects caused by flawed immigration policy. It does not fully explain the bloodbath, but I believe that it is an important reason. The guy [Breivik] went nuts when

he reached his limit. . . . Paraphrasing Wille Rydman [a conservative politician] one could say this despite the fact that extreme Muslims, online speech, too-lax gun laws, women who will not sleep with nerds and even free masons have all been found to be behind the event. I have claimed that too-lenient immigration policy had an effect. In the end, the real guilty party is the deranged psychopath who pulled the trigger. (Hirvisaari, trans. by author)

With this text, the students quickly noticed the rhetorical ambivalence. Initially, it states that immigration policy had an important role in motivating the massacre. Drawing on a spatial understanding of politics, the policy is treated in scenic terms. It encompasses actions and agents. However, toward the end of the text, agent emerges as the root term. It renders the scene less oppressive and makes the qualities of the agent decisive, in this case the mental condition of Anders Breivik. On the other hand, changing the root term from scene to agent is facilitated by referring to the oppressive quality of the scene, which had pushed "the guy to reach his limit." Consequently, there is a rhetorical tightrope strung between immigration policy and the perpetrator, between scene and agent. The scene-agent ratio is again here at work; however, now the scene is "a flawed immigration policy," whereas in the first example the ratio was the same but right-wing populism functioned as the scene. The political ideology that the writers oppose had caused the agent to perpetrate the crime, with the implication that the ones who had crafted such heinous policies were also to be held responsible. By the same token, it is implied that the crime was almost a legitimate reaction to the ill-guided policy. There is thus a scene–agent–act cycle at work in both texts.

Three points emerged in the concluding discussion about what the students had learned about the pentad. First of all, the pentad offered the students a nimble way to bring to the fore how rhetorical motives are connected to ideological differences. For example, in the first text analyzed in class, the emphasis on scene facilitated critique of right-wing populism, while in the latter text, agent was used to turn the focus away from such scenic considerations. The second important insight was related to ambiguity among competing motives. For instance, by teasing out some of the implications, it could be noted that in the first text the initial scene-agent and scene-act ratios were in fact reversed: the poor choices made by voters in the Nordic countries had created the scene that, in turn, had "produced" the mass murderer. Third, the pentad showed how human beings could be presented in a dehumanizing way as a political scene or agency, instead of being agents who act. In the latter text, immigrants constituted a dangerous scene, whereas, in the former, Anders Breivik was an agency or a function of a populist ideology, almost without his own motives.

Independent Analyses

I taught the other Burkean concepts in a similar manner. After that the students chose a topic that they worked on independently for four weeks; then we began our three seminar sessions and our pedagogical debates. In these debates, each student presented their analyses for critique. These class debates showed me that students had learned to conduct Burkean analysis more than satisfactorily. I particularly enjoyed their observations about the ways in which various types of agents were constructed in texts they had chosen: "the nation" or "the society" as humanized agent emerged as a characteristic feature of Finnish political rhetoric. On the other hand, the students occasionally still struggled with teasing out ambiguities. For instance, I needed to help bring to fruition an observation that, in texts that demanded that "the nation" should act in a certain way, the humanized, collective agent was often in fact an agency for the speaker's purpose—and it would, in fact, function as a further scene for ordinary citizens. In addition, I had to occasionally emphasize that the object of analysis is the construction of motives in a given text, instead of making another interpretation of the factual matter.

The students had a week to finalize their work based on peer and teacher feedback. The course essays included a variety of topics ranging from a cluster analysis of Peter Kropotkin's anarchist writings to a logological examination of war rhetoric by George W. Bush and a pentadic analysis of Finnish economic rhetoric. They indicated that the students were able to apply Burke's ideas on their own. Even more delightfully, four of them used Burke successfully in their master's theses. To conclude on a high political note, Finland probably is the first country, at least in Europe, where there is a Burkean member in the state parliament: a participant of the 2012 Burke course won a seat in the Finnish parliament in 2019 elections. Perhaps we will also see Burkean politics in the future!

Conclusion

The cornerstones of my pedagogical creed are based on critical pedagogy (see for example Paulo Freire) and Burke's approach to symbolic action. Most often we learn by observing, usually by seeing and hearing. We learn best, however, by doing together. My pedagogical thinking builds on an application of identification and division: The role of a teacher is to question and to build bridges, and I am a bridge builder when I facilitate the finding of points of contact (similar or dissimilar) between different experiences and aspects, or—as in the pentad course—between observations and their theoretical wording. In addition, I am a questioner when I ask questions that aim at opening new perspectives, often by incongruity. As Burke notes, there is little difference between textual analysis and social analysis: "what equals what," "what follows what," and the accompanying exhortations are important questions in analyzing any phenomena—"human quandaries in general" ("LAPE" 275, 170). In this way, we are hopefully able to understand that we all suffer from occupational psychoses and that "a way of seeing is also a way of not seeing" (*PC* 49).

Although the academic world is constantly required to justify its apparent usefulness, the aim of my course was not to prepare students for the market. Instead, it was a step in developing a critical attitude toward rhetoric and the use of power—in other words, "a technique of preparatory withdrawal, the institutionalizing of an attitude that one should be able to recover at crucial moments, all along the subsequent way" ("LAPE" 273). Or in Paulo Freire's terms, it was action and critical reflection.

I believe that Kenneth Burke offers an important tool kit for political scientists. The dramatistic pentad in particular is vital for teasing out ambiguities inherent in rhetoric. It is these points of uncertainty and transformation that give rise to the substance of the "political barnyard," namely argumentation and struggle. The pentad shows in a fruitful manner how motives are created rhetorically in different ways in relation to one single event and what kind of implications ensue from competing rhetorical constructions. Importantly, the pentad helps us to understand and express in an analytical manner how different rhetorical strategies, such as scenic rhetoric or emphasis on the agent, can be persuasive. For these reasons I find teaching Burke to future political scientists valuable, even if it requires switching between two languages.

Parsing of the Pentad Handout

From Ann George

The Pentad and the Paradox of Substance in *A Grammar of Motives*
(aka dialectic) (aka intrinsic vs. extrinsic problem [p. 23])

- acts or agents can become scenes (7): other characters or past actions become part of the context that motivates action
- scene can be an aspect of agent (10): if hero's state of mind creates the scene; or if body is considered part of the agent's "properties," "as with a dwelling that a man had ordered built in strict accordance with his own private specifications, or as theologians see 'the body' as the dwelling place of 'soul'"
- circularity of terms (19): if an agent acts in keeping with her nature [act-agent ratio], she may change the scene [scene-act ratio] to make it "fit" her nature [scene-agent ratio]
- BUT we are only capable of partial acts, acts that but partially represent us and that produce but partial transformations in other pentadic elements—perfect fit between all elements (esp. act, agent, scene) = static, Edenic symmetry
- the paradox of substance: agent=actor, mover BUT the agent-scene ratio implies that the "passive" agent is motivated, moved by external forces (40)
- therefore, "to consider an act in terms of its grounds is to consider it in terms of what it is not, namely, in terms of motive that, in acting upon the active, would make it passive"
- "paradoxical tendency to slight the term *act*, in the very featuring of it" (65) (that is, as when we try to describe the act by looking elsewhere—at agent, scene, etc.) the intrinsic (act) and extrinsic (other pentadic terms) can change places. See also comments on contextual definition (p. 23–24)
- there's a sense in which an act is "undramatistic"—that is, unmotivated by external factors; act as magical or arbitrary or self-motivating: "there could be novelty only if there were likewise a locus of motivation within the act itself, a newness

not already present in elements classifiable under any of the other four headings" (65). For example: the act of writing may bring up problems and discoveries intrinsic to the act (67)

Some questions and/or answers to think about:

Q1: Given the pentad, how can we understand a good character in a bad scene?

    A. Each act/agent inhabits a variety of scenes, depending on what circumference a critic chooses to look at. "Who is to say, once and for all, which of these circumferences is to be selected as the motivation of his act?" (83–84)

Q2: But where does that leave the critic? Relativism?

    A. the selection of circumference = an act of faith (84) and depends on purpose (86)

    B. Ultimate values in GM = "the ideals of tolerance and resignation to bureaucratic requirements implicit in the structure of modern industry" (318)—moves to tolerance and humility

    C. A terminology of conceptual analysis, if it is not to lead to misrepresentation, must be constructed in conformity with a representative anecdote—whereas anecdotes 'scientifically' selected for reductive purposes are not representative" (510).

Q3: If these terms so easily melt into one another, how do we handle them? How will they be useful to us? Are they tied to an ethical basis that enables us to use them for evaluation?

Q4: KB claims that "the ambiguity of substance affords a major resource of rhetoric" (51). Resource to do what? How so? Examples?

    A. SEE his examples on p. 52—they seem to imply that ambiguity is a way to "legitimately" lie or be vague; of course, that implies that the pentad gives critics tools to expose the lies

III. Equipment for Living

Photo 3. Kenneth Burke delivering a lecture at (then) Central Washington State College, ca. 1967. Photo by John Foster appears courtesy of Dr. James E. Brooks Library, Archives and Special Collections; Central Washington University Faculty Papers, John Foster; Central Washington University.

10 Attitudes toward a Historiographic Seminar on Burke

Ann George

> *Training graduate students to engage with Burke in his rhetorical scene.*

I taught my first graduate seminar on Kenneth Burke in spring 1998 as a shiny, new assistant professor, barely six months after I'd defended my dissertation on *Permanence and Change* (*PC*). If ever a course design was rotten with perfection, it was that one. The drive was toward maximum exposure—a quick march through (or over) Burke's major texts, at a slightly more intense pace than the Burke seminar I'd taken as a Penn State graduate student. We read a book per week, starting with *The Complete White Oxen* and *Towards a Better Life* and ending with *Language as Symbolic Action*, plus a smattering of criticism, archival letters, and shorter magazine articles I'd found during my dissertation research. Still, the seminar was more or less a success: students were game, took up Burkean methods in dissertations, and at least one had fond memories of the class. When I taught it again nine years later, it had been approved as a separate course: ENGL 80603—Seminar in Kenneth Burke. I'd abandoned the "intellectual marathon" in favor of a deep dive into fewer texts. I've taught the seminar three more times since then, most recently in spring 2016; in addition, I regularly teach a seminar on modern rhetorical theory, which features two or three Burke texts. Every iteration of teaching Burke's ideas is built on the same basic premise: that writing theory is a rhetorical act—a purposeful intervention by a particular agent (along with co- and counteragents) into a specific cultural scene. So, although in my teaching I typically use the broader language of the rhetorical parlor when contextualizing—rhetoricizing—Burke's work, what I'm essentially doing in every class is a dramatistic analysis of his texts. That is, I teach students to use Burkean methodology to study Burke.

To what end? I want to move them beyond thinking of Burke as a box to check when they prepare for their comprehensive exams. I hope they will see Burke's theory not merely as something to study, but as something to use—today, in their ordinary lives. So, I'm not primarily in the business of training students to become Burke scholars but to think of themselves as scholars, teachers, *and* citizens who could recognize opportunities to use Burkean theory or methods and feel themselves capable of doing so (Bryan Crable presents another syllabus for this approach in his essay in this volume). Ultimately, I try to hook students on Burke's larger civic mission: education for citizenship, training people to enact the art of living (which necessarily includes working toward the purification of war and establishing social justice), to enact what I've called in my *Critical Companion* a "critical civic pedagogy" (George, *Kenneth Burke's* 11). In this chapter I offer, first, a general discussion of how I pursue those goals followed by a more detailed look at each class session.

Pedagogical Approaches and Methods

Several pedagogical imperatives follow directly from my understanding of theory as a rhetorical act, a cultural intervention. First, we read texts chronologically to place them more clearly in shifting cultural conversations. Second, because my expertise lies in 1930s–1950s scenes, acts, and agents, the course privileges Burke's early texts. More importantly, students need a great deal of information to effectively rhetoricize Burke's texts. Students supply some of this material in contextualizing oral presentations, but it takes a large seminar to make this material go very far, and I end up providing most myself. Supplemental archival documents and correspondence, forgotten historical events and political groups, photos, videos, book reviews, contemporary writers and their texts, Burke's primary periodical publishing venues and news sources—it's a lot for an instructor to compile and for students to absorb, and it sometimes threatens to overwhelm the course—or me. There's an important corollary here, an issue in Burke scholarship that I explicitly present to students: the question of how to represent and study Burke. If he is "the eccentric hermit of Andover farm," close readings of key terms and passages may suffice; if he is a public intellectual and educator, rhetoricizing and archival study are in order (George, "Review" 32). Thus, there's also an explicit historiographic element to the course.

    I've also come to realize that my goal to have students sign on to Burke's civic mission means that I need to make Burke, in students' terms, "relatable." I strive to replace their vision of Burke as imposing Theorist with my vision of him as a fully human, three-dimensional figure. As I think about it, this is just how I got hooked on Burke—not by reading his theory but by reading his archival correspondence and getting to know something of him as a person. On the first day, I show the Chapin Foundation video "KB: A Conversation with Kenneth Burke," as well as photos of his Andover, New Jersy house; his home office; and the "pond"—to locate Burke in a personal space. I've upped the use of shorter, often understudied pieces from the *New Republic* and *Nation*, which are often more accessible than major works and occasionally hilarious (and if students recognize these magazines, they get a sense of Burke's stature). Mostly, students are eager for whatever personal information I can share. They like hearing that Burke nicknamed his five children after parts of the pentad. That he composed music almost every day. That he kept a large garden to feed his family and chopped his own firewood. That he hosted weekend bashes for city friends (among them many modernist luminaries), who shared their latest poems or stories, bawdy songs, and large quantities of the Burkes' homemade rice wine. They like hearing about his writing process and, even more so, that he had bad writing days. They are stunned to learn that Burke got fan mail and that *Permanence and Change* was sold in Macy's. (*New Republic* readers could mail in a coupon and a dollar to get their copy. I show them a xerox of the page.) Even the view of Burke as a writer with a purpose—and, hence, of theory with a purpose, not just free-floating thought experiments—encourages them to engage with his texts more seriously. In short, I serve up what functions for students as a series of perspectives by incongruity on the aloof theory-head who glares at them from the covers of his books. Sometimes there's a tremendous payoff: students who form a personal connection to Burke, who humanize and *play* with him and his ideas, are more likely to commit to his civic mission (see figure 1).

Figure 1. Students at play with Burke. Whiteboard drawing in shared graduate student office by TCU students in 2016 Burke seminar. Photo by author.

Additionally, because I so clearly remember my own struggles with Burke and because many students see the ability to "do" theory as an innate talent, not a learned practice, I offer them the kind of support tools more often associated with undergraduate theory classes: reading questions, worksheets, and handouts. We often apply Burke's theory to current events, and I'll grab any pop culture references I can to explain key terms. (Not necessarily *current* pop culture, though: *Star Trek: The Next Generation* and *Buffy the Vampire Slayer* became unlikely touch points in the 2016 Burke seminar, when several participants disclosed that they owned box sets of these oldies. I'm hoping my Wakanda references will hold up a few more years.) We talk repeatedly about effective reading strategies for Burkean theory, particularly knowing, as one student put it, when to "read intently," zooming in to study important passages, and when to "read softly," zooming out and letting Burke's characteristic strings of disconnected examples flow over you, rather than getting bogged down (James).

Finally, because I hope students will take up Burke in their research, pedagogy, or civic lives, we spend a significant amount of course time focusing on Burke as a methodologist—someone who built analytical tools that would enable people to become better critics of policy, institutions, and the cultural pieties that Burke argued are "so ingrained in our speech" and our habits of being that they have become "as natural as breathing" ("Reading While You Run" 36). We try out, individually and in small groups, perspective by incongruity, as well as pentadic and terministic screen analyses. Similarly, we examine methods used in Burkean scholarship, including pedagogical accounts and my own work as an archival researcher and historiographer.

ASSIGNMENTS AND ACTIVITIES

Because several of my colleagues regularly assign multimodal projects, my seminar assignments are purposely quite traditional: eight brief reading responses posted to our e-learning platform before class so students have articulated—and shared with each other—questions and ideas about the day's text; an oral presentation that offers biographical, historical, or cultural contextualization for Burke's work; and a four-part, scaffolded seminar project (brief topic proposal; annotated bibliography; formal, conference-style project proposal; and article-length research essay or web text). Students' research topics range from *Permanence and Change* as an anti-eugenics text to Burke and the New Critics to terministic screens in environmental rhetoric to using Burke in feminist pedagogy to Burke and optical science.

I've sometimes swapped out parts of the final project (a conference presentation for the bibliography, for instance). My first Burke seminar culminated in a mini conference during the final exam period; seminar members, including myself, presented in three panels. During one serendipitous semester, another local university ran a Burke seminar concurrently with mine, so we organized an all-day, public symposium (complete with keynote address by Gregory Clark), in which students and instructors from both classes presented their work. In another seminar iteration, students were especially passionate about using Burke in their undergraduate teaching, so I adapted the "2MinuteThinker" video project into a "2MinuteTeacher" video, in which students explained one key Burkean concept to an undergraduate audience, honoring Burke's commitment to civic pedagogy.

Seminar meetings typically begin with setting the scene: contextualizing information is provided via either student oral presentations or my own archival documents or cultural research. To foreground students' interests and needs—to give them some control over the day's agenda—the next step is always listing their questions on the board; these guide much of our discussion. Sometimes I have students share a passage they found particularly significant or freewrite about confusions or work in small groups to start discussion of key concepts by choosing and explaining several passages. One of my favorite in-class activities has become sharing our drawings of key terms, especially paired or related terms such as the poetic orientation and the comic corrective or semantic and poetic meaning (see figure 2). I started this practice to appeal to visual learners, and it's taught me two things: (1) trying to draw concepts—that is, make them concrete—shows you precisely what's not coming clear, and (2) some of us can draw an understanding of terms we can't yet articulate.

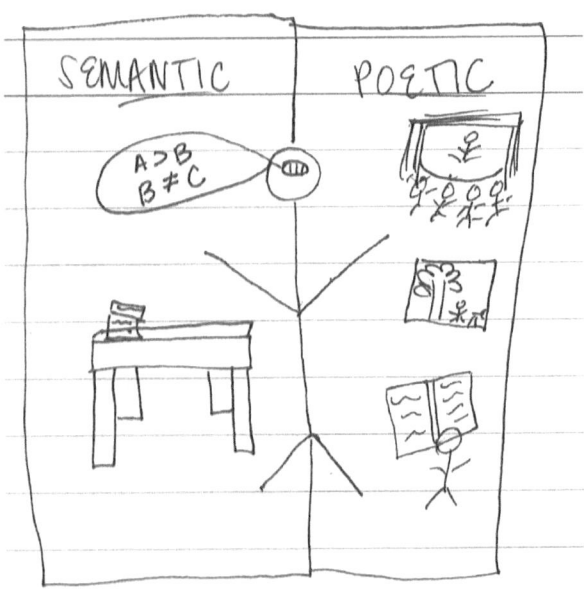

Figure 2. Student drawing of semantic and poetic meaning used by permission of Megan Poole.

Week-by-Week View

Week One: Introduction to Burke and the Seminar

In addition to the usual syllabus overview and getting-to-know-you moves, I want to accomplish two things in this opening session: (1) introduce students to Burke, and (2) create a productive attitude for our study of his work. To achieve the first goal, I provide basic biographical information and theoretical interests and show the Chapin Foundation video (interviews of Burke by his grandson, Harry Chapin), which students enjoy and which helps to both humanize Burke and give them a voice to hear in their heads when they read. Then we read and discuss several short stories from *The White Oxen and Other Stories*, which immediately unsettles some of their assumptions: this highly experimental, *literary* Burke is not at all who they've been expecting, so there's a perspective by incongruity from the get-go. To get at the second goal, I explicitly address the intimidation factor, in part by telling stories about how I came to Burke and my own struggles with his texts. I'm an expert but one who vividly remembers how it felt to be at sea in Burkean waters—or how it *feels*: even rereading texts I often teach and write about, I'm surprised at how many passages I can only shrug at (I share this with students), so I act as coach and cheerleader and explain why Burke is worth the effort.

Week Two: Counter-Statement (CS)

Criticism

- Clark, *Civic Jazz: American Music and Kenneth Burke on the Art of Getting Along* (skim or skip chapters on jazz—much of Ch. 3 and most of Ch. 5)
- Selzer, *Kenneth Burke in Greenwich Village*, Ch. 6

Instructor Contextualization

1930s Literary Wars: Burke-Malcolm Cowley and Burke-Allen Tate correspondence (online), Granville Hicks's review of *Counter-Statement*, Burke's response.

We focus on how the title describes the book's function as a counterstatement to high modernists like Tate, to literary Marxists like Hicks, and to itself—since the essays revisit, elaborate, qualify, and counter each other. For wary students who hope to pin Burke down, *Counter-Statement* is continually vexing, which makes it a great place to start our study of Burke—to begin getting students comfortable with his "undisciplined" theorizings, his deliberate sowing of ambiguity, and positions that shift as Burke learns and/or responds to different scenes, and, ultimately, to understand those qualities as the source of his theoretical power. Selzer reinforces the text as a complex counterstatement; Clark connects *Counter-Statement*'s concept of *form* as a rhetoricized aesthetic experience to Burke's civic mission to build and sustain democratic culture and, in so doing, Clark highlights Burke's continued relevance.

Week Three: Working the Burkean Archive

Archival packet of unpublished manuscripts: "Men of Leisure," "The Principles of Wise Spending," and "A Sure Solution for the Problem of Armaments"

Criticism

- Anderson and Enoch, *Burke in the Archives*. Read Introduction, Ch. 12, and a chapter of your choice. Skim Ch. 1.
- Wible, Scott. "Professor Burke's 'Bennington Project.'" *Rhetoric Society Quarterly*, vol. 38, no. 3, 2008, pp. 259–82.
- George, *Critical Companion*. Pick one: Ch. 4, 5, or 6
- George and Selzer, Ch. 2 (background for next class)

I place this unit early in the semester to encourage students to use archives for course projects. My purpose is to introduce students to the archival turn in rhetorical studies in general and Burke studies in particular, including theories and practices of archival research that range from issues of historiography and representation to finding aids and permissions. Although students know theoretically that archives don't offer unmediated access to "what happened," their questions suggest they haven't yet internalized this premise, so I foreground the researcher's role in archival knowledge making. We follow this up by discussing Burke scholarship that uses archival material, focusing on the kinds of research produced, how scholars make meaning from archival documents, and how they articulate the value of this work. Next, students "become" archival scholars and brainstorm approaches to several unpublished documents, working, first, as a whole class, then in small groups. By the end of class, students have done some theorizing about and analysis of archival research, and they've seen enough of the nuts and bolts of Burke's archives to understand what's involved in such a project—and, perhaps, to see themselves pursuing one. There's an added bonus here that contributes to my larger goal of inspiring further engagement with Burke's civic mission: because I've chosen economic and political satires to study, students are exposed to Burke's wit and his concern as a public intellectual for issues of class, militarism, and quality of life, critiquing some of the same cultural values or institutions they critique.

WEEK FOUR: PERMANENCE AND CHANGE (PC), PARTS I & II, INCLUDING "LOST PASSAGES OF P&C" (ONLINE)

Although I assign Part II for this class, we rarely get beyond setting up context and Part I.

Criticism

- George and Selzer, *Kenneth Burke in the 1930s*, Ch. 3 (for big picture) OR George, *Critical Companion*, Ch. 1 (for help with key terms).

Contextualization

- Burke, "Waste—The Future of Prosperity" (*New Republic*, July 16, 1930, pp. 228–31)
- Tate, "Poetry & Politics" (*New Republic*, Aug. 2, 1933, pp. 308–11)

Oral presentation topics: Communist Party of the USA (CPUSA), Japanese invasion of China, *New Republic*

We approach the text as a proposal argument, using key terms (orientation, piety, trained incapacity) to unpack Burke's claim that a positivistic, mechanistic worldview is the source of cultural disease. Context is fundamental to *Permanence and Change*: the satirical "Waste—The Future of Prosperity" is a hilarious example of Burke's capitalist critique, and Tate's article presents one (proto) New Critical cultural cure that Burke rejects in the text. As I argue in my *Critical Companion*, I understand *Permanence and Change* as part of Burke's *ad bellum purificandum* project; to heighten militarism and systemic cultural violence as central elements of the problem Burke addresses, I read aloud agonized passages from archival documents as Burke contemplates the horrors of the coming world war. Recent stumbling blocks for students include: (1) imagining a time when Americans might take arguments for communism seriously and understanding Burke's approach to communism; (2) appreciating *Permanence and Change* as a groundbreaking text given that much of Burke theorizing—language as ideological and socially constructed and thus constituted by (and constitutive of) networks of power—has become one of the field's foundational assumptions. Additional information about the 1932 and 1936 CPUSA election platforms (short on armed revolution and long on "radical" advocacy for a shorter work week, racial integration, reformed immigration policies, etc.) helps address the first difficulty. The second launches us into discussing, for instance, Burke's theorization of the social text—a way to ground trendy cultural studies programs—and my *Critical Companion* claim that *Permanence and Change* retheorizes both epideictic rhetoric and identity construction in ways that enrich current scholarly conversations.

Week Five: Permanence and Change, Part III

Criticism

- Crusius. "The Question of Kenneth Burke's Identity: And 'Permanence and Change.'" *JAC*, vol.18, no. 3, 1998, pp. 449–61.

Optional: Choose any one for an example of rhetorical criticism using perspective by incongruity:

- Tonn and Endress. "Looking Under the Hood and Tinkering with Voter Cynicism: Ross Perot and 'Perspective by Incongruity.'" *Rhetoric & Public Affairs*, vol. 4, no. 2, 2001, pp. 281–308.
- Demo. "The Guerilla Girls' Comic Politics of Subversion." *Women's Studies in Communication*, vol. 23, no. 2, 2000, pp.133–56.
- Young. "(Re)presenting Gender: Exploring Text-Image Incongruities in Anne Taintor's Artwork." *Women and Language*, vol. 33, no. 1, 2010, pp. 72–93.

Optional for help with terms: George, *Critical Companion* Ch. 2 (metabiology) and Ch. 3 (poetic orientation, art of living, recalcitrance)

Contextualization

- Burke, "Boring from Within" (*New Republic*, Feb. 4, 1931, pp. 326–29)

- Burke, "Reading While You Run" (*New Republic*, Nov. 17, 1937, pp. 36–37)
- Burke, "Revolutionary Symbolism in America" (online)

Oral presentation topics (alternatives to *Permanence and Change*'s proposed cultural cure): First American Writers' Congress; Southern Agrarians, *I'll Take My Stand*; I.A. Richards, *Poetries and Sciences*

We focus on Burke's proposed solution to the technological psychosis: what kind of cultural shift did he hope to engineer and how did he plan to accomplish this reorientation? Burke's proposal for the "good life" consists of a poetic orientation and art of living, ethically grounded by metabiology and perpetually refined via recalcitrance—all extraordinarily challenging concepts. Metabiology makes most sense in tandem with Burke's argument for simplification, so I begin with the archival language I found most helpful: "minimal ethic," "biological imperative." Then we explore how those ideas appear in *Permanence and Change* through the revised language of "nudism" and "rock bottom" thinking (172, 261)—language that signals Burke's attempt to strip things down to the bare essentials: what do people absolutely need to live together well? Students' growing interest in the body has led to interesting discussions of the unlikely choice of embodiment as a site of permanence, Burke's deconstruction of the mind-body binary, and his (likely) ableism. Students get more traction with the art of living than the nebulous-sounding poetic orientation, so we try to make the art of living as concrete as possible: what should we, collectively, become—or do? What attitudes or behaviors does Burke advocate? One added difficulty is that because *Permanence and Change* doesn't fit students' sense of what rhetorical theory looks like, they often read it primarily as cultural critique, missing Burke's argument for an activist rhetoric that pleads with resistant audiences. I, thus, emphasize these rhetorical strategies: perspective by incongruity, graded series, stylistic inducement, and translation, each illustrated in *Permanence and Change* and the three short contextualization essays. Most recently, amidst ongoing mass protests against gender inequality and systemic racism, students are skeptical of Burke's plan to overturn an entrenched dominant culture with what they see as timid rhetorical moves, which launches us into a discussion of just what *are* effective means to create change.

Week Six: Attitudes Toward History (ATH) through p. 215

Criticism
- George and Selzer, Ch. 4
- Hawhee, *Moving Bodies*, Ch. 2.

Oral presentation topics: Burke's relationship with Malcolm Cowley, labor strikes (UAW, US Steel, Longshoremen's Strike [Bloody Thursday], etc.), the Popular Front

Attitudes Toward History is first and foremost a book about critical methodology and attitudes, but it rarely feels that way to first-time readers. Because it proceeds largely by induction, losing students in contestable definitions in "Poetic Categories," minor details of the "Curve of History," and analyses of now unfamiliar or insignificant texts, we attend largely to what Burke *does* rather than what he *says*—or, rather, to passages where he pauses the analysis to tell us what he's doing and why. For example, Burke comments midway through "Poetic Categories" that his "primary purpose" in examining poetic forms is to illustrate how "symbolic structures [are] designed to equip us for confronting given historical or personal situations" (57)—an argument he crystalizes in his 1938 essay "Literature as Equipment for Living." Likewise, students need coaching to understand the "General Nature of Ritual" as an exploration of how *symbolism* functions. Hawhee's argument that Burke enacts a Jamesian mystical methodology—one that values multiple perspectives and attempts to see "around the corner" (*ATH* 222)—both reinforces the text's methodological emphasis and connects Burke's work to current scholarship on the body. One perennial question is how the comic frame deals with true evil (with a Hitler or our own white supremacist institutions), which leads us to discuss the easily overlooked conclusion of "Comic Correctives" where Burke insists that the comic frame isn't passive, that it "should not offer recompense" for intolerable situations but help to alleviate them (175). A second recurring question is the relationship between the poetic orientation and the comic frame—and why Burke seems to have dropped the former. What can he do with—or why does he need—a new term? This question often prompts our first drawing session: depending on time, I ask students to identify a key passage explaining the comic frame, then draw it singly or in relation to the poetic orientation. Students notice, among other things, that the poetic orientation is a vision of (or the scene for) the good life, while the comic frame is the attitude Burke claims is the most effective for analyzing human behavior and persuading audiences. We also discuss Burke's later claim in "Curriculum Criticum," an afterword to the second edition of *Counter-Statement*, that *Permanence and Change* approaches rhetoric as "ideal cooperation" and *Attitudes Toward History* explores rhetorical strategies of "actual human associations" (216).

Week Seven: Attitudes Toward History (finish)

Criticism

- Kastely. "Kenneth Burke's Comic Rejoinder to the Cult of Empire." *College English*, vol. 58, no. 3, 1996, pp. 307–26.

Contextualization

- Burke, "Literature as Equipment for Living" and "Twelve Propositions" (both in *Philosophy of Literary Form*).

Oral presentation topic: Burke and Sidney Hook, *Partisan Review*, reviews of *ATH*. Instructor summarizes reviews of *ATH* if no student presents them.

The "Dictionary of Pivotal Terms" helps us continue discussion of *Attitudes Toward History*, Part III as presenting a methodology to locate, analyze, and modify symbolic attachments. Student favorites include bureaucratization of the imaginative; casuistic stretching; discounting; good life; identity and identification, which deconstructs the single humanist subject ("the so-called 'I' is merely a unique combination of partially conflicting 'corporate we's'" [264]); stealing back and forth of symbols; and symbols of authority. Burke's methodology is designed to counter superficial, scientist Marxist analysis and rhetoric, which fail to acknowledge that symbols are "'vessels' with unchartable emotional implications" (343) and which are saturated with the debunking attitude, attributing malign motives to opponents. This is a rhetorically tricky argument for Burke to make, however, since he presents himself as a Marxist insider, addressing primarily a Marxist audience; *Attitudes Toward History* becomes, then, a sort of "let me show you how to be more persuasive" text. This leads us to discuss Burke's methodological claim to "integrate technical [i.e., literary] criticism with social criticism . . . by taking the allegiance to the symbol of authority as our subject" (331). We use "Twelve Propositions" to pull together Burke's somewhat scattered claims; written in response to a highly critical review, it outlines *Attitudes Toward History*'s argument in an extraordinarily linear fashion, articulating the connections between symbols of authority, individual and collective identities, and material and cultural realms. The final proposition—that we should study human agents as actors and that the most useful rhetorical strategies for social change are the "parliamentary" (313)—provides an effective segue to both *The Philosophy of Literary Form* and *A Grammar of Motives*. Kastely demonstrates how and why to incorporate the comic corrective into undergraduate pedagogy.

Week Eight: The Philosophy of Literary Form (PLF) (title essay and "Longer Articles")

Criticism

- Weiser, "'As Usual I Fell on the Bias': Kenneth Burke's Situated Dialectic." *Philosophy and Rhetoric*, vol. 42, no. 2, 2009, pp. 134–53.

Oral presentation topics: Brooks and Warren, *Understanding Poetry*; Ransom, *The World's Body*; Chicago school of neo-Aristotelians; *Southern Review*

I begin with a key methodological claim on the board: "The main ideal of criticism, as I conceive it, is to use all that is there to use" (23). The purpose of our discussion, then, is to explore what "all that is there" meant for Burke, what such criticism looks like or what it accomplishes (i.e., "Philosophy of Literary Form" and, ultimately, "The Rhetoric of Hitler's 'Battle'") and how—through what conversations—he arrived at this position. We start with Burke's claim in the original Foreword to *Philosophy of Literary Form* that texts should be analyzed "as acts upon a scene" (xvii), without letting either element overshadow the other. Students often have difficulty understanding how the major essays hold together, so we look at Burke's famed rhetorical parlor description (110), then we discuss how Burke's parlor has shifted since *Attitudes Toward History*, in part by looking at publication dates and venues, which I've distributed earlier and which highlight the range of Burke's audiences. The (literary) Marxists Burke addressed in *Attitudes Toward History* have left the parlor (or he has left theirs), and he's now deeply engaged with critics focused either on the act (intrinsic criticism)—such as I. A. Richards, (proto) New Critics, and the Chicago school neo-Aristotelians—or on the scene, such as sociologists and general semanticists. We then explore how Burke cobbles together a critical methodology from a series of agreements with and counterstatements to each group—his "yes, but . . ." response in each essay (what Weiser, following Burke, calls "falling on the bias"). To New Critics and neo-Aristotelians: yes to close reading, especially the importance of form, but what about the agent (Freud) and the scene? To sociologists, yes to scenic motives, but you've neglected the individual and form. "Semantic and Poetic Meaning" has proven to be an especially effective text to focus on, so we outline together Burke's responses to each and then, once again, we draw each term based on specific passages from the text, put them on the board, and compare our understandings.

Week Nine: A Grammar of Motives (GM): Intro, Part I, Part II (skim one section), "Means and Ends of This Grammar" (pp. 317ff), "Our Position Epitomized" (pp. 335ff).

Track key terms on GM worksheet Handout 2: *Grammar of Motives* Key Terms at the end of this chapter.

Criticism

- Crusius, "A Case for Kenneth Burke's Dialectic and Rhetoric." *Philosophy & Rhetoric* 19, no. 1, 1986, pp. 23–37.
- DePalma, Ringer, and Webber. "(Re)Charting the (Dis)Courses of Faith and Politics, or Rhetoric and Democracy in the Burkean Barnyard." *Rhetoric Society Quarterly*, vol. 38, no. 3, 2008, pp. 311–34.
- Weiser, "Burke and War: Rhetoricizing the Theory of Dramatism." *Rhetoric Review*, vol. 26, 2007, pp. 286–302.

Contextualization

- "Statement by the President, August 6, 1945"

Oral presentation topics: general semanticists, atomic weapons programs and/or advances in nuclear physics

A Grammar of Motives is another text for which exigence becomes particularly vital, and I use Weiser's article to set the stage for discussing dramatism. From there we look at Burke's later statements of purpose and central claims—"Means and Ends" and "Our Position Epitomized";

these provide a deductive approach to the text, which students need to connect the parts of Burke's argument, especially the pentad, with the larger, postwar cultural intervention Burke attempts here. At that point, we can productively shift to the beginning, complicating each pentadic term (e.g., agent into coagent, counteragent, collective agents, drives and states of mind, etc.), discussing each as "a locus of motivation" (*GM* 65), as well as the purpose of pentadic ratios. The main sticking points for students are scope, reduction, circumference, and, especially, substance (which students understandably equate with a physical object, not language or motive) and paradox of substance, so we walk through a handout of some key claims and questions I use to highlight the ambiguity and perpetual dialectical action that Burke saw as essential to avoiding monolithic wartime perspectives—and that he built into dramatism (see my "Parsing of the Pentad Handout" at the end of Part II). Crusius's essay clearly reinforces dramatism's goal "to overcome the limitations of any single critical vocabulary" (27), while DePalma, Ringer, and Webber's article provides a much-needed example of pentadic analysis. Ultimately, students most clearly see the pentad's value by doing an analysis themselves, so we work in pairs, then in whole-class discussion, to analyze Truman's short statement announcing the bombing of Hiroshima, a disturbing contemporary text that illustrates the workings and consequences of the monolithic perspective Burke worked to disrupt.

WEEK TEN: GRAMMAR OF MOTIVES, PART III
AND "FOUR MASTER TROPES" (FMT)

Criticism

- Tell, "Burke's Encounter with Ransom: Rhetoric and Epistemology in 'Four Master Tropes.'" *Rhetoric Society Quarterly*, vol. 34, no.4, 2004, pp. 33–54.
- Villanueva, "Blind: Talking About the New Racism." *The Writing Center Journal*, vol. 26, no. 1, 2006, pp. 3–19.

Oral presentation topics: reception of *GM*

By the end of class, I hope we can articulate what dramatism adds to rhetorical theory—specifically, what it does for us as rhetors, rhetorical critics, educators, and citizens. We focus, first, on constitutions as Burke's representative anecdote of human relations, and although they're often puzzled by particular subchapters, students' knowledge of Supreme Court cases and conflicting Constitutional interpretive lenses clarifies Burke's arguments about constitutions as dialectical substances that ground and motivate behavior; Burke's example of the statue of fencers (*GM* 365) is especially helpful. Students enjoy Burke's constitutional analysis and are invariably impressed by its brilliance and relevance. Transubstantiation (dialectical transformation) is the next, more difficult point of discussion, so we often return to Crusius's article. "Four Master Tropes" is our final point of discussion of dialectic. Tell's article, which locates "Four Master Tropes" within Burke's conversations with the New Critic John Crowe Ransom, provides a great gloss on Burke's challenging text and helps students see the "so what?" of the article. Villanueva's article, a student favorite, offers a powerfully relevant "so what?": how tropes function as interpretive lens and, thus, constrain conversations about race. As for the contributions of the pentad and dramatism, given our recent political polarization, students easily appreciate the value of dramatism's proliferation of perspectives for revitalizing democratic discourse. But students still have trouble explaining Burke's claim that "the ambiguity of substance affords a major resource of rhetoric" (*GM* 51). Put another way, they aren't sure how dramatism contributes to Burke's *ad bellum purificandum* project. I suspect the disconnect they feel here reflects their own understandable uncertainty of rhetoric's ability to address current social injustices. We discuss at length how *A Grammar of Motives* offers ways to identify, probe, and transcend the "faulty terminologies" that substantiate and motivate our "absurd ambitions" and Burke's own poignant plea that we "look[] upon the cult of empire as a sickness" (*GM* 317).

WEEK ELEVEN: A RHETORIC OF MOTIVES (RM) PARTS I & II (ONLY PP. 49–110, "CARLYLE ON MYSTERY," AND "METAPHORICAL VIEW OF HIERARCHY")

Criticism

- Clark, *Rhetorical Landscapes in America*, pp. 1–11 and 147–62

Oral presentation topics: Behaviorism (especially B. F. Skinner), Burke and Ralph Ellison, Burke at University of Chicago

We focus on *A Rhetoric of Motives* as continuing Burke's *ad bellum purificandum* agenda—an antidote to the Cold War and the proliferation of incomplete accounts of human motivations by New Critics, Freudians,

Marxists, behaviorists, and positivist social scientists. We look at Burke's purpose clearly defined in the Introduction and carried out in Parts I and II, discussing especially his goal to broaden the scope of rhetorical study not only by embracing other disciplines but also by understanding rhetoric not as a form of discourse (like a campaign speech) but as a function or process at work in all texts. We focus on the one thing students are least apt to feel confused about: identification. Graduate students need help articulating this concept's full implications. Beginning with Burke's observations about "a general *body of identifications* that owe their convincingness . . . to trivial repetition and dull daily reinforcement" (26) and "the ingredient of rhetoric in all socialization" (39), then shifting to Clark's argument that rhetoric is an experiential, relational (not a rational) encounter, we work through identification as an on-going process of identity construction—of ourselves and, hence, of others. In short, Burke is once again exploring the realm of epideictic, exposing the extraordinary power of microprocesses of rhetoric (often lacking a clear agent or persuasive intent) and its implications for rhetorical study and effective persuasion. We linger on Burke's insistence that no activity is autonomous, which is easy to see in the example of World War II nuclear physicists, who (naively, we think) claimed their weapons development was "pure" science, but much trickier when it comes to our relationship with our school, Texas Christian University, a white supremacist, ableist, sexist, heteronormative institution. We also linger on the workings of identification: is it something a rhetor does or something an audience feels or both or something that happens by other means? We end by discussing Burke's goal to "build a whole human society about the critique of ambition" (140) in light of his argument, confusing and uncomfortable for students, that hierarchy is inevitable—which is where we pick up next class.

Week Twelve Rhetoric of Motives, Part III (stop at p. 294)

Criticism

- Crable, "Distance as Ultimate Motive: A Dialectical Interpretation of *A Rhetoric of Motives*." *Rhetoric Society Quarterly*, vol. 39, no. 3, 2009, pp. 213–39.

Oral presentation topics: Burke and the Institute for Advanced Study, reception of *A Rhetoric of Motives*

Students struggle with two things in Part III: (1) Burke's argument that language is inherently hierarchical, partly because they don't follow his logic (that separation of parts necessarily leads to hierarchy) and partly because they have always understood hierarchies as purely cultural constructions, and (2) *A Rhetoric of Motives*' seeming lack of coherent structure. Crable's article becomes our guide. It presents a compelling Platonic through line and locates the source of hierarchy in the archetypal form of appeal, or in Burke's terms, courtship: pure persuasion. Crable argues for pure persuasion, not identification, as the ultimate rhetorical motive upon which Burke hangs his rhetorical theory. Because pure persuasion names a mythic image, which, by definition, resists articulation and because the term is so misleading (pure persuasion isn't opposed to "impure" persuasion), we move slowly through Burke's shifting explanations and tenuous examples. I extend Crable's account of pure persuasion by explicitly rhetoricizing it as part of Burke's *ad bellum purificandum* agenda; it is, I suggest, an attempt to identify a motive of "self-denial" or "distrust of acquisitiveness" hardwired into humans upon which to "build a whole human society about the critique of ambition" (*RM* 271, 140).

Week Thirteen: Language as Symbolic Action (LSA), Chs. 1–3; "Prologue in Heaven" from Rhetoric of Religion (online)

Oral presentation topics: Feminist responses to Burke, Burke at Bennington, Burke's poetry

In the preface, Burke claims that *Language as Symbolic Action* illustrates "a theory of language, a philosophy of language based on that theory, and methods of analysis developed in accordance with the theory and the philosophy," all of which can be summed up as dramatism (vii). We discuss the assigned essays in light of this stated purpose. "Definition of Man" (re)turns our attention to feminist critiques of Burke and his responses, foregrounds Burke's theorizing on the negative (we integrate ideas from "Prologue in Heaven"), and prompts reflection on how humans are "rotten with perfection," often the most confusing definitional element. But we primarily focus on Burke's claim that "however important to us is the tiny sliver of reality each of us has experienced firsthand, the whole overall 'picture' is but a construct of our symbol systems. To meditate on this fact until one sees its full implications is much like peering over the edge of things into an ultimate abyss" (5). So, we meditate on it, trying to articulate things we know firsthand. The more saturated we become with (social) media the smaller that sliver seems. And the political consequences of this constructed reality become ever more visible as we now talk not so much about holding different political ideologies as living in two different worlds. "Terministic Screens" is a natural extension of the first essay. I always start with the Moonwalking Bear Awareness Test video (on YouTube, www.youtube.com/watch?v=Ahg6qcgoay4) which illustrates how powerfully language directs our attention. Since students are familiar with this theory, we analyze how specific terms, as well as whole vocabularies (including those in rhetoric and composition) reflect, select, and deflect reality. (See Terministic Screen Analysis Assignment for Undergraduates at the end of this chapter.) "Poetics in Particular, Language in General" is a useful corrective to students' (and often my own) too-simplistic collapse of categories—that is, it's rhetoric all the way down—which is an accurate but insufficient way to read Burke and cultural texts. He critiques Aristotle for reducing texts to "mere" Poetics (pp. 30–31); scholars in rhetoric should beware of similarly reducing all symbolic action to rhetoric, full stop. To summarize and reinforce our semester's learning, we end by listing Burke's contributions to rhetorical studies and education for citizenship. Specifically: how does Burkean theory change our understanding of texts, life, identity, methods, and objects of study, academic work?

Week Fourteen: Drafts of seminar project
due for in-class peer review

Toward a Better Seminar

Each time I teach this seminar, I update or redesign course content, assignments, and goals to better meet students' interests and needs and to better reflect shifts in rhetorical studies. Since TCU students generally self-identify as teachers, I would next time include readings on Burkean pedagogy—his own teaching and teaching inspired by him, such as we see in this collection. And since many students have—and most rhetoric and composition graduate students need—significant multimodal and web-authoring experience, I've been considering having students collaboratively compose blogs or web pages—"Strategies for Reading Kenneth Burke," our own "Dictionary of Pivotal Terms," "Kenneth Burke for Dummies"—that could be designed for public or undergraduate rhetoric and writing major audiences. Most important, however, I would redesign the course to more forcefully foreground issues of social justice and to enact an antiracist pedagogy, which would include explicitly (1) allowing students to design assignments that create the world they want to live in (so maybe not Burke for Dummies), (2) attending to Burke's position as a canonical white male theorist, (3) discussing the citation politics that can make using Burke to discuss underrepresented groups problematic, and (4) interrogating the value and limitation of Burke's work for our current cultural moment. Burke clearly provides methods for and models of powerful class critiques (in a future semester, we could more formally study unpublished satires like "The Principles of Wise Spending"), ecocriticism ("Towards Hellhaven: Three Stages of a Vision"), redefining work ("Men of Leisure"), and interventions into violence and military aggression (*War of Words*, "Linguistic Approach to Problems of Education")—all of which are still painfully relevant. Burke doesn't do the work of gender, race, and ability critique or intervention—at least, not obviously so—but as Shannon Walter's essay in this volume demonstrates, I believe he continues to give us space and tools to do this work ourselves.

Syllabus for a Graduate Seminar and Topic Handouts

English 80603: Seminar in Kenneth Burke: Rhetoric, Poetics, and Culture

What the Course Is About

This seminar will be a thorough examination of perhaps the most important and interesting American rhetorical theorist of this century. This course will include a careful consideration of Burke's major theoretical with particular emphasis on his writing before 1940 and the ways in which his rhetorical theory and methodologies grew out of his own literary practice and his engagement in modernist/Depression-era conversations about the function of art (and language, more generally) in culture. That is, we will investigate Burkes overriding interest in how language works— what effects texts (of all kinds) can have and how they create these effects. While we will be attending to the canonical Burke, the course will also introduce students to little-known or little-read Burke materials (including magazine articles, short stories, and bits from his massive correspondence).

The overarching concerns of this course are two issues at the heart of Burke studies: how to represent Burke and how to study him. By providing an opportunity to explore both Burke's relationships with other thinkers (particularly other American writers of the first half of the century) and Burke's engagement with contemporary culture, this course problematizes the standard representation of Burke as the eccentric hermit of Andover farm. It also argues that while it's important to study Burkean theory as theory (we'll do plenty of that), it's also important to study his theory as addressed— that is, as a rhetorical act—and to explore why he wrote the kind of theory he did given his particular scene(s).

What I Hope We'll Accomplish (aka Outcomes)

- Students will demonstrate, in class discussion and weekly memos, an understanding of Burkean theory as a rhetorical act—that is, as an intervention in particular cultural scenes.
- Students will develop strategies for reading difficult theoretical texts and demonstrate an ability to critically engage with those texts and key Burkean concepts in class discussion, weekly memos, and final essay.
- Students will demonstrate an ability to articulate and employ key Burkean critical methods (perspective by incongruity, pentadic analysis, terministic screens, etc.) in class discussion, weekly memos, and the final essay.
- Students will practice the academic genres of conference proposals, oral presentations, annotated bibliographies, and either original scholarly arguments or literature reviews.

What We'll Read

(all Burke texts are published by U of California P)

Kenneth Burke, *Counter-Statement* (2nd ed)
Kenneth Burke, *Permanence and Change* (3rd ed)
Kenneth Burke, *Attitudes Toward History* (3rd ed)
Kenneth Burke, *The Philosophy of Literary Form* (3rd ed)
Kenneth Burke, *A Grammar of Motives*
Kenneth Burke, *A Rhetoric of Motives*
Kenneth Burke, *Language as Symbolic Action*
Gregory Clark, *Civic Jazz: American Music and Kenneth Burke on the Art of Getting Along.* Chicago, 2015.

What You'll Be Expected to Do

Say something

The course involves lots of reading, lots of talking, lots of questioning, and lots of responding. It is not a lecture course. Given our topic and the nature of the readings, I expect our class discussions to be lively and interactive. However, seminars are not about showing how smart you are—that is, they're not performative spaces. Seminars are places to collaboratively create knowledge.

N.B.: Attendance: You can't contribute to the class if you're not here, hence, attendance is mandatory. One absence for illness or emergency will not affect your grade; however, two absences may lower your grade substantially, three are grounds for failure. I also expect you to be actively engaged in the class, giving your full attention to me, your classmates, and your work. Cell phones should be turned off and stowed.

Weekly Memos (30%)

Your discoveries in, responses to, and/or questions about our readings will serve as the springboard for class discussion. For any EIGHT classes, write a 1–2 pp., single-spaced memo of your reactions to the week's readings (including classmates' memos, which you should read as well). Post these as either Word files to the Discussion Board on our TCU Online site.

Memos should be analytical, rather than mere "reader response." However, these are also not meant to be primarily performative. You don't need to have all the answers or even fully formed arguments. The memos are spaces to work out ideas—writing is a heuristic process! They can be speculative, tackle things you don't understand—show where and why you're confused—even if you don't reach definitive answers by the end. Or perhaps you'll solve one confusing point only to raise another. It's really OK not to know for sure as long as you're carefully engaging the text and thinking hard. So don't pick "safe" topics that enable you to wrap things up neatly with a bow. Challenge yourself.

Your memos should be a sustained discussion/questioning of one topic (or a few, closely related points) rather than three-four paragraphs on unrelated questions or ideas. (You may, however, end with a short list of unrelated questions that you'd like the class to address.) I will occasionally provide an optional writing prompt. You may use these memos as spaces to work out ideas for your seminar paper. Perhaps you'd like to track a term through Burke's texts (form, substance, identification, dialectic, irony, etc.): line up passages where he uses the term and see what they add up to. Burke's definitions often feel cumulative to me, so I've found it helpful to gather a bunch of passages to see how they reinforce, further explain, push against, or qualify each other. If you're interested in Burke's relationship to a particular thinker or body of thought—John Dewey, say, or William James or mysticism—you might track where these thinkers or philosophies show up and analyze what Burke has to say about them.

Memos are informal and ungraded—this is primarily (though not entirely) a completion grade. If you complete eight thoughtful, engaged, well-written responses, you will earn an A-. If you complete eight responses that consistently demonstrate especially sophisticated and/or challenging analysis, you'll earn an A. Overly brief or sloppy responses will not receive full credit. After you've submitted 2–3 memos, I will give you some feedback and suggestions. Since you have lots of opportunities to submit memos, late ones will not receive credit. You may only write one memo each week, so don't get behind.

Oral Report (20%)

As part of our effort to contextualize Burke within on-going cultural conversations, each of you will give a 15- to 20-minute presentation that helps to familiarize us with some of the magazines Burke read and was frequently published in (such as the Nation, the Southern Review, the New Republic), some of his close friends and their works (such as Malcolm Cowley or William Carlos Williams), key historical or literary events (such as the First American Writers' Congress or nuclear war), or intellectual/political/scientific groups he wrote to and about (such as the Southern Agrarians or behaviorists). If you can make these presentations feed into your research projects, I'll entertain alternative topics if you can make the case. Some of the presentations (such as Burke's poetry, Burke & Cowley) can be moved to alternate dates.

Prepare a one-page handout to accompany your talk. Being able to give a coherent, informative, and well-delivered talk is an essential skill in our profession: as with all academic presentations, I will assess your content and delivery (including new media used; if you plan to use a PPT presentation, make sure you've studied tips for rhetorically effective presentations on the CDEx website). Treat this assignment like a professional presentation and give it the preparation it deserves.

Four-part, scaffolded research project (50%):

1. Topic Proposal (required but not graded): As early in the semester as possible (but no later than Week 7), you should submit a one-paragraph topic proposal, which does just that: proposes a general topic—a text, a concept, and/or a method (archival, rhetorical criticism, theoretical analysis, etc.) for your major project—and provides a brief explanation of why you're interested.
2. Annotated Bibliography of 8–10 sources, using proper MLA citation format (15%). Due Week 10 or 11.

    The purpose of this assignment is to help you identify a conversation you want to enter in your research—to locate your ideas in relation to ongoing discussions in the field. To do that, you need to know what others have said/are saying about your topic or text—and how they've approached it. Hence, most of the sources will be secondary. (This bibliography comes BEFORE not after you write your formal project proposal; indeed, your proposal springs directly from your reading: it says, "here's what other scholars say about this topic, and here's what I want to add to that conversation.")

    Your bibliography should begin with a paragraph that briefly overviews your topic/the conversation you're entering and that explains how you've organized your entries (and why). The best bibliographies will organize sources in a way that indicates the shape of the scholarly conversation—for instance, by theme/sub-area (to illustrate major subsets or debates), by methodology (to illustrate the variety of methodological approaches scholars have taken), by chronology (to show how the scholarship has developed), etc. Many of you will be doing annotated bibliographies as part of your exams, so this is a low-stakes place to practice.

For each source, provide a paragraph (ca. 150 words) that explains its purpose, argument, and methodology/theoretical frame (if appropriate) and that locates it in relation to other sources on your list. You may also include some critical evaluation. NB: Annotations should not simply summarize a source. Explain what it says but also what it does—what does it argue? What other work does it respond to? How does it compare to other texts? Why/how will it be useful for your project? That's a lot to say in a short annotation, so you'll have to make every word count.

3. Project Proposal (required but not graded): A 250-word, conference-style proposal outlining the purpose, scope of, and audience for (specify a journal) your research project. (We'll talk about proposal writing in class.) Due no later than one week after you submit your Annotated Bibliography either Week 11 or 12—the sooner, the better). Please email these to me so I can quickly return them.

4. Research Project Portfolio [includes (revised?) project proposal, rough and final drafts] (35%): The major written project for the course is a 15- to 20-page, original argument, written with a specific journal in mind—indicate which one on your first page. Choice of topic/approach is open: you may engage with Burke's theory, fiction, or poetry; write a piece of Burkean rhetorical criticism; trace/elucidate a key term; contextualize a work; do an archival project; develop a Burkean pedagogy; etc. Good projects—and, hence, publication opportunities—abound.

MA students' paper option: a 15- to 20-page literature review (rather than original argument) on a topic of your choice.

If you don't already have plans for a project, consider a paper on "Burke and . . ." or "Burke as. . . ." That is, explore Burke "and" someone he knew or studied or reacted to: Burke and William Carlos Williams, Burke and I.A. Richards, Burke and George Herbert Meade, Burke and Coleridge, Burke and Augustine, etc. (An excellent example of this type of project is Debra Hawhee's *Quarterly Jour-*

nal of Speech article, "Burke and Nietzsche.") OR explore Burke "as" something or other: Burke as Narrative Theorist, Burke as Poet, Burke as Reviewer. For anyone wishing to trace a term, take a look at Prelli, Lawrence J., Floyd D. Anderson, and Matthew T. Althouse. "Kenneth Burke on Recalcitrance." *Rhetoric Society Quarterly* 41.2 (2011): 97–124. Another increasingly popular approach to Burkean theory is to illuminate it by doing primary research on someone or something Burke references. (The model here is, again, Debra Hawhee's discussion of Burke and endocrinology—Ch 4 in *Moving Bodies*.)

Burke is currently a hot item, and there are vast stretches of unexplored Burkean territory, particularly the first half of his career and his relationships with other prominent writers and thinkers and critical circles. So, there are excellent chances for conference presentations and/or publication. RSQ has a soft spot for Burke scholarship, and the Kenneth Burke Society has an online journal—*KB Journal*. Burke also always plays well at RSA. And of course the next Triennial Conference of the Kenneth Burke Society is always another opportunity.

FINALLY, THESE . . .

A brief note on writing: It should come as no great surprise that it's important for scholars in English studies to write extremely well. I'm always happy to help. Any published scholar will tell you that one key to success is lots and lots of revision: plan on it. If you need help with standard academic moves integrating sources (or even if you just need to remind yourself of their importance), I highly recommend Gerald Graff's and Cathy Birkenstein's little book, *They Say, I Say* (Norton).

A brief (Burkean) note on grades: One of Burke's rhetorical tricks is to use italics to shift the emphasis and, thus, the meaning of a phrase. For example: it goes without saying that *grades are important*; always do your very best work. But it also *goes without saying* that grades are important; grade anxiety is not a conversation that needs to be going on in your head because, ultimately, grad school isn't about grades. It's about professionalization—learning to think, write, and work like an academic. An A paper that gets stuck in a drawer is worth less than a B paper that gets revised and sent out to a journal. (I've also rarely heard a job candidate's grad school GPA mentioned as a factor in search committee meetings. Prospective employers are more likely to look at which courses you took rather than remark upon an A-.) And as important as coursework is, lots of your professionalization goes on outside the classroom. Read journals. Present at a conference. Write a book review. Apply to be an RA or ADC. Go to hear a visiting speaker, attend a job talk or a dissertation defense or a professionalization brownbag. Make it a point to develop a close working relationship with 2–3 professors who'll become your primary mentors, often long after you've graduated.

Handout 1: "Semantic and Poetic Meaning" (Southern Review, 1938)

I. Opening synthesis
- no basic opposition between the ideals of semantic and poetic meaning: difference not antithesis (139)
- And this not altogether straightforward claim: "semantic meaning, that may be considered as a partial aspect of poetic meaning, tends to become instead the opposite of poetic meaning, so that a mere graded series comprising a more-than and a less-than, changes instead into a blunt battle between poetry and antipoetry, or 'poetry vs. science.' Only by a kind of 'synecdochic fallacy,' mistaking a part for the whole, can this opposition appear to exist" (139).
- "Although the semantic ideal would eliminate the attitudinal ingredient from its vocabulary . . . the ideal is itself an attitude . . . semantics itself may be an attenuated form of poetry" (150)

II. The Difference

Semantic	Poetic
"neutral," technical mode of analysis (138)	"strongly weighted with emotional values, with *attitudes*" (143)
envelope address (140): describes or places; doesn't judge	
Ideal = logical positivists evolve a vocabulary that gives name and address of every event (141)	Ideal = "The ideal word is in itself an act" (167).
Test = operational: instructions for performance of desired operations (141); True-false test; syllogism (144)	Test ≠ true or false (144) **Test = "giving body to the perspective"** = "let each show the scope, range, relevancy, accuracy, applicability of the perspective or metaphor [he] would advocate" (145) = what you can DO with the metaphor (i.e., give fuller account, "integrate wider areas of human relationship" (146)
"description by the **elimination of attitude**" (147–48); "*cut away* . . . all emotional factors that complicate the objective clarity of meaning" (148)	"attempt to *attain a full moral act* by attaining a **perspective atop** all the conflicts of attitude" (148). Moral act = "total assertion at the time of the assertion" & "has a *style*" (148); "total summing up" (149)

Semantic	Poetic
Envisions vocabulary **that *"avoids drama"*** (goes around); **observes** battle, prepares CHART for action (149)	Vocabulary **"goes *through* drama"**; true knowledge gained only through battle, through **participation**; prepares IMAGE for action (150)
anesthetic, analgesic: perception without feeling, without judgment (150–51)	**esthetic**: perception with feeling (150)
ultimate example = specific vocabularies of technological specializations" (150)	Ultimate examples = Shakespeare, Eumenides (152)
statement without the suffering/conflict to earn it (158), "a fraud: [an ideal] one may believe in because it is impossible" (159)	**"maximum complexity of weighting"**; "as accurate, in the realistic charting of human situations, as any ideal semantic formula" (159)
"bad" style (159): "serve[s] to prevent the doing of anything" (163)	**call for cult of style** as "campaign base for personal integrity"(161). "Style as the hortatory act, as the example that would prod continually for its completion in all aspects of life" (162).

SUM: Semantic ideal "fosters . . . the notion that one may comprehensively discuss human and social events in a nonmoral vocabulary, and that perception itself is a nonmoral act. It is the moral impulse that motivates perception, giving it both intensity and direction, suggesting what to look for and what to look out for. Only by wanting profoundly to make improvement, can we get a glimpse into the devious personal and impersonal factors that operate to balk improvement" (164).

Handout 2: Grammar of Motives Key Terms

Circumference
Constitution

Constitution-behind-the-Constitution
Dialectic
Dramatism
Dramatism X Dialectic [what's the connection?]
God-term
Paradox of Substance
Pentad

- Act
- Agent
- Agency
- Purpose
- Scene

Ratios
Representative anecdote
Scope
Constitution X Substance X Motive [what's the connection?]

Handout 3: Reading Questions for A Rhetoric of Motives (RM)

Note for instructors: These reading questions are designed for students in an upper-division course on rhetorical theory and criticism. The course attracts writing/English majors and minors, whose majors range from education to business to political science. I typically assign the Introduction and brief excerpts from Part 1.

Use these questions to help guide your reading of Burke. I will not collect your answers, but I will expect you to come prepared to discuss them in class—to be able to point to specific passages—so you should either take notes on this page or make marginal comments on a hard copy of the reading.

1. How does Burke define rhetoric? (You'll find more than one definition.)
2. According to the Introduction of RM, what does Burke intend to demonstrate in the book?

3. Burke argues that all human activity is rhetorical, but what, specifically, does he include under the heading of rhetoric—what kinds of activities? List a few of Burke's examples and see if you can come up with some of your own.
4. What does Burke seem to mean by the term identification? Why does he think it's so important?
5. How do you make sense of Burke's claim that "belonging . . . is rhetorical" (RM 28)?
6. Why does Burke argue that no human activity is "autonomous"?

Terministic Screen Analysis
Assignment for Undergraduates

*Note for instructors: The next time I teach this assignment, I will emphasize audience as an important part of context since terms have very different purposes or effects for different audiences—a point horribly underscored when a student veteran began crying in class during my too-breezy discussion of how initialisms like MIA and KIA work to disguise the humanity of wartime casualties. For her and another student veteran, such shields are necessary psychological tools to blunt the horror of their experiences.

Additionally—and despite Burke's self-identification as a "word man"—I can also imagine allowing students to analyze a "visual screen." Since Burke parallels the effects of terministic screens with those created by photographing the same object with different color filters (LSA 45), students might productively study how different camera angles/lenses or the ways photographs of war are colored (or not), cropped, staged, etc. create particular understandings of war scenes.

What kind of analysis? The concept of a "terministic screen" is easier than it seems: it's a screen made of "terms"—words. As its coiner, Kenneth Burke suggests, you can think of it as a lens we see through, which colors or sizes an image. Or, as the name itself suggests, you can think of terministic screens as filters: a coffee filter, a kitchen strainer, or a window screen. Like these filters, terministic screens will only let certain material pass through. Unlike physical screens, however, terministic screens are mental constructs, and they're often so much a part of our culture, that they're invisible. Hence, we don't realize the effects of these words, nor do we know how to seek alternatives (if, indeed, we realize that alternatives exist). For Burke, as for most modern sociolinguists and philosophers, language is ideologically laden and rhetorical: it persuades us to think and act in certain ways, and it has very real, material consequences.

When a terministic screen works, what's it doing to our thought process? Burke says that terministic screens work by

- reflecting reality—there's probably some truth to the term, so it may seem purely descriptive: war as politics/business fits to the extent that governments do use cost/benefit analyses
- selecting reality—they "turn up the volume" or emphasize one element or point of view; think of the way you "select" a passage in MS Word—it gets highlighted in color
- deflecting reality—they act like blinders on a horse, keeping us from seeing or thinking from different perspectives

If then, as Burke argues, language shapes our attitudes and behavior, it behooves us to examine how particular words/phrases shape what we see, think, feel, and do. Burke was typically interested in the working of whole vocabularies—the way disciplinary or occupational language prompts users to think of people or policies in particular ways. A chemical weapons manufacturer will analyze human bodies and behavior much differently than a military supply chain manager or a Red Cross worker, computer hacker, or peace negotiator. For this short analysis, we'll focus on a single word or phrase. Terministic screens, in and of themselves, are not necessarily harmful (or not intentionally so); we all use disciplinary or specialized language to capture definitional nuances and to speed communication. But terministic screens always limit our ways of seeing, and when the stakes are high and things are ugly (as they are in wartime), when tremendous resources are used to create an "us" versus "them" mentality, language will be used to demonize some groups or practices and valorize others. Some war-related terministic screens have already been brought to our attention and analyzed: in WWII, Hitler's description of the Jews as vermin or insects and America's portrayal of the Japanese as snakes or spiders (it's so much easier to justify killing rats, bugs, and slimy things than human beings) have been well documented.

This assignment asks you to find and analyze a terministic screen used to talk about war. Begin by giving us some basic info: where/when is the term typically, or most recently, used? who uses the term? In other words, words have meanings in particular contexts, so what's the context for your term?* Then discuss its implications and consequences—how does it reflect, select, and deflect reality? (One way to highlight these is to consider other ways of saying the same thing.)

Here are a few other ways to think about terministic screens—ways to help you find a term as well as ways to help you analyze it fully:

- terministic screens can be and/or can function as:
    - a label, classification, or title – the Patriot Act, Operation Iraqi Freedom, Desert Storm, Department of Homeland Security, War on Terror
    - a metaphor – theater of operations, tour of duty, surgical strike
    - language meant to obscure, doublespeak: "transfer tubes," collateral damage, regime change, "clarifying" the Geneva Conventions
    - language that creates binaries—terrorist, axis of evil

Here are some examples that you may write about but feel free to find one yourself (just let me approve it): smart bomb, Shock & Awe, detention programs (or detainees), "alternate set of procedures" or "heightened interrogation" as substitutes for "torture," MIA, KIA, POW (or its latest incarnation: PUC for "Person Under Control"), contractors or security (rather than mercenary), "civil control stations," the surge, ethnic cleansing, preemptive war, police action, WMDs, IEDs.

11 Multiperspectivism: Educating Social Science Students to Become Symbol-Wise Practitioners

Laura Van Beveren and Kris Rutten

> *Encouraging symbol-wise critical reflection with students of clinical psychology and social work.*

In 2015, Ghent University introduced the concept of *multiperspectivism* as its new educational vision and strategy, starting with a quote from Kenneth Burke: *"Every way of seeing is also a way of not seeing. It is better to have a variety of models and archetypes so we stay flexible and open."* According to the university, multiperspectivism implies "a general sort of reflexivity, inviting people to position themselves in history, in a global context, in a network of meanings, a multitude of visions." In its didactical translation, the notion corresponds to a conception of learning as "a reflexive process: a critical revision of theoretical frameworks that starts from a reflection about these frameworks" ("Ghent University's" 1, 5, 9–10).

With its emphasis on notions such as *critical*, *reflection*, and *reflexivity*, Ghent University's educational project can be situated within a wider international trend of forwarding critical reflection as a guiding concept for good and accountable education, research, and practice in the social and behavioral sciences. Despite the increasing implementation of this concept in higher education curricula and professional standards, several questions remain high on the research agenda: *What* are we talking about when we talk about critical reflection? *How* can we and our students reflect critically? And, perhaps the most fundamental question, *why* should we critically reflect? In our research and teaching, we engage with these questions by exploring what it implies to commit to the project of critical reflection from a rhetorical perspective. In what follows, we first discuss critical reflection as conceptualized in the social and behavioral sciences. We then explain how we drew on Burke's and Krista Ratcliffe's work in developing a rhetorical approach to critical reflection and how we implemented it in educational projects with students in clinical psychology and social work. We conclude by reflecting on the implications of educating students in the social and behavioral sciences to become "symbol-wise practitioners" and by providing some suggestions for educators.

Critical Reflection and Reflexivity

Generally, the notions of *critical reflection* and *reflexivity* emphasize that practice and research in the social and behavioral domain are never neutral or ahistorical and are consequently not simply technical or rational endeavors but require normative professional judgment on what constitutes good and desirable courses of action (White and Stancombe 3–15). It is therefore argued that social and behavioral sciences need so-called "critical-normative professionals" who recognize normative professional judgment as central to their profession and who critically reflect on the theoretical, political, and ethical logics that underpin their practice and research.

Reflective approaches to professional practice particularly emphasize that theory and practice are intertwined in social professions and recognize the value of knowledge gained through everyday experience (Schön 55–61). Nevertheless, reflection becomes a *critical* endeavor only if it broadens its focus from the everyday interactions between practitioners and service-users to the wider social, political, cultural, and ethical contexts and implications of one's practice and discipline (Brookfield 297). The related notion of reflexivity invites practitioners to question not only their claims to knowledge but also the process of knowledge creation and the operation of power relations within it more fundamentally (D'Cruz et al. 77–78).

Across social and behavioral fields, it has been argued that social professions are predicated upon *symbolically* mediated interactions (Biesta 34) and that the process of professional judgment itself is relational and *discursive* (White and Stancombe 158). Accordingly, scholars emphasize that attending to the interpretive and discursive dimensions of social and behavioral sciences and professions is essential in developing critical and reflexive professional attitudes (Fook 56). More precisely, developing a critical awareness of interpretive and discursive processes on a *personal level* is crucial if one wishes to develop a self-critical, reflexive understanding of one's professional position, assumptions, and power (D'Cruz et al. 77–80). At the *interpersonal level*, tending to the interpretations and discourses of others is essential in opening up the question of what constitutes good practice as a dialogical and even democratic effort (Parton et al. 18, 21; Biesta 44, 71). Finally, at the wider *societal level*, critical reflection implies an examination of the role that language and symbols play in producing dominant "ways of knowing" and of the ways our practice reproduces or challenges our taken-for-granted systems of interpretation (Brookfield 300–03).

Building on previous insights, some scholars have suggested the study of critical reflection and reflexivity might benefit from a turn to rhetorical studies, as this field's focus on the performative power of discourse is especially relevant in the context of practice-based disciplines (Parton 461; Taylor 203–04; Taylor and White 45–46). In our research and teaching, we respond to this suggestion by developing a pedagogy of critical reflection that draws on the work of rhetorical theorists Kenneth Burke and Krista Ratcliffe. Although their work has been deployed mainly within the field of rhetoric and composition studies, we believe it has a theoretical, methodological, and pedagogical relevance that stretches beyond this domain to the social and behavioral sciences.

More specifically, we argue that by being educated in and from a rhetorical perspective, students are encouraged to take a "researcher's attitude" towards their practice. This occurs less through the rational application of research to practice than by reading and analyzing professional practice as a form of symbolic action and by critically inquiring into the interrelatedness of language and action, of theory and practice in their fields. In addition to being a valuable analytical lens *on* the social and behavioral sciences, we assert that Burke and Ratcliffe provide "equipment" *for* these fields. We specifically claim rhetoric's productive power lies in the fact that in disclosing new interpretations of social, clinical, and educational issues, it simultaneously opens up new orientations for professional action. As such, rhetoric reminds students to view the inevitable contingency of their practice as an opportunity to take a confident risk to act from a specific "way of seeing" while bearing in mind that "another way of seeing" is always possible.

In the next section, we elaborate on how Burke's and Ratcliffe's work offers "equipment" for stimulating in social professionals these critical, reflexive, and "symbol-wise" attitudes towards their practice and discipline.

A Rhetorical Approach: Burke's Symbol-Wisdom

Burke most explicitly and comprehensively discusses the educational relevance of his ideas in his 1955 essay "Linguistic Approach to Problems of Education" ("LAPE"). Our rhetorical approach to critical reflection strongly draws on this essay as well as Jessica Enoch's "Becoming Symbol-Wise: Kenneth Burke's Pedagogy of Critical Reflection," in which she relates "Linguistic Approach" to the concepts of critical reflection and critical pedagogy.

Central to our approach is Burke's characterization of language as a form of symbolic action as well as his argument that "the most direct route to the study of human relations and human motives is via a methodological inquiry into cycles or clusters of terms and their functions" ("Dramatism" 445). While throughout his work, Burke offers many concepts that serve as analytical methods for studying human motivation through language, in "Linguistic Approach," he approaches this endeavor from a pedagogical perspective. As Enoch notes, Burke's essay offers several "linguistic exercises" or "dramatistic practices" with which to operationalize an education in symbol-wisdom (282).

Our rhetorical approach to critical reflection mainly draws on the Burkean concepts of *terministic screen* and *trained incapacity*. For example, implicitly invoking the notion of terministic screens, "Linguistic Approach" proposes that students track down the selections and deflections implicit in news reports and analyze how terms function differently in different contexts, producing other attitudes in audiences (Enoch 284–85). We consider this a highly relevant exercise in the social and behavioral sciences classroom, where we shift the exercise's focus from news media to the professional domain, particularly the rhetorical selections and deflections inherent in disciplinary understandings of complex issues, such as mental health, poverty, or teacher identity.

We furthermore emphasize in our rhetorical pedagogy of critical reflection the performative or socializing effect of terministic screens.

Since clinical psychology and social work are practice-based professions, we consider it of paramount importance that students gain insight into the interconnections between their disciplinary or personal terministic screens and their professional interventions. For example, the complex issue of poverty may be understood in terms of its economic aspects (as a lack of financial resources) or in terms of its social aspects (as a form of sociocultural exclusion), and each terministic screen will direct professional intervention in a particular way. In teaching students that terministic screens offer not only an understanding of the issue at hand but also strategies to encompass it (Burke, *PLF* 61, 293), the rhetorical perspective helps reveal that social and behavioral practices are never theory- nor value-free.

In addition to terministic screens, our rhetorical pedagogy of critical reflection centers Burke's notion of trained incapacities. We consider this notion, which Burke borrowed from the sociologist Thorstein Veblen and which he also refers to as "occupational psychosis," particularly relevant to our pedagogy because it details the way our disciplinary terministic screens simultaneously enable (or train) us to deal with a complex issue while at the same time prevent (or incapacitate) us from approaching the issue in a different way (*PC* 7–10, 48–49). As such, Burke's rhetorical perspective highlights the complexity and ambiguity inherent to social and behavioral professions: as there is never one right, neutral course of professional action, students necessarily need to engage in a normative and political discussion about what constitutes good, desirable, and socially just professional practice.

As summarized by Enoch, the critical educational potential of Burke's work (and "Linguistic Approach" in particular) lies in the fact that it encourages students to engage in such discussions from a position of symbol-wisdom: "an attitude of reflective patience by methodically investigating the ways language functions" in how we understand and conduct our lives (290).

Ratcliffe's Rhetorical Listening

We complemented our Burkean pedagogy of critical reflection with insights from Krista Ratcliffe's theory of rhetorical listening, which both draws on and critically adds to the work of Burke. Ratcliffe defines rhetorical listening as "the performance of a person's conscious choice to assume an open stance in relation to any person, text or culture" (26), a stance that requires that we "consciously stand under discourses that surround us and others, while consciously acknowledging all our particular embodied—and very fluid—standpoints" (28). Rhetorical listening functions as a "trope for interpretive invention" (1), meaning that listening does not designate a passive stance but rather a specific way to be and act rhetorically, a "way of making meaning with/in language" (23).

In bringing Burke's work into conversation with Ratcliffe's, we sought to explicitly include in our rhetorical pedagogy the need for students to interconnect personal, interpersonal, and societal dimensions in their analysis of the terministic screens and "ways of knowing" operating in their fields. On the *personal* level, rhetorical listening implies that social professionals reflexively listen to the presences, absences, and unknowns in their professional discourses and think about how they affect their worldviews and decision-making. Put differently, rhetorical listening requires that we "become self-conscious toward the limitations of [our] own 'imaginary version' of self and other" (Alice Rayner qtd. in Ratcliffe 30). On the *interpersonal* level, rhetorical listening implies that social professionals attend to the discourses and interpretations of service-users from a position of commitment and care.

Moving from the (inter)personal to the *socio-cultural* level, Ratcliffe theorizes how our personal claims operate within wider culturally and historically grounded symbol systems. At this level, understanding how words function as "tropes" is crucial: having multiple meanings, words function differently according to the cultural logics in which they are grounded (33–34). An example from the context of psychology: from a biopsychiatric logic the notion of *being a patient* might function tropologically as "corresponding to a set of pre-defined criteria that determine one has a mental dysfunction," whereas from a psychoanalytical logic the notion of *the patient* is often used to emphasize one individual's experience of suffering as central to the clinical process. Referring to Burke's concept of terministic screens, Ratcliffe furthermore states that cultural logics have a socializing effect because we embody and perform them in specific ways, and they cause us to enact certain cultural scripts (11). However, the gaps and contractions in embodied discourses simultaneously create a place of agency for people to revise or resist them.

Moreover, by "perform[ing] the feminist act of recovering the neglected fourth literacy of listening" (Gerald 142), as a pedagogical approach, Ratcliffe's rhetorical listening challenges the rhetoric classroom's traditional focus on "speaking" and "writing" and its often male-oriented goals of gaining mastery over discourse or "winning the argument." Accordingly, Glenn (4) situates rhetorical listening within her wider concept of rhetorical feminism and teaching, which alludes to a stance and set of rhetorical tactics that recognize vernaculars as a source of (rhetorical) knowledge, create space for the rhetorical appeals of emotion and experience, and value alternative means of rhetorical delivery and invention such as silence and listening. We contend that, as a pedagogical position, rhetorical listening can be fruitfully translated to social and behavioral science classrooms. We consider it especially valuable in renegotiating what counts as expertise and legitimate knowledge in social professions by stimulating professional attitudes that approach professional practice from a position of not (yet) knowing rather than from an incontestable expert position and valuing alternative ways of constructing clinical, social, and educational knowledge.

Critical Case Studies

In the context of our teaching at Ghent University, we set up educational projects to explore the implications, in terms of the critical practices and professional identities they develop, of educating students in and from a rhetorical perspective to become "symbol-wise practitioners." In this sense, we follow what Herbert Simons calls the "rhetorical hypothesis," the idea that "there is potential profit in pursuing rhetorical lines of inquiry to their farthest limits" in the human sciences. In relation to Burke's work specifically, Simons claims that it "was not so much a declaration that all communication is rhetorical as it was an invitation to explore pragmatically the possibilities—the implicit entelechial potential—of viewing communicative acts and artifacts in this way" (256–57). What is needed in exploring the rhetorical hypothesis is not a "scientizing" or a quantification of rhetoric but rather a variety of "critical case studies from across the human sciences," as well as a systematic confrontation of the stories these case studies tell us (271). In what follows, we briefly introduce how we set up such critical case studies by implementing our rhetorical pedagogy of critical reflection in educational projects with master's students in clinical psychology and social work.

Clinical Psychology

Building on theoretical perspectives from the fields of critical disability studies and critical psychology, we argue that future clinical psychologists need to reflect on how the notions of *mental health* and *mental illness* are culturally constructed in their field and in society more generally. Drawing on the growing body of work on mental health rhetoric research (see Reynolds 3), we conceptualized the role of our rhetorical approach to critical reflection as both disclosing mental health and mental illness as value-laden notions grounded in specific cultural constructions of the relationship between mind, body, and society and as stimulating in students an awareness of the different cultural logics in which psychological practice and theory on mental health are inevitably embedded.

As Burke noted, in being "representative of human ways while yet having fixity enough to allow for systematic examination," fiction can function as a site to study human motives and meaning making ("LAPE" 263). We accordingly introduced students to Burke's central ideas (with a focus on terministic screen and trained incapacities) and then asked them to read Ellen Forney's *Marbles: Mania, Depression, Michelangelo and Me: A Graphic Memoir* (2012). In this autobiographical story, Forney paints a complex, nuanced picture of her experiences being a queer woman artist who is diagnosed with "bipolar disorder." The memoir elaborates on Forney's ambiguous attitude toward the labels "bipolar disorder" and "the crazy artist," specifically exploring her search for identity now that her "own brilliant unique personality . . . reflected a disorder, shared by a group of people" (Forney 19). We asked students to draw on Burke's concepts to rhetorically analyze the cultural constructions of mental health and mental illness evident in the Forney's text and to reflect on disciplinary topics such as diagnosis, labeling, client-therapist relationship, medication, and stigma based on their rhetorical analysis.

Based on a qualitative analysis of the students' reflections, we learned that they approached the story of Ellen Forney either from a position of rhetorical listening or a position of what we termed *rhetorical othering*. In the latter case, students located rhetorical meaning making exclusively with Ellen/the Other—"the bipolar person approaches the world in a bipolar way because (s)he is bipolar"—leaving their own as well as their discipline's terministic screens or cultural logics unquestioned. In the former case, they recognized the cultural construction and experience of "mental health (problems)" as a result of the complex interplay between the symbolic actions of the self, the other, and (a disabling) society.

For example, at the interpersonal level, students tried to untangle the different terministic screens operating in the professional interactions between Ellen and her therapist, as well as how these correspond to different cultural scripts to enact. As one student observed, "Ellen considers herself as a member of the 'Club van Gogh': a group of successful bipolar artists that see bipolarity as a complex personality and as the fuel of a creative motor. This contrasts with the screen of the therapist who defines Ellen as a patient with a mental disorder and considers her behavior as corresponding to a cluster of symptoms that constitute 'bipolar disorder' in the DSM.[1] . . . From the therapist's screen, taking medication is a necessary form of self-care to stabilize the symptoms of the bipolar disorder and to avoid risky behavior from the patient. From Ellen's screen, taking medication is an attack on her complex personality." Instances of rhetorical listening additionally ask students to reflexively engage with their own terministic screens. Students predominantly referred to their own screens as "psychological" and considered this screen both enabling, for example in contrast to overtly biomedical and neurological approaches to mental illness, and as incapacitating, for example—as the following quote illustrates—when it functioned to psychologize: "Ellen approaches her 'disease' both as a painful curse and as a source of inspiration and part of her creative personality. This confronted me with my own blind spots regarding bipolar disorder. I'm inclined to only see it as a psychological problem that requires treatment." In some cases, students drew on Burke's concepts (the pentad's scene and circumference especially) to socially and historically contextualize Ellen's terministic screens, for example by situating Ellen's identification as "a member of the Club Van Gogh" within wider cultural logics about mental health and normality: "Our society is much more tolerant towards manic episodes if they are combined with the terministic screen of the 'crazy artist.' Artists' craziness is considered normal, while non-creative people would be considered 'just crazy.'" Reflecting on the process of knowledge construction about mental health more fundamentally, the exercise led some students to conclude that, as one wrote, "narratives can teach students to juxtapose scientific knowledge with subjective experiences in their future clinical practice."

Social Work

Building on critical social work theories about poverty and anti-poverty policy making, we argue that future social workers need both to ex-

---

1. This refers to the American Psychiatric Association's *Diagnostic and Statistical Manual of Mental Disorders*.

plore *poverty* as a contested, situated, and discursively produced notion and to critically engage with the normativity of the social work practices they develop themselves in relation to poverty (Krumer-Nevo et al. 230). We again turned to the fictional domain in our pedagogies: after introducing the students to the rhetorical theories of Burke and Krista Ratcliffe, the class watched Renzo Martens's art project/documentary *Enjoy Poverty* (2008). In the documentary, we follow Martens, a Dutch white man, on his journey through the plantations of the Democratic Republic of Congo. Confronted with the poverty of many plantation workers, he controversially proposes that, given their desperate and structurally hopeless situation, the best option is for the Congolese to "enjoy their poverty" and exploit it on the Western market (e.g., through the industries of humanitarian journalism or developmental work). The documentary specifically inquires into the power of media, artists, and aid organizations in representing and constructing knowledge about poverty, often by enacting the very power differentials they seek to critique.[2] After watching the documentary, we gave our students the assignment to use Burke's and Ratcliffe's frameworks to rhetorically analyze constructions of poverty as a social problem evident in the documentary.

In this project, we sought to align our pedagogies more explicitly with our theoretical rhetorical frameworks. For example, we complemented students' individual reflections with reflective group discussions, in which students could discuss and confront different ways they rhetorically engaged with the documentary and the topic of poverty more generally. Indeed, a pedagogy of rhetorical listening approaches the process of meaning making as an intersubjective process and understands reflection as both an individual and a collective project. We also developed a set of questions to guide students' rhetorical reflections. Firstly, to encourage them to engage with the societal embeddedness of social workers' definitions of poverty, students were asked to relate various terministic screens on poverty to the wider cultural logics within which they functioned.

---

2 Martens's *Enjoy Poverty* has been both praised and critiqued for taking this approach. Although we do not have the space to elaborate on this debate here, we note that students likewise discussed the politics and ethics of representing and artistically engaging with the issue of poverty. For a more extensive discussion of *Enjoy Poverty*, see De Roo's *African Poverty, Taboo or Standardize* on *Episode III: Enjoy Poverty (2008) by Renzo Martens*.

For example, several groups critically discussed how the plantations owners' perspectives on poverty function within a cultural logic of individualization: "The plantation owners said: 'we do pay them enough, it's just, [the plantation workers] don't have the skills to handle their money and this is why they are living in poverty.' It's taking social problems and making an individual, pedagogical problem of it." Another group noted that the cultural logic of individualization corresponds to anti-poverty policies that locate responsibility for being poor with people living in poverty themselves, an approach they recognize in their own government's policies as well: "This individual blaming is also evident in the language of the government, and this has consequences for how we think about social security and rights. . . . If you consider poverty an individual problem, then you will think that the individual has the responsibility to get out of it. Otherwise you would also question structures in society and ask why people cannot access certain resources." Gaining insight into the wider cultural logics in which our professional and political understandings of poverty are embedded may help students reflect on how professional interventions at the interpersonal level can be implicated in the reproduction of dominant societal discourses about poverty.

Secondly, to guarantee that students would critically engage with claims about poverty but also with the process of knowledge construction about poverty more fundamentally, we included a set of questions that focused on the "rhetorical ecology" of humanitarian and social work practices—that is, who is able, allowed, or has the power to speak and who is expected to listen (Glenn 9). Students specifically critiqued the one-sided power relation in Renzo Martens's conception of emancipation as "teaching the plantation's workers how to deal with their situation, how to live." Still, students find it difficult to deal with the tension between trying to avoid imposing one's professional perspective and completely undermining the idea of professional expertise: "This is a difficult issue in social professions: you should not act as if you know best, but you also have to recognize that you do have expertise on some points. That is a difficult balance." For many students, rhetorical listening provides tactics to engage in this balancing act because listening to the life-world of service-users and to their experiential knowledge about their own situation can form the basis for responsible professional practice. In addition, identifying contradictions and gaps between service-users' experiences and the wider cultural logics underlying dominant anti-poverty policy may help social workers to reshape, from the interpersonal level, the exclusionary effects of our "dominant ways of knowing" about poverty: "Policy says that you must activate people in poverty, but you also have the story of the client who is sitting in front of you. If there is a tension between them, as a social worker, you have to use this tension to change something . . . not sitting there and think, the policy is right, and the client has to listen because we know best."

THE SYMBOL-WISE PRACTITIONER

At the outset of this chapter, we postulated that knowledge production and professional practice in the social and behavioral domain can neither be ahistorical nor theory- and value-free, which challenges practitioners to develop critical-normative professional identities, meaning they take a "partial, locatable, critical, reflexive and temporary stance" (Roets et al. 175). Below, we discuss the insights we gained in our critical case studies regarding how we can understand the social and behavioral sciences' "symbol-wise practitioner" as a "critical-normative practitioner."

THE SYMBOL-WISE PRACTITIONER AS A RESEARCHER

By being educated in and from a rhetorical perspective, students first and foremost learned to read and analyze their discipline and practice as a form of symbolic action. The Burkean concept of *terministic screen* and its relation to his notions of *attitude* and *orientation* proved especially valuable for enabling students to grapple with the idea that in social and behavioral fields, theory and practice are always interrelated. Acting as rhetorical critics, students gained insight into both the rhetorical selections inherent in their personal or professional understanding of notions such as *mental health* or *poverty*, as well as the ways these selections direct their professional interventions. Otherwise stated: understanding the performative power of language and symbols implies that students recognize that professional practices are inevitably embedded in certain theoretical and normative assumptions about the problem at hand and about their discipline more generally. Thus, educating students to become symbol-wise practitioners encourages them to take a "researcher's attitude" toward their field and to inquire into its symbolic and interpretive dimensions by "adopt[ing] an attitude of patient reflection and identify[ing] with one another as language users who are both symbol-wise and symbol-foolish" (Enoch 287). Such an "interpretive attitude" (Burke, *PC* 118) is vital to the process of developing critical-normative professional identities that require an awareness of the cultural logics underpinning professional practice and a recognition that these are normative, theory-driven, and open to contestation. As Parker claims, any "attempt to open a 'transparent' window onto the world requires a good deal of theoretical work," and making visible and debatable your part in constructing that window and your reasons for why it should be taken seriously constitute the ethical responsibility of all practitioners and researchers (19).

The Symbol-Wise Practitioner as a Transformative Intellectual

Interestingly, in their reflections, students themselves cautioned not to restrict rhetorical reflection to "an attitude of patience and withdrawal" (Enoch 292) given that social professionals ultimately are expected to *act*. In this vein, it is worth noting that Burke's interpretive attitude has been attributed inventive, productive, and transformative dimensions. Kneupper, for example, argues that the critical potential of Burke's dramatism may develop into a trained incapacity if its analytic use is not complemented with its use as a heuristic device that can produce new discourse (130), while Bennett notes that "it is no small irony then that Burke's many writings are often utilized in pedagogy and research as a systematic approach to criticism, not as a rhetorical heuristic for inspiring invention" (para 1). Ratcliffe's conceptualization of rhetorical listening, too, goes beyond mere analysis, identifying listening as a "trope for interpretive *invention*" (1) and the "*performance* of . . . a stance of openness" (26, emphasis added). To the question of how social and behavioral professionals can develop rhetorical reflection as an inventive, transformational praxis (Enoch 291), the work of Singh and Cowden might be relevant. Challenging the commonsense dichotomy between "thinkers" and "doers," the authors call for social and behavioral practitioners to think of themselves as "transformative intellectuals" (480). Inspired by the work of Antonio Gramsci and Henry Giroux, they reimagine the concept of the *intellectual* as someone who "is concerned with the use of critical skills for the purpose of democratic social transformation, and the nurturance of the capacity to critically evaluate one's own and other's life-worlds" (480). In taking a researcher's stance, the symbol-wise practitioner can thus also find opportunities to reimagine and transform. We contend that rhetorical pedagogies of critical reflection include an orientation toward inventiveness and transformation because, in disclosing new or different interpretations of disciplinary notions such as mental health or poverty, they simultaneously disclose new orientations and strategies for action. Furthermore, inviting students to take a stance of rhetorical listening in relation to, for example, experiential knowledge as developed by service-users or the terminologies of other disciplines may prove a fruitful way to confront them with such new interpretations and to challenge their (disciplinary) trained incapacities. Moreover, turning to culture and the arts in our pedagogies may be particularly valuable in "shaking up students' language" (White 22), as "poetry, broadly defined, is a locus of perspective by incongruity, a place where incongruous metaphors can be pushed together to create new ways of viewing the world—a counter-gridlock" (Hawhee, "Burke and Nietzsche" 139).

THE SYMBOL-WISE PRACTITIONER EMBRACES AMBIGUITY

Clearly, rhetorical pedagogies of critical reflection disclose the multiplicity inherent to notions of mental health or poverty, as well as the social and behavioral sciences more generally. Furthermore, by focusing on the diversity of terministic screens imaginable and on the myriad ways these screens may relate to each other, students were confronted with the ambiguous character of their fields. Through their rhetorical reflections, they learned not only that a rhetor (i.e., a practitioner, service-user, policy maker, etc.) can be motivated differently by different vocabularies but also that "multiple terministic clusters exist and that they can be in agonistic and complementary relationships at the same time" (Angel and Bates 4). This ambiguity implies that some uncertainty is inherent to professional practice since practitioners have to "take action while simultaneously acknowledging that [their] analyses are, to an extent, contingent and fallible" (D'Cruz et al. 71). We assert that in addition to being a valuable analytical lens *on* the social and behavioral sciences, the work of Burke and Ratcliffe provides equipment *for* these fields, especially in relation to the challenge of dealing with their uncertainties in responsible, productive ways. Notably, Burke's dramatistic perspective never aimed at identifying the "right" terministic screen through which to interpret a complex situation and so resolve ambiguity. Rather, Burke aims to open up texts and "multiply the perspectives from which we view motives and thereby expose the resources of ambiguity people might exploit to interpret complex problems" (Blakesley 35). Translated to the domain of the social and behavioral sciences, this implies that the challenge of taking a productive rhetorical stance lies in seizing the ambiguity and uncertainty of clinical and social practice as an opportunity to develop a critical awareness of one's incapacities while simultaneously recognizing oneself as "trained"—as able to formulate a potentially meaningful answer to a problem. For practitioners, this requires a continuous balancing between "being trained" on the one hand and "having incapacities" on the other: taking the "risk" to act from a specific "way of seeing" and, simultaneously, to use mistakes as opportunities for shared learning and upholding "the premise that there are always alternatives" (Lorenz 14). For us, it is here that we find a translation of Burke's trained incapacity from a predominantly psychologically or linguistically oriented notion describing a fundamental characteristic of human symbol-use to a pedagogical notion that, in the context of the social and behavioral sciences, serves as equipment to develop professional attitudes that engage with the ambiguity of professional practice in (self-)critical yet productive ways.

Lessons for Educators

Although Burke notes that "planned incongruity should be deliberately cultivated" (*PC* 119), scholars have pointed to the political and pedagogical risks involved in developing overtly routinized, methodical practices of critical reflection as part of the "tick box exercise" of acquiring individual competences (Galea 247–49). Our recommendations for educators who wish to engage in rhetorical pedagogies of critical reflection in their (social and behavioral sciences) classrooms, therefore, do not take the form of a model or a delineated method of reflection. Rather, we draw on the insights gained in our critical case studies to suggest four vital dimensions of rhetorical practices and pedagogies of critical reflection.

First, we argue that students need to develop a basic understanding of rhetorical theories and concepts (in our case, those of Burke and Ratcliffe) to be able to use them as equipment to "engage on the terrain of language" and discover their agency to "play with/in text" (Ratcliffe 18, 135). This might be achieved through theoretical work and by way of engaging students in small assignments (cf. Burke's linguistic exercises) that focus on the application of specific rhetorical concepts (e.g., for social work students: identify different terministic screens operating in news reports on a specific social problem).

Second, instructors may enact rhetorical pedagogies of critical reflection by translating specific rhetorical concepts into pedagogical and didactical principles and approaches. Developing pedagogies as expressions of rhetorical concepts such as perspective by incongruity or rhetorical listening certainly constitutes a challenging task. Still, it may be in this challenge that rhetoric's ability to serve as "equipment" in various disciplinary contexts is situated. In this regard, there is some very promising recent work. For example, Pycroft studied how the notion of trained incapacity can help criminal justice practitioners navigate the wider social context of their practice and of the barriers and opportunities for creative and critical practice this context presents (25–40). In the domain of history, Knutsen and Knutsen studied how Burke's dramatism might incite in students a "performative historical competence" by reading history as a form of symbolic action (1–12)—something that Ann George demonstrates with her students in the graduate class outlined in this volume. We believe that further work is still to be done here with regard to many of the social and behavioral fields and hope this chapter has provided inspiration for educators and scholars who wish to take on this challenge.

Third, we propose that a rhetorical approach to critical reflection is embedded within a wider critical curriculum that includes relevant (disciplinary) critical theories. These would play a significant role in (a) theorizing where the critical contribution of rhetoric may specifically lie in relation to particular topics or disciplines; (b) resisting, by way of constituting an important part of the "training" of social and behavioral professionals, tendencies to develop rhetorical reflection as a process of engaging only with one's incapacities, which is not only a self-defeating move but ultimately undermines the ability of the profession and discipline to act as a critical agency; and (c) providing historical, sociological, economic, and policy analyses that not only complement Burkean rhetoric as a symbolically oriented approach but also help locate the intersections between the social, the political, the economic, and the linguistic.

Fourth, and finally, we contend that stances of symbol-wisdom and rhetorical listening may be fostered by way of cultivating, in and through our pedagogies, an openness to uncertainty. Such openness would provide students with the opportunity to discover productive ways of (rhetorically) engaging with the inevitable contingency and situatedness of their practice. From a rhetorical perspective, "making [students] at home with uncertainty, celebrating—via perspective by incongruity—the 'heuristic value of error'" (George, *Kenneth Burke's* 223) may be established through "shaking up students' language" and challenging their "final vocabularies" (White 22, 26–27). Once again, we make a plea here for doing so by using culture and the arts, as "the agonistic space of literature allows the conflict of various attitudes without any avowal that there is a correct, final, or totalizing attitude" and, as such, "dramatizes possibility—recalling the Jamesian insight that only the existence of options and the capacity, but not the necessity, to exercise some but not all of those options render action thinkable and desirable" (McGowan 133).

Assignment Prompts

Course

12-week Cultural Studies course for master students in social work and international bachelor and master students in various social and behavioral fields including educational studies, psychology, sociology, communication studies, linguistics, and gender and diversity studies. The course teaches students to approach social topics through the lens of different cultural and interpretive frameworks including Burke's and Krista Ratcliffe's rhetorical theories.

Assignment

Throughout the course, students make several small assignments to get acquainted with the central concepts of the course. Example: "Choose a topic of public debate that engages issues of identity (e.g., #MeToo, Black Lives Matter, Black Pete, hijab-bans in public spaces, disability and inclusion in schools . . .) and identify different 'terministic screens' (Burke) and 'cultural logics' (Krista Ratcliffe) at play in the debate." At the end of the course, students participate in a final assignment that connects the different topics of the course, namely the cultural studies perspective, narrative and rhetorical approaches to social issues, art as a form of anthropological research, and the social role of the arts. The final assignment consists of a screening of Renzo Martens's art documentary *Enjoy Poverty* and processes of individual and group reflection on the documentary and the issue of poverty more generally.

PART I: INDIVIDUAL REFLECTION

Develop a critical analysis of Renzo Martens's *Enjoy Poverty* building on the central theories and concepts of the course. We provide some guiding questions and suggest different concepts that can inspire your analysis.

Poverty as a discursive and normative construct
- What representations of poverty can you identify in the documentary? Which dimensions of poverty are emphasized, which are left out?

- How does Renzo Martens understand poverty? How do other characters understand poverty?
- How do the different characters in the documentary propose that we deal with poverty?
- How is this related to their understandings of poverty?
- Guiding theories and concepts
  - 'Lesson 1: Cultural studies': the symbolic dimensions of social realities
  - 'Lesson 2 & 3: Burke's & Ratcliffe's rhetoric': humans as symbol-using animals, terministic screens, selections and deflections, orientations to act, cultural logics, cultural scripts to act

Poverty and the politics of representation

- Who speaks about poverty in the documentary? Who doesn't?
- What understandings of poverty are considered more/less legitimate than others in the documentary? By whom? How do the characters persuade the audience of this?
- What power relations are at play in the documentary in terms of the representation of poverty and of who speaks, listens, remains silent?
- Guiding theories and concepts
  - 'Lesson 2 & 3: Burke's & Ratcliffe's rhetoric': trained incapacity, the rhetorical situation, rhetorical listening as listening to the other and the self, rhetorical listening as critical analysis—what are the (unequal) consequences of speaking from a specific cultural logic and for whom?
  - 'Lesson 4: The artist as ethnographer': representation as description and delegation, the poetics and politics of ethnography

Poverty in the arts

- Try to widen the scope of your analysis from the content of *Enjoy Poverty* to *Enjoy Poverty* as a specific cultural product that is produced in a specific socio-cultural context. What could have been the aim of Renzo Martens? At what audience is the documentary aimed? What could be positive/problematic consequences of the documentary in terms of our understanding

of poverty (in the Global South)? What power relations are at play in terms of who benefits from this documentary?
- Guiding theories and concepts
  - 'Lesson 2 & 3: Burke's & Ratcliffe's rhetoric': circumference, listening to our own discourses, terministic screens and trained incapacities, situating ourselves and our knowledge
  - 'Lesson 5: The social functions of the arts': in what different ways can the arts take on a social commitment?

From poverty in the arts to poverty in social professions

- Find an account on poverty that is not fictional. This can be a news article, a TV or news report on poverty, a personal confrontation with poverty, an experience during an internship, a policy initiative, a specific (social work) intervention or project focused on poverty, a discussion or conversation about poverty in your personal environment . . .
- Use the above questions about *Enjoy Poverty* to analyse your chosen account on poverty. How is poverty represented in the material you chose? By whom? What orientations to act correspond to the framing(s) of poverty evident in your chosen materials? Are there specific power relations at play? What are the consequences of this representation of poverty and for whom?

PART II: Reflective group discussions

To avoid a reduction of critical reflection to an individual learning process and to stimulate collective reflection, the students' individual assignments were complemented with group discussions consisting of approximately eight students from different disciplinary and geographical backgrounds. In the first part of the group discussion, students shared how they tackled the above questions about the documentary and the topic of poverty more generally as well as how they applied various rhetorical concepts and ideas in the process. In the second part of the group discussion, we focused on what it implies for students to adopt a critical professional attitude and what elements of the course they found (un)helpful in cultivating such an attitude.

12 Muscular Drooping and Sentimental Brooding: Kenneth Burke's Crip Time–War Time Disability Pedagogy

Shannon Walters

Combining Burkean pedagogy and disability studies pedagogy to practice symbolic analysis.[1]

When Kenneth Burke argued in 1955 that a linguistic approach to education could help avoid war, he correlated a tendency toward relentless competition and unquestioning unity in the Cold War international arena with ambitious attitudes nurtured every day in typical classroom settings. Burke offers his linguistic pedagogy, focused on preparing students to be "symbol-wise," as an alternative to overambitiousness and as a way to "cancel off the many prompter ambitions that, given the new weapons, threaten to destroy us" ("LAPE" 273). Ideally, Burke believed that teaching students to study and appreciate language, rather than using it for competition and combat, would lead them to adopt a "technique of preparatory withdrawal" (271). Instead of propelling conflict, a pedagogy of wise symbol use could "make methodical the attitude of patience" (271).

This pedagogy resists existing midcentury approaches to education, which, according to Burke, are primarily "means of preparing students for market" in which courses with humanistic emphases focus on helping "students 'get ahead' as individuals" and vocational courses "perfect technical ability" (271). Burke believes that this goal-driven aim, in

---

1. Chapter copyright 2018 by the National Council of Teachers of English. Reprinted with permission.

which "the serious student enters school hoping to increase his powers, to equip himself in the competition for 'success,' to make the 'contacts' that get him a better-paying job," leads directly to competitive, ambitious drives and "nationalistic emphases in general" (270–71). In a climate rife with competition, with nothing to counter unanimity and "somnambulist[ic]" "automatic responses," these "national 'differences' may become national 'conflicts'" (270, 272). Rather than ambition and competition being a healthy symbol of American strength, Burke ironically positions "ambition as a disease," a perspective he forwards in "Linguistic Approach to Problems of Education" and *Attitudes Toward History* (272, 258). This attitude suggests that nonnormative perspectives on bodies and minds are crucial to understanding Burke's pedagogy and theories of symbolic action, albeit in complicated ways. Burke depends on ableist comparisons to position ambition as a disease while simultaneously questioning the value of ambition.

Burke's nonnormative approach, integral to his larger pedagogical theory, shares important perspectives with current theorists in disability studies who take as their primary objective unsettling accepted assumptions regarding "normal" and "abnormal" and "able" and "disabled" (Davis, *Enforcing*; Linton). In fact, the connection between pedagogy and war in Burke's linguistic approach to education is incomplete without thoroughly understanding how disability functions in Burke's pedagogy and theory. This understanding has critical implications regarding the role of composition in our current context of war and can also advance and be revised by current disability studies pedagogy. Reaching beyond simple alliances between disability studies and Burkean pedagogy, in what follows I both recover Burke as a rhetorical theorist and teacher crucial for disability pedagogy and use current critical disability studies to inform Burkean pedagogy. By exploring Burke's pedagogy from disability perspectives, I situate both disability studies pedagogy and Burkean pedagogy as mutually informing each other, revising positions and advancing critical conversations about language, bodies, pedagogy, and composition.[2]

---

2. In true Burkean fashion, my conversations with a range of invaluable interlocutors have challenged and enriched my analysis. My special thanks to Jack Selzer, whose kind and patient mentoring inspired my interest in Burke. An anonymous reviewer, by asking if there was ableism in Burke's calling ambition a disease, also pushed me to brood more productively with the issue of Burke's ableist language and concept of perfection.

The "serious" student that Burke describes as primed for conflict is an implicitly "able" student—one understood to be powerful, independent, strong, well-equipped, and well-connected. As an alternative to this implicitly able student—one shaped by a competitive and ambitious environment—Burke offers a different model of student. This student "droops" and "broods," which I argue shows Burke to be an educator who values disability, understanding it as generative for learning and changing. Burkean pedagogical practices of drooping and brooding share, advance, and can be critically modified by crip time, which I situate as productively challenging accepted norms in classrooms regarding how bodies and minds "should" perform. After applying a disability studies perspective to Burke's pedagogy and contextualizing pedagogical conversations in Burke's time and our own, I define Burke's linguistic approach to education as presenting a crip method for valuing disability and resisting an ableist model for composition students. I show that this concern is especially exigent in our current global context, which shares with Burke the feeling of war that is "always threatening" ("LAPE" 272). Exploring frequent associations currently made between mental disability, particularly madness, and international conflict, especially terrorism, I show that focusing on disability is as crucial today as it was in Burke's time to understand composition pedagogy's role globally. Throughout, I position Burke as forwarding a proto-disability studies pedagogy that is a valuable resource for current disability pedagogy and necessary for composition teachers to be critically mindful of today. Burke's proto-disability pedagogy, in turn, can be critically revised by disability theories attentive to the underpinnings of ableism in some of Burke's language about bodies, including his notions of perfection in pedagogy and use of disability metaphor.

Disability Studies Perspectives on Burke's Pedagogy

Understanding Burke's linguistic approach to education in relation to disability pedagogy in the current context of war extends recent efforts by scholars to apply Burke's pedagogy to contemporary issues and composition pedagogies. Jessica Enoch understands "Linguistic Approach" as a "pedagogy of critical reflection that speaks not only to [Burke's] 1955 world but also to our own" (273). Using a critically reflective approach, she advocates that "students today should learn to reflect on the language used to move people to action and war" and to "understand how terms like *evil, terrorist* [and] *freedom*" are used (291). Scott Wible contextualizes "Linguistic Approach" in relation to Burke's pedagogical methods at Bennington College, demonstrating fundamental connections between Burke's teaching and scholarship, particularly for showing to students "unexpressed assumptions that propel so much human activity toward competition and, ultimately, physical and social destruction" (259). The stakes of this continuing conversation are high. Referencing *A Grammar of Motives*, which, as Wible shows, closely connects to "Linguistic Approach," Elizabeth Weiser writes that "today the issues on the world scene are strikingly similar to those being debated during the original construction of dramatism and (soon afterward) identification: how best to respond to totalitarianism, extremism, [and] the necessary certainty of war" (*Burke, War, Words* xiv). Exploring Burke from a disability studies perspective furthers this ongoing conversation at the intersection of war, pedagogy, and symbol use.

A critically reflective disability studies perspective on Burke's pedagogy is crucial in this continuing conversation because key Burkean concepts can both advance and be modified by disability studies. Scholar-activists in disability studies define *disability* not as a personal tragedy, regrettable defect, or circumstance to overcome but instead as a valuable and generative way of inhabiting the world. The material-semiotic elements of disability—bodily lived experiences and discourses used to represent disability—are integral to this perspective. Disability scholars are especially concerned with language used to describe disabled people and how terminology affects attitudes. The social model of disability, for example, seeks to "wrest control" of the language from narrow medical meanings and to "reassign meaning to the terminology used to describe disability and disabled people" (Linton 9).

Burke's linguistic pedagogy is also concerned with this nexus of discourse and attitude, exhibiting attention to difference and making it an important critical location for disability. In letters describing his frequently taught course Language as Symbolic Action, Burke identifies his pedagogical goals: to "sharpen awareness of the ways in which terms are related to one another, and of the momentous role that terminology plays in human thought and conduct" (Letter to Bowman). Integral to Burke's pedagogy is dramatism, which aims to "channelize the direction of the terms in which differences [are] expressed" (Letter to Coffin). The expression of difference—discursively and materially—is an abiding concern of disability studies. Nirmala Erevelles identifies disability as "*the ideological linchpin utilized to (re)constitute social difference along the axes of race, gender, and sexuality in a dialectical relationship to the economic/social relations produced within the historical context of transnational capitalism*" (6, original italics). This approach, attentive to economic, material, and social difference, complements linguistic and discursive approaches. Applying a disability studies perspective focused on these differences to Burkean pedagogy in the Cold War and our current time of conflict deepens intersections between pedagogy, symbol use, and war, extending Burke's theories on difference into specific disability-related areas.

Applying a disability perspective to Burke's "Linguistic Approach" also deepens recent efforts exploring Burke's nonpedagogical work in relation to embodiment and its contingencies. As Debra Hawhee notes, "There is ample evidence that bodies (sick bodies, charged bodies, rhythmic bodies) served as important guides for Burke from the beginning" as he repeatedly took up "questions about bodies and language" (*Moving Bodies* 9, 5). Answering these questions meant eschewing binaries between essentialist and constructivist approaches and talking about "nature and language; about movement and pain" (7–8). This approach parallels recent critical moves in disability studies, which recognize that a social model of disability does not have to ignore the body and that medical approaches include sociocultural forces. Disability theorist Tobin Siebers's call for "complex embodiment" theorizes "the body and its representations as mutually transformative" (25). Burke's questions about bodies and language propel this turn toward complex embodiment, uncovering additional analytical sites and pedagogical methods.

Other scholars are beginning to connect Burke to disability studies. Ann George "introduces" Burke to Helen Keller, relating Burke's and Keller's rhetorical praxis. John Duffy and Melanie Yergeau apply Burke's maxim "wherever there is 'meaning' there is persuasion" to their corollary that "wherever there is disability there are meanings." James L. Cherney uses Burke's identification to explore disability, while others, including Elizabeth Brewer and Jordynn Jack, use Burke's terministic screens and definition of man. This valuable work uses Burke's key concepts and well-known theories for general introductions to disability or applied to specific concerns. I extend this by exploring disability in relation to Burke's lesser-explored pedagogical theories, which are connected to cornerstones of his linguistic theory.

Competition and Conflict: Then and Now

To understand Burkean pedagogy as forwarding a proto-disability pedagogy, it's crucial to connect the context in which Burke wrote "Linguistic Approach" to our current global context. When Burke, appealing for a linguistic educational approach aimed at the abatement of war, notes how "man's distinctive trait, his way with symbols, is the source of both his typical accomplishments and his typical disabilities," he positions education and symbol use directly in relation to ability and disability (271). It's tempting to assume that Burke aligns being symbol-wise with "accomplishments" and symbol foolishness with "disabilities." While this positioning would reflect educational assumptions of his time, it's more compelling to understand Burke as challenging this deficit approach. Burke's pedagogy resists a cultural context in which demonstration of ability is equated with international superpower status and pursues an alternative approach that values disability.

The Cold War context of "Linguistic Approach" was rife with international conflict and competition, which was reflected in conversations about education. As Christine Sleeter explores, postwar education emphasized technological invention and military advancement—both "business and the military had a strong interest in schools producing young people trained to carry on military research" (214). Military personnel described educational competition in militaristic terms and language closely connecting intellectual ability to superiority in international relations, as the United States and Soviet Union engaged in a "cold war of the classrooms" (Rickover 19). In early 1957, the United States was understood as losing that battle: "Our schools do not perform their primary purpose, the training of the nation's brain power to its highest potential" (19). After Sputnik, this sense of failure intensified: Sputnik "provided a focal point for debates about schooling, and 'proof' that Americas had allowed schools to be too soft and lax on young people" (Sleeter 215).[3] These educational debates are anchored by predictable assumptions regarding disability and ability. Criticisms of the US educational system are set in terms of lack, deficit, and flaw, with the assumption that students are "disabled" by inadequate schools. American schools, too "lax" and "soft," mean that US "brain power" cannot achieve levels of ability it should.

---

3. Sleeter suggests that forming the "learning disability" category was a direct response to threats of US supremacy during the Cold War.

In 1961, a *Saturday Evening Post* article situated this educational war in stark terms, asking "Can Ivan Read Better than Johnny?" and asserting that "[w]hat Russian students learn in school and what American students learn in school may do much to determine whether the free world will check and defeat Communism, or whether Communism will check and defeat the free world" (Trace 30). This race to secure international superpower status is a contest put explicitly in terms of intellectual ability in education. Freedom, independence, victory, and superpower status are intertwined with the discourse of educational and intellectual ability while defeat, dependence, wasted potential, and inadequacy are connected with educational failure and disability. Beyond simply valuing student ability in the classroom, this discourse promotes a form of ableism, systemically erasing disability or the possibility of contributions from disabled students.[4]

Alternatively, by identifying symbol use with both "accomplishments" and "disabilities" in his linguistic approach to education, Burke presents another possibility, rooted in the generative possibilities of disability. Rather than a simple association of wise symbol use with accomplishments and foolish symbol use with "disabilities," Burke envisions students' abilities and disabilities merging in their symbol use to build intellectual curiosity, pose critical questions, and encourage reflection. He imagines linguistic "education as so conceived would be first and foremost 'of a divided mind,' and would seek to make itself at home in such divisiveness" ("LAPE" 271). Burke's invocation of "disabilities" in the context of symbol use, coupled with his prizing of a "divided mind," shows him to be constructing a proto-disability pedagogy, one that builds disability into the definition of symbol use and that values disability-minded traits in educational enterprise. The divided mind that Burke seeks is not the competitive, unchangeable, and unified mind of the Cold War era educational mission. Instead, Burke sees a mind that is split, undecided, questioning, and doubtful as valuable for the nation.

This alternative approach is as important today as in Burke's time. The spirit of competition and the prizing of ableism in education that Burke identified still dominates the pedagogical landscape. As in Burke's time, competition is constant, ingrained in today's students through high-stakes testing and assessment at every level. Measures of ability are the cornerstones of this competition, promising students the way to, in

---

4. Disabled students didn't gain access to public schools until 1975, via the Education for All Handicapped Children Act.

Burke's terms, "get ahead as individuals." The vocational courses Burke describes narrowly aimed to "perfect technical ability, to teach special skills," sound not unlike the preprofessional tracks at universities, leaving little room for liberal arts, elective, or general education courses. The various "fly-by-night outfits" that "quickly cook up unlikely looking courses" that Burke identified after the G. I. Bill are not far removed from contemporary diploma mills, for-profit colleges, or the recently defunct Trump University, which still depend on the "willingness of the student-consumer to be assured [that] . . . he will somehow have a much better chance to hit the 'jackpot'" ("LAPE" 294). The model of today's corporate university is a direct descendent of the educational approach Burke details. An implicitly able body and mind power today's educational system, as in Burke's day. In the composition classroom, a labor force and student body that is able and virtually interchangeable fits best into this system. What Robert McRuer calls the current "corporeality" of pedagogy means that "instruction is often streamlined across dozens of classes," with standardized tests operating as instruments designed for cultivating "professional-managerial skills rather than critical thought," a model based on "measurement and marketability" (49). This current "corporeality" grows out of composition's complex history with disability. As Jay Dolmage shows, "Composition is not always an accessible space" since it "grew at a time when issues of ability were framed according to a deficit model," during the period of an assumed literacy "crisis" and the rise of open admissions following WWII ("Mapping" 14–15).

Outside of the classroom, the climate of war is different today but seems almost as persistent as it felt during the Cold War. The War on Terror, both domestic and international, is an ongoing, protracted military campaign that most college students have heard about for as long as they can remember. The United States is involved, in varying degrees, in wars in Iraq and Afghanistan, while media outlets continually report of nuclear weapons and potential dangers of countries such as Russia, North Korea, and Syria. Shortly before taking office, President-elect Donald Trump suggested expanding the United States' nuclear capabilities to compete with Russia, prompting a situation that some media outlets call "Cold War 2.0" (Fisher; Osnos et al.) After taking office, Vice President Mike Pence declared the "era of strategic patience is over" with North Korea regarding its nuclear and ballistic missile program (Kennedy). Today, as it was during the Cold War, global dominance and leadership is understood as a demonstration of ability, bravery, strength, and power. In short, we continue to teach and learn at a time when war, as it was when Burke was writing, is "always threatening" ("LAPE" 272).

When Burke identifies symbol use as the source of both "typical accomplishments" and "typical disabilities," he positions disability and rhetoric in a co-constitutive relationship, extending long but fraught connections also articulated by scholars in rhetoric and disability studies. "The concept of disability has . . . been involved since classical antiquity in an enabling/disabling partnership with rhetoric, [often] occupying the less valued side of binary oppositions" (Wilson and Lewiecki-Wilson, "Disability" 6). Focusing on the enabling side of this partnership, Dolmage argues that to "affirm the disabled body is to affirm embodied rhetoric" (*Disability* 191) and advocates for a "view that the body's partiality and incompleteness can be claimed as essential and generative" (91). Burke's placing of symbol use in relation to disability and his overall valuing of disability in a linguistic approach to education contribute significantly to this perspective, revealing new locations for disability rhetoric and pedagogy. Specifically, I define Burke's concepts of *muscular drooping* and *sentimental brooding* as crip-timed pedagogical approaches that value disability and resist the unremitting ambition and competition that lead toward conflict, in the composition classroom and the world.

METHODICAL DISABILITY: DROOPING AND BROODING

As described, one of Burke's primary objectives in "Linguistic Approach" is to show his audience that the serious student presumably at the height of his or her powers, supremely able and accomplished, is deceptive, limiting, and dangerous, particularly in wartime. Burke sees overactive ambition as the main flaw of this implicitly able student and, by ironically defining "ambition as a disease," questions accepted assumptions regarding ability and disability in education (272). Burke uses irony to emphasize the unmarked but assumed hierarchy of ability. Burke's critique of the ambitious, able student illustrates what Siebers calls the "ideology of ability." Noting that "ideology does not permit the thought of contradiction necessary to question it," Siebers writes that "the ideology of ability is at its simplest the preference for able-bodiedness" (8). Burke exercises a critique of the ideology of ability in education by situating excessive ambition as disease, resisting the status quo preference for an able student and offering an alternative pedagogy that values disability in the practices of drooping and brooding.

Ambition in students is not necessarily a sign of ability for Burke but instead is a disadvantage if understood too narrowly, a perspective best understood in connection with his broader concepts of *trained incapacity* and *perspective by incongruity*. These concepts also hinge on questioning typical assumptions regarding ability and disability. In *trained incapacity*, "one's very abilities can function as blindnesses," and "past education" creates a response that "defeats one's interests" (*PC* 7). In other words, education can produce processes by which "people may be unfitted by being fit in an unfit fitness" (10). By using terms of relative ability and disability—"abilities" and "blindnesses," "fitness" and "unfit"—Burke questions accepted norms regarding what kinds of abilities or disabilities represent respective advantages or disadvantages in education, suggesting a more fluid continuum is necessary. This continuum offers pedagogical possibilities for bodies and minds occupying more diverse positions of difference.

Burke's perspective can be understood in relation to today's pedagogical principles of access and inclusion, backed by Section 504 of the Rehabilitation Act and the Americans with Disabilities Act (ADA), which ideally offer different paths to student success that do not necessarily preclude ambition but foster alternative methods for achievement. Saint Louis University's Disability Services, for example, works with students to find campus resources that will "prepare them for academic and personal success" ("About"). Many universities employ similar appeals to disabled students, emphasizing flexible paths to achievement. When success is predicated on principles of inclusion, flexibility, and access, ambition is not the narrowly defined category Burke critiques. Burke's use of disability terminology that hinges on a fluid continuum of ability and disability questions the limited framework for ambition in his current context, particularly in environments restricted to narrow understandings of ability, which persist today (Grasgreen).

For Burke, understanding ambition as a disease is also a form of *perspective by incongruity*, or the "methodic merger of particles that had been considered mutually exclusive" (*PC* lv). This new perspective hinges on the merger of ability and disability, or the situating of heightened ambition—usually considered a sign of ability—as a metaphor for disease. In *Attitudes Toward History*, Burke expands his connection between ambition and disease, writing, "in an ideal society, a man would not go to a doctor when he lacked ambition—he would consult a doctor to help him cure ambition. In the paradoxes of capitalism, inordinate ambition has become the norm" (258). Ambition in the classroom does not necessarily enable students and, in fact, when uncritically accepted and narrowly defined, is destructive. Burke's linguistic approach to education is designed to teach students to "modify" the "intrinsically competitive emphasis" of education and guide us toward curtailing ambition by being "sufficiently exacting in our ambitiousness to cancel off the many prompter ambitions that, given the new weapons, threaten to destroy us" (272–73). Burke, in other words, hopes that a different type of ambition, one rooted in an appreciation of disability, will offer another path.

This alternative path involves forming a model for a non-ableist student, who embodies the generative aspects of disability. Siebers writes that to "reverse the negative connotations of disability" promulgated by the ideology of ability, "it will be necessary to claim the value and variety of disability" (11). Burke's pedagogical methods of drooping and brooding claim the value of disability for education, particularly by encouraging students to be more skeptical, reflective, and forbearing. Under the heading "Educational Aims and Values," Burke describes a method for resisting the "intrinsically competitive emphasis" of education and replacing it with an approach based on the "fear of symbol-using (that is, an ironic fear of the very resourcefulness that is man's greatest boast)" ("LAPE" 272). Questioning one's abilities, in other words, is productive for students. Rather than the unanimity of one's current educational and political scene, this fearsome approach would produce a more critical and reflective "divided mind." By making a way for a "methodic distrust of competitive ambitions which goad us . . . [w]e would try . . . to perfect techniques for doubting much that is now accepted as lying beyond the shadow of a doubt" (272). Burke continues by explaining how to make methodical these techniques for doubting, rooting them further in his appreciation of disability:

> The aim, then, is to droop, at least *ad interim* (within the special conditions of the educational enterprise, considered as but one stage of a person's life)—but to droop so methodically, with such an emphasis upon method, that each day can bristle with assertions, as we attempt to perfect our lore of the human scramble (what Goethe calls the *Zeitenstrudel*, and Diderot the *grand branle*). (273)

"To droop" means "to hang or sink down, as from weariness or exhaustion; to bend, incline or slope downward; to flag, fail, decay," definitions that are typically associated negatively with disability (*OED*). Yet Burke's use of "to droop" is generative and positive, drawing on the possibilities in meaning making that disability and different ways of moving and thinking yield. Drooping, for Burke, is advantageous because it enables a different approach to education, an alternative sense of timing and space. Drooping leaves room for change and flexibility—each day "can bristle with assertions" different from before. Reminiscent of his use of identification to expand the "range of rhetoric" to "lead us through the Scramble, the Wrangle of the Market Place," Burke uses drooping to expand the objectives and aims of education (*RM* 23). Rather than an unyielding sense of right and wrong, drooping leaves space for differences in interpretation. The intermittent or temporary approach to drooping that Burke suggests—one to be adopted at various stages—as well as the different cadence to thought and movement that drooping produces—shares with the experience of disability a nonnormative approach to time.

Disability theorists such as Irving Kenneth Zola and Carol Gill explore "crip time" as a way to acknowledge the flexible approach to normative time that disability occasions and the understanding that disability can redefine time.[5] Margaret Price notes that it is the "notion of flexibility (not just 'extra' time) that matters" in crip time (*Mad at School* 62), while Alison Kafer writes, "crip time bends the clock to meet disabled bodies and minds" rather than the other way around (27). For Kafer, this bending asks the larger question of "how might observations on 'crip time' lead to more expansive notions of both time and futurity" (27)? It's exactly these expansive notions of flexibility, time, and futurity with which Burke grapples in "Linguistic Approach," as he searches for ways to teach in a time when war is "always threatening" and when "the new weapons" in an escalating nuclear arms race "threaten to destroy us" (273). These threats—which call into question the notion of futurity in very real terms—call for a new understanding of time in education for Burke. The flexibility that the attitude of drooping requires and the differences in thinking and moving it invites mean that different scenarios are possible than the one toward which humanity seems inevitably hurtling.

---

5. Time also figures into concepts including the term *temporarily able bodied* and the understanding that categories of disabled/nondisabled can change anytime.

For Burke, drooping's flexible and nonnormative approach to time—a kind of crip time—means that students have different paths forward that take them away from single-minded purpose, ambition, or competition. When students cultivate an attitude of drooping, they move through thinking, reacting, and reflecting differently, imbuing these activities with a sense of crip time that slows them down. Burke writes that the cultivation of methodical drooping in education means "being stopped by such a discipline" (273). In this sense, "education must be thought of as a technique of preparatory withdrawal, the institutionalizing of an attitude that one should be able to recover at crucial moments, all along the subsequent way" (273). Stopping and withdrawal are methods by which Burke seeks to bend the existing normative approach to time, challenging students to check their competitive impulses—in the classroom and beyond—before it's too late. Rather than feeling right and justified in one's path at all times, methodical drooping seeks to cultivate a different approach, finding "crucial moments" to slow down. Students are advised to "watch and wait" while making "methodical the attitude of patience" (271). This slower, alternative approach to timing in education—stopping, withdrawing, waiting—ideally leads to leaders who do not turn "national differences" so quickly into "national conflicts." Working against ableist assumptions associating strength and ability with speed, Burke associates drooping with slowness productively, noting that drooping can be "quite muscular" when it "opens many new vistas" of symbolic activity (274). Drooping is muscular not in a "might is right" way that depends on the traditional hierarchy of strength over weakness. Drooping, instead, is muscular by enabling one to think in new ways, to experience different perspectives and not cling too closely to one point of view. Muscular drooping allows one to bend, flex, and stretch one's mind in new ways, slowly and patiently.

While Burke's drooping represents a disability-friendly and nonnormative approach, it also relies on a problematic notion of perfection that can be critically revised by current disability studies and crip time theories. This critical revision hinges on creative application of disability to pedagogy, which as Brenda Jo Brueggemann, extending Leonard Davis, demonstrates, is "an enabling pedagogy, a theory and practice of teaching that posits disability as insight" (321). In the spirit of understanding revision as a practice of "looking again," disability's insight can revise limits of Burke's disability pedagogy. For example, the concept of *perfection* has historically been a harmful commonplace for a variety of bodies and minds who do not "measure up" to an assumed but illusory state of completeness or flawlessness. Through drooping, Burke seeks "to perfect techniques for doubting" and to "attempt to perfect our lore of the human scramble." This repeated, abstracted focus on perfecting, even its nonnormative aim, may re-entrench ableism if not understood from a disability studies perspective.

Rob Michalko, who writes about "cool blindness time," offers a specific example of disability as insight—unconnected to literal sight—that can be understood to counter this focus on perfecting. Contrasting "blindness time" and "culture standard time," Michalko writes that "blindness time resets its clock to cultural standard time with the mechanism of 'figuring out.' Blindness is the time to figure out sight and the subsequent sighted configuration of the world." Similar to crip time, blindness time's practice of "figuring out" is a flexible, nonstandard practice, focused on the alteration and resistance inspired by disability as insight. Blindness time confronts culture's standard time with questions about the accepted dominance of sight, opting for relationships based on "figuring out" rather than "perfecting." This iterative practice, if aligned with drooping, can mitigate the ableist underpinnings of Burke's focus on perfecting.

To complement the nonnormative embodied technique of drooping, Burke's alternative educational method also includes a nonnormative psychological and emotional technique called brooding. Extending methodic drooping, Burke writes,

> Education, so conceived, would brood, as with the Flaubert who wrote *L'Education Sentimentale*. But in its attempts to perfect a technique of brooding, it would learn to cherish the documents as never before. No expunging of records here. All must be kept, and faithfully examined; and not just that it may be approved or disapproved, but also that it be considered as a challenge to our prowess in placing it within the unending human dialogue as a whole. ("LAPE" 273)

Brooding, like drooping, usually possesses a negative connotation; to brood typically is associated with depressive, anxious, and obsessive thinking patterns and behaviors. Yet Burke's invitation to brood appreciates the productive possibilities of ruminative thought in ways that can be extended by the generative potentials of depression offered by theorists in critical affect studies. Ann Cvetkovich, for example, writes about "political depression" in *Depression: A Public Feeling*, noting that "hope and despair remain entwined as we track the ongoing rhythms of war (in and out of Iraq, Libya, and Afghanistan)" and "financial meltdown" amid other public issues, including "assaults on the university" (2). She recognizes that depression "can take antisocial forms such as withdrawal or inertia, but it can also create new forms of sociality," perhaps serving "as the foundation for new kinds of attachments or affiliation" (6). Aligning herself with scholar-activists in the Public Feelings Project, Cvetkovich notes that this new orientation to depression uses keywords such as "*rest, impasse,* and *sentimentality*," which "provide entry points into social and cultural analysis" (13). The aim is "to be patient with the moods and temporalities of depression, not moving too quickly to recuperate them" and "to let depression linger" (14). Cvetkovich's focus on patience and even impasse resists Burke's repeated focus on perfection through brooding, recognizing that crip time catalyzes new connections through alternative understandings of time.

These new kinds of orientations and relationships to the personal and public feelings of depression can extend what Burke hopes to achieve with sentimental brooding. For Burke, sentimental brooding is an entry point into new ways of thinking and feeling. Brooding is aligned with drooping in that it occasions an alternative, slower approach to thinking and learning. In her study of crip time, Kafer remarks that "depression slow[s] down time," suggesting possibilities for understanding time differently (380). The withdrawal and inertia that Cvetkovich describes, from the perspective of Burke's brooding, is less an "antisocial" behavior and more like a protracted, alternative thought process. Like the flexes and bends of crip time in drooping, brooding encourages students to take their time on documents and cultural records rather than jump into arguments or positions immediately. Brooding is sentimental for Burke in the desire to preserve and treasure a wide range of perspectives. By learning "to cherish the documents as never before," Burke hopes to avoid the kind of sureness, unanimity, and single-mindedness of the postwar cultural orientation in politics and education. By advising that "all must be kept," Burke employs sentimentality to preserve the documents and records that might interrupt this single-mindedness, forming a new archive and cultivating "divided minds" comfortable in their multiplicity. Perspective taking requires patience and the imperative to "watch and wait." Keeping documents for faithful examination is not just the means to argument's end; instead it's "a challenge to our prowess," a reminder that there is an "unending human dialogue" to consider (273). This challenge to ability means other perspectives are possible. In Cvetkovich's terms, new attachments and affiliations are possible for a pedagogy aligned with Burke's sentimental brooding because students are encouraged to linger and be patient with the documents and records of cultural and social analysis.

One way drooping and brooding could productively work in the composition classroom is through rethinking writer's block. Reading strategies focused on lingering with the documents of cultural analysis foster a writing process more tolerant of the time it takes students to carefully consider positions and find arguments. Cvetkovich describes her experience of being "stuck" in the writing process of her dissertation and first book, as well as the methods she found for becoming productive. Pointedly, she asks, "What is going on when you can't write?' (19). In a Burkean pedagogy of drooping and brooding, this question is generative; "being stuck" in writing is not a delay or hindrance but instead an opportunity for reflection, reconsideration, and patience. In Michalko's terms, a writer may be "figuring out" their process. While these experiences of "being stuck" and "figuring out" may not align exactly with Burke's drooping and brooding techniques, the spirit of this pedagogical approach is similar. Students who experience writer's block, rather than being labeled as deficient or failing the assignment, may be understood as inhabiting a form of drooping or brooding and could offer other evidence of their ongoing reflection in nontraditional forms of writing or be allowed alternative timelines for completing work. The reasonable accommodations made for disabled students in writing classrooms often already take these forms and may serve as examples applicable to wider student bodies.

Burke returns to the language of disability to reflect on his educational approach and to anticipate counterarguments, a perspective that can be augmented by critical insights from disability studies on his metaphoric language regarding bodies: "Admittedly, this view of education as a kind of smiling hypochondriasis presents some difficulties. The promissory, by its very nature, likes to look forward" ("LAPE" 273). *A Grammar of Motives* contextualizes this hypochondriac view. Asking "to what extent can we confront the global situation with an attitude neither local nor imperialistic," Burke answers by identifying an "attitude of hypochondriasis: the attitude of a patient who makes peace with his symptoms by becoming interested in them" (442–43). For Burke, hypochondriasis is "an attitude of appreciation" that "would seek delight in meditating upon some of the many ingenuities of speech" (443). While this enjoyment is certainly possible, a current disability studies perspective offers productive resistance and revision regarding Burke's metaphoric language of hypochondria and potential pedagogical practices.

Burke's repeated dependence on illness/disability metaphors in his language about bodies—ambition as disease, abilities as blindnesses, and education as hypochondria—provokes questions and potential resistance. Scholars in disability studies, including Amy Vidali and Sami Schalk, have been critical of the normative use of disability metaphors, while also arguing for approaches to metaphor that integrate transgressive possibilities. While Burke seems to upend some normative assumptions in his comparisons, he is also depending on the premise that equates disability with negativity in order to do so. Burke's own practice of critical reflection and "meditating" on the "many ingenuities of speech" supports a more disability-centered approach to metaphor in pedagogical applications of drooping and brooding. As Vidali demonstrates, "A disability approach to metaphor attends to how diverse bodies impact metaphor acquisition and use, which shifts disability away from something only 'used' or 'represented' by metaphor" (42). Rather than policing metaphor, a critically reflective perspective such as this revises and re-imagines. The diverse bodies of students in the composition classroom can and should provide additional models of drooping and brooding that complement metaphor in Burke's models. A blind student, for example, perhaps one who practices a form of "blindness time," may have alternative strategies to linger with the documents of cultural analysis or approach the productive, "brooding" potential of writer's block that a nondisabled student or a differently disabled student may not necessarily share but can benefit from witnessing. A student with a chronic illness might have specific experiences with crip space-time that generatively shape a "drooping" attitude towards a text or argument based on changes and flexibility. These specific, material practices of disabled students can resist the tendency to metaphorize disability in abstract ways.

Burke is hopeful about a pedagogy that droops and broods because he envisions a new kind of student populating classrooms who is less attached to the competition and ambition that he sees fueling conflict internationally. Consequently, it's useful to remember alternative meanings of *brood*—a "group of young, species group or kind" or "to incubate" and "to warm, protect and cover" (*Dictionary.com*). Doing so supports the possibility that Burke seeks to encourage a different breed of student through a linguistic and disability approach to education, one less likely to measure success by traditional standards based on strength, speed, and ambition and more by the barometers of understanding, fearsomeness, and patience. Disabled students, as part of this new brood, have much to contribute towards this approach.

Pedagogical Techniques for Drooping and Brooding

Burke suggests that his linguistic approach to education could occupy a foundational curricular position, one not unlike composition today. Realistically, he knows that "a whole educational program . . . undertaken in such a spirit" of smiling hypochondriasis is unlikely but suggests "this enterprise could be but one course in a curriculum" (273–74). Burke envisions a "kind of 'central' or 'over-all' course, a 'synoptic' project for 'unifying the curriculum' by asking students themselves to think of their various courses in terms of a single distinctive human trait (the linguistic) that imposes its genius upon all particular studies" ("LAPE" 274). The foundational positioning of this linguistic course parallels the aims of many composition programs; certainly Burke's central and unifying approach is similar to writing courses seeking to introduce students to larger structures of academic discourse and prepare them for writing in the university and beyond. Yet Burke's aim of prodding students to think about the "genius" of humans' distinctive linguistic trait is one that, in relation to his larger educational program, takes on an ironic, fearsome, and nonnormative perspective. Burke does not see the "genius" of symbol use from an ableist perspective; he uses disability–friendly concepts such as smiling hypochondriasis, muscular drooping, and sentimental brooding to imbue a sense of disability into the study of the "genius" of language. In this way, Burke's educational program and pedagogical techniques can be seen to resist the normative "corporeality" of composition that McRuer identifies and the inaccessible space of composition that Dolmage describes.

Burke, in positioning disability as generative for learning, suggests specific pedagogical techniques for drooping and brooding that extend the range of his linguistic approach and model nonnormative ways forward for composition. These techniques, in addition to making composition in general a more accessible space, inform a specific contemporary concern in composition classrooms and disability studies pedagogy. Particularly in the study of disability and the teaching of writing, scholars have become concerned with what Everelles calls the "add-and-stir" method of including disability (93). As Deb Martin relates, when disability is included in composition textbooks, it's often in simplistic terms, such as a pro/con debate or disabled/nondisabled binary. Price explains, following Davis, "Disability in the first-year writing classroom is thus in danger of becoming merely 'the new kid on the multicultural block'" (Price, "Accessing" 54; Davis, *Bending* 35). Therefore, Price states, if "we wish to benefit from the potential power of disability as a topic in the writing classroom, we must go beyond simple inclusion" ("Accessing" 54). Burke's theories and pedagogies of symbol use show him thoroughly engaged with discourses of ability and disability, situating him as an important source for realizing the transformative potential of disability pedagogy in the composition classroom. Now I turn to specific pedagogical techniques of drooping and brooding—the charting of terms and reading the news—that position Burke as a teacher who can speak to concerns regarding overly simplistic inclusions of disability and present opportunities for making the composition classroom more accessible. These techniques are designed to show how all students and educators, disabled or not, are affected by discourses of disability, particularly in a global context of war.

One of the pedagogical strategies that Burke suggests for the abatement of war and ambition, the charting of terms, is well positioned as an exercise in composition classrooms focused on critical literacy. He directs, "When you consult a text, from which you hope to derive insights as regards our human quandaries in general, you begin by asking yourself 'what equals what in this text?'" ("LAPE" 270). These equations can reveal the ways that "certain elements equal 'good' and certain elements equal 'bad' (or, what is often more important, if certain elements equal 'socially superior' and certain elements equal 'socially inferior')" (270–71). This study is a methodical way of keeping an open mind: a "preparatory stage in which one wholly 'yields' to the text" is a "basic admonition" to "watch and wait" since "one cannot know in advance what the 'equations' are to be (what 'hero' is to equal, what 'villain' is to equal, what 'wisdom' is to equal, etc.)" (270–71). Burke outlines a related pedagogical practice called *indexing* that attempts to methodically study connections, assumptions, and extrapolations. Reasserting this exercise's aims, he notes it's "in accordance with our project for methodic drooping" (275) and that "we do this, not just to learn something about the given work, but ultimately in the hope of learning something about the ways in which the 'personality' of the work relates to the 'personality' of the social order" (275).

Current disability pedagogies enact a modified form of Burke's methods of charting and indexing, directing students to find associations between what is assumed as socially inferior and superior in relation to disability and ability. Cynthia Lewiecki-Wilson and Brenda Jo Brueggemann's *Disability and the Teaching of Writing*, for example, includes G. Thomas Couser's common formulas of disability memoir—rhetorics of medicine, triumph, horror, and spiritual compensation. Suggestions for student activities include the possibility that "instructors might make a chart using Couser's terms (his rhetorics) with abbreviated descriptions of each plot type and its embedded rhetorical message" (197). Beyond simple taxonomies, this chart can "encourage conversation and discussion" about equations between disability and rhetorical messages. These exercises, similar to Burke's equation charting, can direct students in composition classes to watch and wait regarding disability stereotypes and formulaic messages. An attitude of disability critical consciousness and skepticism underlies this process of charting, extending Burke's efforts productively. Like Burke's practice of "yielding without demoralization," for example, this charting of disability rhetorics teaches students to yield to the text but also resist it, as they watch and wait, not accepting preconceived stereotypes and generalizations about who should be a hero or villain or what kinds of bodies and minds govern associations of socially superior and inferior.

In related pedagogical pursuits, Burke applies similar methods to reading the news reflectively, modeling the critical reading strategies important to many composition classrooms today. For example, Burke describes an exercise in which students would "read in a newspaper some 'factual' story that obviously produced a pronounced attitude for or against something, [and] while reading it one would try to imagine how the same material might have been presented so as to produce other attitudes" ("LAPE" 286–87). Similar to the exercise of charting equations and indexing, this exercise elicits multiple possibilities and different readings and forestalls the assumption that a singular understanding of "what equals what" is correct. In the composition classroom, reading the news this way ideally leads to students who are more critical readers and reflective writers.

This pedagogical strategy is particularly well suited to uncover equations made between disability and terrorism in current mass media. Shaista Patel employs a practice that models and extends Burke's charting to explore the discourse of the "mad Muslim terrorist." Showing that newspapers are "insidiously powerful texts" that "actively participate in forming 'news' as the 'truth' of our society," Patel explores "links between race/religion, madness, and terrorism discourses with the particular aim of investigating what the label 'mad' is doing to readers' sensibilities regarding the political action of racialized others" (201–02). Patel does not explicitly invoke Burke, but her link of mental disability and madness intersects with race and religion in a Burkean "what equals what" way, leading audiences to identify an inherent connection between "*all* Muslim men . . . psychologized as mad" (205). This discourse shifts according to race: "white terrorists remain as individual white men who committed heinous 'senseless violence' because they were not 'sound of mind'" (205). Implicitly, Patel follows the guidelines of Burke's charting the equations exercise, exploring how terrorism rhetorics map onto larger sociolinguistic categories. Villains are inherently disabled by their association with madness, a categorization that identifies Muslim men as "recognizable figures of danger in our current geopolitical context" and as bodies that must be "incarcerated or eliminated" (202).

A Burkean pedagogical exercise for the composition classroom that takes a complementary perspective on how disability circulates in political discourse might ask writing students to consider the kinds of bodies and minds celebrated in other rhetorics and discourses of terrorism. In the days following the Boston Marathon bombing, for example, President Obama offered comfort to victims and survivors and prayers for Boston at an Interfaith Service. Integral to his message was a discourse of ability and strength that implicitly sought to associate terrorism with disability and weakness. Obama's call, for example, "to push on, to persevere" is put in terms of able-bodiedness, as he urges listeners to "summon the strength that maybe we didn't even know we had, and we carry on; we finish the race." He repeats, adding an identity-based claim, saying, "We finish the race, and we do that because of who we are." Strength, ability, and fortitude are synonymous with American identity in this formulation, with "finishing the race" a metaphor for broader recovery. In contrast, Obama uses a discourse of disability to identify the "perpetrators of [the] senseless violence," who are characterized as "small, stunted individuals who would destroy rather than build." This negative association between disabled bodies and terrorism parallels the associations often made in the media regarding mental disability and terrorism.

Obama's message of unified strength contrasts starkly with the pedagogical practices that Burke suggests, which are based on the fearsomeness of symbol use, an appreciation of disability, and a healthy skepticism of unity. Thinking forward to the following year, Obama concludes his speech by saying that "the world will return to this great American city to run harder than ever and to cheer even louder." Combined with the call to finish the race—an act of competition and completion aimed at wholeness—this appeal increases in intensity as listeners are urged to run even harder. Strength and bravery are integral, as Obama reminds the audience that faith, love, and common creed is "our strength," the reasons why "a bomb can't beat us" and why "we don't hunker down" or "cower in fear." This call to strength is neatly summed up in the "Boston Strong" movement that followed the bombing. The ubiquitous slogan sends the message that the only response to terrorism is an able-bodied response—strength, bravery, and single-mindedness. While it may not be symbol-wise to dismiss a statement that unifies so many, it's worth exploring what other embodied responses are possible, particularly for survivors of violence experiencing disability themselves.[6] Burke's pedagogical practices of charting and indexing and his techniques of drooping and brooding are crucial for exploring alternative responses.

A New Brood

In the sixty-plus years following "Linguistic Approach," the warnings Burke heralded regarding competition, education, and global war are more relevant than ever. "Boston Strong" serves as a shorthand for the implicit list of traits assumed to shape not only the ideal citizen but also the ideal student—strong, fast, aggressive, forward-thinking, and single-minded. This message has significant implications regarding who is imagined as the ideal student and citizen in our classrooms and world stages. Being a "strong" student in today's educational climate frequently involves a denial of disability and difference, just as being a superpower on the world's stage requires constant displays of strength and unanimity. Although more disabled students are attending universities, many

---

6. I do not mean to offer a romanticized view in which disabled people are completely removed from war culture. For examples of complex connections of assistive technologies to military technology, see Kafer 120–21.

choose not to identify as disabled, often forgoing support services for fear of stigma (Lewiecki-Wilson and Brueggemann 2). This ableist environment affects everyone, disabled or not, not only because it limits the minds and bodies deemed suitable for schooling but also because it restricts the range of perspectives needed to address intractable problems such as competition, aggression, and conflict. As Price asserts, "Ableism impairs all of us" (*Mad at School* 8).

Pedagogical methods and exercises based on appreciation of disability such as those designed by Burke and imbued with a critical disability studies perspective provide an opportunity for composition teachers to intervene in ableist learning climates, nurturing a new brood of students more circumspect in their arguments. Students in composition classrooms encouraged to develop ways of drooping and brooding form new patterns for engaging with texts, connecting with classmates, and representing their views to wider audiences. Students who develop techniques for cultivating divided minds are likely to consider wider ranges of perspectives, change their minds more readily, and advance their writing to more complex levels. Burke is an important source for imagining disability studies pedagogies seeking to nurture this new brood of student—those prepared to think, learn, and change in ways that appreciate disability and position them as critically reflective global citizens. This new brood of student is particularly crucial to support now, as in Burke's time, because we continue to live in a time when war is "always threatening."

As Ann George and Jack Selzer show, Burke was not an isolated genius but instead was closely connected to larger intellectual circles and sociopolitical currents of his time. It's time to connect Burke more directly to the study of disability and disability pedagogy in the composition classroom. Recognizing Burke as a teacher of disability pedagogy deepens existing engagement with embodiment, rhetoric, and pedagogy, providing ways to address difficult issues at these intersections. Many of Burke's key concepts—not only *trained incapacity* and *perspective by incongruity*, but also *orientation, symbolic action,* and *piety*—are closely connected to disability and nonnormative approaches to bodies and minds (Jack). These crucial connections indicate that Burke is a critical resource for supporting and advancing disability theory and composition pedagogy.

Critical disability studies pedagogy is also a resource for advancing Burkean theories. Exploring alternative corporealities, McRuer asks,

"Can composition theory work against the simplistic formula of that which is proper, orderly, and harmonious?" (48). Similarly, elaborating on the potentials of disability rhetoric aligned with a "model for adaption, change, critique," Dolmage asks, "What if these were our central educational values (instead of accumulation, retention, comprehension, compliance, reproduction)?" (*Disability* 289). Burke's drooping and brooding, particularly when complemented with critical disability perspectives, reimagine our central educational values, along axes that value disability, resisting order and compliance. Drooping and brooding are additional ways of making disability "visible" in composition (Brueggemann et al.). Together, Burke's techniques of muscular drooping and sentimental brooding and strategies of indexing and reading the news offer comprehensive, whole-bodied pedagogical approaches that value nonnormative embodied, cognitive, and emotional strategies for transformative learning in the composition classroom. Disability studies and Burkean pedagogy can continue to inform and be informed by each other. One potential avenue for future research might focus on resisting privileging what Patricia Dunn calls the linguistic-centric composition approach and ask how Burke's "linguistic approach" might be revised for students not possessing traditional language.

In *The Peaceable Classroom*, Mary Rose O'Reilley raises a critical question posed at a teaching colloquium at the height of the Vietnam War: "Is it possible to teach English so that people stop killing each other?" To a certain extent, Burke's "Linguistic Approach" asks this question; it's a question that has not stopped being relevant today. Part of the answer involves valuing disability—the alternative ways of thinking, feeling, moving, and learning that disability occasions show students different methods for engaging their world. Burke's disability pedagogy is a powerful critique of the ideology of ability in our classrooms that prefers the narrowly able, competitive, and aggressive student, the same student who is primed to escalate conflict locally and globally. The student who droops and broods, in contrast, supported by alternative ways of moving, thinking, and learning in crip time, is prepared to de-escalate conflict, to practice patience in developing arguments, and ultimately to engage more peaceably with students and citizens of different perspectives. This is the student to nurture.

13 Burke for Undergraduates: Equipment for Thinking, Working, and Living

Elvera Berry

> *Demonstrating the lasting power of a general undergraduate seminar on Burke.*

> *Burke is an invaluable gift to college students. College students deserve so much more than education as consumption. They deserve to be challenged with academic content that will engage them, provoke them, and help them grow. Studying Burke helps us to engage in education as true learners—people who are interested in reflecting on what it means to be human, what it means to be symbol makers and users . . . [to] care deeply about how to be in the world. That's what Burke did for me.*
>
> —Katie Sawade Hall

As authors have pointed out throughout this book, Kenneth Burke's corpus poses unwelcome challenges for graduate students and faculty, let alone for undergraduates conditioned by the comfort of empirically concrete information and immediate results. Burke takes a chisel to the cement of our concretized knowledge. Why bother inviting undergraduates into such a project? Because I am not convinced that age matters. A first encounter with Burke at *any* stage is like going on a blind date at *any* age. Some suffer through an uncomfortable introduction and brief encounter, chalking it up to experience; others try a second date, enjoying the conversation but holding in abeyance the possibility of any future contact; a few brave souls enter into a relationship, choosing to hang around the parlor to see what happens. Having hung around Burke's parlor for over thirty-five years and having seen what can happen, I want to convey the possibility—indeed, the urgency—of including Burke in the undergraduate curriculum. To that end, I will describe the influence of Burke in my own educational journey; the development of a Burke seminar in the context of a non-elite, private liberal arts college; and the attendant opportunities and consequences that students have perceived when considering their Burkean journey in retrospect.

Encountering Kenneth Burke

After teaching German for over a decade, I was pursuing a second master's in communication when I discovered Kenneth Burke and completed a Burke-driven master's thesis. On a lark, I sent him a note with a copy of my thesis but, not surprisingly, never received a reply. Several months later, in March 1982, I happened to hear that the man whose work had captured my attention and imagination was going to be in Rochester for a lecture and a public poetry reading. My husband and I arrived early and were waiting when the five foot, four-inch intellectual giant, escorted by a local poet, arrived in the still-empty lecture hall.

She introduced herself and immediately asked: "Are you Elvera Berry?"

To my amazement, I discovered that because he was in Rochester, and the return address on the thesis I had mailed in October was Rochester, Mr. Burke simply assumed I would be there! He immediately engaged me in conversation, indicating that he had recently discovered my thesis in his "layers of civilization." We spoke only briefly, but I was satisfied! However coincidentally, I had met the man, and he had read my work. I was content to hear his afternoon lecture and attend his evening poetry reading.

After the lecture, about a third of which I understood, his friend approached me, asking whether I could possibly spend some time with "K.B." the next afternoon to provide a distraction from what would be a difficult time for him. She explained that he had come to Rochester above all to visit his ailing friend and patron, James Sibley Watson, only to discover Watson had passed away while he was en route. Concerned about whether he would be able to handle his lecture in the wake of this news, she had watched K.B. "come alive" during our brief conversation before the lecture, enabling him to return to his world of ideas. Now, he needed to be ready to participate in Dr. Watson's memorial before leaving Rochester, so she hoped I could offer similar support the next afternoon. Thus began our first encounter: I met a new friend at an old friend's expense.

Apprehensive about spending time with someone whose ideas often rested just beyond reach, I met with Mr. Burke the following afternoon and discovered the *person* behind his ideas. At one point, as I heard myself begin to question one of his ideas, I stopped short and apologized for questioning what I did not fully understand. I learned a lasting lesson as he literally rose from the chair, red-faced, with piercing blue eyes ablaze: "No!" he exclaimed, "You don't understand me at all! *I'm* still trying to figure this thing out!" I witnessed in that moment what is evident throughout his writing: No matter how strong his argument, the point is not the reader's agreement; the point is seeking ever-greater understanding.

As we moved from one topic to another, he periodically returned to what was weighing him down: the death of the man who, as publisher of *The Dial*, had supported him financially and enabled him to work as music critic and *The Dial*'s associate editor. Much later, when the late Dr. Watson was being honored at Rochester Institute of Technology for his many contributions to medicine, photography, science, and the arts, Burke and lifelong friend, Malcolm Cowley, shared the stage: Cowley in a wheelchair, Burke unsteady with his cane. There I witnessed again his painful loss as he struggled to pay tribute to Watson. One question, uttered through tears as we talked, epitomized the depth of his frustration and grief: "How could I do justice to the man who gave me a backbone?"

The vulnerability surrounding our first meeting and reinforced later when we visited over tea in the home of the late Dr. Watson, laid the foundation for far more than academic conversations as we contemplated complexities of life and aging and loss: the death of grandson Harry Chapin in 1981 less than a year before Dr. Watson's passing, daughter "Happy's" (anthropologist Eleanor Leacock) passing in 1987, and myriad old friends "leaving" one by one. We corresponded and connected at conferences; twice he returned to Rochester, and twice my husband and our son, for whom Burke's name and ideas were household terms, and I visited him at the compound in Andover—the last time in July 1993, just four months before his death. It was there, at home, that he shared most adamantly his distress over the degenerating world of politics and ongoing destruction of land, water, and air.

I share a piece of my story not to venerate an imperfect saint but to speak to the uniqueness of every human encounter and the influence of both the academic and the personal in my approach to education. Although I may wish I had met K.B. in his prime, I appreciate having entered his parlor at critical moments when I was able to "just be there" to listen, to learn, to witness his comic correctives, to hear his music, to commiserate—in short, to witness the integration of person and ideas. Behind the printed symbols and within his spoken words resided a wordsmith intent on keeping conversations going and engaging in the drama of human relations. While I do not dwell on the personal in my teaching, I share relevant examples to show connections between agents and their symbolic action.

A Burkean Education

What difference has *identification* with Burke made in my understanding of education and teaching practices? I had long been interested in the transformative potential of education for college students, resisting the notion of the classroom as predominantly a place to deliver the final word. What in much of my own education had been a matter of courses to complete and material to memorize was, instead, becoming a question of how to engage students in their own education, whatever the subject matter. Doctoral study of higher education in philosophy and rhetoric did not include compelling pedagogical insights, but serious study of Burke's 1955 essay, "Linguistic Approach to Problems of Education," in which he examines "the obviously great importance of the linguistic factor as regards both education in particular and human relations in general" (259), provided a direct hit. As he explores his three all-encompassing aims of education—the *pragmatic*, the *admonitory*, and the *appreciative* [sic] (273)—we encounter the drama, or trauma, of education, which to Burke is an inherently linguistic project of teaching and learning. Moreover, he ties this centrality of language in "the ideal dialogue of education" to the ideals of democracy and a truly free citizenry (285).

What if we applied his integrative, language-based perspective on education to our disjunctive approaches to undergraduate education? To education beyond training? To undergraduate curricula? In my dissertation, I fleshed out a theoretical conceptualization consonant with Burke's educational project. I began with a straightforward pentadic statement of a not unreasonable educational goal: "Education (agent) teaches (act) individuals through theory and practice (agency) to function as equals (purpose) in a democratic society (scene)" (Berry 73).

Further examination of that statement, however, in light of Burke's complex sets of terms in "Linguistic Approach" and his many education-related references, yielded the dissertation's guiding perspective for conceptualizing a Burkean model of undergraduate education: Education for Personhood. The personhood model, expounded in my 2010 "The Both-And of Undergraduate Education," rests on a pentadic transformation of Burke's educational "voyage of discovery together" ("LAPE" 276):

> Teachers and students are participatory "joint Agents" who engage in learning (a symbolic "Act") through the "Agency" of identification, interaction, and conflict for the "Purpose" of cooperation despite misunderstandings in a communal, democratic, and universal "Scene." (Berry 81)

Perhaps an argument could be made that Burke's ideas and writings should be allowed to speak for themselves and not be contaminated by personalized interpretations—that looking through a personal lens is tantamount to distortion of texts. While I do not share a contamination perspective, I highly value the goal of doing justice to an author and a text just as we constantly strive to do justice to our personal perspectives. As Jack Selzer's demonstration of the rhetorical parlor in this volume illustrates, Burke's relentless attention to the particulars of all aspects of human communication reflects the goal of doing justice to whatever text he examined, whether myriad others' writings or his own. At the same time, ever conscious of his ability to get in his own way while on the way to yet another brilliant insight, Burke recognized that we are always partially blinded by our own lenses. "At the very start," he quipped in a Flowerish, "one's terms jump to conclusions" (*Collected Poems* 299). He revisited others' as well as his own texts and ideas, not to render final judgment but rather to engage in criticism in order to effect new understandings. He simply never ceased "trying to figure this thing out."

How has Burke informed my approach to teaching, in general, and to "teaching Burke," in particular? Just as the very use of language involves an ongoing act of self-exploration, so, too, does education. In both philosophy and practice, Burke provides a model of "teacher and class on a voyage of discovery together" ("LAPE" 276) that can inform our assumptions, guide our teaching and learning, and speak to the complexity of "joint-Agents" discovering new ways of being. Burke continues to place complicated demands on me as I seek to teach from the perspective he helped me to hone: *Students are capable of learning, education involves their active engagement, and we discover very few final answers.*

Burke in an Undergraduate Context

Roberts Wesleyan College, located in Rochester, New York, is a non-sectarian, Christian liberal arts college with a diverse student body, including a substantial commuter population, international students, and a wide range of sociocultural and theological perspectives; a significant percentage of traditional students encounter the challenges of political and religious diversity for the first time. The college enrolls approximately 1,800 students (half in traditional undergraduate liberal arts and professional programs, half in degree-completion and graduate programs).

In the late 1990s, I developed a special topics Burke seminar to be added to the rigorous, rhetoric-based communication major, which had prepared students for a wide range of graduate degrees and professional employment for over a decade. An elective among 400-level requirements, the seminar has been offered eleven times since 1998, serving approximately 150 students. Enrollment has ranged from nine to eighteen students, primarily communication but also English, psychology, religion, and science majors. The catalog description reads:

> CMC 410 *Special Topics in Rhetoric and Criticism: Kenneth Burke's Rhetoric, Criticism, and Influence* (3 credit hours). This course examines the writing and influence of literary and social critic Kenneth Burke. Students are introduced to Burke's major contributions to rhetorical theory, literary criticism, and sociology, as well as to the "person" behind the scholarship. (Offered alternate years)

Admittedly, the course does not exist in a vacuum. I proposed the seminar after observing student interest in Burke's ideas in my required introductory theory course; in textual references to Burke in my rhetoric, persuasion, or organizational courses; and in his poems that I incorporate in my oral interpretation course. I had also noted student engagement in my occasional anecdotal references to the *person* behind the complicated ideas and fascinating definition of who we are as human beings. In addition, I saw the possibility of opening a scholarly world of primary texts from which students might benefit academically and personally. Since almost all had already encountered the reputedly "tough" professor, they entered knowing they would be expected to take the course seriously; most have chosen the Burke seminar out of interest or peer recommendation: "It's tough but worth it."

Selecting texts is always a challenge fraught with consequences of having said "no" to those not selected. We read the three required texts in this order: Gusfield's *On Symbols and Society*, a collection of primary-text material that introduces students to the range of Burke's major ideas in small doses; the third edition of *Permanence and Change*; and *The Rhetoric of Religion*. I originally assigned *Counter-Statement* because I thought to begin with Burke's first compilation of his innovative criticism. While I continue to refer to *Counter-Statement*, I adopted *Permanence and Change* for two reasons: (1) to provide somewhat greater breadth for students of rhetoric as Burke explores the groundwork for the rest of his corpus, expanding the circumference of literature and the social sciences, and (2) to include Burke's revisiting his own ideas after almost twenty years and again thirty years later. Here, in a critic's criticism of even his own criticism, Burke illustrates the significance of ongoing conversation with ideas. Many Roberts students are drawn to considering the parallel universes of religion, with which they are already familiar, and language which, after ten weeks of Burke, they are beginning to understand differently. The juxtaposition of those universes in *The Rhetoric of Religion* typically leads to unanticipated new, challenging, and often helpful insights.

WHAT TYPES OF ASSIGNMENTS DO STUDENTS TYPICALLY FACE?

1. Daily preparation: Students are expected to come to class having read and seriously considered the assigned material. In addition to note-taking and talking back to the text, they may be asked for a written reflection—either general or regarding a particular passage; reflections discussed in class or occasional in-class quizzes (assessed with check-plus, check, check-minus) are designed to ascertain levels of understanding or misunderstanding rather than to inflict punitive grades.

> **Example**: Students recognize that Burke's "Range of All the Ratios," in Gusfield's chapter 9, places Burke in the middle of cur-

rent politics. Asking students to explain the following statement provides an opportunity both to solidify their understanding of pentadic ratios and to share their resultant interpretations of democracy: "By the scene-act ratio, if the 'situation' itself is no longer a 'democratic' one, even an 'essentially democratic' people will abandon democratic ways" (Burke qtd. in Gusfield 154).

2. Leadership: Once students seem comfortable identifying key ideas and terms, I ask individuals or teams to be discussion leaders for specific portions of readings. They develop their own approach, set of questions, etc., to lead the discussion, and I try to weigh in only to clarify, illustrate, or elaborate.

> **Example**: Assigning specific sections to two or three students provides incentive to work collaboratively in order to raise questions, clarify understandings, anticipate sections with which classmates might struggle, and plan their typically fifteen- to twenty-minute class session. (A helpful variation for "Augustine" and "Genesis" in *The Rhetoric of Religion* is to assign sections to *introduce* to the class, perhaps with a one-page outline to distribute.)

3. Exams after each book: Major portions are completed outside of class with access to texts and personal notes, as well as reflective time to develop coherent responses. Primarily essays, exams emphasize understanding and application of key notions, connections among ideas, or textual analysis.

Two Sample Exam Questions:

1. Kenneth Burke observed: "I am offering my Definition of Man [*sic*] in the hope of either persuading the reader that it fills the bill, or of prompting him to decide what should be added, or subtracted, or in some way modified" (LSA 3). Based on your understanding of Burke's definition, discuss the extent to which Burke's definition "fills the bill" for you and identify any adjustments you might recommend over half a century later.
2. Having read Burke's *Permanence and Change* as well as his 1954 "Appendix" and 1983 "Afterword," construct your own "Afterword: In Retrospective Prospect," in which you:
    - Articulate your overall response to Burke's 1930s book;

- Comment on Burke's notable reflections revisiting his own work; and
- Identify ways in which you are applying, or can foresee applying, what you have gleaned from your study of *Permanence and Change*.

4. Formal paper: Students select a topic of personal interest to explore using Burke sources (articles, books, major sections of books) beyond seminar-required reading. Topics may include, for example, further examination of an idea encountered in the seminar; development of cross-disciplinary connections of personal interest; a Burkean analysis of a non-Burke "text"; or application of Burke to current cultural or sociopolitical issues. Paper topics must be approved; guidance is needed to ensure a topic or research question that is manageable in a short but worthy investigation (typically under ten pages).

What Is It Like for a Diverse Cross Section of Undergraduates to Wrestle with Kenneth Burke?

My goal in teaching is always to invite students into a conversation that started a long time ago and now is theirs to continue. While every course presents challenges on which education necessarily depends, the Burke seminar typically requires more diligent preparation than students are used to. They enter a conversation that I assure them will yield more questions than answers but will be a conversation rich with ideas, connections, and implications. I do not pretend that Burke is easy; I tell students they will encounter many references with which they may not be familiar, and we will not understand everything we read. I let them know that scholars who have studied Burke for decades continue to discover what they had previously overlooked or what makes a different kind of sense in the current "drama of human relations." I remind them frequently to step back from the desired comfort of immediate understanding and embrace a process of discovery as they play with Burke's ideas and consider their implications. Like life, itself, Burke will challenge what we thought we understood. Throughout our study, I try to help students maintain perspective, a sense of humor, and excitement about their *aha* moments. I freely share my own *aha* moments brought about by rereading the texts, and I am delighted when I can share with them an *aha* moment someone just created for me via a question, connection, or observation. That is what makes teaching endlessly meaningful.

What Does a Typical Class Look Like?

I begin with what a class is not: it is not a prerecorded or formal lecture, nor is it a polished set of PowerPoint slides. Gathered in a horseshoe arrangement, a typical class is somewhat messy! I assign specific sections or minimum number of pages (typically twenty-five to fifty) with instructions to "read, take notes, identify questions, posit connections; come to class ready to engage." Depending on the material, I may invite responses to open-ended questions: "What did you find most intriguing or surprising? Where did you get lost?" I listen for the points of common interest and frustration, gradually framing specific questions to engage the class as we examine the text together. At any time, we may wrestle with a particular question in small groups. Or I may open with a simple, content-related question that will soon become complicated, perhaps something that connects with a campus or national event illustrative of Burke's concerns in the day's reading. Or I may immediately hand the class over to the assigned discussion leader. Whatever the means, I aim at uncovering and reinforcing key Burkean notions while also exploring ways in which newly encountered material connects with, expands upon, or even seems to contradict previous material. (Burke revisits; so do we!) I want our conversation with Burke to yield a new respect for words and their power, terms and their implications, language and its personal and collective consequences.

At the end of each iteration of the seminar, I have asked students to characterize their encounter with Burke's ideas, often using the prompt "Burke: So What?" Twice, in 2001 and 2019, I had invited alumni to reflect on Burke in retrospect. Comments below, representing a cross section of graduates from 1999 to 2019, are drawn primarily from those responses; I recontacted them for permission to use portions of their earlier statements. Not surprisingly, they were in universal agreement that Burke was not easy. Nevertheless, while many needed reassurances that they had not lost their capacity to read, students found ways to appreciate Burke's relevance, energizing questions, and layers of complexity. Alumni commented on their "love-hate relationship" with Burke's "practically incomprehensible" texts (A. J. Thomas), as well as enlightenment via his "recurring humor and folksy examples. Of all the theorists I read in undergrad, he was easily the most formative" (Bryan Blankfield). They reflected: "I couldn't believe these ideas were coming from me" (J. Jones) or "all of a sudden words and thoughts became objects of study" (N.C.) or "the symbolic nature of language is always at the forefront of my mind in considering how I will organize a school library collection" (Nicole Morello). Another former student noted:

> I began the Burke seminar with a small dose of recalcitrance about the heavy reading load. I was prepared to dislike the seminar. Yet. There was something that I found in Burke . . . that completely captivated my attention. I started seeing Burke everywhere—in a truly Burkean, interrupting fashion. . . . He continues to complicate, inform, and interrupt the way I see the world and my place in it. (Victoria Houser)

How Have Students Coped?

Explicit reminders that we are not competing with each other but working collaboratively to try to understand the material and consider its implications help reduce anxiety. Students have often referred to informal study groups meeting in dorms, library, and dining hall as Burke became a constant companion—however unwelcome at times. The following comment captures a characteristic progression from isolated to communal learning:

> I remember you, encouraging discussion after discussion in and out of the classroom, helping us draw connections to politics and current events, patiently moving us from "so what?" to "now what?" . . . I remember studying with [two classmates] in the library before the first exam, trying to understand what Burke meant by "circumference"; . . . riding on the track-and-field bus with [athlete classmate], and talking about a passage in P&C; . . . [an alumnus] visiting as a graduate student, chatting about his research on animal rhetoric; . . . presenting alongside [two others] at ECA, and having our papers reviewed by [a university professor]. (BP)

A Student Experience beyond the Classroom

In 1998, having studied Burke, the first of sixty Roberts undergraduates presented papers at the Eastern Communication Association (ECA) convention, a convention regularly including only professors and graduate students. The goal in developing papers and panels has been to contribute to the Burkean conversation by digging deeper into Burke and shedding new light on a topic, issue, or problem. Many projects have involved questionnaires, interviews, or visual illustrations. Even a small sampling of student-selected topics provides a veritable history of popular and burning issues of the era as students embraced the transcendent relevance of unpacking Burke and discovered new ways of understanding and coming to terms with the interests, concerns, and dramas of their own times: In 1999, "Affirmative Action: Guilt and Redemption; Narratives of 'The Other': The Campus Minority Experience." In 2007–08, "Rhetoric of Global Warming: A Burkean Difference." In 2011, "Gender Language: Power in the God-Terms; He Who Must Not be Named: Terministic Power in Harry Potter." In 2016, "Memes of the Barnyard: Limitations of Internet Freedom," "Blue and Black: Buzzwords and Burke," and "Shared Scapegoats: Feeding Racist Disparity." In 2019, "The Role of Twitter in Technological Psychosis: The Spread of Misinformation in a Post-Truth World."

Why Did Students Choose to Take on So Much Extra Work?

The possibility of attending a large professional convention in a major city, encountering scholars mentioned in their textbooks, and talking with professors and graduate students about future possibilities was no doubt appealing. Students often received encouragement from previous ECA convention attendees, including some in graduate programs in business, English, law, library science, psychology, rhetoric, and theology. But above all, for students who have begun to view education beyond hurdles and grades, there is always something enticing about engaging in a new kind of challenge, especially if several peers are also involved. Not connected with a professor's research project, the non-credit-bearing project was theirs to develop individually and together with peers on their joint voyage of discovery, sharing Burke sources, ideas, and frustrations. I became logistics coordinator; resource when needed; cheerleader; reader, only to ensure papers were ready for the outside responder; and coach, hearing their fifteen-minute presentations. ECA introduced them to the rigors of preparation and to a professional world many have since entered.

Burke as Equipment for Thinking, Working, and Living

Beyond the sheer difficulty of Burke's prose, the complexity of his ideas, and the logistics of engaging with his thinking for the seminar or an ECA convention, alumni observations demonstrate three interrelated effects of studying Burke at the undergraduate level. For many students, Burke's works served as equipment for *thinking*: a welcome intellectual challenge and an introduction to the joys of cultural theorizing. Burke's ideas also provided equipment for *working*: insights that held across a variety of fields, a perspective on perspectives, a deep dive into the critical thinking that prepared them for an unknown future. And for some students, the Burkean encounter literally became equipment for *living* as they began to confront and name their own terminological screens, circumferences, trained incapacities, attitudinal motives, and need for correctives. Through Burke, they were slower to judge and quicker to recognize the pieties and abysses of their own *Weltanschauung*. In combination, these three effects hint at both immediate and long-term benefits to undergraduate investment in Burkean thought. Such benefits manifest themselves differently to each recipient, which is why the juxtaposition of my own educational history with the responses of a parlor of alumni reveals Burke's transformational capacity more fully, more intimately, and more eloquently than I alone can convey.

Equipment for Thinking

> Reading Burke "in the raw" was the first time I was encouraged to grapple with difficult material and encouraged to have something to say about it. I was able to do so because you created an environment of curiosity, where we weren't expected to understand everything on the first pass but were taught how to make connections, read carefully, and play with ideas. This approach stuck with me after graduation, and I returned to it over and over as I picked up books of philosophy, cultural criticism, and rhetorical theory. (Annie Laurie Nichols)

> Burke is almost like the "DNA" of communication . . . opening up your mind to something that continues to evolve the longer you think about it. . . . I have a strong ability to understand people on a deep level, to see different sides to every story, and to remain open minded during tense conversations, and I think a

good chunk of that skill comes from studying Burke alongside other comm courses. (Ariel Hummer)

Taking Burke . . . gave me a comfort that I didn't have before in living in the tension of paradox and the unknown. It forced me to think critically about myself, my faith, and my interactions with others. (Kaleb Colosimo).

Burke is constantly unfolding before us, asking to be extended, (re)imagined, and (re)determined. (Cheyenne Zaremba)

Burke's theory of language and the logic we cannot avoid espousing in every living moment had the most far-reaching impact on my thinking as a scholar and human being. (Amy A. Foley)

The biggest long-term influence he's had on me as a scholar (not working in communication or even in the humanities, but as a social scientist), was in inspiring me to be ambitious in making new connections to make sense of the world. . . . One of my strengths as [an economist] is in seeing connections and patterns that others don't, and that habit of thought was massively influenced by my exposure to Burke's writing. (Russell Toth)

Equipment for Working

Language as always reflecting, selecting, and deflecting (a la terministic screens): I invoke this all the time when explaining to people how the same story can be told in so many different ways, the same arguments defended by so many different methods. . . . So much of my thinking and writing life is influenced by the belief that language needs to be treated as an ever-shifting terrain. . . . "It's more complicated than that." (Greg Coles)

Concepts I attribute to my graduate theological education actually had their roots in some very Burkean soil. . . . Those who traffic in words are handling powerful stuff. (A. J. Thomas)

My experience in the legal profession may exaggerate this . . . but understanding the multifaceted effect of words in a profession which seeks to create singular meaning . . . helps me to find ways of approaching a legal issue that others may not see. (Courtney Hitchcock)

Burke can serve as a gateway into the many philosophic schools that offer perspectives of reality . . . a study of the philosophical undertones and intellectual weight that imbue language. . . . [Burke] should be included within the undergraduate curriculum—the earlier the better. (Matt and Susan Mancino)

I can remember [2007] underlining the phrase "morals are fists". . . . I dog-eared countless pages and underlined several, seemingly standalone sentiments. . . . Recently as a PhD student in Sociology, I have been engaging with different questions and different source materials in a project that looks at the social organization of carework [sic]. When I submitted a comprehensive exam, a professor's first response was, "I have recently been engaging with the work of Kenneth Burke. You are a closet Burke scholar!" I hadn't read Burke in ten years but had somehow imbibed it. And "it" was more than standalone sentiments, but a radical way of attending to social relationships, to knowledge production, and to the social or material aspects of meanings. Aha . . . [Three years later] I'm working on a major national grant application for a five-year study and have just steered the research team (of profs from other universities) towards drawing on rhetorical theories. (Janna Klostermann)

Equipment for Living

I wrote [ECA] about the competing ideals faced by Bertolt Brecht and how it influenced his plays. Today, I see the need to find that same balance in my own life whether that means balancing between friends who say Black Lives Matter and friends who say All Lives Matter or trying to navigate all viewpoints in an office. Thankfully studying Burke showed me that I don't have to choose sides or live in an either/or world but can exist in a both/and world that we so desperately need. (Daniel Snyder)

Burke created a visual metaphor for viewing human interaction and communication that has seeped into every area of my life . . . people gathering together to peer over the abyss, or avoid it completely, interacting through the structures they create. . . . This particular metaphor has influenced my faith, my social calling, my role as parent, and my role as admin for a number of groups. Burke was hard to fully grasp, yet that seemed to be his goal of always reaching and asking, living in the questions. Burke himself pulled thoughts and images from many others, gathering them in a way that crafted glasses for viewing all humans in interaction and thought. His style was encouragement for me to also seek out notes of resonance in every person, book, and work of art, to craft my own multicolored lenses. (Marlise Flores Boedeker)

Kenneth Burke changed my life. . . . There is nothing that has changed, broadened my views and perspectives and allowed me to see the world in new frames more than reading Burke. The concept that language is world-making is something that I had never thought of before I read *Permanence and Change* for the first time. Here is why: Growing up in a sheltered conservative environment gave me a certain set of grammars for dealing with the world. Then, Burke taught me that my grammars were products of my upbringing, culture, and the vocabularies . . . both given to me and . . . restricted. . . . Burke gave me the tools to make up my own mind about the things of the world and turned me into the person I am today with the convictions that I am proud to carry. (Micki Burdick)

Burke was an academic challenge for me in a time when I was excited to learn. It was also a time when my life in college was consuming, and I had lost some perspective. My relationship with my parents was in trouble, partially because education, the most important thing in my life, was something they did not see as valuable. Neither of them had ever dreamed of attending college, and felt higher education was valuable only for getting me a better job someday. They didn't care to hear about what I was learning, and often interpreted my 'ah-ha!' moments as unwelcome critiques of the way I was raised or of their traditional beliefs. My dad and I got in a fight one evening (after a conversation about gender) that resulted in both of us crying. I had never seen him cry. . . . Then I took Burke, and I realized that my dad didn't need to understand why I loved learning or why I loved talking about gender and society and critical thinking. It didn't mean he loved me less. . . . it just meant he was seeing life through a different screen. I learned, through some of the most complex studies I encountered in college, that the man that had equipped me to live was interpreting life with a different set of tools. He had not encountered some of the equipment for living that I, as a college educated woman, had now encountered. Most importantly, I chose to accept that that was ok. Burke taught me to step out from behind my terministic screens and to dig into the people around me to learn what experiences had molded them. I'm grateful for Burke because he taught me those skills when I needed them most. (Anonymous)

So What?

I close with my own response to "Burke: So What?" Having introduced the complex work and equally complex person of Kenneth Burke to 150 undergraduates and attempted to help them discern what might be useful to them, I am convinced that Burke should not be reserved for graduate students. While his prose is not necessarily for everyone, educators would do well to provide exposure to an eminent thinker of the twentieth century whose insights ring as true and whose equipment remains as valuable today as eighty years ago. Through shared engagement with Burke, students have taught me that they are fully capable of learning, engaging in their own education, and becoming partners on a voyage of discovery together. What more could an educator ask for?

Undergraduate Theory Syllabus

CMC 410 Kenneth Burke's Rhetoric, Criticism, and Influence

Texts

Burke, K., and J. Gusfield. *On Symbols & Society*
Burke, K. *Permanence and Change*
Burke, K. *The Rhetoric of Religion*

Recommended Resources

Burke, K. *A Grammar of Motives*
—. *A Rhetoric of Motives*
—. *Attitudes Toward History*
—. *Counter-Statement*
—. *Language as Symbolic Action*
—. *The Philosophy of Literary Form*
Blakesley, D. *Elements of Dramatism*
Rueckert, W. *Kenneth Burke and the Drama of Human Relations*

Kenneth Burke was one of the foremost critics, if not the foremost literary and social critic, of twentieth-century America. Committed to language as the primary defining human characteristic, Burke embodies a liberal arts perspective and challenges his readers to grapple with both timeless and immediate human concerns. Students will examine Burke's major contributions to rhetorical theory, literary criticism and sociology, and will encounter the "person" behind the scholarship.

The Seminar is grounded in the assumption that rhetoric is more than the art of "effective communication." As an academic discipline, rhetoric is related to meaning, values, motive, and knowing. Participants are encouraged, therefore, to examine Burke not only on his own terms but also in relation to the discipline. Through course assignments and seminar experiences, students are encouraged to meet three primary objectives:

- Understanding of Kenneth Burke's major areas of interest, criticism, and concern;
- Increased awareness of the relationship between rhetoric and other academic disciplines;
- Focused study/application of Burke-scholarship beyond required Seminar texts.

ASSESSMENT OF STUDENT PERFORMANCE

- Class attendance (on time) and active, respectful classroom involvement/participation (more than two absences = grade reductions; repeated tardiness = "absence");
- Timely completion of all course assignments ("assignments" are not optional; they are due as indicated by the professor. Late work is accepted only by agreed-upon arrangement with the professor; grade reductions ensue);
- Ongoing oral and written reflection, analysis, and synthesis in response to reading and discussion (a learning community depends on each participant's preparation prior to class);
- Evaluation of assignments, quizzes, exams, research paper, and overall performance (all aspects of the course are considered in final assessment);
- Evidence of taking personal responsibility for learning (while others serve as catalysts for learning, only individuals can "learn").

The three primary sources of learning in this course are the required texts, serious engagement with assigned material, and full participation in seminar discussion. To those ends, you must have a copy of the three textbooks and attend class. You are expected to read and prepare written reflections to assigned material prior to class, come to seminar ready to share observations and questions (questions are as important as possible answers), listen and respond to others' ideas, and practice respectful civil discourse. In Kenneth Burke's terms, our goal is to "keep the conversation going" as we engage in education as "a voyage of discovery together."

The seminar format of the course will require taking personal responsibility for learning and shared "teaching." Other than possible quizzes to keep us on a learning track, there will be no surprise assignments; homework and assignments will be clarified throughout the semester, and you will always know in advance what is due and when. When in doubt, ask!

Clearly, you will play a major role in the development and success of the course—both for you and for your classmates. Be prepared for challenge, reward, and the fun of exercising your intellect.

Appendix A: Further Resources on Burkean Education and Teaching Burkean Concepts

Allister, Mark. "A Marriage of Pedagogy and Theory: Sequencing and the Pentad." *The Writing Instructor*, vol. 2, no. 3, 1983, pp. 129–36.

Arrington, Phillip. "A Dramatistic Approach to Understanding and Teaching the Paraphrase." *College Composition and Communication*, vol. 39, no. 2, 1988, pp. 185–97.

Beasley, James P. "Demetrius, Deinotes, and Burkean Identification at the University of Chicago." *Rhetoric Review*, vol. 29, no. 3, 2010, pp. 275–92.

—. "'Extraordinary Understandings' of Composition at the University of Chicago: Frederick Champion Ward, Kenneth Burke, and Henry W. Sams." *College Composition and Communication*, vol. 59, no. 1, 2007, pp. 36–52.

Beasley, James P., and Jack Selzer. "Present at the Creation: Kenneth Burke at the First CCCC." *Rhetoric Review*, vol. 38, no. 1, 2019, pp. 39–49.

Beers, Terry. "The Knack for Art: The Why and Wherefore of Combining Strategies of Invention." *Freshman English News*, vol. 17, no. 2, 1989, pp. 25–29.

Blakesley, David. "A Burkeian Reading of *White Noise*." *Approaches to Teaching DeLillo's* White Noise, edited by Tim Engles and John N. Duvall, Modern Language Association of America, 2006, pp. 169–79.

—. *The Elements of Dramatism*. Longman, 2002.

Branch, Kirk. "What Work Requires of Schools: Literacy and Control in Education for the 'High Performance Workplace.'" *Journal of Teaching Writing*, vol. 16, no. 2, 1998, pp. 295–332.

Briggs, John C. "Peter Elbow, Kenneth Burke, and the Idea of Magic." *JAC: Journal of Advanced Composition*, vol. 11, no. 2, 1991, pp. 363–75.

Brummett, Barry. "Form, Experience, and the Centrality of Rhetoric to Pedagogy." *Studies in Philosophy and Education*, vol. 34, no. 1, 2015, pp. 377–85.

Butler, Shannan H. "Teaching Rhetoric Through Data Visualization." *Communication Teacher*, vol. 25, no. 3, July 2011, pp. 131–35.

Cahill, William. "Kenneth Burke's Pedagogy of Motives." *KB Journal*, vol. 7, no. 2, 2011.

Clifford, John. "Burke and the Tradition of Democratic Schooling." *Audits of Meaning: A Festschrift in Honor of Ann E. Berthoff*, edited by Louise Z. Smith, Boynton/Cook, 1988, pp. 29–40.

Coe, Richard M. "Beyond Diction: Using Burke to Empower Words, and Wordlings." *Rhetoric Review*, vol. 11, no. 2, 1993, pp. 368–77.

—. "Critical Reading and Writing in the Burkean Classroom: A Response to Mary Salibrici." *Journal of Adolescent & Adult Literacy*, vol. 42, no. 8, 1999, pp. 638–40.

Comprone, Joseph. "Kenneth Burke and the Teaching of Writing." *College Composition and Communication*, vol. 29, no. 4, 1978, pp. 336–40.

Cypher, Joy M. "Shark Attacks and Wedding Rings: Teaching Kenneth Burke's Theory of Language as Entitlement." *Communication Teacher*, vol. 17, no. 1, 2002, pp. 12–14.

Dobyns, Ann. "The Ethics of Argument: Kenneth Burke's Influence on the Teaching of Writing." *Rhetoric and Ethics: Historical and Theoretical Perspectives*, edited by Victoria Aarons and Willis A. Salomon. Lewiston, Edwin Mellen, 1991, pp. 101–19.

Enoch, Jessica. "Becoming Symbol-Wise: Kenneth Burke's Pedagogy of Critical Reflection." *College Composition and Communication*, vol. 56, no. 2, 2004, pp. 272–96.

Enos, Theresa. "'Verbal Atom Cracking': Burke and a Rhetoric of Reading." *Philosophy & Rhetoric*, vol. 31, no. 3, 1998, pp. 64–70.

Feyerherm, Joel. "Application of Kenneth Burke's Theories to Teaching Technical Writing." *Technical Writing Teacher*, vol. 17, 1990, pp. 41–49.

Fife, Jane. "Peeling The Onion: Satire and the Complexity of Audience Response." *Rhetoric Review*, vol. 35, no. 4, Oct. 2016, pp. 322–34.

Fillion, Bryant. *Rhetoric as Symbolic Action: An Explication of Kenneth Burke's Theory of Rhetoric and Its Implications for the Teaching of Rhetoric in Secondary Schools*. 1970. Florida State U, PhD dissertation.

Fleckenstein, Kristie S. "Imitation and Symbolic Synthesis: Preparing a Face for Rhetorical Agency." *Texts of Consequence: Composing Social Activism for the Classroom and Community*, edited by Christopher Wilkey et al., Hampton, 2013, pp. 181–208.

Fogarty, Daniel. *Roots for a New Rhetoric*. Russell and Russell, 1968.

Fox, Catherine. "Beyond the 'Tyranny of the Real': Revisiting Burke's Pentad as Research Method for Professional Communication." *Technical Communication Quarterly*, vol. 11, no. 4, 2002, pp. 365–88.

Hassett, Michael. "Constructing an Ethical Writer for the Postmodern Scene." *Rhetoric Society Quarterly*, vol. 25, 1995, pp. 179–96.

—. "Increasing Responsibility through Mortification: A Burkean Perspective on Teaching Writing." *JAC: A Journal of Composition Theory*, vol. 15, no. 3, 1995, pp. 471–88.

Hawhee, Debra. "Kenneth Burke and American Studies: A Response to Giorgio Mariani." *American Literary History*, vol. 21, no. 1, 2009, pp. 123–27.

—. "Language as Sensuous Action: Sir Richard Paget, Kenneth Burke, and Gesture-Speech Theory." *Quarterly Journal of Speech*, vol. 92, no. 4, 2006, pp. 331–54.

Head, Samuel L. "Teaching Grounded Audiences: Burke's Identification in Facebook and Composition." *Computers and Composition*, vol. 39, 2016, pp. 27–40.

Helmbrecht, Brenda M. *A Mediatic Pedagogy: Rhetoricizing Images within Composition Curriculum*. 2004. Miami U, PhD dissertation.

Hunter, Paul. "Synecdoche Against Metonymy: Burke, Freire, and Writing Instruction." *Freshman English News*, vol. 18, no. 2, 1990, pp. 2–9.

Isaksen, David E. "Indexing: Kenneth Burke's Method of Textual Analysis." *KB Journal*, vol. 12, no. 2, 2017, www.kbjournal.org/isaksen-indexing.

—. *Visions of Nuclear Weapons: Kenneth Burke's Consummation Principle and the Manhattan Project*. 2020. Texas Christian U, PhD dissertation.

Jacobi, Martin James. *Literature as Equipment for Writing: Applications of Kenneth Burke's Dramatism to the Teaching of Composition* (Rhetoric, Education). 1984. U of Oregon, PhD dissertation.

Johnson, Rose M. "A Ratio-nal Pedagogy for Kate Chopin's Passional Fiction: Using Burke's Scene-Act Ratio to Teach 'Story' and 'Storm.'" *Conference of College Teachers of English Studies*, vol. 60, 1996, pp. 122–28.

Karis, Bill. "Conflict in Collaboration: A Burkean Perspective." *Rhetoric Review*, vol. 8, no. 1, 1989, pp. 113–26.

Kastely, James L. "The Earned Increment: Kenneth Burke's Argument for Inefficiency." *JAC: A Journal of Composition Theory*, vol. 23, no. 3, 2003, pp. 505–23.

—. "Kenneth Burke's Comic Rejoinder to the Cult of Empire." *College English*, vol. 58, no. 3, 1996, pp. 307–26.

Keith, Philip M. "Burke for the Composition Class." *College Composition and Communication*, vol. 28, no. 4, 1977, pp. 348–51.

Krueger, Ben. "Burke Bingo: Using Active Learning to Introduce Dramatism." *Communication Teacher*, vol. 25, no. 2, Apr. 2011, pp. 81–85.

Lynn, Kristen. "Developing Syllabi According to Kenneth Burke: Form Versus Information." Conference Papers—National Communication Association, Nov. 2007, pp. 1-21.

Mailloux, Steven. "Jesuit Eloquentia Perfecta and Theotropic Logology." *Studies in Philosophy and Education*, vol. 34, no. 1, 2015, pp. 403–12.

Murray, Jeffrey W. "Peace Talks: A 'Dialogical Ethics' Model of Faculty–Student Collaboration in the Undergraduate Classroom." *Cogent Education*, vol. 3, no. 1, 2016.

Nelson, J. "Using the Burkean Pentad in the Education of the Basic Speech Student." *Communication Education*, vol. 32, pp. 63–68.

Pigott, Margaret B. "'And Gladly Wolde He Lerne, and Gladly Teche': Using Burke's Grammar of 'Perspectives' as Course Design." *Michigan Academician*, vol. 27, no. 4, Aug. 1995, pp. 515–29.

Quandahl, Ellen. "'It's Essentially as Though This were Killing Us': Kenneth Burke on Mortification and Pedagogy." *Rhetoric Society Quarterly*, vol. 27, no. 1, 1997, pp. 5–22.

—. "'More than Lessons in to Read': Burke, Freud, and the Resources of Symbolic Transformation." *College English*, vol. 63, no. 5, 2001, pp. 633–54.

—. "What Stands for What: Kenneth Burke on Spirit and Sign." *Reclaiming Pedagogy: The Rhetoric of the Classroom*, edited by Patricia Donahue and Ellen Quandahl, Southern Illinois UP, 1989, pp. 113–27.

Quinn, Arthur. "Teaching Burke: Kenneth Burke and the Rhetoric of Ascent." *Rhetoric Society Quarterly*, vol. 25, 1995, pp. 231–36.

Quinn, David. "The Four Master Tropes as Informing Principles." *Hispania: A Journal Devoted to the Teaching of Spanish and Portuguese*, vol. 66, no. 2, May 1983, pp. 242–52.

Ramage, John D. *Rhetoric: A User's Guide*. New York: Pearson/Longman, 2006.

Rand, Erin J. "'What One Voice Can Do': Civic Pedagogy and Choric Collectivity at Camp Courage." *Text and Performance Quarterly*, vol. 34, no. 1, 2014, pp. 28–51.

Richards, Jennifer. "Equipment for Thinking: or Why Kenneth Burke Is Still Worth Reading." *Studies in Philosophy and Education*, vol. 34, no. 1, 2015, pp. 363–75.

Robertson, Jacob L. *Towards a Rhetoric of Roles—Self-Fashioning as Invention Strategy in the Rhetoric and Composition Classroom*. 2016. U of Houston, PhD dissertation.

Rood, Craig. "'Understanding' Again: Listening with Kenneth Burke and Wayne Booth." *Rhetoric Society Quarterly*, vol. 44, no. 5, 2014, pp. 449–69.

Rountree, Clarke, and John Rountree. "Burke's Pentad as a Guide for Symbol-Using Citizens." *Studies in Philosophy and Education*, vol. 34, no. 1, 2015, pp. 349–62.

Rutten, Kris, and Ronald Soetaert. "Attitudes towards Education: Kenneth Burke and New Rhetoric." *Studies in Philosophy and Education*, vol. 34, no. 1, 2015, pp. 339–47.

—. "Revisiting the Rhetorical Curriculum." *Journal of Curriculum Studies*, vol. 44, no. 6, 2012, pp. 727–43.

—. "Narrative and Rhetorical Approaches to Problems of Education: Jerome Bruner and Kenneth Burke Revisited." *Studies in Philosophy and Education*, vol. 32, no. 4, 2012, pp. 327–43.

Rutten, Kris, Dries Vrijders, and Ronald Soetaert. "Rhetoric as Equipment for Living: Part II [Special Section]." *KB Journal*, vol. 11, no. 1, 2015.

Salibrici, Mary M. "Dissonance and Rhetorical Inquiry: A Burkean Model for Critical Reading and Writing." *Journal of Adolescent & Adult Literacy*, vol. 42, no. 8, 1999, pp. 628–37.

Slater, Jarron B. *Style Unbounded: Somatic Figuration, Play, and Sublimity in the Stylistic (Re)Turn and Kenneth Burke's Writings about Style*. 2018. U of Minnesota, PhD dissertation.

Smudde, Peter M., editor. *Humanistic Critique of Education: Teaching and Learning as Symbolic Action*. Parlor, 2010.

Soetaert, Ronald, et al. "Intermediality, Rhetoric, and Pedagogy." *CLCWeb: Comparative Literature and Culture*, vol. 13, no. 3, 2011, article 11.

Sproat, Ethan McKay. *Inexorable Burden: Rhetoric and Togetherness*. 2014. Purdue U, PhD dissertation.

Stroud, Scott R. "John Dewey, Kenneth Burke, and the Role of Orientation in Rhetoric." *Trained Capacities: John Dewey, Rhetoric, and Democratic Practice*, edited by Brian Jackson and Gregory Clark, U of South Carolina P, 2014, pp. 47–64.

Walsh, Lynda, et al. "The Burkean Parlor as Boundary Object: A Collaboration between First-Year Writing and the Library." *Composition Studies*, vol. 46, no. 1, 2018, pp. 102–23.

Weiser, M. Elizabeth. "National Identity Within the National Museum: Subjectification Within Socialization." *Studies in Philosophy and Education*, vol. 34, no. 1, 2015, pp. 385–402.

Weiser, M. Elizabeth, Joseph J. Horak, and Debra Monroe. "Beyond Shame: The Dialogic Narrative and Comic Cognition." *JAC: A Journal of Composition Theory*, vol. 27, no. 3–4, 2007, pp. 563–90.

Wible, Scott. "Professor Burke's 'Bennington Project.'" *Rhetoric Society Quarterly*, vol. 38, no. 3, 2008, pp. 259-82.

—. "'Talk about How Your Language Is Constructed': Kenneth Burke's Vision for University-Wide Dialogue." *Burke in the Archives: Using the Past to Transform the Future of Burkean Studies*, edited by Dana Anderson, et al., U of South Carolina P, 2013, pp. 178–95.

Williams, Mark T., and Gladys Garcia. "Crossing Academic Cultures: A Rubric for Students and Teachers." *Journal of Basic Writing*, vol. 24, no. 1, 2005, pp. 93–119.

Winterowd, W. Ross. "Dramatism in Themes and Poems." *College English*, vol. 45, no. 6, 1983, pp. 581–88.

Wright, Courtney J. *The Forensic Burke: A For(u)Mative Member of the Parlor*. 2013. Eastern Michigan U, PhD dissertation.

Works Cited

"About Disability Services." *Saint Louis University*, 10 September 2018, www.slu.edu/life-at-slu/student-success-center/disability-services/index.php.

Adams, Douglas. *The Hitchhiker's Guide to the Galaxy*. 1979. Rpt. in *The Ultimate Hitchhikers Guide: Five Complete Novels and One Story*. Douglas Adams. Random House, 2002.

Alcoff, Linda. "Cultural Feminism versus Post-Structuralism: The Identity Crisis in Feminist Theory." *Signs: Journal of Women in Culture and Society*, vol. 13, no. 3, 1988, pp. 405–36.

Anderson, Benedict. *Imagined Communities*. Verso, 1983.

Angel, Adriana, and Benjamin Bates. "Terministic Screens of Corruption: A Cluster Analysis of Colombian Radio Conversations." *KB Journal*, vol. 10, no. 1, Summer 2014, kbjournal.org/angel_bates_terministic_screens_of_corruption. Accessed 4 April 2020.

Arendt, Hannah. *The Human Condition*. U of Chicago P, 1998.

Atkins, Rodney. "It's America." *It's America*, Curb Records, 2010.

Beasley, James P., and Jack Selzer. "Present at the Creation: Kenneth Burke at the First CCCC." *Rhetoric Review*, vol. 38, no. 1, 2019, pp. 39–49, doi:10.1080/07350198.2019.1549406.

Bennett, Jeff. "'Kenneth Burke's Attitude at the Crossroads of Rhetorical and Cultural Studies' by Sarah Mahan-Hays and Roger C. Aden." *KB Journal*, n.d., www.kbjournal.org/node/48. Accessed 4 Apr. 2020.

Berry, Elvera. "The Both-And of Undergraduate Education: Burke's 'Linguistic' Approach." *Humanistic Critique of Education: Teaching and Learning as Symbolic Action*, edited by Peter M. Smudde. Parlor, 2010, pp. 61–91.

Biesta, Gert. J. J. *Good Education in an Age of Measurement: Ethics, Politics, Democracy*. Routledge, 2010.

Birdsell, David S. "Ronald Reagan on Lebanon and Grenada: Flexibility and Interpretation in the Application of Kenneth Burke's Pentad." *Quarterly Journal of Speech*, vol. 73, no. 3, 1987, pp. 267–79.

Blakesley, David. *The Elements of Dramatism*. Longman, 2002.

Booth, Wayne. Reasons for Not Liking Burke/Reasons for Liking Burke. Box 94 (Unprocessed Collection). Rhetorical Theory Notes, Wayne Booth Papers. U of Chicago Special Collections Research Center, Chicago, IL.

Brewer, Elizabeth. "Community." *Multimodality in Motion: Disability and Kairotic Spaces*, special issue of *Kairos: A Journal of Rhetoric, Technology and Pedadgogy*, vol. 18, no. 1, 2013, kairos.technorhetoric.net/18.1/coverweb/yergeau-et-al/index.html.

"Brood." *Dictionary.com Unabridged*, www.dictionary.com/browse/brood. Accessed 15 June 2016.

Brookfield, Stephen. "The Concept of Critical Reflection: Promises and Contradictions." *European Journal of Social Work*, vol. 12, no. 3, 2009, pp. 293–304, dx.doi.org/10.1080/13691450902945215.

Brooks, Meagan Parker. *A Voice That Could Stir an Army: Fannie Lou Hamer and the Rhetoric of the Black Freedom Movement*. U of Mississippi P, 2014.

Brown, Theresa. *Critical Care: A New Nurse Faces Death, Life, and Everything in Between*. New York, HarperCollins, 2010.

Brueggemann, Brenda Jo. "An Enabling Pedagogy." *Disability Studies: Enabling the Humanities*, edited by Sharon L. Snyder, Brenda Jo Brueggemann and Rosemarie Garland-Thomson, Modern Language Association, 2002, pp. 317–36.

Brueggemann, Brenda Jo, Linda Feldmeier White, Patricia A. Dunn, Barbara A. Heifferon and Johnson Cheu. "Becoming Visible: Lessons in Disability." *College Composition and Communication*, vol. 53, no. 3, 2001, pp. 368–98.

Burke, Kenneth. *Attitudes Toward History*. 1937. 3rd ed., Berkeley, U of California P, 1984.

—. *Collected Poems 1915–1967*. Berkeley, U of California P, 1968.

—. "Counter-Gridlock: An Interview with Kenneth Burke." *On Human Nature: A Gathering While Everything Flows, 1967–1984*, edited by William H. Rueckert and Angelo Bonadonna, U of California P, 2003, pp. 336–89.

—. *Counter-Statement.* 1931. 3rd ed. Berkeley, U of California P, 1968.
—. "Dramatism." *International Encyclopedia of the Social Sciences 7,* edited by David L. Sills and Robert K. Merton, Macmillan and Free Press, 1968, pp. 445–52.
—. *Dramatism and Development (Heinz Werner Lectures, 1971).* Barre, Clark UP/Barre Publishers, 1972.
—. "Fact, Inference, and Proof in the Analysis of Literary Symbolism." *Symbols and Values: An Initial Study,* edited by Lymon Bryson, Louis Finkelstein, R. M. MacIver, and Richard McKeon, Harper and Brothers, 1954, pp. 283–87.
—. *A Grammar of Motives.* 1945. 2nd ed., Berkeley, U of California P, 1969.
—. *Language as Symbolic Action: Essays on Life, Liberty, and Method.* Berkeley, U of California P, 1966.
—. Letter to C. M. Coffin. 25 Apr. 1950, Kenneth Burke Papers, Eberly Family Special Collections Library, Pennsylvania State U.
—. Letter to Charlotte Bowman. 3 June 1952, Kenneth Burke Papers, Eberly Family Special Collections Library, Pennsylvania State U.
—. "Linguistic Approach to Problems of Education." *Modern Philosophies and Education. The Fifty-Fourth Yearbook of the National Society for the Study of Education, Part 1,* edited by Nelson B. Henry, U of Chicago P, 1955, pp. 259–303.
—. "The New State." Letter to James Abell, letter enclosure, 7 April 1933. Kenneth Burke Papers, Series Burke 2, Eberly Family Special Collections Library, Pennsylvania State U.
—. *On Symbols and Society,* edited by Joseph R. Gusfield. Chicago, U of Chicago P, 1969.
—. *Permanence and Change: An Anatomy of Purpose.* 1935. 3rd ed., U of California P, 1984.
—. *The Philosophy of Literary Form: Studies in Symbolic Action.* 1941. 3rd ed., U of California P, 1973.
—. "The Rhetoric of Hitler's 'Battle.'" *The Philosophy of Literary Form: Studies in Symbolic Action.* 1941. 3rd ed., U of California P, 1973, pp. 191–220. First published in *Southern Review,* vol. 5, 1939, pp. 1–21.
—. *A Rhetoric of Motives.* 1945. 2nd ed., U of California P, 1969.
—. *The Rhetoric of Religion: Studies in Logology.* 1961. 2nd ed., U of California P, 1970.

—. "The Tactics of Motivation, Part I." *Chimera*, vol. 1, no. 4, 1943, pp. 21–33.
—. "A Theory of Terminology." *On Human Nature: A Gathering While Everything Flows, 1967–1984*, edited by William H. Rueckert and Angelo Bonadonna, U of California P, 2003, pp. 229–46.
—. "War and Cultural Life." *American Journal of Sociology*, vol. 48, no. 1, 1942, pp. 404–10.
—. *The War of Words*, edited by Anthony Burke, Kyle Jensen, and Jack Selzer. U of California P, 2018.
Butler, Judith. *Bodies That Matter: On the Discursive Limits of Sex*. New York, Routledge, 1993.
Carlson, A. Cheree. "Gandhi and the Comic Frame: 'Ad Bellum Purificandum.'" *Quarterly Journal of Speech*, vol. 72, 1986, pp. 446–55.
—. "'You Know it When You See it': The Rhetorical Hierarchy of Race and Gender in *Rhinelander vs. Rhinelander*." *Quarterly Journal of Speech*, vol. 85, 1999, pp. 111–28.
Caswell, Michelle, and Marika Cifor. "From Human Rights to Feminist Ethics: Radical Empathy in the Archives." *Archivaria*, vol. 81, no. 1, 2016, pp. 23–43.
Charon, Rita, et al. *The Principles and Practices of Narrative Medicine*. New York, Oxford UP, 2017.
—. "Narrative Medicine: A Model for Empathy, Reflection, Profession, and Trust." *Journal of the American Medical Association*, vol. 286, no. 15, 2001, pp. 1897–1902.
—. *Narrative Medicine: Honoring the Stories of Illness*. New York, Oxford UP, 2006.
Cherney, James L. "The Rhetoric of Ableism." *Disability Studies Quarterly*, vol. 31, no. 3, 2011, dsq-sds.org/article/view/1665/1606.
Clark, Gregory. *Civic Jazz: American Music and Kenneth Burke on the Art of Getting Along*. Chicago UP, 2015.
—. *Rhetorical Landscapes in America: Variations on a Theme from Kenneth Burke*. U of South Carolina P, 2004.
—. "'Sinkership' and 'Eye-Crossing': Apprehensive in the American Landscape." *KB Journal*, vol. 2, no. 2, 2006, kbjournal.org/clark.
Cole, Thomas R., Nathan Carlin, and Ronald Carson. *Medical Humanities: An Introduction*. Cambridge UP, 2015.
Condit, Celeste Michelle. "Post-Burke: Transcending the Sub-Stance of Dramatism." *Quarterly Journal of Speech*, vol. 78, no. 3, 1992, pp. 349–55.

Couser, G. Thomas. "Conflicting Paradigms: The Rhetorics of Disability Memoir." *Embodied Rhetorics: Disability in Language and Culture*, edited by James C. Wilson and Cynthia Lewiecki-Wilson, Southern Illinois UP, 2001, pp. 78–91.

Crusius, Timothy. "A Case for Kenneth Burke's Dialectic and Rhetoric." *Philosophy & Rhetoric*, vol. 19, no. 1, 1986, pp. 23–37.

Cvetovich, Ann. *Depression: A Public Feeling*. Duke UP, 2012.

D'Cruz, Heather, et al. "Reflexivity, Its Meanings and Relevance for Social Work: A Critical Review of the Literature." *British Journal of Social Work*, vol. 37, no. 1, 2007, pp. 73–90, doi.org/10.1093/bjsw/bcl001.

Davis, Lennard. *Bending over Backwards: Disability, Dismodernism and Other Difficult Positions*. New York UP, 2002.

—. *Enforcing Normalcy: Disability, Deafness, and the Body*. New York, Verso, 1995.

Dolmage, Jay. "Mapping Composition—Inviting Disability in the Front Door." *Disability and the Teaching of Writing*, edited by Cynthia Lewiecki Wilson and Brenda Jo Brueggemann, Bedford/St. Martins, 2008, pp. 14–27.

—. *Disability Rhetoric*. Syracuse UP, 2014.

"Droop." *Oxford English Dictionary*, www.oed.com. Accessed 15 June 2016.

Duffy, John. "Virtuous Arguments." *Inside Higher Ed.*, 2012, www.insidehighered.com/views/2012/03/16/essay-value-first-year-writing-courses. Accessed February 2021.

Duffy, John and Melanie Yergeau. "Guest Editor's Introduction Special Issue of Disablity Studies Quarterly: Disability and Rhetoric." *Disability Studies Quarterly*, vol. 31, no. 3, 2011, dsq-sds.org/article/view/1682/1607.

Dunn, Patricia. *Talking, Sketching, Moving: Multiple Literacies in the Teaching of Writing*. Heinemann, 2001.

East, James H., editor. *The Humane Particulars: The Collected Letters of William Carlos Williams and Kenneth Burke*. U of South Carolina P, 2003.

Ellentuck, Matt. "The Moment Zion Williamson Almost Killed Me." *SBNation*. 30 Mar. 2019, www.sbnation.com/2019/3/30/18288200/zion-williamson-reporter-loose-ball-march-madness-duke.

Ellison, Ralph. *Invisible Man*. New York, Vintage International, 1980.

Enjoy Poverty. Directed by Renzo Martens, Inti Films/The Image and Sound Factory, 2008.

Enoch, Jessica. "Becoming Symbol-Wise: Kenneth Burke's Pedagogy of Critical Reflection." *College Composition and Communication,* vol. 56, no. 2, 2004, pp. 272–96, doi:10.2307/4140650.

Enoch, Jessica, and Cheryl Glenn. "Drama in the Archives." *College Composition and Communication,* vol. 61, no. 2, 2009, pp. 321–42.

Everelles, Nirmala. "In Search of the Disabled Subject." *Embodied Rhetorics: Disability in Language and Culture,* edited by James C. Wilson and Cynthia Lewiecki-Wilson, Southern Illinois UP, 2001, pp. 92–111.

Falk, John. *Identity and the Museum Visitor Experience.* Walnut Creek, Left Coast Press, 2009.

Farman, James, editor. *The Mobile Story: Narrative Practices with Locative Media,* New York, Routledge, 2014.

Finnegan, Cara. "What Is This a Picture of? Some Thoughts on Images and Archives." *Rhetoric and Public Affairs,* vol. 9, no. 1, 2006, pp. 116–23.

Fisher, Max. "Trump's Nuclear Weapons Tweet, Translated and Explained." *The New York Times,* 22 December 2016, nyti.ms/2il3Am7.

Fogarty, Daniel. *Roots for a New Rhetoric.* Russell and Russell, 1968.

Fook, Jan. *Social Work: Critical Theory and Practice.* New York, SAGE, 2002.

Forney, Ellen. *Marbles: Mania, Depression, Michelangelo, and Me: A Graphic Memoir.* New York, Penguin, 2012.

Foss, Karen A., and Cindy L. White. "'Being' and the Promise of Trinity: A Feminist Addition to Burke's Theory of Dramatism." *Kenneth Burke and the 21st Century,* edited by Bernard L. Brock, SUNY Press, 1999, pp. 99–110.

Foss, Sonja K., and Cindy L. Griffin. "A Feminist Perspective on Rhetorical Theory: Toward a Clarification of Boundaries." *Western Journal of Communication,* vol. 56, no. 4, 1992, pp. 330–49.

Frank, Arthur. "Five Dramas of Illness." *Perspectives in Biology and Medicine,* vol. 50, no. 3, 2007, pp. 379–94.

Franks, Myfanwy. "Feminisms and Cross-ideological Feminist Social Research: Standpoint, Situatedness, and Positionality—Developing Cross-ideological Feminist Research." *Journal of International Women's Studies,* vol. 3, no. 2, 2002, pp. 38–50.

Freire, Paulo. *Education for Critical Consciousness*. Translated by Myra Bergman Ramos, Seabury Press, 1973.
Galea, Simone. "Reflecting Reflective Practice." *Educational Philosophy and Theory*, vol. 44, no. 3, 2012, pp. 245–258, doi.org/10.1111/j.1469-5812.2010.00652.x.
George, Ann. *Kenneth Burke's* Permanence and Change*: A Critical Companion*. U of South Carolina P, 2018.
—. "Mr. Burke, Meet Helen Keller." *Rhetoric: Concord and Controversy*, edited by Antonio de Valesco and Melody Lehn, Waveland, 2011, pp. 340–47.
—. Review of *Landmark Essays on Kenneth Burke*, by Barry Brummett. *Rhetoric Society Quarterly*, vol. 26, no. 1, 1996, pp. 90–93.
George, Ann, and Jack Selzer. *Kenneth Burke in the 1930s*. U of South Carolina P, 2007.
Gerald, Amy S. "Review: Rhetorical Listening: Identification, Gender, Whiteness." *Journal of Composition Studies*, vol. 35, no. 1, 2007, pp. 142–145, www.jstor.org/stable/43501695. Accessed 18 Feb. 2020.
"Ghent University's Educational View and Strategy: Multiperspectivism as Philosophy of Education." *Ghent University*, www.ugent.be/en/ghentuniv/principles/educational-strategy/multiperspectivisme_eng.pdf. Accessed 15 June 2020.
Gill, Carol. "A Psychological View of Disability Culture." *Disability Studies Quarterly*, vol. 15, no. 4, 1995, pp. 16–19.
Glenn, Cheryl. *Rhetorical Feminism and This Thing Called Hope*. Southern Illinois UP, 2018.
Glenn, Cheryl, Margaret M. Lyday, and Wendy Sharer, editors. *Rhetorical Education in America*. U of Alabama P, 2009.
Grasgreen, Allie. "Dropping the Ball on Disabilities." *Inside Higher Ed*, 2 April 2014, www.insidehighered.com/news/2014/04/02/students-disabilities-frustrated-ignorance-and-lack-services.
Hawhee, Debra. "Burke and Nietzsche." *Quarterly Journal of Speech*, vol. 85, no. 2, 1999, pp. 129–45, doi.org/10.1080/00335639909384250.
—. *Moving Bodies: Kenneth Burke at the Edges of Language*. U of South Carolina P, 2009.
Hirvisaari, James. Comment on "Räjähdys Oslon keskustassa (Breivikin iskut)." Homma web forum, 25 July 2011, 11:23 p.m., hommaforum.org/index.php/topic,53242.1680.html. Accessed 30 August 2020.

Holbein, John. "Why So Few Young Americans Vote." *The Conversation*, 11 March 2020, theconversation.com/why-so-few-young-americans-vote-132649. Accessed February 2021.
Hsi, Steven D. *Closing the Chart: A Dying Physician Examines Family, Faith, and Medicine.* U of New Mexico P, 2004.
Hunter, Kathryn Montgomery. *Doctors' Stories: The Narrative Structure of Medical Knowledge.* Princeton UP, 1991.
Hyvärinen, Matti. "Huuto symbolina 1970-luvun opiskelijaliikkeessä." *Myytit ja symbolit: Kirjoituksia suomalaisista kulttuuritulkinnoista*, edited by Ulla-Maija Peltonen and Kirsti Stenvall, Tummavuoren kirjapaino, 1991, pp. 80–107.
"Illegal Aliens. Ineligibility for Public Services. Verification and Reporting. Initiative Statute." California Proposition 187. Sacramento, CA, 1994.
Jack, Jordynn. "On the Limits of Human: Haggling with Burke's 'Definition of Man.'" *Burke in the Archives: Using the Past to Transform the Future of Burkean Studies*, edited by Dana Anderson and Jessica Enoch, U of South Carolina P, 2013, pp. 84–98.
James, Whitney Lew. Personal communication with author. 7 May 2021.
Japp, Phyllis M. "'Can This Marriage Be Saved?': Reclaiming Burke for Feminist Scholarship." *Kenneth Burke and the 21st Century*, edited by Bernard L. Brock, SUNY Press, 1999, pp. 113–30.
Jay, Paul, editor. *The Selected Correspondence of Kenneth Burke and Malcolm Cowley, 1915-1981.* U of California P, 1988.
Jokisalo, Jouko. "Rasistisen oikeistopopulismin aave kummittelee Euroopassa." *Rauhan puolesta*, Mar. 2011, rauhanpuolustajat.org/arkisto-raput/rasistisen-oikeistopopulismin-aave-kummittelee-euroopassa/. Accessed 1 September 2020.
Kadetsky, Elizabeth. "Bashing Illegals in California." *The Nation*, 17 Oct. 1994, pp. 416–21.
Kafer, Alison. *Feminist Queer Crip.* Indiana UP, 2013.
"Katainen pyysi anteeksi oppositiolta." *Yleisradio*, 5 Feb. 2009, yle.fi/uutiset/3–5720913. Accessed 30 Aug. 2020.
KB: A Conversation with Kenneth Burke. Directed by Harry Chapin and Dylan Skolnick, interviews by Harry Chapin, Old Crowe Production, n.d.
Kendi, Ibram X. "A Battle between the Two Souls of America." *The Atlantic*, 11 Nov. 2020, www.theatlantic.com/ideas/archive/2020/11/americas-two-souls/617062/. Accessed Feb. 2021.

Kennedy, Merrit. "Pence Tells North Korea: 'The Era of Strategic Patience is Over.'" *NPR*, 17 April 2017, www.npr.org/sections/thetwo-way/2017/04/17/524316419/pence-tells-north-korea-the-era-of-strategic-patience-is-over.

Kenny, Robert Wade. "A Cycle of Terms Implicit in the Idea of Medicine: Karen Ann Quinlan as a Rhetorical Icon and the Transvaluation of the Ethics of Euthanasia." *Health Communication*, vol. 17, no. 1, 2005, pp. 17–39.

—. "The Rhetoric of Kevorkian's Battle," *Quarterly Journal of Speech*, vol. 86, 2000, pp. 386–401.

Keskinen, Riku. *Suomalaisen Puhetaidon Kirjallisuuden Lähtökohdat*. 1998. Jyväskylän yliopisto, licentiate thesis.

King, Andrew. "Kenneth Burke as Teacher: Pedagogy, Materialism, and Power." *Humanistic Critique of Education: Teaching and Learning as Symbolic Action*, edited by Peter M. Smudde, Parlor, 2010, pp. 42–60.

—. "Pentadic Criticism: The Wheels of Creation." *Rhetorical Criticism: Perspectives in Action*, edited by Jim A. Kuypers, Lexington Books, 2009, pp. 165–80.

Kneupper, Charles W. "Dramatistic Invention: The Pentad as a Heuristic Procedure." *Rhetoric Society Quarterly*, vol. 9, no. 3, 1979, pp. 130–36, doi.org/10.1080/02773947909390535.

Knutsen, Ketil, and Ingunn Knutsen. "Performative Historical Competence: Use-of-History as Symbolic Action." *Journal of Curriculum Studies*, vol. 52, no. 5, 2020, pp. 673–84, doi.org/10.1080/002 20272.2019.1636138.

Kook, Christian, and Lisa S. Villadsen, editors. *Rhetorical Citizenship and Public Discourse*. Penn State UP, 2012.

Krueger, Ben. "Burke Bingo: Using Active Learning to Introduce Dramatism." *Communication Teacher*, vol. 25, no. 2, 2011, pp. 81–85, doi:10.1080/17404622.2010.528002.

Krumer-Nevo, Michal, et al. "Poverty-Aware Social Work Practice: A Conceptual Framework for Social Work Education." *Journal of Social Work Education*, vol. 45, no. 2, 2009, pp. 225–43, dx.doi.org/10.5175/JSWE.2009.200600144.

Lewiecki-Wilson, Cynthia, and Brenda Jo Brueggemann, editors. *Disability and the Teaching of Writing: A Critical Sourcebook*. Boston, Bedford/St. Martin's, 2008.

Linton, Simi. *Claiming Disability: Knowledge and Identity*. New York UP, 1998.
Lorenz, Walter. "Rediscovering the Social Question." *European Journal of Social Work*, vol. 19, no. 1, 2016, pp. 4–17, doi.org/10.1080/13691 457.2015.1082984.
Mangino, Heather. "Narrative Medicine's Role in Graduate Nursing Curricula: Finding and Sharing Wisdom Through Story." *Creative Nursing*, vol. 20, no. 3, 2014, pp. 191–93.
Martin. Deb. "Add Disability and Stir: The New Ingredient in Composition Textbooks." *Disability and the Teaching of Writing: A Critical Sourcebook*, edited by Cynthia Lewiecki-Wilson and Brenda Jo Brueggemann, Bedford/St. Martin's, 2007, pp. 74–92.
McAdams, Dan P. "Identity and the Life Story." *Autobiographical Memory and the Construction of a Narrative Self: Developmental and Cultural Perspectives*, edited by Robyn Fivush and Catherine A. Haden, Lawrence Erlbaum, 2003, pp. 187–207.
McGhee, Heather. *The Sum of Us: What Racism Costs Everyone and How We Can Prosper Together*. New York, Penguin Random House, 2021.
McGowan, John. "Literature as Equipment for Living: A Pragmatist Project." *Soundings: An Interdisciplinary Journal*, vol. 86, no. 1-2, 2003, pp. 119–48, www.jstor.org/stable/41179088. Accessed 18 Feb., 2020.
McRuer, Robert. "Composing Bodies; Or, De-Composition: Queer Theory, Disability Studies, and Alternative Corporealities." *JAC: A Journal of Composition Theory*, vol. 24, no. 1, 2004, pp. 47–77.
Micciche, Laura R. "Feminist." *A Guide to Composition Pedagogies*, edited by Gary Tate, Amy Rupiper Taggart, Kurt Schick, and H. Brooke Hessler, 2nd ed., Oxford UP, 2014, pp. 128–45.
Michalko, Rod. "What's Cool about Blindness?" *Disability Studies Quarterly*, vol. 30, no. 3-4, 2010, dsq-sds.org/article/view/1296/1332.
Nichols, Annie Laurie. *No Tangle So Hopeless: Toward a Relational Cluster Analysis*. 2018. U of Maryland, PhD dissertation.
O'Reilley, Mary Rose. *The Peaceable Classroom*. Heinemann, 1993.
Obama, Barack. Cathedral of the Holy Cross, 18 April 2013, Boston, MA. Interfaith Service. obamawhitehouse.archives.gov/photos-and-video/video/2013/04/18/president-obama-speaks-interfaith-prayer-service-boston.
Obermark, Lauren. *Engaging Museums: Rhetorical Education and Social Justice*. Southern Illinois UP, 2021.

Osnos, Evan, David Remnick and Joshua Yaffa. "Trump, Putin, and the New Cold War." *The New Yorker*, 6 March 2017, www.newyorker.com/magazine/2017/03/06/trump-putin-and-the-new-cold-war.

"Our Universes: Traditional Knowledge Shapes Our World." *National Museum of the American Indian*, americanindian.si.edu/explore/exhibitions/item?id=530. Accessed 25 May 2020.

Overington, Michael. "Kenneth Burke and the Method of Dramatism." *Theory and Society*, vol. 4, no. 1, 1977, pp. 131–56.

Palonen, Kari. *Kootut Retoriikat: Esimerkkejä Politiikan Luennasta*. Jyväskylä, Finland, SoPhi, 1997.

Parker, Ian. *Qualitative Psychology: Introducing Radical Research*. Maidenhead, UK, Open UP, 2005.

Parton, Nigel. "Some Thoughts on the Relationship Between Theory and Practice in and for Social Work." *British Journal of Social Work*, vol. 30, no. 4, 2000, pp. 449–63, doi.org/10.1093/bjsw/30.4.449.

Parton, Nigel, et al. *Social Work: A Constructive Approach*. Antwerp, Belgium, Standaard Uitgeverij, 2006.

Patel, Shaista. "Racing Madness: The Terrorizing Madness of the Post-9/11 Terrorist Body." *Disability Incarcerated: Imprisonment and Disability in the United States and Canada*, edited by Liat Ben-Moshe, Chris Chapman, and Allison C. Carey, Palgrave Macmillan, 2014, pp. 201–15.

Penuel, William R., and James V. Wertsch. "Vygotsky and Identity Formation: A Sociocultural Approach." *Educational Psychology*, vol. 30, no. 2, 1995, pp. 83–92.

Perelman, Chaïm and Lucie Olbrechts-Tyteca. *The New Rhetoric: A Treatise on Argumentation*. Translated by John Wilkinson and Purcell Weaver, U of Notre Dame P, 1969.

Philipsen, Gerry. "Mayor Daley's Council Speech: A Cultural Analysis." *Quarterly Journal of Speech*, vol. 72, no. 3, 1986, pp. 247–60.

Plato. "Gorgias." *Plato: Complete Works*, edited by John M. Cooper, translated by Donald J. Zeyl, Hackett, 1997, pp. 791–869.

Porter, James. *Audience and Rhetoric: An Archaeological Composition of the Discourse Community*. Longman, 1992.

Price, Margaret. "Accessing Disability: A Nondisabled Student Works the Hyphen." *College Composition and Communication*, vol. 59, no. 1, 2007, pp. 53–76.

—. *Mad At School: Rhetorics of Mental Disability and Academic Life*. U of Michigan P, 2011.

Pycroft, Aaron. "From a Trained Incapacity to Professional Resistance in Criminal Justice." *Multi-Agency Working in Criminal Justice: Theory, Policy and Practice*, edited by Aaron Pycroft and Dennis Gough, Bristol Policy Press, 2019, pp. 25–40.

Ratcliffe, Krista. *Rhetorical Listening: Identification, Gender, Whiteness*. Southern Illinois UP, 2005.

Reynolds, Fred. "A Short History of Mental Health Rhetoric Research (MHRR)." *Rhetoric of Health & Medicine*, vol. 1, no. 1, 2018, pp. 1–18.

Rickover, H. G. "Let's Stop Wasting our Greatest Resource." *Saturday Evening Post*, 2 March 1957, pp. 19, 108–11.

Roberts, Lisa C. *From Knowledge to Narrative: Educators and the Changing Museum*. Smithsonian Institution Press, 1997.

Roets, Griet, et al. "Du Choc des Idées Jaillit la Lumière: Thinking with Eric Broekaert's Integrated and Holistic Paradigm of Education." *The International Journal of Therapeutic Communities*, vol. 38, no. 3, 2017, pp. 169–76, www.emerald.com/insight/content/doi/10.1108/TC-03-2017-0010/. Accessed 20 May, 2020.

Rountree, Clarke. "Instantiating 'The Law' and its Dissents in Korematsu v. United States: A Dramatistic Analysis of Judicial Discourse." *Quarterly Journal of Speech*, vol. 87, no. 1, 2001, pp. 1–24.

—. "Revisiting the Controversy over Dramatism as Literal." *KB Journal*, vol. 6, no. 2, 2010, www.kbjournal.org/content/revisiting-controversy-over-dramatism-literal. Accessed 10 June 2020.

Roy, Abhik. "The Construction and Scapegoating of Muslims as the 'Other' in Hindu Nationalist Rhetoric." *Southern Communication Journal*, vol. 69, 2004, pp. 320–32.

Rupiper-Taggart, Amy. Personal communication with author. April 2008.

Schalk, Sami. "Metaphorically Speaking: Abelist Metaphors in Feminist Writing." *Disability Studies Quarterly*, vol. 33, no. 4, 2013, dsq-sds.org/article/view/3874/3410.

Schiappa, Edward, and Mary F. Keehner. "The 'Lost' Passages of *Permanence & Change*." *Communication Studies*, vol. 42, 1991, pp. 191–98.

Schön, Donald. "The Crisis of Professional Knowledge and the Pursuit of an Epistemology of Practice." *Journal of Interprofessional Care*, vol. 6, no. 1, 1992, pp. 49–63, doi.org/10.3109/13561829209049595.

Secor, Marie, and Davida Charney, editors. *Constructing Rhetorical Education*. Carbondale, Southern Illinois UP, 1991.

Selzer, Jack. "Rhetorical Analysis: Understanding How Texts Persuade Readers." *What Writing Does and How It Does It: An Introduction to*

Analyzing Texts and Textual Practices, edited by Charles Bazerman and Paul Prior, Erlbaum, 2003, pp. 279–307.

Shakespeare, William. "As You Like It, Act 2, Scene 7." *The Folger Shakespeare*, shakespeare.folger.edu/shakespeares-works/as-you-like-it/act-2-scene-7/. Accessed 12 Nov. 2019.

Sheilds, Laurene E. "Narrative Knowing: A Learning Strategy for Understanding the Role of Stories in Nursing Practice." *Journal of Nursing Education*, vol. 55, no. 12, 2016, pp. 711–14.

Siebers, Tobin. *Disability Theory*. U of Michigan P, 2008.

Siebler, Kay. *Composing Feminisms: How Feminists Have Shaped Composition Theories and Practices*. Hampton, 2008.

Silko, Leslie Marmon. "The Border Patrol State." *The Nation*, 17 Oct. 1994, pp. 412–15.

Simons, Herbert. "The Rhetorical Legacy of Kenneth Burke." *A Companion to Rhetoric and Rhetorical Criticism*, edited by Walter Jost and Wendy Olmsted, Blackwell Publishing, 2004, pp. 152–67.

Singh, Gurnam, and Stephen Cowden. "The Social Worker as Intellectual." *European Journal of Social Work*, vol. 12, no. 4, 2009, pp. 479–93, doi.org/10.1080/13691450902840689.

Slater, Jarron. "Attitudes of Collaborative Expectancy: Antithesis, Gradatio, and *A Rhetoric of Motives*, Page 58." *Rhetoric Review*, vol. 37, no. 3, 2018, pp. 247–58.

Sleeter, Christine. "Why Is There Learning Disabilities? A Critical Analysis of the Birth of the Field in Its Social Context." *The Formation of School Subjects: The Struggle for Creating an American Institution*, edited by T. S. Popkewitz, Palmer Press, 1987, pp. 210–37.

Sontag, Susan. *Illness as Metaphor*. Farrar, Straus and Giroux, 1978.

St. John, Jeffrey. "Assessing Citizenship: Foundation, Identity, Place, and Obsolescence." *Review of Communication*, vol. 8, no. 4, 2008, pp. 409–19, doi:10.1080/ 15358590802276051.

Stenberg, Shari J. *Composition Studies Through a Feminist Lens*. Parlor, 2013.

Stygall, Gail. "Women and Language in the Collaborative Writing Classroom." *Feminism and Composition Studies: In Other Words*, edited by Susan C. Jarratt and Lynn Worsham, Modern Language Association, 1998.

Summa, Hilkka. *Hyvinvointipolitiikka ja Suunnitteluretoriikka*. 1989. University of Helsinki, PhD dissertation.

—. "Kolme Näkökulmaa Uuteen Retoriikkaan. Burke, Perelman, Toulmin ja Retoriikan Kunnianpalautus." *Pelkkää Retoriikkaa: Tutkimuksen ja Politiikan Retoriikat*, edited by Hilkka Summa and Kari Palonen, Vastapaino, 1996, pp. 51–83.

Taylor, Carolyn. "Narrating Significant Experience: Reflective Accounts and the Production of (Self)Knowledge." *British Journal of Social Work*, vol. 36, no. 2, 2006, pp. 189–206, doi.org/10.1093/bjsw/bch269.

Taylor, Carolyn, and Susan White. "Knowledge, Truth and Reflexivity: The Problem of Judgment in Social Work." *Journal of Social Work*, vol. 1, no. 1, 2001, pp. 37–59, doi.org/10.1177/146801730100100104.

Tell, David. "Burke's Encounter with Ransom: Rhetoric and Epistemology in 'Four Master Tropes.'" *Rhetoric Society Quarterly*, vol. 34, no. 4, 2004, pp. 33–54.

Thames, Richard H. "Preaching What We Practice: Course Design Based on the Psychology of Form." *Humanistic Critique of Education: Teaching and Learning as Symbolic Action*, edited by Peter M. Smudde, Parlor, 2010, pp. 127–42.

Tilli, Jouni. *The Continuation War as a Metanoic Moment: A Burkean Reading of Lutheran Hierocratic Rhetoric*. 2012. University of Jyväskylä, PhD dissertation.

Tirrell, Jeremy. "Latourian *Memoria*." *Thinking with Bruno Latour in Rhetoric and Composition*, edited by Paul Lynch and Nathaniel Rivers, Southern Illinois UP, 2015, pp. 165–81.

Trace, A. S., Jr. "Can Ivan Read Better than Johnny?" *Saturday Evening Post*, 27 May 1961, pp. 30–68.

Vidali, Amy. "Seeing What We Know: Disability and Theories of Metaphor." *Journal of Literary & Cultural Disability Studies*, vol. 4, no. 1, 2010, pp. 33–54.

Weinberg, Richard B. "Communion." *Annals of Internal* Medicine, vol. 123, no. 10, 1995, pp. 804–05.

Weiser, M. Elizabeth. "Burke and War: Rhetoricizing the Theory of Dramatism." *Rhetoric Review*, vol. 26, no. 3, 2007, pp. 286–302.

—. *Burke, War, Words: Rhetoricizing Dramatism*. U of South Carolina P, 2008.

—. *Museum Rhetoric: Building Civic Identity in National Spaces*. Pennsylvania State UP, 2017.

—. Review of *The War of Words*, by Kenneth Burke. *Rhetorica: A Journal of the History of Rhetoric*, 1 May 2021, pp. 242–44.

"Welcome to 2MinuteThinker!" *YouTube*, uploaded by 2MinuteThinker, 28 May 2011, www.youtube.com/watch?v=IhOPPXDFqY0.

Wess, Robert. *Kenneth Burke: Rhetoric, Subjectivity, Postmodernism.* Cambridge UP, 1996.

White, Sue. "Unsettling Reflections: The Reflexive Practitioner as 'Trickster' in Interprofessional Work." *Critical Reflection in Health and Social Care*, edited by Sue White, et al., McGraw-Hill Education, 2006, pp. 21–39.

White, Sue, and John Stancombe. *Clinical Judgement in the Health and Welfare Professions.* McGraw-Hill Education, 2003.

Wible, Scott. "Professor Burke's 'Bennington Project.'" *Rhetoric Society Quarterly*, vol. 38, no. 3, 2008, pp. 259–82.

Wilson, James C. and Cynthia Lewiecki-Wilson. "Disability, Rhetoric and the Body." *Embodied Rhetorics: Disability in Language and Culture*, edited by James C. Wilson and Cynthia Lewiecki-Wilson, Southern Illinois UP, 2001, pp. 1–24.

"Wrongful Conviction Day." *Innocence Network 2020,* intlwrongfulconvictionday.org. Accessed 20 June 2020.

Zola, Irving Kenneth. "The Language of Disability: Problems of Politics and Practice." *Australian Disability Review*, vol. 1, no. 3, 1988, pp. 13–21, www.disabilitymuseum.org/dhm/lib/detail.html?id=813&page=all. Accessed 15 June 2016.

Contributors

ANN GEORGE is a professor of English at Texas Christian University, where she teaches courses on rhetorical history, theory, and criticism; editing; and style. Her publications include *Kenneth Burke's Permanence and Change: A Critical Companion*, *Women and Rhetoric between the Wars*, and *Kenneth Burke in the 1930s*. She was introduced to Burke in 1993 as part of Jack Selzer's first Penn State Burke seminar; she approaches Burke via archival research, feminist historiography, and critical pedagogy.

M. ELIZABETH WEISER is a professor of English at The Ohio State University, where she teaches rhetoric, professional and creative writing. She authored *Burke, War, Words* and *Museum Rhetoric*; she has co-edited *Engaging Audience*, *Women and Rhetoric between the Wars*, the *The Fertile Earth and the Ordered Cosmos*, and the forthcoming *Taboos in Museology*. Beginning serious study of Burke in a dissertation project with Ann George, she was treasurer of the Burke Society from 2014–2021 and is now on the executive board of the ICOM International Committee for Museology.

JAMES BEASLEY is an associate professor at the University of North Florida where he teaches rhetorical history, theory, and research. His 2010 article, "Demetrius, *Deinotes*, and Burkean Identification at the University of Chicago" won the Theresa J. Enos Award for best essay in *Rhetoric Review*. He is the author of *Rhetoric at the University of Chicago* and the co-author of *Dramatism and Musical Theater: Experiments in Rhetorical Performance* with Kimberly Eckel Beasley, both published by Peter Lang Publishing.

ELVERA R. BERRY, a professor of communication at Roberts Wesleyan College, teaches rhetorical theory and criticism; classical rhetoric and persuasion; and communication-grounded studies of organizations, leadership, gender, and oral interpretation. A regular participant and presenter in KBS/NCA/ECA, she initiated ECA's Kenneth Burke Interest Group and undergraduate panels. She connected with Burke in the early 1980s, contributed "The Both-And of Undergraduate Education" to *Humanistic Critique of Education*, and incorporates Burkean perspectives on higher education throughout her teaching.

DAVID BLAKESLEY is Campbell Chair in Technical Communication and Professor of English at Clemson University, as well as a fellow of the Rhetoric Society of America. His publications on Burke include *The Elements of Dramatism*, *The Terministic Screen: Rhetorical Perspectives on Film*, and, with Julie Whitaker, *Burke's Late Poems 1968–1993*. In classrooms, he learned much about KB from William A. Covino, W. Ross Winterowd, and Ellen Quandahl. In 2021, he began his term as president of the Kenneth Burke Society.

BRYAN CRABLE is a professor of rhetorical studies and director of the Waterhouse Family Institute at Villanova University, and the immediate past president of the Kenneth Burke Society. In addition to numerous articles and chapters on Burke, he is the author of *Ralph Ellison and Kenneth Burke: At the Root of the Racial Divide*, and the editor of *Transcendence by Perspective: Meditations on and with Kenneth Burke*. Although he never took a formal class on KB (beyond an independent study with William K. Rawlins), he owes his education in Burke to Denise Bostdorff, Larry David Smith, and Robert Wade Kenny.

RACHEL CHAPMAN DAUGHERTY is a senior lecturer at Texas Woman's University, where she serves as assistant director of first-year composition. She teaches courses in writing, research methods, technical communication, and writing program administration. Her essays have appeared in *Peitho*, *Innovative Higher Education*, and *Reinventing Rhetoric Scholarship*. She began her study of Burke in 2010 and later in a seminar with Ann George, approaching Burkean theory as a feminist rhetorical teacher-scholar.

ANNIE LAURIE NICHOLS learned "it's more complicated than that!" in Elvera Berry's rhetorical theory classrooms, a lesson that equipped Nichols to live in Russia for several years before studying Burke at the University of Maryland, first with Jim Klumpp and then with Damien Pfister, who directed their dissertation on cluster analysis. An officer in the Burke Society at ECA, NCA, and KBS, Annie Laurie now teaches

Burke in visual communication, media criticism, and rhetorical argument courses at Saint Vincent College, a working Benedictine monastery with honeybees in the walls.

KRIS RUTTEN works as an associate professor in the Department of Educational studies of Ghent University, Belgium, where he leads the research group Culture & Education. His fields of expertise include rhetoric and education, the rhetoric of cultural (il)literacy, and the pedagogical role of cultural institutions. He served as the president of the Rhetoric Society of Europe from 2017–2023 and is currently the vice-president of the Kenneth Burke Society and an associate editor for *Critical Arts*.

JACK SELZER, before he retired in 2018 after forty years on the faculty at Penn State, had the good fortune of teaching at a university that houses the Kenneth Burke Papers and that supplied a succession of outstanding graduate students to his Burke seminars. So, he eventually authored, coauthored, edited, or coedited several books and articles about Burke. He now administers a website devoted to the rhetoric of the civil rights movement.

JARRON SLATER was introduced to Burke in an undergraduate class taught by Greg Clark in 2009 in which *A Rhetoric of Motives* was a required text. He started implementing and teaching Burke as a master's student in 2010. His publications about Burke include articles and chapters in *Rhetoric Review*, the *Journal of Religion and Communication*, *Style and the Future of Composition Studies*, and *Teaching Writing in the Health Professions*.

JOUNI TILLI is a researcher at The University of Jyväskylä, Finland. He teaches rhetorical criticism and political theory. His research interests include rhetorical theory, racism and biopolitics, history politics, and religious rhetoric. Tilli has published in *Nations and Nationalism*, *Journal of Communication and Religion*, and *War in History*. He co-edited *National Rhetorics in the Syrian Immigration Crisis: Victims, Frauds, and Floods* with Clarke Rountree. Tilli received the KBS Emerging Scholar Award in 2017.

LAURA VAN BEVEREN is a postdoctoral research fellow at Ghent University, Belgium. She was introduced to Burke in a cultural studies course for students in social sciences. Her research studies the work of Burke as a methodological and pedagogical framework to inform critical-reflexive professional attitudes in the social and behavioral sciences. She has published her research in *Teaching & Teacher Education*, *British Journal of Social Work*, *Qualitative Health Research*, and *Disability & Society*.

SHANNON WALTERS is an associate professor of English at Temple University, where she researches and teaches in rhetoric and composition, disability studies, and gender studies. She is the author of *Rhetorical Touch: Disability, Identification, Haptics*. Her work has appeared recently in *PMLA*, *Research in the Teaching of English*, *Composition Forum*, and *The Journal of Literary & Cultural Disability Studies*.

Index

1965 Immigration Act, 12
2Minute Thinker, 88
2MinuteTeacher, 209

ableism, 215, 262–263, 267, 274
abnormal, 262
abortion, 147, 150
acts, xxi, xxii, xxiii, 138, 140, 146, 150, 169, 180, 186, 190, 192–194, 196, 200, 206, 218, 247
ad bellum purificandum (toward the purification of war), xvii, 15, 206, 213, 221, 223
Adams, Douglas, 24–25
aesthetics, xxvii, 129, 133, 134, 139–140, 212
agency, 144, 150, 152, 169, 172, 174–178, 180–182, 191, 195–196, 198, 246, 255–256, 289
agent, 70, 169, 172–175, 177, 179–180, 191–192, 194–201, 205, 219–220, 222, 289
algorithms, 143
alienation, xvii, 66–67; spiritual, 65
Almanac of the Dead, 9, 11
Alterra, Aaron, 136
ambiguity, 77, 117, 194, 197, 201, 212, 220–221, 245, 254–255
ambition, 222–223, 262, 269–271, 273, 277–279
ambivalence, 197
American Writers' Congress (1935), 87, 215, 229
Americans, xx, 12, 29, 30, 63, 117, 148, 214, 270
Americans with Disabilities Act (ADA), 270
Anderson, Benedict, 117–120, 133, 212, 232

Andover, NJ (Burke's farm), 56, 84–85, 88, 206–207, 226, 287
antiracism, 69, 75, 225
antistrophos, 132
anti-vax discourse, 52
appeals: ethical, 8; identity-based, xxvii, 143, 146, 155; rhetorical, 156, 164, 247
archival methods, 168, 170
archives, xxvii, 105, 166, 168–169, 171–172, 177, 212–213; digital, 168
Arendt, Hannah, 190
argument, xxv, xxvi, 6, 8– 9, 12, 18, 43–44, 55, 57, 59–62, 68, 71, 107, 115, 124, 146–147, 151, 158, 162–164, 186–187, 199, 213, 215–218, 220, 222–223, 231, 244, 247, 275, 277, 287, 289
Aristotle, xxiv, 5–6, 53, 89, 185, 224
arrangement, 9, 19, 114–115, 294, 303
art of living, 14, 206, 214– 215
artifacts, xxi, xxvii, 4, 14–15, 18, 22, 27–28, 111–114, 118–119, 124, 159, 171–172, 177–178, 179, 247
Asen, Robert, xiv
atheism, 115–116
attitude, xvii, xviii, 65–66, 82, 91, 115, 121, 139, 148, 199, 211, 217, 233–234, 243, 245, 248, 252–253, 257, 260–262, 264, 272–273, 276–277, 280
audience, 4, 11, 50, 84, 102, 108–109, 114–115, 117, 119, 122, 125, 129–131, 134–135, 137, 142, 144, 146, 153–154, 156, 158,

331

162, 180, 186, 190, 193, 209, 217, 222, 231, 238, 259, 269, 282
awareness: rhetorical, 156, 163–164
Azerbaijan, 29, 31–32, 34

Beasley, James, xix, xxvii, 22, 77, 166
behaviorism, 222, 229
Bennington College, xxi, 6, 22, 212, 223, 264
Berry, Elvera, xxviii, 14, 34, 285–286, 289
better life, xiv–xv, xxvii
bioethics, 131
biologism, 62–63
bipolar disorder, 248–249
Black bodies, 26, 172
Black Lives Matter, 51, 258, 299
Blakesley, David, xxv, xxvi, 6, 52, 73, 94–95, 170, 189, 254, 302; *Elements of Dramatism, The*, xxv, 6, 94, 99, 189, 302
bland strategy (tactic), xix
blindness time, 274, 277
blog posts, 55
bodies that learn language, 63
body, the, 18, 134, 200, 215–216, 265, 269
Booth, Wayne, xxv, 166–168, 186
Boston Strong, 282
Breivik, Anders, 194, 195, 196, 197, 198
Brewer, Elizabeth, 265
British Museum, 110
Brock, Bernard, xviii
brooding, 263, 270–271, 274–279, 282–284; sentimental, 269, 275, 276, 278, 284
Brown, Theresa, 135, 136, 141
Brueggemann, Brenda Jo, 273, 280, 283–284
bureaucratization of the imaginative, 217

Burke, Kenneth: *Attitudes Toward History*, xvi, xxvi, 20, 23–24, 28, 50–52, 62, 64–65, 67–71, 94, 140, 216–218, 227, 262, 270, 302; *The Complete White Oxen*, 205; *Counter-Statement*, 94, 211–212, 217, 227, 291, 302; *Dramatism and Development*, 21; *A Grammar of Motives*, 5, 8–9, 23, 85–86, 94, 109–110, 121, 166, 169, 189, 191–194, 200–201, 218–221, 227, 264, 276, 302; *Language as Symbolic Action*, xiii, 5, 94–95, 205, 223, 227, 264, 302; *Permanence and Change*, xvi, xxvi, 24, 51, 58–59, 62–64, 69, 76, 94, 117, 205, 207, 209, 213–215, 217, 227, 291–293, 300, 302; *The Philosophy of Literary Form*, xxii, 5–6, 23–24, 30, 74, 128, 132, 137, 139, 189, 217–218, 227, 245, 302; *A Rhetoric of Motives*, xix, xxi, xxiv, 5, 23–24, 76–77, 94, 107, 113, 115, 119, 121, 131, 135, 138–139, 143, 146, 221–223, 227, 236–237, 272, 302; *The Rhetoric of Religion*, 28, 95, 223, 291–292, 302; *Towards a Better Life*, 5, 7, 205; *War of Words*, xix–xx, 5, 15, 76, 94, 225; *The White Oxen and Other Stories*, 211
Burke, Libbie, 128
Burkean debate, xxii, xxiii
Burkean pedagogy, xiv, 148, 224, 231, 245, 261–262, 265–266, 276, 284
Burklow, Elaine, 85–86
Bush, George H. W., 12, 198
Butler, Judith, 149
Butts, Jimmy, 90

campaigns, 27, 34, 54, 156, 160–165, 187, 222, 235, 268

Canvas, 78, 94, 100, 103
Carlson, Cheree, 68–70, 87–88
Carlson, Kylie, 68–70, 87, 88
Carrico, Victoria, 88, 90, 92
Carson, Ronald, 131
case studies, 139, 191, 247, 252, 255
casuistic stretching, 67, 217
Chapin, Harry, 84, 88, 207, 211, 287
Chapin, Sandy, 88
Charney, Davida, xviii
Charon, Rita, 132, 134–135
Cherney, James L., 265
Christianity, xiv, 111, 222, 290
Cicero, 89, 185
circumference, 193–194, 201, 220, 249, 260, 291, 295
citizen engagement, xiv–xv
citizenship, xiii–xvi, xix, xxi, xxiii, xxvii, 8, 12, 136–137, 140–141, 151, 153, 170, 198, 206, 220, 224, 283–284, 288
civic pedagogy, 76, 206, 209
civil rights, xxvii, 11–12, 16, 169, 170, 177–179, 180; activism, xxvii
Civil War, 169
Clark, Gregory, xvi, 16, 91, 118–119, 136, 139, 209, 211–212, 221–222, 227
clinical psychology, 247
Clinton Administration, 12
Clinton, William Jefferson, 12
close reading, xxiv, 3, 5, 134, 206, 219
cluster analysis, 6, 19, 20–24, 26–32, 35, 37, 189, 198; equational, 21; relational, 21– 22
cluster maps, 27–28
Cold War, xvii–xxviii, 221, 261, 265–268
Cole, Thomas, 12, 128, 131

Coleridge, Samuel Taylor, 5, 10–11, 231
collaboration, 73, 143, 146, 150, 155
collaborative expectancy, 139
comic corrective, 65, 216, 288
comic frame, 65–67, 69–70, 216
common sense, 29
communal life, xiv, xx
communal orientation, 59
communication, xiii, xv, xvi, xxiv, 5, 7, 10, 21, 62, 73, 78, 96, 131, 154, 161, 186, 239, 247, 258, 286, 289–290, 297–298, 300, 302
communism, 60, 214
community engagement, 143, 156
competition, xvii, xxiii, 15, 17, 261–262, 264, 266–267, 269, 273, 277, 282–283
competitive cooperation, 78–79
composition, xv–xvi, xviii, xix–xx, xxiv, xxvii, 3, 14, 20, 39, 43, 96, 148, 262–263, 268–269, 276–277, 278–281, 283–284
compositional logic, 19, 21, 37
Condit, Celeste, 144–145
Conference on College Composition and Communication (CCCC), xix–xx
consubstantiality, 91, 145–147, 150–152, 154–156, 165
contextual criticism, 5, 7, 10
contextual readings, 4
contextualism, 6
Contract with America, 13–14
contradictions, 251
COVID-19, 119
Cowley, Malcolm, 7, 24, 52–53, 56, 166, 183, 211, 216, 229, 287
Crable, Bryan, xxvi, 50, 95, 206, 222–223
credibility, 9
crip method, 263

crip time, 263, 272–275, 284
critical awareness, xv, xvii–xviii, 243, 255
critical reflection, xiv, xxvii, 128, 148–150, 154–155, 199, 241–245, 247, 248, 253–256, 260, 263, 277
criticism, xvi, xxiv–xxvi, 3–5, 7, 10, 21, 26, 38, 108, 186,–188, 190, 205, 214, 217–218, 230–231, 236, 253, 289–291, 297, 302, 303
cultural critique, 59–61, 66, 215
cultural history, 24
cultural identity, 7
cultural logics, 246, 248–249, 250–251, 253, 258–259
cultural studies, 96, 186, 214, 258
curation, 108–109, 115, 122–123
Cushman, Ellen, 157
Cvetkovich, Ann, 274–276

Daugherty, Rachel Chapman, xxvii, 77, 143
Deam, Todd, 87
death penalty, 152, 153
debunking, xix, 217
decentering of teacher authority, 150
deconstruction, 215
definitions, 39, 43, 85, 193, 200, 223, 236, 265, 267, 291–292
deflection (tactic), xix
deliberative engagement, xiv
delivery, 158, 230, 247
Demo, Anne, 40, 43, 214
Derrida, Jacques, 187
Diagnostic and Statistical Manual of Mental Disorders (DSM-MD), 249
Dial, The, 287
dialectical inquiry, xv–xvi, 78
dialogue, xv, xvii, xxiii–xxiv, 78, 109, 116–117, 194, 274–288
Diderot, Denis, 271

digital humanities, xxvii, 170
disability: pedagogy, xxviii, 261–263, 266–267, 273, 278–279, 283–284; rhetorics, 7, 82, 132, 262, 264, 266–267, 269, 270, 272, 276–277, 279, 280–283; stereotypes, 280; terminology, 270
disability studies, xxviii, 247, 261–265, 269, 273–274, 276–278, 283
discourse communities, 109
discursiveness, xx, 70, 147, 150, 242–243, 258, 265
diseases, 15, 131, 213, 249, 262, 269, 270, 277
Display of Me (Weiser assignment), 108, 110, 123
division, xv– xvi, xxiv, 22, 24, 46, 53, 63, 96, 107, 143, 148, 199, 236
dog whistles, xxi
Dolmage, Jay, 268–269, 278, 284
Donne, John, 134
doublespeak, 240
drama, xx, 132, 134–135, 139, 168–169, 177, 190, 235, 288, 293
dramatism, xxiv–xxv, 96, 120, 168, 189, 190, 196, 219–221, 223, 253, 256, 264
dramatistic ratios, 176, 192
drooping, 263, 269–279, 282–284
Duffy, John, xviii, 265

Eastern Communication Association (ECA), 295–296, 297, 299
economic rhetorics, 193, 198
economics, xv
Edson, Margaret, 134
education, xiii–xiv, xvii–xix, xxiii, xxv, 12, 20, 36, 50, 128, 148, 206, 224, 236, 241, 244, 261–263, 266–273, 275–278, 282, 285, 288–290, 293, 296, 298, 300–301, 303; graduate, xiii,

xxvi, xxvii, 50, 52, 57, 73, 74,
    81, 170, 185–187, 188, 205, 208,
    224, 256, 285, 290, 295–296,
    298, 301; rhetorical, xiv–xv, xviii,
    xxiii, xxiv, xxv, 72; undergraduate, xxiv, 288–289
Elements of Dramatism, The
    (Blakesley), xxv, 6, 94, 99,
    189, 302
Eliot, T. S., 90
Ellison, Ralph, 57, 68–69, 221
Emancipation Day Parade, 171
emotional growth, 133
emotions, 8, 60, 247
empathy, xxvii, 116, 128–134, 136,
    138, 140
engagement, xiv, xvii, xxiii–xxiv,
    xxvi, 16, 52, 58, 61, 64, 72–76,
    77–78, 81–82, 96, 98, 101, 130,
    143–145, 147, 154–155, 213, 226,
    283, 290, 301, 303
Enoch, Jessica, xiii–xiv, xvii, xxii–
    xxiii, 148–149, 169, 175–180,
    212, 244–245, 252–253, 263
entelechy, xxii, 188
entitlement, xxii
epideictic rhetoric, 214
equality, xvi, 130, 176
equipment for living, 64, 68, 133,
    297, 301
essence, xxii, 61, 64, 108, 119–
    120, 122
ethics: racial, 79
ethnic pride, 9
ethnicity, 143–144, 146, 152
ethos, 5, 9, 163
etymology, 137, 191
Everelles, Nirmala, 279
exigency, 75, 77

fact-checking, xix
faith, xv, 111, 116, 201, 282,
    298, 300
Falk, John, 109, 114

Farman, Jason, 170
feminism, 115; inquiry, 145; pedagogy, 143–144, 154–155, 209
feminist rhetorics, 247
feminist theory, xxvii, 22, 75,
    143–147, 149, 150–151, 154, 155,
    209, 223, 246
film, 7, 11, 16, 27, 88, 90–
    91, 96–97
Finland, 185–188, 190, 192,
    195–196, 198
Finnegan, Cara, 168, 171–172
first-year composition, xiii, xviii,
    14, 279
Flaubert, Gustave, 274
Florida, 12, 169–170, 177–178
florilegia, 39, 42
Fogarty, Daniel, xxii
form, xvii–xix, xxiii, xxv, 13,
    19–22, 26, 28, 65–66, 72, 76,
    82–83, 87, 90, 102, 107–108,
    122, 123, 128–130, 134,
    137–139, 152, 154, 156, 171, 181,
    189, 207, 212, 219, 222–223,
    229, 233, 243–245, 249, 251–
    252, 255–256, 258, 267, 270,
    276–277, 280, 283; conventional,
    130; universal appeal of, 138
Forney, Ellen, 248
four master tropes, 187
frames, 53–55, 60, 64–71, 84, 180,
    216–217, 231
Frank, Arthur, 135
Franks, Myfanwy, 145
freedom, 9, 176–177, 264
Freedom of Information Act
    (FOIA), 87
Freire, Paulo, 199
Freud, Sigmund, 57, 219

Geisler, Cheryl, xiv
gender, 65, 69, 143–144, 146, 152,
    215, 225, 258, 265, 300–301
generative principles, 77

genre, 161, 164
George, Ann, xiii, xv, xxvii, 7, 52, 57, 76–77, 200, 205, 256, 265, 283; *Kenneth Burke's* Permanence and Change; *A Critical Companion*, 57, 94
getting along, xvi, 140
Ghent University, 241, 247
Gill, Carol, 272
Gingrich, Newt, 13
Giroux, Henry, 141, 253
Glenn, Cheryl, xxiii, 94, 169, 175–180, 247, 251
god-terms, 9, 189
Goethe, Johann Wolfgang von, 271
good life, the, xvi, xxiii, 140, 215–217
Google, 151, 156, 158,– 159
Gramsci, Antonio, 253
Gray, Freddie, 31
guilt, xxii, 187, 189
guilt-redemption cycle, 187, 189
gun control, 151
gun violence, 147
Gusfield, Timothy, 291–292, 302

habits of mind, xviii, xxiii
Hamer, Fannie Lou, 3
Hannah Gadsby: *Nanette* (comedy special), 65
Harvard University, xxi
hate speech, 30, 195
Hauser, Gerard, xiv
Hawhee, Debra, 86, 134, 216, 231–232, 254, 265
health professionals, 127–128, 132, 134–135, 138–140
health professions, xiii, 128–130, 132, 135–137, 139
heuristics, 52, 228, 253, 256
historiography, 212
history, xxvii, 10–11, 17, 39, 111, 114, 142, 166, 169, 170, 174, 177–179, 182, 186–187, 195, 241, 256, 268, 296–297
Hitler, Adolf, xv, 5, 10, 20, 21, 28, 30, 37, 56–57, 216, 218, 239; *Mein Kampf*, 10, 57
Holbein, John, xxiii
Hook, Sidney, 217
Hsi, Steven, 137
human barnyard, 76–77
human relations, 288, 293
Humanistic Critique of Education: Teaching and Learning as Symbolic Action (Smudde), xxv
humanities, xxvii, 128, 131, 132, 139, 186, 298
hypochondria, 127, 277
Hyvärinen, Matti, 186–187

identification, xxiv, xxvi–xxvii, 6, 22, 24, 46–47, 57, 67, 96, 107–108, 115–116, 118–122, 127–129, 135–139, 143–147, 149, 151–152, 154–156, 158–159, 163, 189, 199, 217, 222–223, 229, 237–238, 249, 264, 265, 272, 288–289; emotional, 135; theory of, 135, 144
identifications: body of, xxi, 222
identity, xviii, xxvi–xxvii, 11, 30, 32, 50, 53–54, 67, 108–114, 116–120, 122–124, 126, 129, 136, 138, 143–147, 149–150, 152, 154–155, 214, 217, 222, 224, 244, 248, 258, 281; construction, 214, 222; narratives of , 122; national, xxiii, 34, 117–118, 187, 194
identity formation, xviii, xxvii, 32, 108, 114, 120
ideological assumptions, 19
ideology, 158, 195–198, 269, 271, 284; of ability, 269, 271, 284
illness narratives, xxvii, 127–128, 129, 137, 141
illness/disability metaphors, 277

illumination, 74–75
immigration, 8–13, 147, 196–197, 214
Immigration and Naturalization Service (INS), 8–9
indexing, xxi, xxii, 6, 279–280, 282, 284
Indigenous Nations, 63
indoctrination, xvii, 20
information, xv, xviii, 4, 18, 36–37, 58, 73, 85–86, 98–99, 109, 130, 133, 161–162, 169–170, 173, 177, 179, 184, 206–207, 210–211, 214, 285
injustice, xv–xvi, xxiii, 153, 176–177
Instagram, 27, 153
institutions, xvi, 64, 150, 170, 209, 213, 216
intersectionality, 143, 152, 154
invention, 19, 21, 77, 246–247, 253, 266
Iron Curtain, 8
irony, 5, 229, 253, 269

Jack, Jordynn, 265
Jenner, Caitlyn, 51, 71
Joyce, James, xxi; Portrait of the Artist as a Young Man, xxi
justice, xv, 131, 153–154, 256, 287, 289

Kadetsky, Elizabeth, 12–13
kairos, 171, 181
Katainen, Jyrki, 190
KB Journal, 83, 87–88, 90, 91, 95–98, 101–102, 232
Keehner, Mary F., 59, 60
Keller, Helen, 265
Kendi, Ibram X., xv
Kennedy, Ted, 12, 268
Kenneth Burke in the 1930s (George and Selzer), xv, 95, 213

Kenneth Burke Literary Trust, 88, 90
Kenneth Burke Society, 55, 88, 90, 98, 103, 232
Kenneth Burke's FBI Files, 87
Kenneth Burke's Permanence and Change: *A Critical Companion* (George), 57, 94
Kenny, Wade, 69–71
Kevorkian, Jack, 69–70
key terms, xxi–xxii, 22, 27, 82, 189, 206, 208, 210, 213, 219
King Jr., Martin Luther, 176–177
knowledge, xvii, 10, 75, 76, 129, 150–151, 153–154, 156, 159–161, 168, 175–176, 178–179, 182, 188, 212, 220, 228, 235, 242, 247, 249–252, 254, 260, 285, 299
Kook, Christian, xiv

Lahti, Yannick, 187
Landmark Essays on Kenneth Burke, 6
language, xiii–xiv, xvii, xix, xxii–xxiii, xxvii, xxviii, 13, 43, 46, 58, 59, 62, 107, 117, 120, 131, 135, 144, 147, 149, 151, 164, 188–192, 205, 214–215, 220, 223–224, 226, 238–240, 243–246, 251, 252, 254–256, 261–262–266, 276–278, 284, 288–289, 291, 294, 298–300, 302
language of disability, 276
Lawrence, D. H., 63
League of American Writers, 87
learning from one's opponent, xviii
legal theory, 186
Lewiecki-Wilson, Cynthia, 269, 280, 283
LGBTQ+, 65
Lincolnville Museum and Cultural Center, 169–171, 178, 180, 182–183
Lind, Stephen, 88–89

338 *Index*

linguistic skepticism, xix, 189
listening, 30, 32, 35, 118, 129–130, 132, 134, 138, 141, 148, 245–247, 251, 253, 259–260
literature, 65, 70, 73, 132–134, 139, 186, 227, 231, 257, 291
logomachy, 82

MAGA, 62
making the connection (tactic), xx
marginalia, 75
Martens, Renzo, 250–251, 258–259
Martin, Deb, 176–177, 279
Marx, Karl, 57, 66
maximum consciousness, xvi
McAdams, Dan, 112
McGhee, Heather, xvi
McRuer, Robert, 268, 278, 283
Meade, George Herbert, 231
medical education, 128, 131
medicine, xv, 30, 128–134, 135, 137–139, 280, 287
Mein Kampf (Hitler), 10, 57
memorabilia, 178
mental health, 244, 248–249, 252, 254
mental illness, 248–249
metabiology, 62–63, 214–215
method, xvii, 6, 19–24, 30–31, 35,–37, 77, 86, 134, 149, 186, 189, 230, 255, 271, 274, 279
Micciche, Laura, 144, 149
Michalko, Rob, 274, 276
Mikkola, Ilkka, 187
military, 9, 115, 188, 225, 239, 266, 268, 282
Milton, John, 5, 10
mind-body binary, 215
mindmapping, 37
misinformation, xv, xviii–xix
Moonwalking Bear Awareness Test, 224
morals, 60, 120, 131, 234–235
mortification, 188

motives, 22, 26, 58–59, 77, 110, 190, 200, 220, 223, 302; collective, 110
multiperspectivism, 241
museology, xxvii, 107–108
Museum of Us (Weiser assignment), 107–108, 116, 118–126
museum rhetoric, 110, 120
museums, xxvii, 10, 107–111, 117–120, 123, 177–178, 180–182
Muslims, 69–70, 111, 197, 281
mystery, xxii, 181
myth, 82, 134

narrative, 20, 32, 90, 109, 112–114, 119–120, 127, 132, 134–135, 138–139, 141–142, 170, 179, 182, 258; illness, 20, 32, 90, 109, 112–114, 119–120, 127, 132, 134–135, 138–139, 141–142, 170, 179, 182, 258
Nation, The, 7, 10–12, 111, 123, 125, 207, 229
National Museum of American History (NMAH), 111–112, 118, 123
National Museum of the American Indian, 117, 122
nationalism, 15, 31, 32, 70, 76
nationality, 143–144, 146, 152
nationhood, 117
Native Americans, 8, 11–13
Nazis, 30, 70
Nemerov, Howard, 91
New Criticism, 6
New Republic, The, xxi, 7, 207, 213–215, 229
New Rhetoric (movement), xxiv, 76, 185–187
New School for Social Research, xxi
news bias, xxiii
newspaper articles, 55
Nichols, Annie Laurie, xxvi, 6, 19, 20–21, 28, 297

nonnormative perspectives, 262
normal, 4, 24, 27, 29–31, 35, 43, 249, 262

Obama, Barack, 281–282
occupational psychosis, 59, 186, 245
Odenkirk, Bob, 65
oral cultures, 20
orientation, 31, 36, 52, 58–64, 82, 140, 210, 213–216, 252–253, 275, 283
orthodoxy, 64, 66–67
othering: rhetorical, 248

Palonen, Kari, 185, 187
pandemic, 116, 118, 120
paradox, 110, 120, 200, 220, 298
paradox of substance, 200, 220
Parker Brooks, Meagan, 1, 3, 203, 218
Parkland shooting, 115
parlor metaphor, xxvi, 3, 6, 109, 218, 289
Parvikko, Tuija, 188
Patel, Shaista, 281
pathography, xxvii, 127–132, 135–141
pathos, 5, 8
Patriot Act, 192, 240
patriotism, 148
pedagogical tools, xxi
Peele, Jordan, 52
Pence, Mike, 268
Penn State University, xxi, 205
pentad, xxi, 6, 20, 22, 86, 168–169, 171–172, 174–182, 184, 186, 188–190, 192–194, 196–197, 199, 201, 207, 220–221, 249; ratios, 193, 195–196, 220, 292
pentadic analysis, xxvi, xxvii, 22, 166, 178, 185, 198, 220, 227
Penuel, William, 108–109
Perelman, Chaïm, 185–187

personalizing of essence, 108, 119, 122, 126
perspective by incongruity, xxiv, xxvi, 39–40, 43, 61, 65, 67, 171, 177, 179, 209, 211, 214–215, 227, 254, 256, 270, 283
persuasion, xx–xxi, 9, 46, 53, 108, 115, 135, 143–144, 186–187, 222–223, 265, 290
Philipsen, Gerry, 29
piety, xxiii, 20, 22, 24, 29, 36–37, 52, 60–61, 82, 168, 179, 209, 213, 283, 297
planned incongruity, 255
plantation owners, 251
poetic metaphor, 62
poetry, 11, 103, 129, 131, 139, 185, 223, 229, 231, 233, 254, 286
poets, 129, 137
political science, xiii, xxvii, 185–186, 188, 190, 236
politics, xv, xxiii, 7, 11, 53–54, 190, 193–195, 197–198, 225, 239, 250, 259, 275, 288, 292, 295
Porter, James, 109
positionality, 145,–151, 154–155
poverty, xxviii, 244–245, 249–252, 254, 258–260
PowerPoint, 123–124, 294
prewriting, 21
Price, Margaret, 272
Princeton University, xxi
privacy, xxii, 136
professional judgment, 242
professional practice, xxvii, 242–243, 245, 247, 251–255
Proposition 187, 13–14
proto-disability studies pedagogy, 263
proverbs, 132
psychology of form, 130, 133
psychology of information, 130, 133

public deliberation, xiv
Purge, The (film), 62
purpose, xiv, 4, 8, 16–17, 164, 169, 175–178, 186, 191, 194–196, 198, 201, 207, 212, 216, 218–220, 222–223, 230–231, 253, 266, 273, 289
purposive forgetting, 82

queer theory, 52
quiescence, xvi
Quinlan, Karen Ann, 69–71
Quintilian, 185

race, 15, 27, 31, 52, 54, 57, 68–69, 143–144, 146, 152, 221, 225, 265, 267, 272, 281–282
racism, 176, 178, 215
Ralph Ellison and Kenneth Burke (Crable), 57, 95
Ransom, John Crowe, 218, 220–221
Ratcliffe, Krista, 19, 144, 149, 242–246, 250, 253–255, 258–260
realism, 63
reasons for liking Burke, 166, 168
recalcitrance, 62–63, 214–215, 295
reduction, xx, 8, 125, 220, 260
reflection, xxviii, 21, 23, 91, 114, 119, 136, 143, 146, 148–149, 154, 158, 165, 169, 176–177, 180, 223, 241–244, 250, 252–253, 255–256, 258, 260, 267, 276, 291, 303
reflexivity, 64, 154, 241, 242–243
rejection: attitude of, 66
religion, 57, 62, 131, 281, 290–291
religious discourse, 194
remaking the world, 77
Republicans, 13
revising the news, xxii
revision, xvi, 50, 60, 232, 241, 273, 277

rhetoric, xiii–xiv, xix–xxi, xxiv, xxvii, 3, 7, 16–17, 43, 50, 52–53, 56, 57, 72–77, 79, 82, 88, 96, 97, 99, 102, 107–108, 111, 117–118, 135, 139, 144, 166, 185–188, 190, 193, 195–196, 198–199, 201, 209, 217, 221–222, 224, 236–237, 243, 246,–248, 256, 259–260, 269, 272, 283–284, 288, 290, 291, 295, 296, 302, 303; activist, 215; scientific, xx; spiritual, 188; toxic, xviii
rhetoric and composition, 3, 73, 144, 224, 243
rhetorical analysis, xxvi, 3–5, 7, 11, 14–15, 151, 185, 187, 248; assignment, 16
rhetorical beings, 53
rhetorical listening, 19, 21, 38, 245–251, 253–256, 259
rhetorical studies, xv, xxiv, xxvi, 83, 212, 224, 243
rhetorical theory, 77
Richards, I. A., 215, 218, 231
rituals of rebirth, 67–68
Road to Victory (MOMA exhibit), 85–86
Roberts Wesleyan College, 290
Roberts, Lisa, 109, 290–291, 295
Rorty, Richard, 187
Ross, Jerry, 84–85, 214
Rountree, Clarke, 6, 190–191
Russia, 29, 268
Rutten, Kris, xxvii, 128, 241

Sacks, Oliver, 136
Sandburg, Carl, 86
Sawade Hall, Katie, 285
say the opposite (tactic), xx
scapegoat principle, xv, xvi, 5–6, 22, 56, 70
scene, xv, xxii, 75–76, 109–110, 122, 169, 172–175, 179–180, 183, 185, 190–198, 200–201,

205, 210, 216, 218–219, 226, 249, 264, 271, 289, 292
scene-agent ratio, 195, 197, 200
Schalk, Sami, 277
Schiappa, Edward, 59–60
scientific knowledge, 249
scientistic orientation, 61–63
scope, xxiv, 53, 113, 125, 146, 149, 152, 160–161, 179–180, 193–194, 220, 222, 231, 234, 259
Secor, Marie, xviii
self-care, 249
Selzer, Jack, xv, xix, xxvi, 3, 7, 77, 94–96, 211–213, 216, 262, 283, 289
sexuality, 143–144, 146, 152, 265
Shakespeare, William, 65, 95, 189, 235
shrewd simplicity (tactic), xx
Siebers, Tobin, 265, 269, 271
Simons, Herbert W., 187, 247
situations, xx, xxiii, 50, 58–59, 133, 139, 147, 159, 186, 216, 235
slanting (tactic), xix, xxiii
Slater, Jarron, xxvii, 108, 127, 139
Sleeter, Christine, 266
Smudde, Peter, xviii, xxv; *Humanistic Critique of Education*, xxv
social change, 53, 58, 60, 64, 66, 144–145, 155, 218
social justice, xxvi, 76, 179, 206, 225
social media, 29, 78, 143, 157, 163
Sontag, Susan, 136–137, 141
Southern Agrarians, 215, 229
Soviet Union, 188, 190, 193, 266
spiritualization (tactic), xix
spokesman (tactic), xx
Springsteen, Bruce, 118
Sproat, Ethan, 88, 91
Sputnik, 266
St. Augustine (FL), 169, 170, 172, 174, 176–179, 183, 184

St. Augustine (person), xxvii, 231, 292
St. Augustine Historical Society, 169–170, 174
stakeholders, 145, 146, 149–156, 161–162
Stanford University, xxi
Statue of Liberty, 12
stealing back and forth of symbols, 67, 217
Stenberg, Shari, 154
stereotypes: disability, 280
strategies: rhetorical, xviii, 156, 161, 162, 199, 215, 217, 218
Stygall, Gail, 150
style, 9, 10, 18, 21, 24, 53, 164, 209, 231, 234, 235, 300
Styron, William: *Darkness Visible*, 136
sub-stance, 144, 145, 148, 155
substance, xxiv, 15, 22, 53, 146, 188, 192, 199, 201, 220–221, 229
Summa, Hilkka, 186–187
Supreme Court, 14, 32, 220
symbol-foolish, xiii, 252
symbolic analysis, xiv–xv, xviii, xix, xxv, 261
symbolic mergers, 23, 68
symbols and values (tactic), xxi
symbols of authority, 22, 217–218
symbol-using animals, xix, 138, 140, 187, 259, 271
symbol-wisdom, xiii, 244–245, 256
symbol-wise, xiii–xiv, xxi, xxiii, xxv, xxvii, 148, 151–152, 241–242, 244, 247, 252–253, 261, 266, 282

Taliban, 62
Teach for America, 51
technologies, 62, 64, 73, 77–78, 91, 103, 131, 282
temporizing of essence, 188
terministic screens, xxiii–xxv, xxviii, 22, 96, 168, 209, 227,

238–240, 244–246, 248–250, 252, 254–255, 258–260, 265, 298, 301
terminology, xiii, xiv, 14, 23, 24, 57, 201, 264
terms of order, 22
terrorism, xxiii, xxvii, 192, 194, 240, 263, 264, 281–282
textual analysis, 3, 8–10, 26, 38, 160, 199, 292
theater studies, 186
therapy, 133, 135
Thompkins, Phillip K., 85
Tilli, Jouni, xxvii, 22, 146, 185, 188
Tirrell, Jeremy, 171, 181, 183–184
tolerance, xxiii, 9, 201
tools: rhetorical, xix, 144–145, 147, 154
Toulmin, Stephen, 185, 187
toward the purification of war (*ad bellum purificandum*), xvii, 15, 206, 213, 221, 223
tragic frame, 69–70, 196
trained incapacity, xxviii, 58, 78, 177, 178, 186, 213, 244, 253, 255–256, 259, 270, 283
transcendence, 66–67, 79
translation, 191, 215, 241, 255
Treaty of Guadalupe Hidalgo, 13
Trump, Donald, 57, 187, 268
truth, xvii, xix, 3, 20, 53, 134, 177, 239, 281
Tweetdeck, 81–82, 97
Twine, Richard, 170–172, 174–175, 181
Twitter, 78, 81, 97, 102, 161, 296

underrepresented groups, xxvi, 225
undo by overdoing (tactic), xx
unending conversation of history, 74, 84
United States, 12, 14, 69, 169, 192, 266, 268

University of Chicago, xxi, 166–167, 221
University of Jyväskylä, 186, 187

values, xviii, xxviii, 9–10, 12, 24, 34, 37, 40, 46, 108, 111, 115–116, 134, 140, 201, 213, 216, 234, 263, 266–267, 270, 284, 302; American, 8–9, 34
Van Beveren, Laura, xxvii, 128, 241
Veblen, Thorstein, xxi, 245
veterans, 148–149, 171–172, 194
Vidali, Amy, 277
Villadsen, Lisa Storm, xiv
violence: cultural, 213
visual rhetoric, xxvi

Waitman, Jason, 180, 181
Walking Dead, The (TV show), 62
Walters, Shannon, xxviii, 261
war, xv–xvii, xx, 13, 15, 54, 66, 86, 109, 148, 172, 188, 190, 192–194, 198, 214, 229, 238–240, 261–269, 272, 275, 279, 282–283
War on Terror, 268
Washington, James, 183, 184
Watson, James Sibley, 286–287
ways of knowing, 134, 243, 246, 252
ways of seeing, xxviii, 54, 69, 239
Weaver, Richard, 89
Weinberg, Richard, 134
Weiser, M. Elizabeth, xiii, xx, xxvi, 15, 19, 96, 107, 110, 120, 144, 218–219, 264; *Burke, War, Words*, 15, 19, 96, 264
Wertsch, James, 108, 109
what equals what, xxii, 199, 279, 280–281
what goes with what (piety), xxiii, 24
white privilege, 79
white supremacy, 216, 222
white terrorists, 281

White, Eartha, 170, 211, 242, 243, 254, 256
Wible, Scott, xvii, 6, 22, 212, 264
Wikileaks, 51
Williams, William Carlos, 127–129, 229, 231
Williamson, Zion, 26–27
word man (Kenneth Burke), xiv, 238
World War II, 5, 8, 15, 86, 193–194, 222

wrangle of the market place, 76–77, 272
writing-to-learn, 133

Yellowdig, 78–80, 82, 96, 98, 103
Yergeau, Melanie, 265
yielding aggressively (tactic), xx

Zola, Irving Kenneth, 272
Zoom, 73, 77–78, 81–82, 100, 115

www.ingramcontent.com/pod-product-compliance
Lightning Source LLC
Chambersburg PA
CBHW020742020526
44115CB00030B/751